BRAIN, ATTACHMENT, PERSONALITY

BRAIN, ATTACHMENT, PERSONALITY

An Introduction to Neuroaffective Development

Susan Hart

KARNAC

First published in Danish in 2006 by
Hans Rietzels Forlag
Sjaleboderne 2, 1045 Copenhagen, Denmark

First published in English in 2008 by
Karnac Books Ltd
118 Finchley Road, London NW3 5HT

British Library Cataloguing in Publication Data

A C.I.P. for this book is available from the British Library

ISBN-13: 978 1 85575 588 8

Translated by Dorte H. Silver

Edited, designed and produced by The Studio Publishing Services Ltd
www.publishingservicesuk.co.uk
e-mail: studio@publishingservicesuk.co.uk

www.karnacbooks.com

CONTENTS

ACKNOWLEDGEMENTS

Some six years ago, when I was working at the psychiatric children's ward at Gentofte County Hospital in Copenhagen, I told my
supervisor at the time, Administrative Chief Doctor Karl Johan
Rump, about my enthusiasm for the integration of recent neuroscience and developmental psychology. He shared my excitement,
a rare occurrence at the time, and helped motivate me to continue
down this path, for which I am grateful. I would also like to thank
Chief Psychologist Rikke Schwartz, whom I met through my work
at Gentofte County Hospital, for her important contributions to my
understanding of the link between relationships and the development of personality disorders. Thanks are also due to body psy-
chotherapist Marianne Bentzen, who originally introduced me to
the latest developments in neuroscience, and who has remained a
faithful source of inspiration and discussion partner during the
writing process. Both Rikke and Marianne have been tremendously
helpful in relation to the creation of this book and have patiently
offered relevant comments and corrections. My secretary, Hanne
Mølgaard, also deserves my heartfelt thanks for her loyalty, hard
work, and patience in typing up the manuscript. Finally, I would
like to thank Henriette Thiesen, my editor at the Danish publishing

house Hans Reitzels, where the book was originally published, for stimulating collaboration in connection with putting the final touches on the text. She has patiently contributed to ensuring what is hopefully a readable and accessible text. I would also like to take this opportunity to apologize to my husband and my children for the time-consuming process of writing this book. My daughter expressed that she no longer really feels that she knows me, and I now hope to make up for this.

> Thou straggler into loving arms,
> Young climber-up of knees,
> When I forget thy thousand ways
> Then life and all shall cease.
>
> [From "A child", by Mary Lamb (1765–1847)
> *The Oxford Book of English Verse: 1250–1900*, 1919]

Susan Hart, a psychologist, has been the director of a municipal family therapy centre; her experience also includes work in municipal social services and in a children's psychiatric ward. Today, she has an independent practice and works mainly with professional supervision of psychologists, visiting nurses, and social workers in child and family departments, personnel in child psychiatric wards, and advisers to foster families. Susan Hart is the author of several books and articles on neuroaffective developmental psychology, and frequently gives lectures and courses on the topic.

FOREWORD

"I hope I have indicated that we are currently at one of the most exciting junctures in the history of our field. We are now, or soon will be, in a position to begin mapping relations between individual differences in early attachment experiences and changes in neurochemistry and brain organization. In addition, investigation of physiological "regulators" associated with infant-caregiver interactions could have far-reaching implications for both clinical assessment and intervention"

(Main, 1999, p. 881)

During my many years as a clinical psychologist working with adults, families, and children, I have always marvelled at the way that personality patterns appear as a kaleidoscope of life experiences. I have never doubted the link between family dynamics, interactions, personality, and inner psychological structure, and it has been equally clear to me that the personality is constructed within the context of social interactions or attachment. It has, however, been difficult to describe the processes of transmission from the interpersonal to the intrapsychological. It is not always an easy task to document the relationships between observable behaviour and personality structure.

Van Ijzendoorn (1995) used the term "transmission gap" to describe the difficulty of explaining the transmission between the intrapsychological and interpsychological fields. The theories of attachment and development psychology have helped me to gain an understanding of the nature of this transmission. In particular, John Bowlby's epigenetic understanding has contributed to my learning process. He pointed out that children's psychological development takes place in a dynamic interaction between genetic predispositions and the environment, which shape each other in a mutual process that begins at conception. Bowlby's work was done during a very fruitful period for the development of psychoanalytic theories in the mid 1900s, which sought to understand the individual as part of a system instead of viewing him or her as an isolated energy system. Bowlby had a very wide field of interest—animal studies, systemic theories, cognitive psychology, and behavioural psychology—and he integrated these theories in order to bring Freud's motivational theories into a dynamic relational context. He developed his theories from the mid 1950s and stands, in many ways, as the founder of developmental psychology. He developed his theories on the basis of mammalian attachment behaviour and pointed out that maternal care and a sense of security form the foundation for psychological development. He viewed the environment as a crucial factor in shaping the personality, and his theories made him the target of sharp criticism from psychoanalytic circles in England.

The integration of developmental psychology and recent neuroscience

According to Bowlby, infants organize their experiences with their closest care-givers in so-called "internal working models" at an early stage. These internal working models become critical for the children's formation of future relations and form the basis for their future view of everything that happens in life. This view is shared by many developmental psychologists, including Daniel Stern, who has been the most influential developmental psychologist of the past twenty years, partly due to his theories on self-experiences and affect attunement.

John Bowlby did not have the opportunity to integrate his theories with sophisticated knowledge about the brain, but he was aware that a deeper understanding of the complexities of normal development *vs.* psychopathology would only be possible through an integration of developmental psychology, psychoanalysis, biology, and neuroscience (Schore, 2000a,b).

Sigmund Freud also hoped for a closer link between biology and psychology, but he, too, lacked the opportunity. When setting out, he lacked both a psychological theory and a neuroaffective theory, and he chose to restrict himself to psychology. In his letters to Wilhelm Fliess, he expressed his desire to unite the two disciplines, and he did send Fliess a draft, which was published in English in 1950 as "Project for a scientific psychology" (Freud, 1954). In this text he sought to dissolve the duality that continues to separate psychology from neurology to this day. Freud never gave up the notion that one day psychoanalysis would merge with neurophysiology. He was convinced that the science of psychoanalysis could be reconciled with biochemical and neurological theories, although the time was not yet ripe, and he cautioned against allowing neuropsychological theories to take over with reductionist explanations on purely biochemical or neuropsychological terms. In a more current context, Glenn Gabbard (1992) has issued a similar caveat: "To lose the psychodynamic perspective is to lose the complexity and richness of human functioning in the quicksand of neurotransmitters and molecular genetics" (pp. 996–997). Surely, by now, we should give up a view that reduces the mind to mere biological processes, and be ready to integrate neuroscience and psychology with science and culture, instead of continuing to fluctuate between an aetiology that is either purely sociopsychological or purely biological in nature.

Combining the wisdom of developmental psychology with neuroscience poses a challenge to both disciplines. Psychological theories are often based on philosophy and consist of observations, analyses, and interpretations. Neuroscience is related to exact and objective knowledge, preferably validated knowledge. Due to its philosophical moorings, psychological knowledge is often difficult to objectify and standardize, while science is often rigid, difficult to subjectify, and misses the wisdom contained in the philosophical considerations. Thus, an integration of the two domains will be a challenge for both.

Although modern neuroscience still has a long way to go before it is able to offer a complete understanding of neurological processes, much progress has been made, and new information continues to be added every day. Today, neuroscience has much to contribute to our understanding of affects, emotions, and personality. New imaging technology—SPECT, PET, MEG, MRI, and fMRI—has enabled us to measure activity in the living, active brain. Granted, brain-imaging technology is not yet accurate enough, in particular when it comes to studying the many subcortical neural circuits that control our fundamental psychological processes. Part of the reason for this is that the circuits in this area of the brain are very closely interwoven, especially in the deeper-lying areas in the brain stem. The images we obtain with modern imaging techniques are not snapshots, but depictions that represent complex data, and that require a great deal of statistical processing. The data collected in this manner are difficult to interpret, even for experts.

Despite its relatively short existence, developmental psychology also has much to offer neuroscience, because it describes the relationship between interpersonal dynamics and the processes of personality formation. In my view, to understand the mature and fully developed brain we must first understand the gradual development of the brain, a process that takes place in close interaction with the infant's care-givers. Much research is still needed to understand the developing human brain, while we now have a far greater body of knowledge about the mature brain. We have only just unearthed the Rosetta stone of neuroaffective understanding, but I am confident that, within the foreseeable future, we shall be able to decipher the "hieroglyphs" and gain insight into the relationship between neurons and nurture, and the way that nature and nurture affect each other in an interdependent process.

Neuroaffective developmental psychology

My aim with this book is to bring together theories concerning the relationship between brain functions, behaviour, and personality by exploring the way the brain matures in close interaction with the social and physical environment. I saw an opportunity for theoretical integration some twelve years ago when I first encountered the latest developments in neuroscience as presented by Antonio Damasio and Joseph LeDoux in particular. Although the literature at the time was limited, my encounter with the works of these two scientists inspired me to address the integration of neuroscience and the theory of developmental psychology. This topic has continued to engage me ever since, and today I am even more convinced that a combination of the two bodies of theory would be both important and groundbreaking.

In their first books, Joseph LeDoux and Antonio Damasio offered a thorough introduction to certain aspects of the emotional or feeling brain. Their experience was based partly on work with adults with brain injury, partly on laboratory experiments with animals. At the time, there were no published works concerning the impact of the environment on brain development. In his 1994 book, *Affect Regulation and the Origin of Self*, Allan Schore made a first attempt at integrating and linking these theoretical fields. Schore had completed the important task of assembling research articles that indicated such links. Schore's work was and is the foundation for my own attempts to integrate the theories of neuroaffective development with the understanding that characterizes relational development psychology; an integrated theory that I have called "neuroaffective developmental psychology".

In the years to follow, it became common to integrate attachment and psychoanalytical theory, and to incorporate neuroaffective knowledge in this integration. In the 21st century, Peter Fonagy has been a particularly outstanding figure. To me, he has been a great source of inspiration in my efforts to expand this integration.

As a psychologist, I had always believed that it was only in the human sciences that theories were difficult to validate, and where theories had to rely on conviction to a certain degree. I was convinced that the natural sciences were exact and, thus, made it far easier to find precise and validated answers. However, after studying neuroaffective literature, I find many of the theories confusing, complicated, at times self-contradictory, and very much the object of polemics and debate. Recent neuroscience, with its "rapprochement" to developmental psychology, depends, like any science, on the cumulative effort of thousands of scientists. We still have a long way to go before we can move from general hypotheses to an exact, validated theory on the relationship between brain functions, behaviour, and personality. For now, we must be cautious and approach the theories as hypotheses, some of which might, one hopes, one day be validated. This book does not offer exact answers; rather, it describes hypotheses formulated by scientists with many years of experience in their field and offers additional hypotheses based on this understanding in combination with my own clinical experience. In all likelihood, the hypotheses will have to be readjusted and altered as neuroscience progresses further. For now, this attempt at integration should be viewed as a theory in line with other preliminary theories in an ongoing process of change and refinement.

An outline of the book

This book is intended as an inspiration and as an introduction to what I have called neuroaffective developmental psychology. As an underlying theme throughout the book, I seek to emphasize the importance of attachment for the formation of personality in all its diversity. The book presents a merger of systems that are not normally brought together in a structured psychodynamic context. Thus, the book operates on three levels: a neurobiological level, an intrapsychological level, and an interpersonal level.

This combination of different bodies of theory has made it a constant challenge to maintain a consistent terminology, in particular because certain concepts are not in themselves very clearly defined. One key example of this is the lack of a clear distinction between the concepts of affect, emotion, and feeling. In this context, I use "affects" to refer to the underlying neurological basis for the formation of emotions, while "emotions" and "feelings" are used synonymously. Bowlby introduced the term "internal working models", while later authors, including Daniel Stern, use the term "internal representations", which is also the term that I use. The terms "self" and "personality" may also be hard to distinguish from one another, and in this book they are used synonymously. Translated quotes are marked "translated for this edition". The brief stories about Matt in Chapter Ten are fictitious, while other case stories without a source reference stem from my clinical practice.

The book focuses on the brain structures that are essential for the formation of relationships, personality development, and emotions. It attempts to provide an understanding of the way that the uniquely human nervous system develops capacities for empathy, mentalization, and reflection that enable us to address such aspects as past and present, interpersonal relations, ethics, art, and aesthetics. I have endeavoured to make the text meaningful and comprehensible in order to make the topic interesting and inspiring to the reader and to spark an interest in further studies. Each chapter seeks to present the necessary knowledge for an understanding of our inherent neural basis for interpersonal interactions. The individual chapters can be read independently. Some passages will be more demanding than others and may be safely skipped without rendering the rest of the text meaningless. The outline of the book is as follows:

Chapter One discusses the relationship between nature and nurture. Both nature and nurture have substantial impact on brain development and, hence, on personality. This chapter looks at the mutual interactions between these two factors. The chapter also discusses Paul MacLean's model of the triune brain, which states that the brain has evolved in a hierarchical manner and can be divided into three distinct but interrelated layers, which, roughly put, handle sensations, emotions, and cognition. Since the environmental influences begin while the foetus is still in the womb, Chapter Two discusses the preconditions for brain plasticity, environmental influences on the nervous system during gestation, and the importance of embryology for the development of the nervous system. In order to provide an understanding of the complexity of the brain and its "landscape", Chapter Three takes the reader through brain anatomy, biology, and chemistry, as well as the maturation process of the brain. Chapter Four discusses the plasticity of the brain, but also the assumption that there are so-called windows of opportunity that are only open at certain times during the maturation process. This chapter discusses various theories concerning phases and stages, critical and sensitive periods. Since the human nervous system relies on outside influences to mature, Chapter Five examines the basis for the attunement of the nervous system through rhythm and resonance phenomena. As mentioned above, the brain may be divided into three levels, and these are the topics of Chapters Six, Seven, and Eight. Thus, Chapter Six describes the sensory brain, the lowest level in this triune model, Chapter Seven addresses the emotional level, the middle of the three levels, and Chapter Eight discusses the rational level, the top level of the triune brain. The brain is composed of neurochemical compounds that affect motivation, stress-management skills, and emotional flexibility, and Chapter Nine addresses the most important of these messengers: neurochemical regulation is crucial for the development of personality and is achieved through interactions with the external environment. The current view is that mental processes in the brain are based on the establishment of neural circuits, and that certain brain structures activate certain emotional categories. Chapter Ten examines the main affect-regulating circuits, although our knowledge about these circuits is far from complete. Men and women display behavioural differences, and sex hormones play an important part in brain development and are released at specific developmental stages. It is difficult to find distinct anatomical differences between male and female brains, but there are some minor deviations, and both the impact of sex hormones and these minor differences in brain anatomy may explain certain sex-typical features, which are described in Chapter Eleven. As mentioned earlier, the vertical structure of the brain may be viewed as triune, but the brain is also lateralized and consists of two separate hemispheres. The two hemispheres are in charge of different functions, and Chapter Twelve describes this functional lateralization, the integration of the brain through the corpus callosum and anterior and posterior commissures, and the effect of lateralization on personality functions. All personality development and learning are based on memory functions. Chapter Thirteen describes various theories on memory functions and our many memory systems, which are mutually integrated in the triune brain. Self and consciousness are often treated as self-explanatory terms, but they are essentially symbolic markers of deep and complex internalized sensations and actions. Chapter Fourteen describes various representations of consciousness or mental organization, partly based on the notion of the triune brain, and addresses the role of these levels as prerequisites for the emergence of the ego or self that we know from our waking state.

The day and the hour

> When
> at what day
> at what hour
> surely there must have been
> a day an hour
> when development
> however slowly
> imperceptibly
> was initiated
> did we stop
> being who we had been
> and became those
> who have already
> begun
> not to be.
>
> (Maria Giacobbe, "De fire læretider", 1981,
> translated for this edition)

CHAPTER ONE

The dynamic brain in a dynamic environment: an epigenetic understanding

> Just as everything about our minds is caused by our brains, everything about our brains is ultimately caused by our evolutionary history. For human beings, nurture is our nature. The capacity for culture is part of our biology, and the drive to learn is our most important and central instinct
>
> (Gopnik, Meltzoff, & Kuhl, 1999, p. 8)

From the moment of conception there is a dynamic interaction between our genetic and hereditary properties and our environment. From birth, infants are predisposed to establish attachment and to engage in interactions with their care-givers. They initiate and control interactive situations and have an intuitive basis for sharing other people's feelings and grasping their intentions. Three-week-old infants are able to imitate other people's facial expressions, and two-day-old infants are able to reliably imitate a face that smiles, frowns, or looks surprised (Field, Woodson, Greenberg, & Cohen, 1982; Meltzoff & Moore, 1977; Stern, 1985).

The discussion of nature *vs.* nurture seems never-ending and is, in many respects, meaningless, since nature and nurture can be only expressed through intimate interaction. Nature and nurture are expressed at the moment of conception, throughout gestation, during childhood and youth, and in adulthood. A mother, father, or other primary care-giver affects the development of the infant's affect-regulating system, which is neurally conditioned, and which later helps regulate other attachment functions. John Bowlby viewed attachment as the part of human biology through which social bonds are enacted. The attachment process enables the development of complex mental functions through complex actions from the primary care-giver. Many of these mental functions are uniquely human (Fonagy, Gergely, Jurist, & Target, 2002).

In this first chapter, I address the issue of nature *vs.* nurture and discuss man's inherent biological properties as tailor-made to provide us with the capacity for interacting with our environment or culture; I also look at the evolution of the human nervous system. Paul MacLean's view of the triune brain will be incorporated in a discussion of the human nervous system as consisting of different forms of mentalization, which are capable of functioning independently but usually function in close interaction through a sprawling and tight-knit network of neural paths. At the end of the chapter, I offer a brief introduction to brain development from birth and to the importance of stimulation as the key driver of, and condition for, this development.

Nature and nurture

Howard Gardner (1996) notes that our potential capacities are expressed through the basic structures of the brain, i.e. through heredity, but that environmental factors mobilize these latent capacities by altering the efficiency of the existing neural pathways and causing new behavioural patterns to emerge. We are born with physiological and psycho-biological equipment that must be exposed to human culture in order to reach its potential; our innate potential can only be realized through culture. Our life experiences are critical for the differentiation of brain tissue. The innate structure of the nervous system determines children's interactions with their surroundings, and the resulting responses in turn affect the structure. Thus, there is no inside and outside in relation to the nervous system; as Daniel Stern (2001) has pointed out, we are all born to engage in each other's nervous systems.

The neural structure determines the potential, but experience gives it its specific form. As humans, we are predisposed to develop language, for example, but the specific language that we acquire depends on our environment. The specific information derived from experiences is incorporated into the neural structures. The structure that the nervous system has from birth determines the opportunities and the changes that environmental influences can lead to. Nature and nurture are not each other's opposites; they interact in an interdependent process and are inseparable. Some genes only express themselves under certain life circumstances, and individuals who are particularly genetically vulnerable are also more receptive to psychological damage from environmental factors. We respond differently to similar stress stimuli, and environmental factors affect our personalities in different ways (Rutter & Rutter, 1997).

The human biological capacity for participating in culture

No individual can be divorced from his or her history and culture; we are not fully contained within our own skin. We have a biological capacity for taking part in social interactions and communication because we are born with the predisposition for forming attachments and interacting with our care-givers. Humans are social beings, and our psychological functions depend on interactions and transactions with the social environment during infancy. Biology does not determine a person's actions and experiences—biology determines what is possible. Culture shapes the human mind. It is impossible to determine how much of a child's psychological function is the child's own, and how much is a product of the child's relationships. Culture consists of an infinite number of ways of being together, through language, narrative explanations, etc., in a shared life where people rely on each other. Culture makes actions meaningful by imbuing these actions with intentions within a particular interpretive system that is active from birth (Bruner, 1986). The child arrives with certain innate abilities for participating in culture, and the resulting life and personality are derived from a developmental process that unfolded under particular historical circumstances.

The human brain is the most complex and plastic natural system in the known universe. Humans and mammals have many instinctive operational brain systems, but in the mature adult human brain the instinctive processes are difficult to observe because they are no longer expressed directly but are filtered and modified by higher cognitive activity. The instinctive operative systems form the basis for our sophisticated abilities. The human ability to acquire language, for example, is genetically determined, but the genetic programming concerning language is unusually open and susceptible to environmental influences. The construction of mammalian brains is governed by genetically dictated rules that include innate development programmes. Specific genes are expressed at specific developmental stages. There are programmes for selective cell death, which selectively kill off surplus neurons in order to make room for new and more advanced possibilities. These processes are controlled by chemical substances and molecules that foster optimal neuronal growth patterns. Darwin (1872) mentioned that certain primary emotions arose through genetic dictate, but that they matured and were shaped by environmental influences through personal experiences throughout the lifespan. Neuronal migration and the formation of billions of synapses follow a set of general principles, which cannot be exclusively under genetic control because we simply do not have that many genes. Our genes enable us to feel and behave in certain ways, and cultural learning enables us to effectively utilize these abilities and navigate in a complex world. These trends are combined in motor skills, sensory perception, affect, motivation, emotion, thinking, behaviour, etc.—all the aspects that we define as personality.

The relationship between genetic predispositions and environmental factors

Many hereditary phenomena require transactions with the environment in order to be expressed, and the care-givers' behaviour plays an important role in determining which hereditary predispositions actually unfold, and how (Plomin, 1983). Heredity defines the basic parameters for our development, but many other factors determine the actualization and expression of these hereditary elements. All learning depends on a genetically programmed capacity for learning and involves environmental influences on hereditary properties. Genes contribute to, but do not dictate, the formation of synapses. Schizophrenia is a case in point: if one identical twin develops schizophrenia, the other twin has a high likelihood of also developing the disorder. On average, about one per cent of the population develops schizophrenia. The non-identical twin of a person with schizophrenia has a seventeen per cent risk of also developing the disorder, while the risk for a non-twin sibling is nine per cent. The risk that the identical twin of a person with schizophrenia also develops the disorder is only about fifty per cent, although they share the same genetic material (LeDoux, 2001; Plomin, 1999).

The Finnish psychologist Pekka Tienari (1991) compared adoptive children who had schizophrenic birth mothers with adoptive children whose biological parents had no psychological disorders. He found that the adoptive children with schizophrenic birth mothers were somewhat more likely to develop a personality disorder than the children in the other group—but only when they lived in homes that were considered emotionally dysfunctional. Even a high genetic risk does not necessarily mean that the consequences of a given behaviour are linked with this risk. If, for example, child abuse were found to be conditioned by genetic factors, the damage that the child suffered would still happen, via the child's loss of trust in the environment. Similarly, criminal behaviour only seems to be related to genetic risk if the child spends the first few years of life in a dysfunctional family. Whether the genetic risk manifests itself depends on the quality of the child's family network (Fonagy, 2003).

Genetic factors and the way they are expressed are more amenable to environmental influences at certain developmental stages. These are often referred to as particularly sensitive or critical periods. Genes do not exercise their full influence at birth, but are boosted periodically by maturational progress and through interactions at the various developmental stages. The human brain develops about seventy per cent of its final content and potential after birth (Schore, 1994).

Certain innate dispositions are more susceptible to outside influences than others; for example, experiments with monkeys have showed that monkeys' innate fear of snakes requires not only exposure to a snake but also to the mother's expression of fear when encountering the snake. A single exposure is sufficient to trigger fear in the young monkey, but without the mother's fear response the young monkey's innate fear will not be activated. Thus, the unconscious reaction to snakes has both an innate and an acquired component, and these are interconnected somewhere deep inside the unconscious system (Damasio, 2003). The biological factors create the predispositions and conditions for our interactions with our surroundings, which in turn shape our behaviour. In addition, some of these elements may become symbols, laden with meaning. For example, snakes, bears, and other powerful animals play an important role in the myths and storytelling of most communities. When these symbols are applied they affect us on a deep emotional level.

Our genes are environmentally responsive

Edelman and Tononi (2000) point out that the specific environment that a child is born into determines which neural networks and synapses are formed and strengthened. Already, at birth, the stimulation that the child is exposed to initiates and strengthens certain specific patterns of neural activity. In this manner, genetic and environmental factors interact at every stage of brain development. The environment plays a key role in the establishment and strengthening (selection) of synaptic connections after birth. Because the human brain is so relatively unfinished at birth, the care-givers have a major impact on the detailed structure and functions of the brain. The care-givers affect the unfolding of the brain's genetic programmes through experience-dependent influences and development. The genetic potential plays out on a background of specific social experiences that impact the way that neurons interconnect. Human contact creates neural connections. For example, although the ability and desire for play is a genetically programmed behaviour, these traits are only expressed under the right circumstances. Anxiety and hunger, for example, inhibit play. Most mammals only play when they are in a warm, supportive, and safe setting with engaged and involved care-givers. Thus, environmental stimuli regulate the anatomical and cellular organization in the developing nervous system (Schore, 1994).

Previous experiences affect development on both a psychological and a neurophysiological level. The infant's early care-givers help create a personality foundation, which enables the infant to engage in many other future human relations. The quality and nature of these relationships determine the infant's opportunity for unfolding his or her genetic potential.

An example of the interdependence of nature and nurture is illustrated in experiments with rhesus monkeys, where Stephen Suomi (1985, 1991, 1997, 2000) studied different monkey personalities. Suomi found that young monkeys often display personality features that resemble those of their fathers, even though, in many cases, they had never met their fathers. He also found that maternal care can effectively turn particularly vulnerable and unfortunate personality features around and that such traits as shyness or a reactive temper are innate features that may unfold in advantageous or disadvantageous ways, depending on the monkey's upbringing. Thus, temper is hereditary, but open to both positive and negative influences through environmental factors—*our genes are environmentally responsive*. Suomi found that a caring rhesus monkey mother might make up for difficult temperamental aspects; for example, by taking the time to teach the young monkey coping strategies. The young monkey learns how to seek support from others, and as an adult it will often command a high position in the group hierarchy. In monkeys, the effect of early experiences may be reversible, even in extreme cases, although this is not an easy process. In humans, too, the early social environment has substantial impact on subsequent behaviour, and even the "best genes" in the world cannot ensure that an individual will grow up to be socially competent if he or she is raised in a harmful environment. On the other hand, even the best or the worst environment imaginable cannot prevent certain innate features from appearing at specific times in the child's development and being integrated into the child's behavioural repertoire.

Vulnerability and environmental influences

Temperamental components such as passivity or hyperactivity, for example, may be induced by either innate or environmental manipulations. Several studies (including van Ijzendoorn, Goldberg, Kroonenberg, & Frenkel, 1992) conclude that parental factors have a much greater influence on the infant's attachment pattern than the infant's temperamental characteristics. There is also documentation that innate factors help determine an infant's attachment competencies in the form of secure or insecure attachment (Brodén, 1991). Children are born with different temperaments, which affect their encounter with the world.

As Allan Schore (1994) has pointed out, humans have an innate template for engaging in interactions with a primary care-giver and for unfolding their potential through specific interactions with this person. The mother regulates interactions with the infant, regulates the infant's endocrine and nervous system, and acts as an external regulator of the neurochemistry in the infant brain, as has previously been pointed out by Plomin (1983), Hofer (1983), and others.

Sroufe (1979, 1996) has studied infants with depressed, inattentive mothers and found a clear connection between the degree and character of the interaction and a progressive deterioration of the conditions of these infants. At three months, the infants' responses were unremarkable, at six months, they seemed anxious or passive Around the age of one year, half the children showed an insecure attachment to their mothers, and at age eighteen months all the children had an insecure attachment. The mother's personality has been found to be a more reliable predictor of the child's future attachment pattern than the child's own temperament. The child's temperament—responsiveness, activity level, attention management, etc.—influences the expression of a particular attachment pattern but not the nature of the pattern. Other studies have shown that parents may have difficulty establishing a safe and secure base for children with difficult innate temperaments: for example, children who are difficult to regulate or children with an innate temperament that differs from that of their parents (Belsky & Isabella, 1988; Chess & Thomas, 1987; Karen, 1998).

According to Rutter and Rutter (1997), there is no evidence that specific behavioural patterns are hereditary. From birth, children have individual temperamental differences, and some infants are more amenable to emotional regulation than others. Temperamental differences affect the interaction with the care-giver, and difficulties in the interaction may stem from the mother's personality, the child's personality, differences between the two, or social and societal conditions. The parents' appreciation of the child may be weak, and the interaction may damage the development of the neural circuits.

Humans are social creatures—hence we are also the source of each other's stress. Stress often has roots in close relations and has a substantial impact on brain development. Abuse or neglect in the early stages of life in combination with innate vulnerability in the child has been found to increase the risk of a deterioration of the stressful state. Children who are prone to developing aggressiveness will unfold these aggressive tendencies if they grow up in high-risk families. Children with an innate disposition for depression will develop depression if they are unable to cope with abuse or neglect and chaos.

The way that children process experiences and perceptions of the environment has a great impact on their behaviour, including the expression of genetic dispositions. Internal and external stimuli are crucial to brain development, and such factors as hormones, stress, learning, social interaction, etc., will affect the neural structure. The child's experiences and evaluations are closely associated with attachment relations, and the quality of early relationships is a key influence on the child's processing capacity. Children's understanding of their surroundings is more amenable to modification than the environment itself or the genes with which the environment interacts (Fonagy, 2003).

The triune, hierarchical brain

In 1949 Paul MacLean (1967, 1970, 1973, 1990) published his first article as a precursor of the theoretical construction that he would continue to elaborate on throughout the 1950s and 1960s. In 1970 he had completed a model of cerebral organization that he called "the triune brain". MacLean sought to point out anatomical structures and neural circuits that are crucial to our emotions. He was inspired by James Papez, who had suggested a functional split between the cognitive and the emotional processing of sensory input as early as the 1930s. MacLean divided the brain structures into three tiers, which he viewed as quantum leaps in the evolution of the human brain. In his view, the brain had evolved for millions of years from the bottom up, with higher centres evolving as superstructures on top of lower and older sections (Figure 1.1). Throughout the 1970s

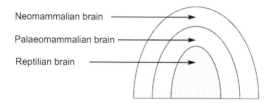

Figure 1.1.   The three levels of the triune brain.

and 1980s he continued to refine this theoretical construct, and in 1990 he published his principal work, *The Triune Brain in Evolution: Role in Paleocerebral Functions.*

MacLean saw the three cerebral structures as essentially different both structurally and chemically, and he viewed them as evolutionarily distinct. They have vast neural interconnections and function as three brains in one. He uses the term "triune" to emphasize that the whole is greater than the sum of its parts because the exchanges between the three brain structures contain more information than the sum of the individual brain structures would if they operated independently. MacLean compares the structure to three individual but interconnected computers, each with its own intelligence, its own subjectivity, its own sense of time and space, its own memory, its own motor functions, etc. Despite the close links between the three cerebral structures they all function as partially independent systems. The lines between the three structures are somewhat blurred, however, and it may be difficult to define a specific function as belonging exclusively to one single structure. MacLean divided the three brain structures into three different mentalization forms and labelled the most primitive layer protomentation, the middle layer emotomentation, and the third layer ratiomentation. These three forms of mentation exist on three different levels in the brain, which he labelled the reptilian brain, the palaeomammalian brain, and the neomammalian brain.

The reptilian brain

The most primitive layer, the reptilian brain, processes instinctive impulses and handles basic motor planning. The term reptilian brain stems from the assumption that this brain was predominant in the age of the reptiles. This part of the brain consists of instinctive functions and very primitive reflexive "emotional" reactions such as seeking, aggression, sexuality, and certain aspects of anxiety behaviour. In the modern human brain, this structure may be related to the brainstem and middle brain structures, which regulate breathing, heart rate, and other vital functions. The reptilian brain controls stereotypical reactions and movements, receives sensory input, and co-ordinates movement. It has a limited cortex and is therefore not capable of learning to handle more complex novel situations.

The palaeomammalian brain

The next layer, the so-called palaeomammalian (older mammalian) brain, is also known as the limbic system. In MacLean's view, this brain became predominant at the stage in evolution when the first mammals appeared on the scene. The older mammalian brain made the basic reptilian affects more subtle through the development of social emotions and generally added further mental and non-reflexive activity to the brain's repertoire. In time, the limbic system also provided memory and the possibility of learning emotional responses, which added a new dimension to situations that involve choice. Both the reptilian brain and the palaeomammalian brain lack the neural circuits required for verbal communication.

The neomammalian brain

The third layer and the latest evolutionary stage is the neomammalian (new mammalian) brain. The explosive growth that took place late in evolution is believed to have been one of the most dramatic examples of evolutionary transformation known in anatomy. This area, which mainly consists of the neocortex, processes mental and cognitive reasoning. The neocortex arose millions of years after the limbic system, as the mammalian brain evolved further. The neomammalian brain is also called "the thinking brain", and further development of the neocortex has added what is specifically human. The neocortex contains the areas that integrate and make sense of sensory experiences. It enables a more complex emotional register, where an emotion is combined with the thoughts concerning this emotion. This is the area that enables abstract thinking, the creation of abstract fictitious worlds where emotional values are attached to real-world phenomena. It expands a given emotion with the thoughts concerning it, which makes it possible, for example, to have feelings concerning ideas, art, and symbols and enables us to imagine what others are feeling. The evolutionary advantage of the neocortex must have been the ability to strategize and make long-term plans. While limbic structures give rise to sensations of pleasure, fear, grief, sexual desire, etc., the neocortex enables us to process this emotional content. The separation of the limbic structures from the neocortex corresponds to the separation of feelings from knowledge.

The hierarchical brain

The extensive functional interaction between the three cerebral layers defined by MacLean, despite their respective "focus areas", has given rise to criticism (LeDoux, 1998). Many neuroscientists reject the model as overly simplistic, because they see it as undermining the understanding of the brain as a highly integrated entity. Despite the criticism, I choose to use the model as a useful synthesis that may help bring order to the many complicated structures of the brain. For, as Professor of Psychobiology Jaak Panksepp (1998) writes,

> Although the triune brain concept is largely a didactic simplification from a neuroanatomical point of view, it is an informative perspective. There appear to have been relatively long periods of stability in vertebrate brain evolution, followed by bursts of expansion. The three evolutionary strata of the mammalian brain reflect these progressions. [p. 43]

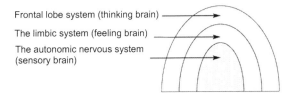

Frontal lobe system (thinking brain)
The limbic system (feeling brain)
The autonomic nervous system (sensory brain)

Figure 1.2. The triune brain.

Thus, the model is merely a "map", which should not be mistaken for the "landscape"; it is not a snapshot of the brain.

Thus, in a somewhat simplified version, the hierarchical functions of the brain may be organized as described above. In a simplified sense, the hierarchical system of the brain implies that higher-order functions are always based on lower-order functions, while lower-order functions may be independent of higher-order functions. As Damasio (1994) points out, nature has not simply superimposed the neural structures for logic and rational thinking on top of the existing structures for physiobiological–sensory regulation and emotional structures; rather, these new structures are developed from and together with the older structures. Thus, it is not only the neomammalian brain that has evolved, but also structures in the palaeomammalian brain and in the reptilian brain. Memory functions were not always a part of the limbic system, and the limbic system has evolved in terms of both mass and neuronal density.

The emotional systems probably hold a key position in the imprint of many higher and lower brain activities. Owing to the interactions of the limbic systems with higher brain regions, no emotion is unaccompanied by thought, and many thoughts produce emotions. The innate emotional systems interact so intensively with higher brain systems that the normal animal brain is probably incapable of having an emotional condition without cognitive processes (Panksepp, 1998). Owing to the interaction of the limbic system with lower brain regions, there are no emotions without physiological or behavioural consequences, and many of the resulting bodily changes might also regulate the tone of the emotional system in a feedback loop.

In this section, I have described the hierarchical brain and the interactions of the various parts of the brain from a phylogenetic point of view, based partly on Paul MacLean's theory of brain evolution. In the following section, I describe some of the general considerations concerning brain maturation throughout the lifespan—the ontogenetic development.

The "user-friendly" brain

At the beginning of the previous century, the English neurologist John Hughlings Jackson (1835–1911) pointed out that the human brain consists of functional hierarchical levels where top-level functions are volitional and able to inhibit non-volitional, lower functions, although they are not unaffected by these lower levels. Through distinct developmental stages, the structures that develop early in life are progressively subordinated and incorporated into later developing structures, which increases the brain's complexity. The functions that were present at the previous levels become subordinate to the higher, later emerging levels (Schore, 2003b). As John Bowlby pointed out, this hierarchical structure makes the brain more adaptable and efficient, but it also renders the developing nervous system more vulnerable and susceptible to the risk of actually losing efficiency. As development progresses, ever more brain structures can be activated simultaneously in support of each other, but there is also a risk of brain structures dissociating or competing against each other (Mortensen, 2001).

All behavioural changes are reflected in the nervous system, and all major changes in the nervous system are reflected on all neural and behavioural levels. Everyday sensory experiences, sensory deprivation, and learning may weaken certain synaptic connections under certain circumstances, or strengthen them under a different set of circumstances (Kandel, 2005). External stimuli influence the brain's affect-regulating systems, which in turn affect hormones and neurotransmitters. The social environment changes during infancy, which leads to the disorganization and reorganization of brain structures. The range of interactions between care-giver and infant is imprinted on the infant's developing nervous system. Various types of stimulation trigger affective interactions and are embedded in certain physiological and psychobiological patterns in the infant's nervous system. Early affective exchanges between infant and care-giver form the basis for the self-regulating mechanisms that remain an important organizing principle throughout life (Krystal, 1988; Schore, 1994).

Initially, infants express themselves through reactions that are both created by innate temperamental contours and triggered and shaped by external stimuli, and, as previously mentioned, they adapt in a number of ways. Some infants handle affect regulation with greater ease than others, and the ability to maintain flexible and organized behaviour in the face of high levels of arousal or excitation is essential in relation to the individual differences in personality organization (Sroufe, 1996).

All synapses throughout the nervous system are open to experiential modification. Emotional systems develop through association or classic conditioning, including the avoidance of unpleasant
experiences and attraction to pleasant ones. The activation of neural
circuits has a direct impact on the development of connections in
the brain. The specific information that is derived from experience
is incorporated into the neural structures, including the formation
of new synaptic connections and cellular changes.

The brain is simultaneously resilient and malleable

In many regards, the brain is plastic, but in other areas it does seem
to adapt to its environment so specifically that certain behaviours
become change-resistant. Thus, one ongoing discussion concerns
the relationship between the so-called "resilient brain" (limber, elastic) and the "malleable brain". Resiliency implies that the brain is
able to recover from a stressful period and return to a previous
condition like a seed that has been stepped on. Malleability implies
that the brain is shaped by the influences it receives, and that it is
able to adapt to its surroundings, like putty. The emerging consensus seems to be that the brain is characterized by plasticity as well as
malleability. It adapts, but not under all circumstances. The human
brain is designed to mature on the basis of experiences. Early neglect
and stress causes adaptive adjustments in neural development. The
evolutionary benefit would be to prepare the adult brain to survive
and reproduce in hazardous surroundings. There may be a high
price to pay if the child is later to manage in an environment that
appreciates other values. Sufficient care allows the brain to develop
a higher level of self-regulating skills, which eventually leads to the
development of empathy and self-reflection and the expression of
creative abilities. Any society reaps as it has sown with regard to the
care it provides for its young (Perry, 1997; Teicher, 2002).

The human brain is unfinished at birth, and many of its capacities unfold only after birth. It is designed to survive in particular
environments, cultures, languages, and climates, and the parents
shape their child's brain in unique ways. In good cases, with good
parents, early brain development equips the child with benefits for
life. In bad cases, for example in the case of parental psychopathology, the brain is shaped in a way that causes the child to develop

maladaptive sides, which he or she will have to struggle with throughout life.

Cerebral development

The brain differs from most other organs by having a growth spurt that begins before birth and lasts until a few years after birth. One consequence of this timing is that in some regards the brain is most sensitive to both beneficial and harmful influences during this period. The brain's development process stretches over several overlapping phases. Its basic structure is formed during gestation, but its development is far from complete at birth.

Human infants are born with more neurons than they need. During childhood, about half of the unused neurons are eliminated (pruning), while the neurons that are frequently used and activated become part of specialized neural circuits and are strengthened (parcellation). Cell death serves to fine-tune function and appears to be associated with increased specialization of the functions managed by the various parts of the brain. The final stage of neural maturation, growth and differentiation, depends on stimulation.

Plasticity and vulnerability

Animal studies show that learning causes growth in synaptic connections and gene activation and, thus, genetic expression (Kandel, 2005). Thus, external stimulation shapes neural connectivity, and in the long term it builds experience that remains modifiable throughout the lifespan. The circuits are not only sensitive to the results of early experiences but are constantly affected and modified by new experiences. The external stimuli determine which connections are strengthened and which are pruned, and the neural pattern is constantly changing. Those connections that are activated most frequently are maintained and developed. This process enables the brain to adapt to its surroundings whether the person grew up in the tropical desert or in the Arctic.

Dysregulation that occurs during a particular critical phase for the development of neural circuits is not always evident until the symptoms emerge. For example, Varela and Maturana (1992) write that if a newborn lamb is separated from its mother for a few hours and then reunited with her, the lamb will appear to develop normally until it begins to interact with other lambs. A lamb that had been separated from its mother does not know how to play, and it becomes isolated. This animal's reaction patterns and nervous system clearly differ from those of other lambs due to its brief separation from its mother, perhaps because the mother licks the newborn lamb incessantly during the first few hours after birth. Because it was separated from its mother, the newborn lamb was deprived of this tactile stimulation and, possibly, the release of certain neurotransmitters that would have been triggered by this interaction. The lamb's interaction with the mother immediately after birth appears to have substantial impact on the development of the nervous system, and the consequences are evident in the lamb's behaviour in areas that are far removed from the licking behaviour.

The magnificence of the nervous system lies in its plasticity in relation to the environment, and neural circuits can develop only when they receive optimum levels of arousal and stimulation. Both the nature and the timing of experiences are important for development. Children and parents reflect the world they have been born into, and the human brain has immense capacity for developing in a user-friendly manner. The brain grows, organizes, and functions in relation to unique life experiences, and experience modifies all human behaviour. But the complexity of the brain also makes it a vulnerable and fragile structure.

Environmental influences

At first, an infant's affectivity is regulated by others, but, through the process of early development, affects gradually become self-regulatory as a result of stimulation and neurophysiological development (Thompson, 1990). Animal studies show that a stimulating and enriched environment has a long-term effect on neurological structure and neurochemistry. Stimulation can physically enlarge, diminish, or alter the brain. Experiments with rats have shown that rats that grew up in an enriched, stimulating environment developed more brain mass than rats that were left in an empty cage without playmates or toys. When the deprived rats were moved to stimulating settings their brains developed, but they never reached the same levels as the rats that had been exposed to the stimulating environment from the beginning. The researchers even found a hereditary effect that was passed on to the next generation. Gopnik, Meltzoff, and Kuhl (1999) describe how rat pups with parents that grew up in enriched environments are born with a thicker cortex than rats whose parents were deprived.

From nature to culture

Environmental influences on the stimulation of neurological growth is so robust that even malnourished rats that grow up in an enriched and stimulating environment have larger brain mass than well-fed but less stimulated rats (Cozolino, 2000). The brain regions that are used are the ones that develop, which is evident, for example, in active musicians who have a higher neuronal density in the brain areas that control the fine motor skills they use for their particular instrument. A study of London cab drivers found that the brain regions that enable the drivers to find their way are strengthened after six months of navigating the streets of London (Maguire et al., 2000). Understimulation causes apoptosis as well as a reduction in the number of neural circuits and their connectivity and branching. The growth in the number and complexity of circuit connections is the result of ongoing stimulation in a varied environment, which is probably the biological basis for all subsequent behavioural, emotional, motor, and cognitive development.

From an evolutionary point of view, the extended childhood is beneficial to humans. The long period of dependency is adapted to match creatures whose main speciality is the ability to learn (Gleitman, 1995). Human nature is culture, and culture is important in relation to the transfer of experience from one generation to the next. Humans are born to communicate and share ideas, and we depend on social exchanges. The infant enters this world and has to engage in human contact, adjust, and learn systems of meaning through constant interactions with the care-givers. Without this exchange, development runs awry, and the humanization process is stunted. Emotional and cognitive communication is a characteristic of our species.

In the USA in 1970, a thirteen-year-old girl was discovered who had been strapped into a chair most of her life and been deprived of sensory, emotional, motor, and language stimulation. In many regards she was retarded, and Russ Rymer wrote poetically about the development of the human brain:

> Brain maturation is not about the way the brain grows . . . It's about the way it dies. As it ages, its neurons disappear. As the brain sheds neurons, it sheds its plasticity, its blank potential. But at the same time the shape of its character and skills is revealed, the way a sculpture is revealed by the chipping away of stone. The process is known as stabilization. [Rymer, 1993, p. 169]

Summary

The discussion about nature *vs.* nurture seems never-ending, and the lack of a conclusion affects the views on maladaptive behaviour and personality disorders. In this chapter, I proposed a combined view of nature and nurture, where heredity (nature) and the environment (nurture) interact as inseparable aspects. Next, I discussed the triune, hierarchical brain, a model that I will continue to refer to in subsequent chapters. The evolution of the brain influences brain maturation and personality formation, and I have discussed the unfolding of the brain's plasticity against the background of the available environment. Our genetic make-up is important for the potential of the nervous system, and among the topics of the following chapter are the relationship between genotype and phenotype and the effect of gestation on the nervous system.

CHAPTER TWO

Genetics and embryology:
the cradle of personality

"Genes may play an essential role in placing a function in the brain of every human, and at the same time make a relatively small contribution to differences in the way that function is wired in individuals."

"Genes contribute to, rather than solely dictate, synaptic connectivity"

(LeDoux, 2001, p. 91, p. 296)

Introduction

Environmental influences begin during the foetal stage as the mother's hormonal balance, nutrition, and possible intake of stimulants or medication affect foetal development. The child's innate or genetic characteristics begin to unfold in interaction with the environment from the moment of conception. In this chapter, I outline the most recent findings in genetic research and discuss the current view of genes as a more or less open system whose function is determined by multiple factors. Only some genetic aspects unfold in a human life, and this chapter looks at the mutual influence of genes and environmental factors during gestation and their impact on the development of the nervous system.

Genes: the building blocks of the organism

The genes that make up our human genome have developed and adapted throughout human evolution. The genes are the basis for the development of an individual, and they ensure continuity as well as variation from generation to generation. The interaction between genes and the environment begins during gestation when the foetus develops sensory organs and the beginnings of motor control. Some genes take effect from the first cell divisions or at certain times during the foetal period, while others take effect late in life. During the development process, genes combine their information with information from other genes; they regulate each other and are affected by the environment, and sometimes they mutate.

Genes contain hereditary information that determines the properties and function of the cells. Genes consist of long spiral strands of DNA (deoxyribonucleic acid). The genetic code is embedded in the sequence of the building blocks of the DNA. Chromosomes contain genes, which always occur in pairs. Human sperm and egg cells both contain twenty-three chromosomes. When these merge at conception they form one cell with twenty-three pairs: forty-six chromosomes in total. Thus, all the cells in the human body contain forty-six chromosomes arranged in pairs, except for the sex chromosomes, where women have two X-chromosomes while men have an X- and a Y-chromosome. Each chromosome consists of a single strand of DNA, and the gene is the DNA segment that determines the construction of a particular property. Through cell division and specialization, the single cell that results from the merger of an egg cell and a sperm cell grows into an adult body with some 100 trillion cells. The genes are the building blocks of the chromosomes, and each chromosome pair consists of some 1,500 genes. Thus, every cell contains some 34,500 genes (1,500 × 23), a unit that is referred to as the genome, which contains the total sum of a person's genetic makeup (Gjærum & Ellertsen, 2002; Tetzchner, 2002).

Thus, genetic or hereditary material is the information that is passed on with the genes contained in the sperm cell and the egg. From each pair a random chromosome is passed on, which implies that any human may produce some eight million different chromosome combinations. A sperm cell and an egg cell each have eight million potential variations, and thus their merger leads to a total of sixty-four trillion possible combinations. Cells develop from stem cells, early stages of cells that all contain the same genetic information (with the exception of the sex cells). Stem cells are activated at a given time to perform their given function in processes that are not yet fully understood; these processes might be determined by genetic information as well as by extracellular environmental factors. Animal studies have shown that cells that are moved from one brain area to another at an early stage function smoothly in their new environment. For example, cells that normally process visual sensory input may be moved to an area that normally processes auditory input. Thus, the function of the individual cell is affected by the cell's environment, and the function is modified accordingly. Cells that are damaged or non-functioning may, to some extent, be replaced by others, which improves the individual's chances of survival. Cells do not divide and specialize according to a rigid pattern but are capable of differentiated development—plasticity. At the same time, the genes restrict the range of possible modifications in order to keep development on the right track (Evrard, Marret, & Gressens, 1997; Tetzchner, 2002).

In 2003, the so-called Human Genome Project was completed, an endeavour to map the human genome in detail. Previously, the genome had been considered a sort of blueprint that described our protein construction in full, but today this view is considered too static or linear. Molecular biologists now believe that it is more useful to begin to analyse the workings of the interaction between genes. Thus, the genes appear to act more as essential blueprints for the structure of the nervous system than as instructions for a predetermined structure.

We now know that we have some 34,500 different genes, but still we know little about the ways that genes connect into networks and spark activity in every single living cell. The main reason that it is so difficult to fully uncover the workings of these processes is that the myriad of components keep altering their condition from one moment to the next, which makes it impossible to study any single part in isolation. Like many other phenomena in the universe, genes seem to operate according to non-linear principles (Strogatz, 2003).

The Human Genome Project found remarkable similarity among individual human beings: 99.9% (Kandel, 2005). Some genes are predetermined and unchangeable. Skin colour, eye colour, etc., are genetically determined, as are certain diseases, e.g., Huntington's Chorea. Other genetic dispositions are influenced by the environment. For example, a newborn infant will smile regardless of outside stimuli, but the social smile, which is triggered by the human face, appears some forty-six weeks after conception (when the child is about six weeks old). We must assume that genetic disposition or biological potential underlies both the innate smile and the social smile. The interaction of the social smile with the environment is governed both by the child's innate properties and by the given context. Many diseases are characterized by a connection between genetic and environmental factors. Many genes interact with environmental factors. For example, both nature and nurture are now believed to play a part in obesity, nicotine addiction, alcoholism, etc.

Genotype/phenotype

Genes have two main functions. First, they are templates for information that is passed on from one generation to the next. This transmission function is outside any individual or social control. Second, the genes are expressed in close interaction between nature and nurture. The expression of many of our genes hinges on other genes and on certain environmental stimuli. The specific stimulation received by an individual plays an important part in determining which genes are activated; this is the so-called epigenetic factor. One's hereditary genetic combination is referred to as one's genotype, while the outcome of genetic activation provides the phenotype. The phenotype depends both on the available genes in the genotype and on environmental influences on the cells of a given individual. Only some 10–20% of the genes are expressed through the phenotype. Other genes are effectively suppressed. For example, a brain cell is a brain cell because this cell type only expresses a subset of the vast amount of information that it contains. Even though its reproductive capacity is not influenced by its environment, it is highly regulated by environmentally responsive factors. In humans, the modification of genetic expression through learning is particular efficient and has led to cultural evolution. Humans change much more through cultural evolution than through biological evolution (Kandel, 2005).

Research shows that many factors go into determining the expression of genotypes as phenotypes (Rutter & Plomin, 1997). For example, rat pups that are separated from their mother during the first few weeks after birth express a permanent increase in the gene that controls the hormone for attachment stress, and they develop lifelong sensitivity to stress. Conversely, rat pups that are licked and cared for by their care-giver develop lifelong protection against stress. Suomi (2000) studied a particular chromosome with an allele (a DNA-sequence in a particular location on a chromosome) that transports the neurotransmitter serotonin (the 5-HTT gene). The normal allele is long, but rhesus monkeys (and humans) may be hereditarily disposed for having a short allele, which reduces serotonin levels. The rhesus monkeys that had a short allele for serotonin fell into three categories in the study. One group displayed signs of anxiety, while the second group had problems with impulse control. They were fearless, engaged in conflicts, and their play quickly escalated to aggressive behaviour. Both these groups spent much of their time in isolation and were at the bottom of the hierarchy, and characteristically they had all suffered under early neglect. These two groups displayed lifelong and permanent changes in their serotonin levels. The third group had been raised by attentive and caring mothers. These monkeys developed normal serotonin levels despite their short allele. They channelled their impulsivity into constructive attention and managed to achieve and maintain positions at the top levels of the hierarchy. The deprived environment seemed to trigger their genetic predisposition, and early trauma is indeed capable of activating certain genes that lead to a reduced capability for interpersonal adjustment, which makes both primates and humans more sensitive to later trauma. In humans, some 43% have at least one short allele for serotonin. Individuals who have a short allele respond more strongly to negative experiences and crises, and in persons with two short alleles this response is even more pronounced. The risk of developing depression and acting out is far greater for persons with short alleles for serotonin (Hamer & Copeland, 1998; Sørensen, 2006).

All the cells in an organism carry a sort of gene-related memory. The expression of certain genes is shaped through complex psychological processes. The collective experience of a species may be reflected through the genome, but individual subjective experiences are reflected through the expression of the genome—the phenotype (Gopnik, Meltzoff, & Kuhl, 1999; Perry, 1999a). Among other things, the genes create the basis for our emotions, and they are involved in determining the constitution of the nervous system and the sorts of mental processes that we are capable of engaging in. But our exact actions, thoughts, and feelings in a given situation are affected by many other factors, not by genetic programming alone. Our emotions have a biological basis, but environmental factors are essential for their development. Genetic studies have shown that genetic expression relies on multiple factors, and the features that emerge are a combination of multi-factor genetic combinations and multi-factor environmental influences. A person may be born with a sensitive nervous system that is easily overwhelmed, but it is the interaction of nervous system and environment that determines how the personality actually unfolds.

Innate regulatory circuits

Some genes are vital to physical survival; they are more or less fixed and operate as closed systems within the basic structure of the organism. Innate circuits have a powerful impact on practically all the circuits that can be modified by experience. The regulatory circuits are related to survival and affect what happens in the later emerging areas of the brain. They respond to the quality of a situation and influence the way later emerging brain circuits are shaped, seeking to efficiently contribute to survival (Damasio, 1994). The brainstem contains so-called modulator neurons that are affected by activities inside the organism. Among other things, these modulator neurons distribute neurotransmitters to far-flung sectors of the central nervous system. The modulator neurons help control activity levels within the organism and define the temperament that shapes our behavioural development. Temperamental qualities, however, are not purely genetically determined; chronic stress, for example, may alter a neurochemical condition both before and after birth.

Temperament describes some aspects of innate characteristics. For example, the temperament is indicative of the environmental responsiveness of the organism, the intensity of emotional responses, basic mood, the ability to enter into a biological cycle, and the attraction to or avoidance of novel situations. A child's temperament can trigger certain parental responses and lead to a self-fulfilling reinforcement that helps promote or inhibit innate features, and the child's temperament may predispose the child for a particular orientation towards the environment. In a child with a sensitive nervous system, even small violations may be overwhelming and trigger a cascade of complex and unpredictable reactions that influence brain development and behavioural patterns (Cicchetti & Tucker, 1994). Many scientists now define individual differences in relation to the strength of the nervous system. Kagan, Snidman, and Arcus (1992) have argued that uninhibited children perhaps have a hereditary component of aggression, but that the likelihood that this aggressiveness develops into a behavioural disorder depends on the environment.

As early as 1890, in considering children's innate dispositions, William James concluded that everything was predetermined. He was looking at structures or patterns that are mainly but not exclusively determined by the genome, structures that newborn infants draw on in order to achieve homoeostatic regulation (Damasio, 1994). Children come equipped with an innate, instinctive behavioural repertoire, which they are able to employ immediately after birth, but they are also born with mechanisms for decoding particular behaviours when they have reached the right developmental stage and conditions require it. For example, children have an innate potential for learning the particular variation of universal human language that is selected in their family and culture. Children are equipped with an innate tendency to seek stimulation and to arrange their experiences into increasingly complex hierarchies. Infants are born with a number of inherent, fixed perceptual preferences, motor patterns, cognitive tendencies, and an ability to express themselves emotionally; further, they are able to recognize their mother's voice and face, among other things. One of the first inherent features that ensure adequate stimulation is the newborn infant's ability to focus visually on objects that are about 20 cm away. This means that it is the mother's face, especially her eyes, that the child is most likely to look at and see. A newborn child is born with a capacity to be fascinated with the human face. The structure of the human face matches inherent visual stimulus properties for which the infant has developed preferences. Our brains are pre-programmed to process certain sorts of input. These innate properties probably developed because they offer evolutionary advantages and have thus become encoded into our genetic material (Siegel, 1999).

Experience and genetic expression

Certain genes appear to be essential for establishing certain aspects of a given behaviour, for example, emotionality, but experience plays a key part in modifying, activating, and deactivating genes. The genes determine what properties are available—the hand that one was dealt, so to speak—but experience determines how the hand is played. Many scientists have found that good basic early care can defuse a vulnerable and particularly reactive temperament. Being raised in a loving and caring setting leads to verifiable objective changes in the genetic expression. On the other hand, being raised in a setting characterized by abuse and unpredictability will have negative effects on even the most resilient nervous system. For example, studies have shown that exposing a particular structure in the limbic system to massive and persistent activation causes a great number of anxiety-provoking neurobiological changes that contribute to altering the genetic expression (Post, Weiss, Smith, Li, & McCann, 1997). If the mother suffers from stress during pregnancy, she releases large quantities of stress hormones, which may affect the infant's brain, for example in the limbic regions, and consequently the child's attention, learning, and temperament (Taylor, 2002).

As previously mentioned, all genes are not expressed at the same time. Schore (1994) mentions that approximately 70% of the genome is expressed after the child is born. The timing of gene expression depends partly on the child's neurophysiological development and partly on the child's interaction with the environment. Certain genetic expressions may not become evident until adulthood, or even old age. Genetic expression is translated into the emergence of new neurons and the strengthening of existing neurons. Throughout the lifespan, environmental stimulation continues to construct the brain. This ongoing adjustment is believed to be based on the fact that all genes have a section with binding areas for outside signal substances that regulate the activity of the gene, which in turn activates a particular type of RNA called mRNA (messenger ribonucleic acid). It is through RNA activity that environmental stimulation leads to continued learning and adaptation (Cozolino, 2006).

The genes are important for our adjustment, vulnerability, resilience, etc. However, the foetal period has also been found to have a significant impact on the development of the nervous system; this influence includes the outside factors to which the mother exposes the foetus during pregnancy.

Embryology—foetal development

Foetal development is commonly divided into three periods. When the egg and sperm cells merge a small cluster of cells is formed, called the morula. The *germinal period* includes the first ten to fourteen days. During this period a number of cell divisions take place, and the morula becomes attached to the mucous membrane in the uterus. The so-called gastrula gradually forms three different tissue layers: the *ectoderm*, the *mesoderm* and the *endoderm*. The outer layer (the ectoderm) turns into skin and nervous system, the middle layer (the mesoderm) turns into skeleton and muscle, while the inner layer (the endoderm) turns into the internal organs. Around three weeks after conception the *neural plate* is formed from the ectoderm; it later folds to form the *neural tube*. From the front end of the neural tube five protrusions extend, corresponding to the five main sections that the brain is traditionally divided into. If the shift from neural plate to neural tube is not completed properly, the result may be spina bifida. The *embryonic period* lasts from two to eight weeks after conception, until the neurons have formed in the brainstem and spinal cord. During the late embryonic period, the motor cells form in the spine, and the foetus begins to develop autonomic reflexes. The neurotransmitter systems that eventually come to regulate motivation and emotion are also neuronal and develop along with the neurons during the late embryonic period. The beginning of neuronal development in the cortex marks the beginning of the *foetal period*. Ten to eighteen weeks after conception, neocortical neurons develop. During the first ninety days, the cells in the neural tube move from the cell division area to their final destinations in the nervous system in a process called *cell migration*. After some eight weeks, the cortex and the early beginnings of the nervous system have formed, and after some twenty-one weeks the crease that separates the two brain hemispheres has developed. Eighteen weeks after conception most of the brain neurons have formed and found their final location. This is when axons and dendrites begin to emerge. This process begins in the second trimester and continues long after birth (Gjærum & Ellertsen, 2002; Huttenlocher, 1994; Trevarthen, 1990).

Establishing the architecture of the nervous system

The neural tube develops neurons and support cells (glial cells). During the first twenty weeks of the foetal period, cell migration and the formation of neurons take place by way of the support cells. In this process, neurons migrate from the innermost layer of the cortex toward the outside. Cell migration is likely to be vulnerable to both genetic and acquired disorders, and the different brain regions have different growth periods. The area with the largest growth is also the area that is most vulnerable to unfortunate influences. For example, both cerebral palsy and severe mental retardation may be caused by adverse influences during the initial three months of the foetal period, while damages around the time of birth may cause disorders in the spatial and temporal coordination of movements. Cerebral palsy and mental retardation may also be caused by severe birth trauma. No other time in human development matches foetal growth in speed and complexity, so this is a very vulnerable time indeed (Karr-Morse & Wiley, 1997).

Cells continue to develop by sending out branches that connect with other cells to form cell clusters, and superfluous neurons in all areas are removed through cell death (apoptosis) and pruning to achieve sufficiently precise connections. When neuronal production is at its highest, some 250,000 neurons develop every minute. This process is controlled by hormones that spread via the neural tube to switch on particular genes that produce proteins that in turn regulate neuronal production through various early cellular stages. After the end of the cell division period, around the fifth month of gestation, few new neurons are formed (Gjærum & Ellertsen, 2002; LeDoux, 2001). As soon as the neurons reach their destination, they begin to develop neuronal connections that enable them to influence each other (LeDoux, 2001). The mature brain consists of some 100 billion neurons and an even larger number of support cells, which are created during the first few months of foetal life. The entire nervous system is established just before birth.

During the foetal period, the brain structure becomes functional when enough neuronal connections are created. Around the sixth month of gestation, the myelination of axons begins, the formation of an insulating layer of fat around the neuronal extensions called axons. This myelination continues well into adolescence, and perhaps all the way into adulthood, at varying degrees of intensity and speed in the various parts of the nervous system. Myelin functions as insulation. It triples the speed of transmission and increases neuronal efficiency and precision (Figure 2.1).

It is not completely clear how neurons specialize for different functions and form neural networks, nor do we know the exact timing of structural differentiation. For example, we know that the

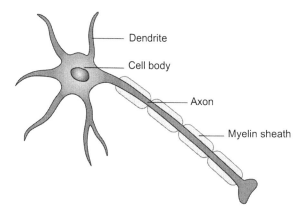

Figure 2.1.   Neuron, axon, and dendrite.

visual cortex is formed between the twenty-fifth and thirty-fifth week of the foetal period, while the structure of the cerebellum is not developed until much later and is not fully mature until after puberty. Superfluous connections between cells disappear as functional circuits are established. During this process, many neurons die through a pruning process. Cell death, pruning, and specialization processes are important aspects of brain development, which take place through an interaction between genetic programming and environmental influences. Neuronal death and pruning are assumed to be as essential to the development of the nervous system as cell division (Hansen, 2002; Karr-Morse & Wiley, 1997; Tetzchner, 2002).

Neurons and their structural architecture do not become specific until the neural connections are fine-tuned and establish their connections, a process that is already well underway in newborn infants. After their establishment, neurons depend on continued activation for their survival and differentiation, and if this continued activation is not present the neurons eventually die. An increase in the emergence of neural connections and myelination marks the beginning of a new developmental stage.

As early as some eight weeks after conception, the foetus is 2–3 cm long and weighs one gram, and it is possible to make out the beginnings of a fully formed human with limbs, a nervous system, and inner organs. After twelve weeks the circulatory system is in place, and after twenty-four weeks the child is able to breathe, but the lungs are still too immature. In human foetuses, all the sensory systems are functioning after week twenty-six. The senses develop in sequence: touch, balance, smell, taste, hearing, and eventually, vision (Tetzchner, 2002).

The nervous system needs stimulation to develop, and the foetal period is no exception. In the following section we shall look at the stimulation of the nervous system through its own motor activity and the mother's movements.

Foetal dependency on activity

New techniques have made it possible to study neurons during the earliest stages of foetal development. Studies using these techniques reveal that the formation of circuits depends on activation. Neurons begin to fire spontaneously and form connections through electric charges that trigger chain reactions and activate other neuron groups. Neurons that fire simultaneously become interconnected. In the late 1940s, neurophysiologist Donald Hebb theorized that neurons that fire simultaneously become interconnected: "Neurons that fire together wire together". It is believed that all learning operates according to this principle, and that neurons that fire often also develop stronger mutual connections. Neurons will always seek to create connections, and neurons that fail to connect into circuits will die (Gopnik, Meltzoff, & Kuhl, 1999).

During the foetal stage, animals learn through conditioning, i.e., they become accustomed to new stimuli. This habituation function is probably established around the time that the senses develop. Sensory stimulation helps activate the neurological system, but at the same time it must be toned down enough that the immature system can handle it. Stimulation during pregnancy functions as a preparation for the more intense and lasting stimulation that the child encounters right after birth, and premature infants often need help to shield themselves from excessive stimulation. The mother's voice is a prominent sound for a foetus because it is transmitted through the body, and it is some 32 decibels above any background noise (Tetzchner, 2002).

Foetal activity strengthens the body and develops the senses, and neural development is activity-dependent. Long before birth, the foetus begins to engage in spontaneous motor activity, and even if these movements may appear random they do seem to serve a developmental purpose. Hamburger (1977) has shown that the formation of sensorimotor connections during the foetal period is activity-dependent and arises through spontaneous motor patterns. At first, these motor patterns can best be characterized as rhythmic. When the most appropriate selection of sensorimotor connections has been accomplished, behaviour is modified by a sort of feedback control, which ensures the constant interaction of sensations, motor activity, and movement. The motor patterns that are involved in selecting the sensory connections are indicative of the neural plasticity of the brain at this early stage. During the early foetal stages, sensorimotor networks are involved in shaping brain anatomy. When the environment begins to play a key role in selecting neural circuits, this process takes place within a nervous system that is already well-structured (Cicchetti & Tucker, 1994; Trevarthen, 1990).

During the final trimester, the brainstem undergoes drastic development and processes take place that are prerequisites for the ability to regulate heart rate, blood pressure, body temperature, and respiration. The main environmental sensation is the persistent and rhythmic sound of the mother's heartbeat, which the foetus senses through motion and sound. Cross-cultural studies show that after birth, mothers often rock their babies in the same frequency as their resting pulse (Perry, 1999a).

Sensorimotor development

The motor and sensory systems are interrelated, and the primary task of the brain is to produce movements at the service of the organism. As in primitive vertebrates and fish, the development and organization of motor systems in the foetus begins with movements of the entire body, while relatively independent single movements do not appear until after birth (Mathiesen, 2004).

The mother's movements stimulate the foetus's vestibular or balance system, and her physical activity may lead to pressure or vibrations on the foetus. The foetus responds to tactile stimulation of its hands and arms around week 10–11, and after fourteen weeks it responds to touching all over the body except for the crown of the head. At a late stage in the foetal period, the neurological structures and chemical substances necessary for the perception of pain, for example, are active. The foetus may have reactions that resemble pain responses, but it is unclear that pain is in fact perceived at this stage. Around seven weeks, the foetus begins to move, and the grasping reflex appears around twenty-eight weeks (Tetzchner, 2002). When the foetus is four months old, it may grimace, for example, if it is tickled. It kicks aggressively when the mother drinks cold water, and in the fifteenth foetal week it begins to perceive flavour. Somewhere between the tenth and fifteenth foetal week, the foetus shifts when the mother coughs, and in the twenty-fourth foetal week, the foetus is able to hear the parents' voices if the father is close to the mother's stomach, and it is able to differentiate these voices at birth. The foetus is light-sensitive from the sixteenth foetal week, and if a light is shone directly at the mother's stomach, the foetus shifts. In the thirty-second foetal week, the foetus has vision, a capacity that is active from birth (Karr-Morse & Wiley 1997). Anders and Zeanah (1984) describe how the infant responds to the mother's voice from birth, and they conclude that channels of communication are ready from birth. Thus, all our senses are developed and in use even before we are born.

The foetus's interaction with environment

As early as at the moment of conception, the mother's environment is a part of the foetus's environment. The foetus is affected by everything the mother does and by everything that happens to her. Cell migration is influenced by genetic factors but is also sensitive to harmful effects passed on by the mother, such as alcohol or medication. Even small amounts of alcohol affect the development and function of the nervous system. Strong alcohol influences inhibit cell division and growth, delays neuronal migration, and disturbs the production of neurotransmitters and other substances. Substance abuse has a particularly harmful effect if it happens at an early stage in foetal development, and may lead to severe malformation. Behavioural consequences in childhood may involve intellectual deficiency, hyperactivity, and concentration difficulties (Rutter & Rutter, 1997). Hormones and other chemical substances affect brain development, and, as mentioned in the previous chapter, the migration of individual neurons and the formation of millions of synapses are not governed purely by genetics, since we simply do not have enough genes for that. Instead, development is believed to be governed by general principles that enable the construction of a highly developed neural organization through a combination of growth and reduction processes. This leads to selective fine-tuning with a remarkable degree of precision. Hormones from the mother help to regulate the expression of genes in the foetal brain. Acute changes in the mother's hormone condition cause changes in genetic expression in the foetal brain, and, under certain circumstances, these changes can last a lifetime (Schore, 2001a,b).

Much research in the 1980s and 1990s focused on the effect of stressful experiences on foetal development: for example, in relation to the emergence of anxiety or aggression later in life. Experiments carried out by Clarke and colleagues (1996a,b) showed that when pregnant monkeys were injected with a stress hormone, the hormone passed from mother to foetus, and the offspring later developed emotional and attention disorders as well as deficient motor co-ordination. Schore (2001b) also points out that there is evidence that stress stimulation from the mother may have a negative effect on stress regulation in the foetus, which may lead to lasting neurophysiological vulnerability.

The birth process also affects ongoing brain development. Major adjustments take place with the triggering of breathing reflexes and the activation of reflexes for controlling the cardio-vascular system; in addition, external influences in the form of light, sound, and touch change dramatically. The new sensorimotor patterns play a key role in the subsequent development of motor, sensory, perceptual, emotional, and mental functions. From the moment of birth, newborn infants have a sense of their own existence. Sensory perceptions in the form of taste, smell, warmth, light, touch, etc., are holistic experiential contours with no detailed structure because the cortex is still immature. Based on their innate active reflexes, newborn infants prefer structured to unstructured stimuli, select novel stimuli over familiar ones, actively explore their environment, and try to figure out how it works (Bergström, 1998; Rutter & Rutter, 1997).

Summary

In this chapter I have explored the interaction between genes and environment and the significant impact of foetal development and environmental interaction during gestation on the development of the nervous system. In the next chapter, I will look at the structure and main operating principles of the nervous system. In Chapters Six, Seven, and Eight, I shall return to the topic of brain structures in relation to MacLean's theory of the triune brain.

CHAPTER THREE

The brain: a complex and dynamic structure

In short, the brain is a system of systems. Each system is composed of an elaborate interconnection of small but macroscopic cortical regions and subcortical nuclei, which are made of microscopic local circuits, which are made of neurons, all of which are connected by synapses.

(Damasio, 1999, p. 331)

The human brain is an amazing structure, the result of previous evolutionary developments and adjustments. The nervous system developed from a primitive neural tube, as nerve connections were formed between remote parts of the body and a central structure that eventually gained overall control. In an evolutionary process, the nerves slowly developed into specialized modules, which made up what MacLean later called the reptilian brain, a reflexive structure without consciousness. On top of this system, a number of modules developed, including structures that enabled the simultaneous use of various senses, structures that made up a primitive memory, and structures that enabled the organism to respond to internal stimuli. The areas that underwent the greatest development in humans are the ones related to think-ing, planning, organization, and communication. In order to give an impression of the brain's plasticity and complexity and describe the "landscape" that this book addresses, this chapter is dedicated to a very general review of the complex structure of the brain with an emphasis on understanding the brain's ability to connect different structures through a maturation process based on psychological processes.

Brain anatomy

Even though the brain only makes up some 2% of our total body weight, it consumes about 25% of our total metabolic energy and about 40% of our blood glucose. About one third of the human genome is dedicated to controlling brain development, and during the first year of life we use about 50% of our metabolic energy exclusively on constructing and refining brain structures (Fisher, 2004). The average adult brain weighs about 1,300 grams and consists of the cerebrum, the cerebellum and the brainstem (Figure 3.1).

The central nervous system is divided into the spinal cord, the brainstem with the cerebellum, the diencephalon, and the two brain hemispheres. The brainstem is the structure closest to the spinal cord; it controls vital functions, including the cardio-vascular system with heart rate and blood pressure and breathing and swal-lowing reflexes. The brainstem also contains an activation system that regulates the activation level of the cerebrum, i.e., arousal and consciousness. Inside the hemispheres lies the limbic system, with functions related to emotions and memory. The hemispheres are divided into four lobes, all named after their location in the cranium: the frontal lobe, the parietal lobe, the temporal lobe, and the occipital lobe (Figure 3.2).

Each lobe has its own functions. The occipital lobe contains the visual cortex, which receives sensory input from the eye. Visual impressions result when light is converted to electrical and chemical signals and transmitted via the optic nerve to a structure called the thalamus and on to the occipital lobe. After an analysis of colour, movement, depth, etc., the impression is passed on for more

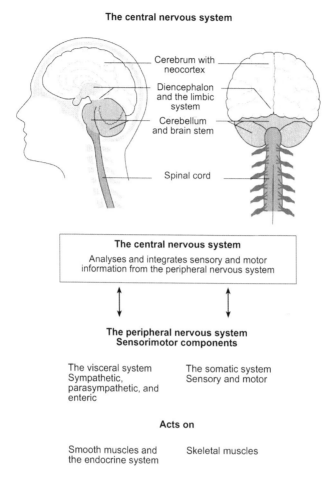

Figure 3.1. The central nervous system and peripheral nervous system.

complex analysis, including the "where" stream in the parietal lobe, which assesses spatial relationships, and the "what" stream in the temporal lobe, which deals with object recognition and identification (Cozolino, 2006). The parietal lobe contains the somatosensory cortex, which processes sensory impressions from our skin, muscles, and joints, and discriminates between different types of sensory input. Under the parietal lobe and on both sides of it lies the temporal lobe. It decodes and interprets what we hear and see and

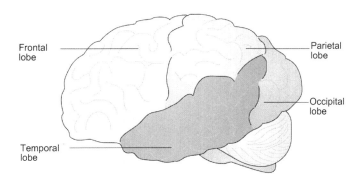

Figure 3.2.   Frontal lobe, parietal lobe, temporal lobe, and occipital lobe.

processes sensory messages. The left temporal lobe is particularly important for our understanding of linguistic concepts (Austin, 1998). The auditory cortex is located in the top section of the temporal lobe. The two language areas are located in the back section of the parietal lobe and the lower frontal section of the frontal lobe (typically in the left hemisphere). The back section of the frontal lobes contains the motor cortex with its neural connections to the brainstem and spinal cord, which controls the skeletal muscles. Directly in front of it is the pre-motor cortex, which co-ordinates impulses into motor patterns. Thus, the motor cortex is placed in front of the central sulcus and behind it is the somatosensory cortex. The motor area is part of the frontal lobe, and the somatosensory neuronal networks are situated in the parietal lobe. At the very front lies the prefrontal cortex, which contains functions for the planning of action sequences. Activity in this structure controls actions, inhibits impulses, and enables us to make choices. This part of the brain is the source of reasoning and plans or long-term actions. The purpose of all components of the brain, except for the frontal lobes, is to provide the basis for action (Gade, 1997).

The cerebellum co-ordinates body movements in relation to the surroundings.

The peripheral nervous system consists of motor and sensory nerve fibres that connect the "periphery", i.e., skin, muscles, and inner organs, to the spine. Pathways for skin and muscles make up the somatic nervous system, while pathways to the inner organs (e.g., heart, lungs, and digestive system) make up the autonomic nervous system. The autonomic nervous system regulates vital processes, e.g., heart rate, digestion, etc., while the somatic system controls the skeletal muscles and transmits information from the sensory organs.

The brain is made up of so-called white matter (neural pathways) and grey matter (the neurons themselves). The white matter consists of neural circuits, whose functions include connecting the cortex with deeper-lying sections and connecting the various regions of the cortex. The grey matter is a vast network comprising 70–80 per cent of our neurons. The cortical surface layer is often called the neocortex because it is the most recent evolutionary development. All grey matter beneath the neocortex is called subcortical (Figure 3.3). The neocortex is highly folded and accounts for about half of the cerebral hemispheres. It is folded into ridges and fissures (gyri and sulci), and if the neocortex were stretched out, it would cover a surface of some twenty square metres. The neocortex is an amazing structure, only 1.5–4.5 mm thick and containing some twenty billion neurons. It is a highly organized structure, and most regions contain six separate layers. Every single neuron connects to thousands of other neurons through axons, an indication of the flexibility and potential of our nervous system in relation to information processing and storage (Gjærum & Ellertsen, 2002).

Apart from the pineal gland in the centre of the brain, each brain module is doubled, i.e., every structure is represented in both hemispheres. The two hemispheres are linked by thick bundles of long

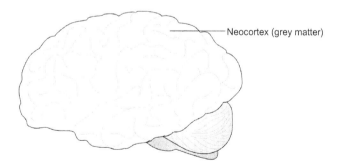

Neocortex (grey matter)

Figure 3.3.   The neocortex. The surface layer consists of grey matter and is called the neocortex. All grey matter beneath the cortex is referred to as subcortical areas.

nerve fibres through the corpus callosum, and the anterior and posterior commissures.

MacLean's triune structure

The brain is internally connected through countless circuits, and, as MacLean and others have described, it is a hierarchical structure with three main tiers. The brainstem (the reptilian brain), which MacLean viewed as the lowest level in the triune system, is the system that regulates arousal and the physiological equilibrium of the organism. The limbic system, which manages the balance between the inside and the outside world, interprets and modulates impulses from the brainstem, while the neocortex interacts with and analyses experiences from the outside world (Figure 3.4). The brainstem, the basic forebrain, and the limbic system modify somatic regulation and all the neural processes that form the basis for mental phenomena.

The nervous system is complex in function and anatomy. I have described the most important and fundamental structures in order to provide an impression of the complexity of the brain. Let us now examine the nervous system on a more basic neurobiological level.

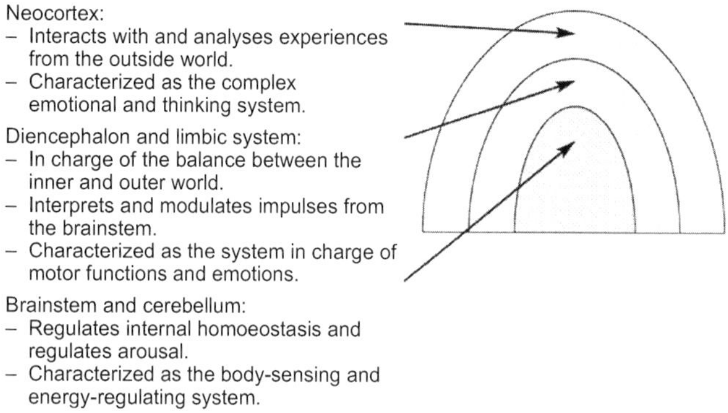

Neocortex:
– Interacts with and analyses experiences from the outside world.
– Characterized as the complex emotional and thinking system.

Diencephalon and limbic system:
– In charge of the balance between the inner and outer world.
– Interprets and modulates impulses from the brainstem.
– Characterized as the system in charge of motor functions and emotions.

Brainstem and cerebellum:
– Regulates internal homoeostasis and regulates arousal.
– Characterized as the body-sensing and energy-regulating system.

Figure 3.4. The triune brain.

Neurobiology and chemistry

Brain tissue consists of a dense cellular network. Most of these cells are so-called support cells (glial cells), whose main purpose is to support the neurons. The ratio of neurons to support cells is approximately 1:10, and support cells account for about half the brain's volume. Among other things, support cells release growth factors that keep the neurons fit, mobilize energy, and convert certain neurotransmitters to waste that is transported out of the nervous system. Some support cells form the white fatty sheaths (myelin) that surround and insulate the long axons (white matter) (see Figure 3.5).

Most neurons are closely related to numerous other neurons. The axon is an extension of the individual neuron that carries the signals emanating from the cell. The neuronal dendrites receive incoming information from other neurons through the synaptic gap (see Figure 3.5).

The axons are particularly branched out, connecting with many other neurons. The pathways vary in length and carry both electric impulses and neurochemicals. The many short neuronal dendrites receive signals from the axons of other neurons and convey them into the cell core. In the myelinated axons, nerve impulses travel at a speed of 100 metres per second or 360 kilometres an hour. Certain neocortical neurons have up to 30,000 neuronal terminals on their dendrite branches. Axons myelinate (form fatty sheaths) as they develop, and this makes it possible to measure the maturity of neural networks based on their degree of myelination (Cozolino, 2000; Siegel, 1999).

Damasio (1994) has calculated that the total length of the neuronal pathways in the human brain corresponds to four times the circumference of the earth. The myelinated nerve fibres make up about 40% of all brain tissue, and the connections between the neurons provide endless possibilities for communication, which is the essential organizing principle of the brain.

Between the neuron and the dendrite is a gap called a synapse (see Figure 3.5). The signal is able to cross this gap because every axon is able to release a transmitter substance through the neuronal terminal. All neuronal communication takes place through the synapses, and the formation of synaptic connections is controlled by an

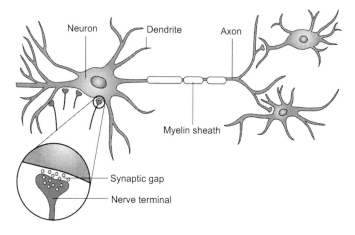

Figure 3.5.   Neuron, axon, dendrite, synapse, and myelin sheath.

intimate interaction between genetic and environmental factors (Perry, 2002).

Neurotransmitters may be excitatory, which implies that the receiving neuron is stimulated, or inhibitory, which implies that it becomes more difficult for the following neuron in the sequence to give off a nerve impulse. Inhibitory synapses are important for the brain's ability to suppress information that is not considered relevant. Excitation (activation) and inhibition are the two basic processes in the brain, and it is the sum of excitatory and inhibitory effects reaching a given neuron that determines whether it passes on a nerve impulse (Tetzchner, 2002) (Figure 3.6).

The grand symphony of the brain

The brain consists of some 80–100 billion neurons. On average, each of the twenty billion neurons in the cortex is connected to 10,000 synapses that switch on and off in a varied and grand symphony that creates a virtually limitless number of possible associations. The neurons interconnect to form extensive neural networks, partly in order to prevent erratic neuronal activity. The brain is activated or calmed down in keeping with this neural symphony, which helps enable learning and the accumulation of mental experiences (Gjærum & Ellertsen, 2002; Siegel, 2004).

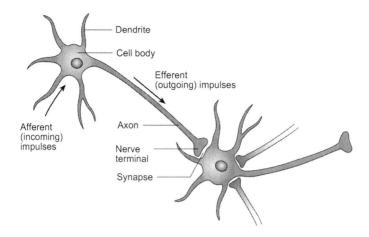

Figure 3.6.   Efferent impulses (outgoing) and afferent impulses (incoming).

Neurons fire irregularly a few times per second; this is referred to as the background activity of the brain. Activated neurons fire at a frequency that is normally between 50 and 100 charges per second. Neurons are constantly affected by impulses from thousands of other neurons and, in turn, affect thousands of other neurons, etc. Through this activity, millions of neurons are interconnected in vast networks that form the basis for all brain processes. Neurons that begin to fire in close temporal sequence, for example due to outside influences, become connected. With each time they are activated in the same pattern, either simultaneously or in short order, the bond between them grows stronger, and the likelihood that they will fire together the next time is increased. This is the underlying mechanism of all learning and the basis of Hebb's (1949) axiom that "neurons that fire together wire together".

Neurons are able to adapt to each other; i.e., synchronize their activity. The larger the number of neurons that respond to a stimulus, the stronger and, thus, the clearer is the signal. Before this synchronization or co-ordination takes place, the connections are weak. The networks grow in regular cycles that go from inter-network competition over network co-ordination to networks becoming components in increasingly complex systems. Increasing co-ordination means increasing influence on the shaping of a particular skill. Each network consists of many interrelated components that often work in parallel. They interact dynamically and are regulated through a feedback system. The more dendrites a neuron has, the more signals it is able to receive from other neurons, and the faster a neuronal group fires, and the more neurons transmit the same piece of information at the same time, the more prominent is the signal in relation to other signals. By inhibiting the activity in nearby cells a signal is better able to stand out in relation to the surrounding activity. Without the inhibitory processes, our mental life would be chaotic, and we would be overwhelmed by sensory perceptions, feelings, and thoughts. The brain constantly has to inhibit vast amounts of neural activity in order to function efficiently (Schacter, 1996).

Synchronization means that different types of sensory impressions that are processed in different brain locations and on different levels are perceived as aspects of the same overall phenomenon. Through the structured synchronization of various relatively smaller neuron groups the individual effects of these neuron groups come to make up one unified whole (Andresen, 2002b; Edelman & Tononi, 2000).

Hebb (1949) writes that all forms of perception, motor activity, learning, and memory are governed by communication between neurons that are co-activated repeatedly. Each neuron is a component in an infinite number of networks. This implies that no neuron ever utilizes its full potential. The more the brain is used, and the more the neurons communicate with each other, the easier it is for learning to take place (Eriksson, 2001)—this is the basis of all psychological development. All types of learning, memory, and motor, cognitive, and emotional development can be explained as an increase in existing neural circuits, changes in existing neurons and neural circuits, and the addition of new neurons. These possibilities reflect the plasticity of the brain or the ability of the nervous system to change.

Polymodality and the association cortex

From birth, infants are able to integrate events and experiences. They recognize sound patterns and visual and tactile impressions as distinct phenomena with particular temporal and coherent structures. The brain seems to be designed to attempt to make sense of experiences and perceive them holistically, even when they are made up of many, partially independent, elements. For example we are exposed to experiences that consist of sound, movement, colour, touch, etc. These distinct perceptions are processed by different parts of the brain but are integrated through particular circuit groups and related neuron groups that respond specifically to higher-order information. These circuits are established as the result of activity during the first years of brain development. The mental system is able to carry out parallel and partially independent processing of the many simultaneous mental events that take place during any interpersonal interaction (Stern, 1985, 1995).

Any form of complex activity, for example the handling of visual, auditory, and emotional impressions, is processed in many different brain regions, and many brain regions collaborate in order to produce any complex activity. The parietal lobe, the temporal lobe and the occipital lobe, also called the PTO area, is where the three lobes meet. This is the area that combines sensory impressions, for example input from vision, hearing, and touch. Brain regions that only handle stimuli from one sensory modality are called unimodal, primary and secondary, while brain regions that are able to combine stimuli from several sensory channels are polymodal. The polymodal regions are also referred to as the association cortex, or convergence zones, and they are the most complex system in the brain. The unimodal regions, which only process one type of sensory input, fuse with other unimodal areas in the association cortex to form an overall perception of a mental event that consists of a symphony of perceptions from many sensory modalities (Panksepp, 1998).

Levels of complexity in the association cortex

Higher levels in the hierarchical structure of the brain have more complex polymodal areas. For example, the polymodal regions in the brainstem are simpler, more basic, and less plastic in terms of their adaptation potential than the limbic system, whose more complex polymodal areas are capable of interpreting emotional signals. The neocortex, and in particular the frontal lobes, consists almost exclusively of polymodal areas; this increases complexity and enables a high degree of plasticity, adaptation, and the potential for abstract thinking (Perry, 1999a).

In humans, the prefrontal cortex and the PTO area are much larger than they are in other primates, and the polymodal areas are more developed. These areas carry out an intensely complex form of information processing and enable the handling of abstract concepts. The associative network of the prefrontal cortex is particularly evolved and complex, and this higher degree of complexity means a greater potential for carrying out sophisticated information processing (LeDoux, 2001).

The polymodal areas make it possible to form mental representations that are independent from specific stimuli, while the associative regions in the prefrontal cortex enable us to form abstract inner representations and to use metaphors and symbols. The associative areas enable the organism to create an integrated holistic perception of itself in relation to its surroundings. Without the association cortex in the parietal and temporal lobes in collaboration with the frontal lobes, cognition would not be possible, and without the association cortex in the occipital lobes, we would not be able to produce mental images. In relation to psychopathology, it is likely that many disorders arise due to a dissociation in associative areas that filters out certain modalities.

The prefrontal cortex consists mainly of an association cortex that processes information from other neural systems and "directs" motor activity. When the language function develops, it connects to areas throughout the frontal lobes, and this eventually enables language to guide behaviour and regulate affect. Our ability to create narratives and recall stories requires polymodal areas that are able to combine the quality of an experience with language. The narratives acquire an organizing function for personal experiences because linguistic concepts are related to inner representations. The narratives are created through the care-givers' communication of social understanding and enable us to process and share information, to create a common history, and to pass knowledge on through the generations and over time and great distances (Bruner, 1990). The association cortex links narratives and emotions, and without these connections words could not spark an emotional response. Children who have been exposed to massive early neglect are often unable to put their emotions into words (alexithymia) and to correct their own behaviour or regulate affects through language, and soothing words provide them no comfort.

The maturation of the brain

Compared with many other species, humans are born with under-developed and immature brains. An average infant's brain weighs about twenty per cent of an adult brain; by comparison, a newborn chimpanzee's brain weighs about sixty per cent of an adult chim-panzee's brain—this despite the fact that the infant brain has more neurons than the adult brain. An infant's brain quickly grows from about 300 grams at birth to 900 grams around the age of one year. At that time it has reached about sixty per cent of the weight of an adult brain. At the age of ten years, it weighs as much as an adult brain: an average of 1,400 grams for men and 1,250 grams for women (Lecours, 1982).

The various regions of an infant's brain contain 15–85 per cent more neurons than the same regions in an adult brain, and during the first two years of life the number of neurons is reduced to that of the adult brain. At birth there are relatively few neuronal connections and synapses, but the number increases rapidly. The brain increases in size due to neuronal growth and the increase in the number of axons and dendrites that follows from the growing number of connections. The brain is not fully developed until the age of 20–23 years. The primary sensory and motor areas are fully formed, but not fully functional, around the second year of life, and all major neural pathways are identifiable at the age of three years. In children under two years of age, the right hemisphere is larger in volume than the left. Even though the brain changes little in size or appearance, the neural circuits continue to develop and trans-form throughout the lifespan (Perry, 2002; Schore 2003b; Shatz, 1999; Tetzchner, 2002; Trevarthen, 1990).

During early childhood, excess synapses are removed (pruning), and many neurons die. Certain neural circuits specialize (parcella-tion), and neurons that do not get sufficient use fail to connect into circuits; they die or the dendrites lose their branches. Neurons that receive frequent use and exercise grow larger, and their dendrites expand. Apoptosis serves to fine-tune the system and continues for many years after birth.

Both excessive and deficient numbers of synapses hamper brain function. Learning and memory seem to take place through the pruning of already formed synapses, the strengthening of existing synapses, and the formation of new synapses. When new synapses form they must be maintained through stimulation. The Greenough team's rat experiments showed that the neural mechanisms that form the basis of experience-dependent brain plasticity allow us to learn and form new memories throughout life (Greenough, Black, & Wallace, 1987).

The first two years after birth are characterized by the emergence of supporting cells, including the formation of myelin sheaths around the axons, and during this development major changes take place in the fat and protein structure of the myelin, which increases the speed of transformation. This improvement in transformation speed continues throughout childhood and puberty and even into adulthood. Neural connections for reflexes, among other things, are myelinated first, while structures in the cerebellum, the limbic system, and the neocortex take longer to develop. Through the myelination of more developed brain regions, primitive behaviour is gradually replaced by volitional acts. The regions that co-ordinate behaviour and attention are not fully myelinated until after puberty. During childhood, the cortical surface becomes increasingly folded to make room for approximately twenty billion neurons (Gjærum & Ellertsen, 2002; Trevarthen, 1990).

The various layers in the brain grow increasingly complex and group into activity patterns. Activity patterns that are repeated frequently develop a particular neural circuit profile. The activation of certain conditions, such as shame, hopelessness, etc., is more likely to recur once the circuit has been formed. Slowly, states develop into personality features (Siegel, 1999).

Top-down a10nd bottom-up processes

Neural circuits function both through top-down and bottom-up processes (Gade, 1997). Bottom-up processes are sensory input or perceptions that move through the lower levels of the brain towards higher, more complex levels. For example, when various sensations combine to form affects, which in turn combine to become moods, a bottom-up process has taken place. But moods also involve top-down processes that run in the opposite direction. A sensation or a perception also depends on expectations, and a prior notion or thought may affect perceptual impressions. Thus, emotions and mentalization are characterized by bottom-up as well as top-down processes. Structures in the brainstem create a generally raised activation, i.e., a cortical readiness in the form of arousal, a raised awareness level, and also prepare a body state to match the situation in terms of body temperature, breathing, and heart rate. The brainstem regions have extensive connections to the limbic system and the neocortex. The limbic system is deeply involved in the regulation of certain emotions. Among other things, this region handles motivational and goal-directed behaviour and the assessment of social experiences.

Emotional processing, which is involved in the preparation of actions, involves previous experiences. Emotional awareness develops through subjective sensations of pleasantness or unpleasantness in relation to particular experiences. When an event takes on particular meaning or value, the awareness is focused, and the emotional experience provides increased energy and awareness. On a fundamental level, the event is perceived as good or bad, and the organism responds by either engaging or withdrawing. Thus, temperament and learning affect emotional responses (Siegel, 1999). The neocortex processes complex information through thinking and reasoning, which enables us to have complex perceptual notions, abstract representations, and sophisticated thinking processes.

Structures in the brainstem emerge early and have limited complexity and plasticity, while structures in the neocortex are characterized by a high degree of complexity and plasticity and emerge later. With development in the neocortex comes extensive development in the connectivity of subcortical regions, which enables top-down processes. These networks contribute with the potential for reflex inhibition and bring subcortical functions under cortical control. For example, over time, children develop an increasingly potent delayed response function, partly due to the maturation of the neural connections from the neocortex to the limbic system.

Summary

Brain structure and function are difficult to grasp, and in this chapter I have only touched briefly upon aspects that I hope will provide a sense of the complexity of the brain. I have provided a structural description to help the reader navigate in this difficult landscape. Many of the structures discussed in this chapter are revisited and described in a variety of ways as we examine structures within the triune brain in Chapters Six, Seven, and Eight. Before returning to the triune model, I will use the next chapter to describe the critical and sensitive periods for the developmental of the nervous system; in Chapter Five I look at the ability of the nervous system to develop through relations with other nervous systems via the phenomena of resonance and synchronicity.

CHAPTER FOUR

Windows of opportunity: the programmable hardwired system

> "The growth of the brain occurs in critical periods and is
> influenced by the social environment ... [D]evelopment ...
> is literally being built on a daily basis during the time of
> accelerated and continuing brain growth in infancy"
>
> (Schore, 1994, p. 10)

T he general consensus now is that the growth of specific brain structures takes place during critical periods in infancy, that brain development relies on stimulation and experiences, and that it is shaped by the person's social environment. Brain development is driven by environmental influences, and this implies that a lack of relevant experiences may have lasting influence on brain development. Stern (1998) points out that, just as food is necessary for the body to grow, stimulation is necessary to provide the brain with the raw materials needed for perceptual, cognitive, and sensorimotor processes to mature. This chapter addresses brain plasticity and the crucial role of stimulation for the brain to unfold its potential; specifically, it looks at the ways that this potential unfolds during sensitive and critical growth periods that are hierarchically connected through levels of mental organization. The total sum of experiences affects brain structures, circuit connectivity, and neurochemistry, and it is the interaction between biological and cultural factors that shapes the unique personality of every single individual.

Brain plasticity

As described previously, most of the functional capacity of the brain develops after birth. Correspondingly, brain plasticity is at its highest during the developmental stages—children are most sensitive to early life experiences. At the foetal stage, neurons and their connections may adapt to handle other functions, while the neurons in the mature brain are much less open to this sort of adjustment: the younger the nervous system, the greater its versatility. There are critical periods for growth and differentiation, and it is crucial that the various systems and functions receive the proper stimulation at the proper time. The degree of flexibility varies between the various parts of the nervous system, and brain plasticity may vary from person to person. Areas that develop in late childhood, such as the frontal lobes, are more susceptible to environmental damage than systems that are fully developed at birth. Large parts of the neocortex are surprisingly unspecialized and plastic, open to the influence of different types of activity during early childhood. Neural plasticity causes a shift from genetic predetermination to so-called epigenetic control and leaves room for the development of individual personalities.

Not all brain structures are equally plastic. Some areas of the brain are more open, others more closed to environmental influences, but all areas appear to have sensitive periods during which synapses develop in the neural circuits. The neural networks compete with each other, and the most active networks survive, in Darwinian style. The purpose of apoptosis is to strengthen the connections between the surviving neurons. The process of strengthening neural circuits through the formation and preservation of synapses (synaptogenesis) and the weakening or elimination of other connections (apoptosis) is referred to as "neural Darwinism"—only the fittest circuits survive as the result of environmental pressures on brain structure. This process enables a fine-tuning of neural circuits, and that is what makes the neural architecture of every single individual unique. Experience-dependent plasticity enables humans and animals to gain knowledge specific to the exact environment that they are a part of (Chugani, 1996; Greenough & Black, 1992). Undoubtedly, the amazing plasticity of the human brain is what has given the human species the necessary adaptability to survive anywhere on the planet.

Neural plasticity and permanence

Inadequate sensory stimulation may inhibit maturation. Hubel and Wiesel (1970) showed that kittens had irreversible neural changes in the visual cortex when they were deprived of normal visual impression for a limited period early in life. The neurons that would normally perceive visual impressions from the deprived eye instead received impressions from the other eye, and the changes were permanent if the absence of normal visual impressions lasted for a certain period of time. This damage did not occur when the experiment was carried out on adult cats. Sensory deprivation of the eye only had an effect when it occurred during the first three months of the kitten's life. Thus, deprivation has major consequences for the development of the nervous system, but, fortunately, deprivation is rarely so extensive or has such far-reaching consequences. Even if development is supposed to take place at particular times, neural flexibility is substantial, and the potential for change is often present throughout the lifespan. Lack of learning during sensitive periods is usually not irreversible, but some forms of learning are more reversible than others.

Children are often able to compensate for previous deprivation at later stages in their development. Disorders that arose at an early developmental stage can often be repaired at a later time, provided the earlier damage did not cause serious irreversible damage to the nervous system. The brain has resources and inherent reparative capacities, provided that the person was able to engage in a childhood relationship with a minimum of attachment, stimulation, and regulation (Rutter & Rutter, 1997; Stern, 1985). In extreme cases, children who are born with a vulnerable nervous system and who were raised in an environment characterized by severe abuse or neglect, for example in the form of deprivation, inadequate attachment experiences, or overwhelmingly traumatic experiences, may suffer irreversible changes to their neurobiological structure and corresponding functions. Both a lack of necessary care from a care-giver and excessive exposure to psychological trauma affect a child's nervous system. There is overwhelming documentation that severe cases of inadequate stimulation or misattunement during the critical period of attachment formation will result in permanent anomalous or maladaptive behaviour. This damage is irreversible and does not respond to correction through normal experiences later in life—the deprived children in the Romanian orphanages are a case in point. Thus, there is a limit to the resilience of the human nervous system. For example, severely deprived children may be unable to learn to speak, they may use their immediate sense of smell for recognition, and both laughter and smiles may be absent. These symptoms can also be observed in young monkeys that have been socially isolated from birth. The monkeys are excessively fearful, attack unexpectedly, and display stereotypic, self-stimulating behaviour. This form of deprivation leads to an absence of play behaviour and later to the failure to develop care functions. To some extent, monkeys are able to compensate for this social isolation later in life. It is still debated as to which brain circuits maintain their development potential throughout the lifespan, and which become fixed or "hard-wired" after an initial period of development (Harlow, 1958; Karr-Morse & Wiley, 1997; Perry, 1997, 2001).

Fortunately, very few children experience such massive neglect that brain plasticity is not able to overcome the effects of developmental social deprivation, for example through training and social stimulation. Even deep-seated subcortical regions are believed to be plastic and susceptible to sensory influence. Brain circuits change in order to adapt to environmental changes (Cozolino, 2000). Only in the most extreme cases is it impossible to reverse a development through exposure to new experiences and active self-organization.

Innate instincts and reflexes are based on neural circuits in the deepest layers of the brain and concern biological regulation that is vital to survival. Darwin introduced a set of primary emotions that he believed to be innate. The acquisition of new response patterns and experiences relies on the ongoing modification of and expansion of basic response patterns, and while basic affects are innate,

the environment plays a crucial role in the regulation and comprehension of basic affects (Damasio, 1994).

Stimulation and the maturation of the nervous system

The user-dependent character of the brain necessitates a capacity
for learning and memory (Perry, 1997). Through evolution the brain
has come to "expect" certain stimuli during critical or sensitive
periods—stimuli of the type that is frequent and widespread within
the pattern of development that is normal for our species. The odds
that children will manage to fine-tune their brain circuits during
these critical or sensitive periods are very favourable indeed. It is
only in the face of genetic or environmental aberrations from the
normal pattern that "nature's expectations are frustrated", and
neural development goes awry (Bruer, 1999).

As the central nervous system develops, children are "pushed"
forward towards higher levels of complexity in terms of mastering
themselves and their surroundings. Each new coping level seeks
stability, until development drives the nervous system on to the
next level. Stability is constantly upset, which leads to the increasing differentiation of skills (Brazelton & Cramer, 1990). Deprivation
is the lack of experiences that would normally occur during development, and which occur so frequently that nature has almost come
to take them for granted.

Certain functions are essential to our species and develop
through maturation without requiring training. Other functions are
culturally conditioned and require training and stimulation. All
functions require a certain developmental maturation of the nervous system before the activity can be induced. Children will begin
to walk (provided they are not deprived of the possibility) at more
or less the same age, regardless of stimulation, while language does
rely on stimulation. Blinking, yawning, and breathing are closed
systems in most animals, but in humans these reflexes are not
completely closed but subject to some degree of volitional control.
Emotional systems may be closed systems in lower mammals, but
evolution has enabled increasingly open systems with the emergence of increasingly sophisticated brain regions. Brain systems
that transfer emotional tendencies are more open to environmental

influence than systems in charge of physical survival. Systems that are situated at the base of the subcortical regions in the brain are more instinctive, and their openness is far more limited than that of higher areas such as the cortex. The more open a brain system is, the more pronounced the influence of environmental factors. For example, the most open programmes in the brain are the regions that handle language and cognition, but even these areas are subject to biological restrictions (Panksepp, 1998).

Developmental stages, developmental lines, or mental organization

Historically, scientists have disagreed as to whether children go through distinct developmental stages or phases. Stern, for one, rejects the developmental phase model proposed by Freud and Piaget, which in his view is based on mechanical and non-dynamic predictability and fails to consider individual and environmental differences. Phase theories based on psychosexual and operational stages are criticized for failing to view development in a sufficiently psychodynamic context and for not incorporating the mutual effects that relationships have on each other. Phase theories cannot be rejected altogether, however; obviously, one cannot teach a four-month-old baby to walk, or explain the intricacies of the theory of relativity to a six-year-old. Developmental stages or phases must be viewed as a way of structuring certain skills at particular age levels, and any given child may simultaneously be at one developmental stage for one set of skills and at a higher or lower stage for another.

Stern states that there is no particular period in life devoted to the formation of a definite, irreversible determination or version of issues for the lifespan such as trust, attachment, autonomy, control, self-regulation, etc. These are issues that we continue to grapple with throughout our lives, but the way in which we approach them and the form that they assume are constantly changing. Stern finds it more appropriate to talk about developmental lines rather than stages or phases, and he says that "The battleground constantly shifts, but the war may stay the same" (Stern, 1995, p. 70). Development is not a matter of successive phases that replace each other but rather of developmental lines that continue each other (Stern, 1985).

The way in which issues for life are addressed and the forms that they take will change throughout the developmental phases, depending on the child's maturity level (Stern, 1995). Humans have an innate capacity for self-organization, and, once they have become organized, the sensory impressions and emotions received by the child will last a lifetime. For example, basic trust and self-regulating abilities will integrate with subsequent phases.

Mental hierarchical levels of organization

Based on theories maintaining the inherent human capacity for self-organization and the hierarchical structure of the brain, I find it more relevant to talk about mental organization than general developmental stages or phases. MacLean divides the brain into three forms of mentation, each shaped by and adapted to specific tasks and areas. He categorizes the different forms of mentation according to his theory of the triune brain, but, in fact, the hierarchical functions can be divided into an endless number of mental organization levels. Children develop adaptation patterns that correspond to their current level of mental organization. This takes place through functional differentiation and hierarchical integration. For example, children have an innate grasp reflex. Later, they learn to grasp a pencil with the entire hand; gradually this develops into the pincer grip, and later into writing skills. As for children's emotional development, they have an innate ability to imitate other people's behaviour; later, they are able to engage in protoconversations, and later again, in mutual attunement with other people's feelings and, eventually, to empathize with and comprehend other people's feelings and intentions. The child's early adaptive patterns are successively reorganized at different times in life.

Through hierarchical integration and differentiation, the quality of solutions is co-ordinated with a previous mental organization. Thus, every developmental, mental organization is based on the outcome of previous mental organizations in an ongoing hierarchical integration process. The child develops as a result of neural reorganization and increasing complexity (Schore, 1994). Multi-neural circuits develop according to a certain timeline. They develop in separate stages, and later developed higher cortical levels inhibit earlier developed lower subcortical levels.

At birth, brainstem functions responsible for regulating breathing and heart rate, among other functions, must be in place, while the cortical areas responsible for abstract cognition do not need to be in place until much later. A frustrated three-year-old will have difficulty regulating arousal states, while an older child is capable of impulse control thanks to cortical development.

Innate and genetic potentials and the interactions that the child engages in are combined on every mental organization level, creating new potentials that help shape the next mental organization level. If interactions at a given level are deficient or absent, the subsequent developmental mental organizations will be affected. On the other hand, each new mental organization level enables the person to address features from previous stages. Thus, one is neither unaffected nor completely controlled by one's early experiences. The child actively seeks adjustment and development, and new experiences always lead to a reorganization of the child's nervous system. Every single developmental task is incorporated into the personality. The way in which the child handles a particular developmental task is co-ordinated with subsequent mental organization. Inadequate handling of one or more developmental challenges will result in a developmental delay in the biological systems. If inadequately developed areas have difficulty adjusting to and integrating with other areas, functions will remain isolated or underdeveloped and fail to integrate with later developing structures. Over time, deficient development in a particular mental organization might lead to difficulties at other levels, and the hierarchical organization will not be adequately integrated, which may cause psychological disorders and maladaptive behaviour (Cicchetti & Tucker, 1994; Sroufe, 1989b).

Critical and sensitive periods

The notion of critical developmental periods stems from embryology, where critical or sensitive periods are initiated and completed by the activation of specific genes at specific times. Critical periods offer additional possibilities for acquiring competencies, but they are also sensitive: The development in question should take place during a particular period of the child's life, partly because the learning process is ideal during this time, and partly because experiences at this time enter more easily into the child's natural competence.

Our genes are not fully expressed at birth, but are strengthened at certain maturational stages. As mentioned previously, the nervous system matures according to epigenetic principles. It develops through stimulation, and previous activities trigger the shift to the next developmental stage. Much of what happens in the development of the organism is due to factors in the environment of the cell, such as signals from other cells that activate certain genes. In order for the genes to be triggered, other genes must be, or have been, active. In normal development, epigenetic maturation may explain the chronological appearance of certain mental organizations at certain ages. Certain types of behaviour occur at certain developmental times, such as separation anxiety and attachment behaviour at 6–8 months, and experiences that can be tolerated by a twelve-year-old may be disastrous for an infant.

In studies of geese, biologist Konrad Lorenz showed that newly hatched goslings bond with the first large moving object they see and hear—a bond that lasts the rest of the bird's life. A gosling's nervous system has a relatively short "window" for the formation of attachment—it is only open for about a day. If the gosling is not exposed to appropriate attachment stimulation during this period it will fail to bond at all, but once the bond is formed it is irrevocable, and the gosling will follow even inappropriate attachment objects (Bowlby, 1969). In experiments with monkeys Harry Harlow (1958, 1959) showed that monkeys need certain attachment experiences in order to develop normally, and that monkeys, like humans, have an innate need for maternal care and an innate template for the requirements of this mother figure. Both monkeys and gosling have a window of opportunity for attachment formation, but in monkeys the critical period is longer (Purves et al., 2001). Substantial research and clinical experience suggest that humans also have a window of opportunity for attachment formation, and that it remains open for longer than that of other primates.

The consequences of maternal deprivation

Harlow (1958, 1959) showed that the consequences of maternal deprivation in rhesus monkeys were more serious if the deprivation occurred when the monkeys were ninety days old than when they were fifty or ten days old. The most likely reason is that the part of the rhesus monkey's nervous system that relates to attachment is not developed until this stage. In humans, separation anxiety begins at the age of 6–8 months. Therefore, humans are believed to be most vulnerable to separation from their primary care-giver during this period. Before this time, the child's attachment is undifferentiated.

Early attachment experiences have a major impact on later behaviour, as much of brain growth takes place while the child is dependent on a close primary care-giver. After birth, the close caring contact regulates brain development, and this early experience is crucial for later behaviour. The growth and differentiation of the nervous system is based on daily interactions during the brain's development period. The final stage of neural maturation, growth, and differentiation depends on appropriate and timely stimulation.

Neural maturation

The infant forms billions of synaptic connections, and, during the first eight months, synaptic density increases approximately eight-fold. Subsequently, there is a selective elimination of synaptic connections, and rhesus monkeys, for example, lose some two billion synapses during the first five years of their life. This explosion of new synaptic connections (synaptogenesis) and subsequent elimination allows the brain to maintain a flexible organization based on countless potential possibilities (Perry, 2002; Tetzchner, 2002). In connection with this, Perry (2002) comments, "While experience may alter the behaviour of an adult, experience literally provides the organizing framework for an infant and child" (p. 87). Early life experiences have tremendous impact on the eventual architecture of the brain. The timing of cell death, apoptosis, varies between brain regions, corresponding to time differences in the development of various functions.

Chugani and colleagues (Chugani & Phelps, 1986; Chugani, Phelps, & Mazziotta, 1987) used PET-scans of infants to measure the glucose metabolism in various brain structures. They found that a high glucose metabolism corresponds to a high level of neural activity accompanied by circuit formation. A decrease in glucose metabolism signals the pruning of superfluous connections, which also marks a decrease in developmental plasticity. The pruning period is followed by a period of reorganization, where new connections integrate with the rest of the system. However, neurophysiologists are still unsure about the relationship between the appearance of a skill and the specialization of circuits, as skills continue to develop and become more advanced throughout the lifespan, even after the sensitive period. Much learning takes places only after the sensitive period, and the periods come to a gradual rather than an abrupt end.

According to Chugani, Phelps, and Mazziotta (1987), brainstem functions, primary sensorimotor cortex, parts of the thalamus, and the cerebellar vermis are highly active at birth. A common feature in these structures is that they are all relatively old in an evolutionary sense. The brainstem, in particular, regulates such functions as arousal, sleep patterns, and the brain's neurochemistry. It is an energy-mobilizing system, which regulates attention and affect on a basic level (Schore, 1994). This level includes reflexes, e.g., the Moro (startle) reflex and the grasp reflex. Visuomotor skills, such as eye-hand coordination are also present (Chugani, 1994). At the age of 2–3 months, the primitive reflexes reorganize and the visuospatial and visuomotor functions integrate and mature. This happens as the basal ganglia, the rest of the cerebellum, the cortex in the parietal, temporal, and occipital lobes, and the affect-regulating limbic structures mature. The last area to mature is the frontal lobes, a process that is initiated at the age of 6–12 months. The prefrontal cortex begins to develop towards the end of the first year, and this development process is particularly influenced by the stimulation embedded in the child's emotional exchange with the primary caregivers. Based on MacLean's theory of the triune brain, the Chugani group's studies can be summarized as follows: from birth until the age of two months, activity occurs mainly in structures in and around the brainstem, i.e., the protomental area. At the age of 2–6 months, the next structure in the triune brain becomes active, and the area for emotomentation develops. Development of the highest level, the area of ratiomentation, begins at the age of eight months and continues well into adolescence.

With normal progression, neural development goes from low intensity to high intensity and then reverts to low intensity. For example, mentally retarded children may have higher synaptic density than normally developed children. An abnormally high synaptic density later in life may be just as unfortunate as an abnormally low density. Eliminating irrelevant synapses improves the signal-to-noise ratio in the brain.

Some structures develop slowly and have prolonged sensitive periods. Rapidly growing tissue is particularly sensitive to environmental stimulation, while late maturing systems, such as the prefrontal structures, are particularly open and consequently sensitive to environmental influences at later stages in development. The cortical systems, which are very involved in managing volitional acts, develop slowly, and consequently have a very long critical period.

Childhood development progresses in stops and starts. Quantitative leaps are followed by the consolidation of new skills. Stern (1995) describes that during the first year of life, these leaps occur around the age of 2–3 months, at 5–6 months, between eight and twelve months, and around eighteen months. After infancy, the intervals increase, with increased growth and activity at the ages of four and seven years (Mathiesen, 2004). Recent research has found a renewed process of cortical neural activity and pruning around puberty, which helps increase the development potential at this time. Each leap forward produces new social, affective, motor, and cognitive skills that reorganize the child's interaction with the parents. Issues for the lifespan, such as trust and autonomy, are negotiated in new ways, based on the child's newly acquired skills.

With increasing age, the brain structures become increasingly fixed, while the biological processes become more flexible. Partly thanks to the development of the prefrontal cortex, the brain becomes able to handle a huge number of different stimuli.

Stem cell research

Until the 1980s, the human brain was believed to be unable to develop new brain cells. The brain was plastic in terms of its ability to acquire new skills, develop new memory tracks, and, to a limited extent, compensate for minor brain injury. This plasticity was ascribed to changes in the synaptic connections that developed over longer or shorter periods of time. Nerve cell division was believed to be definitively over by the time the brain was fully developed. We have long known that mature cells do not divide, but, in the 1980s, this assumption was challenged, and certain areas of the brain were indeed found to form new neurons from immature early stages. Research found that new neurons were being produced in the brains of adult songbirds, especially in the areas involved in song production.

The formation of new neurons has been found in the brains of adult mice, rats, monkeys, and humans. The formation of new cells takes place in stem cells, which contain the basic structure of many cell types, and which are capable of reproducing themselves an infinite number of times. The formation of new neurons is believed to occur in connection with learning and with the formation of new memory tracks. In 1998, it was discovered that new neurons continually form even in the mature brain, and that this occurs in people who are well into their sixties—a finding that opens new research perspectives (Goleman, 2003; LeDoux, 2001). brainstem cells rely on structures that were founded during the foetal stage, and which have been preserved in the mature brain. Stem cells are self-renewing, and each cell is able to divide symmetrically and produce an infinite number of identical cells. When cells are exposed to the appropriate signals, they are also able to divide asymmetrically and produce new stem cells as well as differentiated cells such as neurons or support cells. Newly formed neurons only connect with local circuits. Cell growth has been found in particular in an area within the limbic system (the hippocampus) that plays a key role for memory. Most stem cells do not survive to become neurons. However, studies suggest that stimulation increases the chances of a stem cell to survive and become a fully developed neuron (Goldberg, 2001). Today, it is possible to isolate stem cells, and ongoing research is exploring the possibility of transplanting stem cells to other brain regions in order to repair damaged brain tissue (Cozolino, 2000; Purves et al., 2001).

Although some neurons are able to regenerate, certain action and thought patterns do dominate at certain ages, and there are sensitive periods where it is particularly important to learn particular skills—certain essential windows of opportunity.

Windows of opportunity

As mentioned previously, critical and sensitive periods are times that are optimal for learning or development; these are usually periods characterized by great plasticity. Language acquisition is one area that has often been used to explain and pinpoint critical periods. Although it is possible to acquire a language after the age of twelve years, it is difficult to learn to speak a new language without an accent. Children who learn a language at a young age form prototypes that describe the unique sound system of language in question. Children are able to learn the prototypes of many different kinds of language. Around puberty, the sound representations become fixed, and it becomes more difficult to perceive distinctions between the sounds of a foreign language.

The notion of critical or sensitive periods does not imply that learning after the critical period is impossible. Certain types of learning will be easier at certain levels of mental organization than on others, and the consequences of inadequate stimulation vary with age. For example, pre-school children are more vulnerable to stressful experiences than older children, and a lack of opportunity to form selective attachments during the first years of life has a more lasting effect on the character of social relations later in life.

A critical period implies a certain degree of vulnerability. If the organism depends on a certain stimulation at a certain time the function is lost if later stimulation fails to make up for the missed opportunity; this occurs in highly deprived institutionalized children, or children with early brain injury, for example to the prefrontal cortex. Early environmental or organic brain damage can have grave consequences because it interferes substantially with the development process in the deep subcortical areas (Tetzchner, 2002).

The neural circuits that are formed at an early stage in development are unique and have a powerful impact on the rest of development. Chugani (1999) points out that the time from birth until the age of three years is a critical or sensitive period when the caregiver's influence on brain development is essential, but brain development continues well into puberty. The synapses continue to connect also after the third year of life, and activity remains high until after puberty. During this period, experiential input fine-tunes the neural circuits and provides each personality with its unique neural architecture. Stimulation and stimulus processing are important for establishing brain circuits and for keeping desirable circuits alive. It is crucial for the child to receive appropriate stimulation during childhood, and with increasing age it becomes increasingly difficult to alter the circuitry. The first three years of the child's life are important for the formation of circuits in deep-lying subcortical layers.

Long-term effects of neuronal maturation

Early experiences have an extensive long-term effect on the child's development, but it is not maturation alone that limits plasticity or flexible learning. Once neural circuits are formed, it may be difficult to view the world in any other way. The circuits that are established during childhood are evolutionarily constructed to resist change when they have proved successful at an early time in life. We do not know to what extent these critical or sensitive periods are determined by a biological clock, and to what extent they are based on the difficulty of altering established structures. For example, Edelman (1987) suggests that even though the modification of established neuron groups is always possible with exposure to significant changes in environmental experiences, the selected neural patterns have a tendency to stabilize and, to some degree, resist change. When certain circuits and neuronal groups have been established, they tend to be favoured when the brain is exposed to stimuli that resemble previous stimuli.

Critical periods are not windows that slam shut; rather, they are complex transition phases. When the period of cell death and circuitry specialization is over, there is a period of stabilization where, for example, dysfunctions caused by early negative experiences may change. The organism remains plastic beyond the sensitive or critical period, and, in the case of abuse or neglect, for example, the organism often has sufficient plasticity to benefit from new experiences. Structures can still be influenced and partially changed with the right intervention and timing, even after the window has "closed". Emotional development never ends, but it slows down over time. The number of receptors in the brain can be changed and reduced, and neural circuits may change as the result of social deprivation and the severance of attachment bonds, but the nervous system remains capable of change and development throughout the lifespan—it is never too late to develop neural circuits (van der Kolk, 1987).

Damasio (1994) points out that neural circuits are not only sensitive to the results of early experiences but are also constantly affected and modified by new experiences. In adults, too, neural circuits may change with exposure to new challenges, new surroundings, or situations that are difficult to comprehend. Early learning is the foundation of ongoing learning, and ongoing development happens when new experiences connect with previous memories. Development consists of learning, but learning cannot take place before the synapses are ready. As the synapses begin to form they are influenced by environmental experiences (Gopnik, Meltzoff, & Kuhl, 1999; LeDoux, 2001).

At this point, research has limited insight into sensitive or critical periods in relation to the development of social and emotional skills. The brain's malleability and capacity for reorganization probably varies from person to person and between different brain structures. We know that learning remains possible throughout the lifespan, and if a skill is practised over a long period of time there are measurable neurological changes. Reorganization is a fundamental feature in mammalian nervous systems, and the adult brain retains this capacity for reorganization. Experiments with monkeys have shown that extensive training may alter neural structures, for example in primary sensory areas, but this reorganization only takes place when the animal pays attention to the task. It seems that structural reorganization in the adult brain requires motivation for learning (Bruer, 1999). There is still much research to be done into the treatment possibilities for children exposed to early emotional frustration. Studies of the Romanian orphans who did not go into adoptive families until after 8–12 months of age showed that some sixty-three per cent of the children displayed insecure attachment patterns five years after adoption, but we do not know whether dedicated interventions will be able to make a difference (Chisholm, 1998; Marcovitch et al., 1997).

If children are raised in an under-stimulated, loveless setting, will they be emotionally damaged for life? The answer is probably that a child raised in an extremely emotionally under-stimulated or disorganized setting will acquire irreversible emotional damage if there is no intervention while the window of opportunity is still open, so to speak. If the child received even minimal care, and his or her nervous system is sufficiently resilient, there is a possibility of intervening to support the child's development, provided there is a sufficient and deliberate effort to promote attachment within a relevant relationship. The brain is resilient and malleable, but there is a limit to what the nervous system can be exposed to before it loses its resilience.

Summary

The shaping of the personality and the structuring of the nervous system depend on experiences. In this chapter, I have described how the brain develops by reorganizing neural structures on various levels of organization, which eventually shapes the personality structure. This maturation process takes place during critical and sensitive periods, while the neural structure is forming. Missing a window of opportunity may result in irreversible damage to the nervous system, although in most cases the brain is open to stimulation and reorganization at later times. In the following chapter, I describe how neural circuits are stimulated through the phenomena of resonance and synchronicity, and how they connect with other nervous systems.

CHAPTER FIVE

Resonance, synchronicity, and mirror neurons: the basic units of brain circuitry and affect attunement

"At the heart of the universe is a steady, insistent beat: the sound of cycles in sync. It pervades nature at every scale from the nucleus to the cosmos. Even our bodies are symphonies of rhythm, kept alive by the relentless, coordinated firing of thousands of pacemaker cells in our hearts. In every case, these feats of synchrony occur spontaneously, almost as if nature has an eerie yearning for order"

(Strogatz, 2003, p. 1)

Neural systems develop through stimulation, which consists of resonance and synchronicity phenomena. Resonance means that activated neurons cause other neurons to activate, which increases the overall activity, while synchronicity means that groups of neurons are activated simultaneously.

As early as during the foetal period, the child engages in movements that synchronize motor activity and sensory perception, the precursor of walking, talking, gesturing, etc. For example, we know that synaptogenesis in children is enhanced when, through play and contact, the child enters into a field of resonance with the

care-givers via facial expressions, eye contact, prosody, body movements, and timing. At an early stage, the infant is able to imitate the
care-giver's facial expressions, vocalization, etc. The human brain is
able to integrate expressive body movements, especially in the form
of facial expressions, hand gestures, postures, and vocalization. Our
affective and emotional expression is constructed to enter into fields
of resonance with other people's expressions, and through these
fields of resonance we attune with each other. The workings of our
nervous system are based on rhythm, resonance, and synchronicity,
which means that the nervous system is a constantly changing
organism. In this chapter, I discuss theories explaining the basic
principles governing the development of the nervous system and
our ability to enter into mutually attuned interactions. In the first
section the concepts of rhythm, resonance, and synchronicity are
explained and related to non-linear theory.

Rhythm, resonance, synchronicity

Resonance and synchronicity provide the underlying pulse for
everything that our brains engage in and for our mutual attunement and interactions.

Rhythm means that a behaviour pattern is repeated at regular
intervals, while synchronicity means that two things happen simultaneously. The distinction between the two concepts is often
missed, as synchronization often arises through rhythmic structures. Synchronization may take place arhythmically; for example,
when all the violins in an orchestra come in at the same time and
remain synchronized, not by playing the same passage over and
over but by interacting. Arhythmical synchronization has the capacity for affecting the organism emotionally and moving us. That is
what creativity and art is often about.

Cascading synchronicity

As mentioned above, neuronal connectivity grows stronger when
neurons fire simultaneously. Resonance phenomena occur when a
neuron group fires simultaneously, because this makes the circuit
stand out in relation to the background noise from other, individual

neurons. For example, when a group of people begin to sing at the same time, the singing stands out in relation to general chatter. When the electrical activity of synchronous neurons is co-ordinated, their message is enhanced and becomes more prominent. If the network is too loosely connected, the fragments will not be able to come together, and the delicate circuit risks splintering into "islands". When the firing reaches a critical level, one "island" may suddenly connect with other "islands", and a larger cascade of neural activation may ensue, if conditions are right. In this manner, one tiny seed may spark widespread change. Even neurons that are anatomically far removed from each other may enter into perfect synchronicity. That is what happens in primitive forms of cognition, memory, and perception, where the brain is able to distinguish between two scents or discover a mismatch between auditory and visual impression, sound and image. Whether activity is possible in distant brain areas depends on neuronal coherence. The rapid integration of activity is the condition of a conscious experience. Consciousness requires constantly changing neural activity. If many neuronal groups are firing in a rigid and fixed rhythm, the state becomes too homogenous, and the person loses consciousness; that is what happens in epilepsy. Aspects that lie outside the field of attention are not firing synchronously. Focused attention requires that a large number of neurons connect at the same time while remaining in constant motion. A lack of attention may cause learning difficulties, and problems with maintaining synchronicity causes attention deficit disorders (Edelman & Tonini, 2000).

Synchronicity and chaos theory

Through non-linear theory and chaos theory, we are now closer than before to explaining how synchronicity may occur. Chaos theory relates to phenomena in relation to order and chaos. Chaos consists of cryptic patterns and is governed by rigid rules. Chaos never repeats itself, and behaviour is not periodical. In chaotic systems different patterns of movement are present at the same time, and even small initial changes may alter the course of events. We have all seen small things make a huge difference in our lives, and even simple stimuli may cause changes in the smallest systems. Everything is connected, whether we are talking about neurons, people, or planets. Complex networks create highly developed forms of self-organization (Strogatz, 2003).

Scientists have long been puzzled by the existence of spontaneous order in the universe. Somehow, cells as well as galaxies and humans have managed to get themselves organized. For unknown reasons, the tendency towards synchronicity is one of the most persistent driving forces in the universe. Synchronicity is crucial for the organization and maintenance of life. Even non-living things may synchronize; for example, two clocks placed next to each other at a distance of one to one and a half metres will synchronize their pendulums (Strogatz, 2003). When neurons fire simultaneously, they are forever bound together because they have established identical dynamics and have linked up with other cells. When they are activated, they remain synchronized because they are linked. Neural firing leads to a chain reaction that involves many brain regions. This synchronization happens abruptly, and when neurons synchronize, they organize in time. Synchronization in neurons or external behaviour may take place without forethought and does not require intelligent life.

The integration principle of neural patterns

Brain systems organize in hierarchical patterns that are connected in complex circuits. The interaction between the patterns takes place through spatial and temporal patterns of neural activity that turn on and off constantly and determine what is encoded. The neural circuits connect through stimuli and experience, and, once a neural pattern is formed, the neural activation caused by outside stimuli will attempt to link up with already acquired experiences or a particular neural pattern. When the neural activation that was caused by an outside stimulus fails to match a previous experience exactly, without, however, completely missing the mark, it sparks a new process or a new experience. The difference between the new and the old experience creates learning or development, which makes the circuits involved in the experience more differentiated and stronger and causes them to connect in growing networks within an integrated system. When new and old experiences match, the involved circuits synchronize and integrate, which leads to a coherent mental state. This principle of neural development is used in all successive learning. For example, children have an innate grasp reflex, which gradually develops into the volitional ability to grasp a toy, open one's hand to let go of it again, picking up an object with a pincer grip, holding a pencil, mastering drawing techniques, working with fine mechanics, etc.

The brain as a non-linear system

In non-linear systems the whole is different from the sum of the individual parts. Non-linear systems will strive for synchronization but risk remaining disorganized for ever. At times, the system fails to synchronize at all, even though it seems to have all the prerequisites for synchronization. It is as if there is nothing to attach to, no pull towards anything, no rhythm to fall into. Similarly, some systems only achieve partial synchronization. Life depends on non-linear systems, and biology uses them everywhere. Non-linear systems are difficult to analyse, because the sum of the individual parts does not correspond to the whole. The entire system has to be analysed at once as a coherent structure that is internally connected in giant networks.

Neural circuits, to a large extent, consist of complex non-linear systems, and non-linear systems are predisposed for chaotic states. Small changes in complex non-linear systems may suddenly change the state of the entire system (Bergström, 1998). The system consists of a driving force away from simplicity and towards complexity. Childhood development, for example, may be viewed as the development of patterns that grow increasingly complex, both in children's interaction with their surroundings and in brain development. If personality is viewed as a complex system, dysfunction on one level of the organism may cause significant functional changes on other levels and in the system as a whole. Dysfunctions may arise due to an error message from one single brain component, and the reactions may be unpredictable and widespread. Functions that operate according to non-linear principles are capable of causing major negative or positive changes through just a few changes. Brain systems walk a fine line between continuity and flexibility because they have the ability to modify what is given through the genome. Our brain has a high degree of plasticity and is capable of altering neural circuits through influences from environmental interaction (Siegel, 1999).

In a system that strives for complexity, two processes must be balanced: differentiation and integration. The balancing of differentiation and integration is a principle found in and among all living organisms at every level, from neurons to social structures. Differentiation means that the components of a system are unique and different, as in a family where each person has his or her own opinion, and consensus is unattainable. Integration means that the components function in unity, as in a family that requires everybody to agree and do the same things. In a family, the balance between differentiation and integration may, for example, be to respect individual differences but still be together (Siegel, 2004).

When a system is in a coherent complex state, balanced between differentiation and integration, it is said to be in harmony. The nervous system is unable to maintain this state of complex harmony at all times and then either goes to a rigid state, where everything is predictable, or becomes chaotic, unpredictable, and disorganized (Siegel, 2004). When the system fails to maintain the harmonious state, initially it often seeks to maintain the rigid state until the chaotic state eventually ensues. The integration of neural connections is strengthened through countless waves of learning, and the nervous system keeps switching between rigidity, chaos, and harmony. At times there are quantum leaps in learning, at other times development progresses slowly and imperceptibly. Every new wave of neural organization dissolves the former organization, so there are inevitable periods of transition where the old approach no longer works while a new approach has not yet been established.

The next section explores the integration of neural circuits through neuronal resonance and synchronicity and the way that neural circuits form complex coherent systems in the process.

Neural circuits

The integration of brain circuits takes place through activities in the organism over time, as the organism attempts to self-regulate in relation to its environment. When neural circuits are activated and synchronized on the basis of activities relating to the environment, resonance phenomena occur between internal and external circumstances. Because of its complexity, the brain is capable of rapid shifts in state that enable constant self-adjustment in relation to the environment. The brain seeks to integrate one moment with the next, which promotes flexible adaptation. Synchronized neuronal integration creates coherent experiences, and a change in state involves a phase shift, which involves the disorganization and subsequent reorganization of synchronized integration. Neural networks do not engage in random activities because behaviour is governed by patterns established through previous learning. When a phase shift occurs, the nervous system will seek towards previous familiar levels of integration before it is able to reorganize at higher level. The nervous system always tends towards structure and familiarity. For example, experiments have shown that the human brain is unable to produce random sequences of numbers; the brain inevitably falls into a pattern that imposes some sort of order on the sequence (Cozolino, 2000).

The process of re-entry

Gerald Edelman and Giulio Tononi have formed a theory that explains the occurrence of the neural process through a re-entry process. According to this theory, resonance in the neural process occurs when neuron A transmits signals to neuron B, which in turn transmits signals back to A and on to C in a re-entry loop. C then reaches D, goes back to B and A, etc. In this re-entry process, several elements within the system affect each other's states. A and B connect in an integrated system the moment they signal each other and enter into a state-dependent process. In other states, the activation of neuron A may have very little effect on B. Different components within the neural circuits are functionally linked in an integrated system when a re-entry system exists between them. Coherent neural systems arise when many layers of neural functions are activated simultaneously. Neurons strengthen and weaken their connections depending on the individual electric patterns of activation (Edelman & Tononi, 2000; Siegel, 1999). This process creates a complex, functionally linked system, where one complex system is capable of becoming a component in a growing and increasingly complex system—a process that can be utilized in therapy, for example. Neural regulation is learned in affectively synchronized interactions. Interacting persons are drawn into each other's emotional world; they become emotionally attuned and thus affect each other. The integration and reintegration of neural circuits requires the nervous system to connect with another nervous system and enters into a field of resonance with it. Successful attunement with another person's nervous system enables the nervous system to develop flexibility and integrate neural patterns that may spread hierarchically throughout the brain (Bentzen & Hart, 2005).

The re-entry process is fleeting and takes place in a quarter of a second, which is the time it takes to feel intuitive comfort or discomfort. Rapid and repeated activation stabilizes the re-entry process, and once it has stabilized it can be experienced and fixed in the person's consciousness. The experience is created by a temporal organization unfolding in the present, which is the basis for affective experiences (Stern, 1995, 2004).

Like the re-entry process, neuronal activation, too, is fleeting, lasting only one thousandth of a second. The precise formation of firing neurons determines what the brain represents at any given moment. The past rests in the network structure. The silent or dormant connections of every formation represent or express a potential for previous combinations to be revived or recalled. The structure of past, present, and future is shaped by neural networks in a living time machine. Even tiny changes reshape neural circuits through experience. Thus, experience becomes a part of the brain's microscopic structure and creates a constant transformation from who we were to who we are and who we shall become. Neurons that fire simultaneously tend to do so over and over again; they come to depend on each other and connect more closely. Neurons that have not fired together for a long time may begin to suppress each other. This may lead to the dissolution of networks that previously fired together, which leads to dissociative states. At any given time, any single neuron receives stimulation from "allies" and inhibitory signals from "enemies". In this manner, every single neuron finds its own level of activation, and the neural circuit to which the neuron is connected forms particular patterns of active and inactive units. The manner in which neurons join together and inhibit or activate each other determines the structure of the nervous system and the ways in which the neural systems achieve harmony or disharmony. A nervous system consisting of many unconnected or dissociated circuits will be vulnerable to strong influences, and many of its neural circuits will function independently of each other.

In therapy, one may attempt to awaken dormant or dissociated circuits. This is what happens when one neuron group activates another neuron group that has not been activated along with the first group in a long time. This resembles the way that a high-pitched note may make physical objects vibrate at a particular frequency. For example, a soprano may break a glass when she hits a high note at just the right frequency. Similarly, emotional "tones" in the brain resonates with the past. When an "emotional tone" is struck, it touches on old memories that have the same emotional tone. If an emotional tone is powerful enough it will activate adjacent networks and make the content accessible (Lewis, Amini, & Lannon, 2001).

Countless simultaneous re-entry processes cause the brain waves that we know from EEG-readings (electroencephalographic scans) of electrical activity in the brain surface. The principle at play here is that a match between the top-down signals and the input from bottom-up signals in a neural network creates a field of resonance that supports a specific activation pattern during a given period of time (Mathiesen, 2004). Our knowledge of brain waves is still fairly limited, but in the next section I briefly describe some of the facts we have established so far.

Brain waves

Neural activation consists of electric rhythms that are affected by environmental stimulation. Brain wave activity is mainly due to synaptic connections in the deepest subcortical layers and consists of many different kinds of rhythm. Perception, cognition, sensations, etc., are all closely linked to a wave of electric rhythms that creates neural synchronicity. Neural activation takes place in a split second and then dissipates until there is a new impression, at which time the event is repeated. Brain neurons are constantly oscillating, and they vibrate and harmonize within different parts of the brain.

The different waves come from different places, and some synchro-nize in relation to, for example, a sensation, a movement, a sound, etc. The overall integration of all mental factors in the brain is achieved through fleeting formations of synchronized neuron groups. The brain actively recreates itself by introducing a space to mark the transition from one moment to the next.

In 1995, the biologists Welsh and Reppert discovered that neurons have different frequencies, which they use to pull each other into synchronicity. Even small changes in the energy mass in one part of the brain may sometimes have radical self-increasing effect (Strogatz, 2003). There are five known categories of human brain waves: delta, theta, alpha, beta, and gamma rhythms. The slowest rhythm is delta, which occurs when we are asleep. It is believed to express somatic healing processes. Next is the theta rhythm, which occurs during meditative and non-conscious pro-cesses and in REM sleep (dream sleep). Theta rhythm indicates information and memory processing, while theta rhythm in dream sleep reflects active information integration. Theta rhythms also often occur when we are examining our surroundings, indicating that the circuits are systematically encoding information; for exam-ple, that recent experiences are being translated and entered into long-term memory. Theta rhythms during REM sleep are therefore believed to reflect information processing that integrates temporary memory stores (Panksepp, 1998). Apart from deep sleep, theta and delta rhythms (4–7 Hz) are also found in certain pathological states. Alpha rhythm (8–13 Hz) occurs when the organism is at rest; it is considered a basic state, it occurs in the waking state when one's eyes are closed, and it is probably linked to visual processing. Alpha activity rises especially when someone is focusing their attention, eyes closed. The alpha rhythm disappears when the person grapples with a difficult problem. To Einstein, even the most difficult mathematical problem was so trivial that his brain continued to generate alpha rhythms. Bio-feedback techniques train people to achieve relaxation by making them maintain alpha rhythm and tone down their beta rhythm. Alpha rhythm supports feelings of well-being. Theta rhythm takes over with drowsiness when day-dreams and fantasies take over (Austin, 1998). Beta rhythm (14–60 Hz) occurs when the person is attentive and mentally active, i.e., engaged in cognitive processing or emotional activation. Gamma rhythm (40 Hz) is activated when the person engages in high-intensity processing of perception and cognition. Various brain regions are believed to have their own characteristic rhythm, and brain waves are believed to differ between processing in the visual cortex, sensorimotor cortex, etc. (Purves et al., 2001).

Synchronous waves and learning

In the 1930s, the brain frequency in animals was observed to fall into a steady alpha rhythm (10 Hz) once the animal had become accustomed to a conditioned stimulus. When the conditioned stimulus was linked to a novel stimulus, for example when one type of ringing tone was replaced by a new one, the brain wave activity changed drastically to a new desynchronized pattern in a higher frequency, which spread over many different brain regions in reflection of the learning process. When the reconditioning was complete, and the novel stimulus appeared to have been integrated with the new response, so that the animal had learned, for example, to relate the new ringing tone with a reward, continued desynchronization was found to exist for a long time in those areas of the cortex that integrated the new response with other brain areas (Edelman & Tononi, 2000). This is probably the case in all learning. As long as our nervous system only encounters familiar stimulation, the electric activity remains low, but when we address novel material, many brain areas are activated, and there is an increase in electric activity. This is the difference, for example, between learning to ride a bicycle and being able to ride a bicycle, or between learning to speak English and speaking it fluently. In 1999, Francisco Varela did a study where volunteers were asked to look at patterns of faces (Rodriguez, George, Lachaux, Martinerie, Renault, & Varela, 1999). He found that the brain synchronized around a rhythm of 40 Hz in various cortical regions when the subjects looked at the faces. In Varela's interpretation, this means at that the moment when the brain combines several stimuli to achieve a holistic perception, there is an unconscious epiphany. The 40-Hz-rhythm occurs when millions of neurons dispersed over an area suddenly change their rhythm, synchronize, then disconnect again and allow the next perception to occur. A moment of insight consists of a cascade of electric synchronization that occurs when various parts of the brain harmonize with each other. A rhythm of 40 Hz corresponds to the time it takes to shift one's attention from one perception to another. Different neuron groups compete to engage in a common rhythm, corresponding to various activities competing for focus. The focus of one's concentration corresponds to the neuron groups that fire synchronously, and when synchronicity can no longer be sustained focus will shift to a new object (Strogatz, 2003). No wonder that it can be difficult to maintain attention for extended periods of time!

When particular brain regions are stimulated, various neuronal groups throughout the brain enter into synchronous patterns, capable of triggering the recognition of a stored memory unit. Thus, tiny changes in environmental events, such as a change in tone of voice or in gaze can affect a mood. For example, my son tells me that when he hears someone saying, "Good heavens!" he immediately envisions a series of images of his grandmother, has a warm, fuzzy feeling inside, and recalls the nice afternoons they had with lemonade and pastries from the baker's.

Brain wave theories have often been used to explain how the various parts of the brain connect, and they offer an understanding of the sense of continuity that we have despite the abrupt nature of the individual brain processes. Brain waves occur independent of any conductor or executive function. The basic mechanism is a passing formation of synchronized, widespread neuronal groups. The specific patterns vary from person to person and depend on the individual person's unique history, experiences, and learning. In EEG-readings, electrodes are placed on various parts of the scalp to measure cortical oscillations. Depending on the location of a given electrode, it is possible to record various oscillation signals that suddenly become synchronized. When neurons are close to each other they are almost bound to synchronize because they are interconnected (Goleman, 2003).

We have now seen how the individual brain structures connect on a neural level and how they synchronize to form coherent neural circuits and create oscillations that can be measured as brain waves. In the next section, we look at the application of this principle in the synchronization of our own nervous system with the nervous systems of others, which eventually leads to attachment bonds.

Oscillating neurons, biorhythms, and time

The human infant's most important development task is to form close attachment bonds with the care-givers. Scientists believe that internal representations are constructed on the basis of small repeated interaction patterns on the basis of the structured experience of self interacting with another. Research has shown oscillating neurons (oscillators) that enable us to synchronize our movements with those of others. Apparently, we have internal clocks built into various systems that fire in particular rhythms, but which can be zeroed by outside stimuli; for example, the movements of another person. This zeroing allows our nervous system to synchronize and remain synchronized with that of another person over time. Thus, we have an innate biological capacity for perceiving temporal forms in other people's actions, which essentially allows us to develop a sense of the other person's intentions (Stern, 1985; Torras, 1985).

The existence of oscillating neurons and internal (endogenous) clocks was unknown until the 1950s, when Halberg defined biological rhythms as a statistically proven physiological change that occurs in wave form, and which constantly reproduces itself (Anders, 1989). The endogenous clocks are controlled by cells that follow a circadian rhythm, and consequently are called circadian cells. These cells keep us synchronized with our surroundings on an ongoing basis. Most scientists believe that we have many different kinds of oscillating neurons. Some only function for a short period of time and are zeroed at regular intervals, others follow a twenty-four-hour cycle, for example the sleep–wake cycle, while others are life-long. Evolution has given our organism the ability to harmonize in relation to a day–night cycle. When rhythmic firing occurs in the various areas of the nervous system, the information is bound in time. Rhythmic neuronal activity provides a time frame for information, and the oscillating neurons are crucial for the effect of perceptions, sensory input and motor functions, among other things (Andresen, 2002a,b).

In interpersonal interactions, we attempt to adapt to or synchronize with each other's nervous systems. We enter into a resonance pattern by unconsciously synchronizing with the other, and the oscillating neurons are probably involved in co-ordinating this interaction. When people move synchronously or in temporal co-ordination, they are taking part in an aspect of each other's experience. The infant is born with the ability to perceive time and is able to assess the duration of seconds and fractions of seconds. A two-month-old infant is able to perceive variations of approximately twenty-five milliseconds, to perceive sequences in time and unforeseen events, and to form expectations of imminent actions. The infant quickly recognizes that events that share a time structure are tied together. For example, the child prefers synchronized speech and lip movements over asynchronous movements, and failure to achieve synchronicity with the care-giver distresses the child. Adult monkeys that are strangers to each other quickly synchronize their behaviour and share the same cyclical activity patterns when they are placed in the same cage (Beebe & Lachmann, 2002; Stern, 2004).

The organization of all sorts of biological rhythms, from the circadian rhythm to time structures, is an integrated part of the infant's life. For example, the infant quickly regulates itself in relation to a cycle of light and dark, the three-to-four-hour hunger cycle, and the micro-rhythmic organization in relation to interactions with the care-giver. The basis for rhythms arises endogenously but is regulated by outside circumstances. In the next section, I provide some examples of the ways in which the nervous system regulates itself from birth based on the early care-giver–infant relationship.

Self-organization

The brain is a complex, self-organizing system, which is organized on the basis of environmental interaction. Brain complexity provides plasticity and the ability to adapt to the environment over generations. All living systems are able to respond and adapt to their surroundings. Certain synchronous patterns might be efficient for adapting to certain environmental conditions at a certain time, but might restrict the development potential under a different set of circumstances. For example, a nervous system that has adapted, from the outset, to simple survival in a dangerous and chaotic world where it has to maintain a constant readiness just to stay alive, might have difficulty changing at a later time to adjust to an environment or a culture that requires adaptation strategies aimed at mutual consideration, understanding, and respect.

If the brain fails to integrate, conflicts often ensue between different synchronous neural patterns, a situation that leads to an incoherent nervous system and internal turmoil. The brain constantly seeks to increase its complexity, a process that concerns both the self-organization of the nervous system and its interaction with other people's nervous systems. The brain has to constantly balance between rigidity, i.e., activity held within familiar patterns, and the dissolution of patterns, which in turn leads to renewed chaos. Integration is a process with no predetermined goal (Siegel, 1999). The rhythms and biological principles established from the outset in a self-regulating organization, such as the brain, determine its self-regulation in interaction with the environment. In a human context, biological and psychological levels are first linked through the infant's internal experiences of the organization that arises through interactions with the environment. The infant's states self-regulate on the basis of the way that the care-giver holds the child, her vocalization, etc. (Sander, 1985).

The basis for self-organization—the physiobiological regulation

Sander (1977) has suggested that the basis of the infant's capacity for self-regulation is formed during the first weeks of life in relation to this early environment. If the infant does not engage in physiological regulation, other developmental dimensions will not proceed appropriately. Early basic regulation takes place through repeated and regular sequences of sleep–wake cycles and hunger cycles. These states are regulated during the first days and weeks of life, as care-giver and infant mutually influence each other and establish predictable sequences. The feeling of relatedness or rapport arises through the mutual influence of care-giver and infant during the first six months, a process that is considered the precursor of empathy.

Even though the infant has the capacity for organizing states, Sander (1977, 1983) has shown that this system requires appropriate interactive regulation between infant and care-giver to be established. In a normal caring environment, newborn infants who spend time with their mothers will establish a differentiation between day and night within four to six days. The mother is sensitive to changes in the child's state, and the infant responds to the mother's attempts at increasing or reducing the child's arousal.

Sander studied newborn infants who had been put up for adoption, and who had spent their first ten days in a regular hospital with fixed rules and cared for by many different nurses. These infants did not develop a differentiation between day and night or stable sleep–wake patterns. For the following ten days of their lives each child had more contact with one particular nurse, and child and nurse entered into a mutually regulated process. During those ten days all the infants established a differentiation between day and night and a stable sleep–wake cycle.

During the first ten days of life, infants adapt specifically to their care-giver. Replacing the care-giver with someone else at this point will be associated with significant changes in crying and eating behaviour. The regulation is based on individual differences both in the infant and care-giver, which results in a specific and unique pattern of interaction and regulation. To study the infant's early perceptual processing, researchers have tried masking the mother's face on the seventh day throughout an entire waking period. In this situation the child displayed reactions of surprise when fed by the mother, and remained affected throughout the meal. The individual way in which care-giver and child adapt to each other is the beginning of attachment formation. Infants who are exposed to many different care-givers, or to an unpredictable care-giver who does not engage in a mutually regulated process, will fail to develop synchronized temporal organization; they also develop a disturbed sleep–wake pattern and are far more prone to crying and irritability (Sander, 1977).

The ability of the nervous system to regulate affects in interaction with others is initially based on physiobiological regulation, which is later replaced by psychobiological regulation. In the next section, I describe how repeated events organize rhythms and help the nervous system self-organize.

The basic units of affect attunement

In a complex organism such as the human nervous system, affects emerge slowly on the basis of mutual temporal, synchronized regulation. The attachment capacity is established through the dyadic or mutual regulation of affect (Damasio, 1998; Sroufe, 1996).

At every moment, the brain processes a new pattern of neural activity, depending on its interaction with the environment. For example, when a mother smiles at her baby, the child forms a pattern of neural activity; when they both burst out laughing a new pattern is formed, etc. The pattern resembles but is never quite identical to the previous pattern, because momentary sequences are never quite identical. Patterns arise in interaction with the environment, and patterns or states that are established through repeated experience and with great emotional intensity reactivate more easily. Repetition helps the system to self-organize and stabilize. The integration of many rhythms that come together synchronously creates interconnected circuits in the nervous system in a lifelong process.

Development does not take place according to any acquired or predetermined programme. Development is self-organizing and takes place within a particular set of developmental circumstance defined by the conditions that are genetically embedded in the nervous system from the outset. However, development does require a set of initial conditions, for example a particular biological rhythm and attachment cry in the child's innate skills and an attachment response from the parents (Bertelsen, 1994). It is not the environment that establishes emotions, but the environment does trigger built-in affective potentials within the nervous system.

Rhythms and resonance

Two nervous systems that are activated at the same time create a resonance phenomenon that lets these two systems amplify and co-regulate each other's activity. These resonance phenomena, which occur in the dyadic state, form the basis for the brain's capacity for developing new integrative skills. When the interpersonal communication is fully engaged, the connection is extremely strong, causing an overwhelming sensation of a "now-experience", which Stern (2001) calls a "present moment". When two people's nervous systems are connected over time and energy is allowed to flow freely between them, there is a possibility for new communicative patterns, which increases the complexity of both brain systems. Brain development depends on dyadic communication.

The child's physiobiological rhythms in interaction with an optimum environment develop self-regulatory systems. The child spontaneously creates a physiological rhythm, which is expressed through fluctuations in arousal states such as sleep, drowsiness, attention, tension, etc. Sander (1988) describes the manner in which infants organize their sleep–wake rhythms as one of the most distinct indicators of an infant's vulnerability. A normal, well-organized infant wakes up four to six times every twenty-four hours. As described above, the waking state clearly displays different arousal states, and then the child goes back to sleep.

Over time, fluctuations in arousal states develop into the form of affective states that Stern (1985) calls vitality affects, which are best described through kinaesthetic terms such as surging, fleeting, explosive, etc. From the moment the child is born, he or she is exposed to bodily experiences on a daily basis; for example, breathing, sucking, moving, swallowing, etc., all with their own temporal form and vitality affect. Vitality affects occur all the time and relate to associative networks in the nervous system. Vitality affects give the child a sense of whether a given emotional quality is pleasant or unpleasant, and they are experienced through the interaction between own behaviour and bodily sensations and by observing, testing, and responding to other people's behaviour patterns. Vitality affects manifest all the time; they are a ubiquitous force in relation to the sensation of moods, and we use them to attune with others. Vitality affects only arise when the child "clicks" with a temporal rhythm, and the child must have incorporated rhythms in order to exist in the flow of time (Stern, 1984, 2004).

Physiobiological rhythms are fundamental to all living systems. In humans, this ability is not purely instinctive, and repeated events are important for the organization of these rhythms. The caregiver–infant system is an example of repetitive events that help to organize physiobiological rhythms in the infant's nervous system. Repetitive or rhythmic events lead to habituation and adaptation. Different rhythms develop over time and combine to form ever larger entities. Synchronicity is important for brain development, and there is no one place where perceptions, sensorimotor functions, cognition, and affects combine into a whole (Damasio, 1999; Sander, 1988).

Regulated interaction

In a series of experiments with infants, DeCasper and Carstens (1980) demonstrated the importance of an environment with a rhythm that the infant is able to perceive and comprehend. This affects the infant's subsequent emotional life and capacity for attention, memory, and learning. When a regulated interaction develops into a predictable pattern it becomes an organized event and part of an expectation-based pattern that involves both infant and care-giver. Early on, the infant forms expectations of the care-giver's actions and responds to them, just as the care-giver soon develops expectations of the infant's reactions. Affect-regulating mirroring enables infants to regulate their own impulses through the care-giver's predictable actions. In infancy, the care-giver has a crucial influence on the affect-regulating process. As children develop a greater capacity for independent affect regulation they become able to display their internal states, for example through play, without help from the care-giver. An unpredictable environment hampers the infant's chances of organizing experiences within a dyadic relation, as seen in disorganized children with attachment disorders.

It is impossible to interact with others without the ability to read or deduce their motives or intentions. Researchers have long wondered how this ability can be explained on a neural level, and perhaps the answer lies in the theory of mirror neurons.

Mirror neurons and affect mirroring

At an early stage, the infant imitates affective stimuli, and right from birth arousal regulation is associated with social interactions that the infant finds pleasant or unpleasant. The infant uses affective expressions through facial expressions, motor activity, and vocalization directed at the care-giver, and there seems to be an innate structure in the central nervous system for imitating behaviour.

In the 1990s, Italian neuroscientists (Gallese, 2001; Gallese & Goldman, 1998; Gallese, Fadiga, Fogassi, & Rizzolatti, 1996; Rizzolatti & Arbib, 1998; Rizzolatti, Fadiga, Fogassi, & Gallese, 1999) discovered through experiments with monkeys and by coincidence that premotor neurons were activated when the monkeys were still and observing. The scientists were studying neurons in the frontal lobe system when they suddenly discovered that the same neurons were activated in the monkey's frontal lobe system both when the monkey observed the scientist carrying out an activity and when the monkey itself carried out a similar activity. These neurons were dubbed "mirror neurons", and they provided a neurological basis for understanding the imitation of other individuals. Mirror neurons are interesting because they offer an insight into the ability of the nervous system to imitate others. The Italian scientists suggest that the mirror neurons are part of a larger brain system that enables us to predict future actions and that they offer a neural basis for our ability to understand other people's behaviour—to put ourselves in their place. The neurons in our nervous system fire in relation to the other person's actions, and this is the basis of empathy. We have always known that both humans and primates are able to learn from observation; we just have not known the neurological basis for this ability. The mirror neurons connect observation and behaviour and imply that "the other" is represented in our brain patterns. When we meet others whom we have met before, we recreate each other on the basis of the related neural structures. This includes other people's prosocial behaviour as well as rejections. The mirror neurons discovered by the Italian neuroscientists were situated in the premotor system close to the language centre. Subsequently, Fogassi and colleagues (2005) found mirror neurons in the inferior parietal areas and the insula, and mirror neurons have also been located in the area of the temporal lobe that deals with optic planning and interpretation of body movements, facial expression, mouth movements, and gaze of living beings (STS—sulcus temporalis superior). Fogassi and colleagues believe these mirror neurons to be responsible for not just mirroring and encoding motor patterns, but also for understanding the other's intention with the act. There may be reason to presume that this is the case, since imitative behaviour can be observed shortly after birth. Thirty-six hours after birth, infants have been found to be able to distinguish between happy, sad, and surprised facial expressions (Field & Fogel, 1982; Field, Woodson, Greenberg, & Cohen, 1982). Even very young infants are able to imitate such things as oral movements. Infants will stick out their tongue or purse their lips when they see someone else doing the same, even if they have never seen their own tongue or lips directly. Thus, the neurons establish the connection between the motor cortex, felt lip and tongue positions from sensors in mouth (proprioception), and the sight of another person's lips and tongue (Ramachandran, 2003).

When an observed act is particularly interesting, the premotor system in the frontal lobes is activated, which prepares an action that is not necessarily enacted. This impulse or preparation to act is not volitional, but indicates that the observation of the other person's acts has been perceived. The activation of the premotor system in the observer is recognized by the person who acts, which influences the behaviour of both. The capacity for controlling the "mirror system" is important in relation to activating volitional signals. The mirror neurons are a fundamental mechanism for sensing another person's actions without necessarily doing the same. Mirror neurons let us take part in the another person's acts and mental life without having to actually imitate him or her, which offers a sense of sharing or understanding the other person's intentions and feelings (Stern, 2004).

But how does the nervous system prevent us from being constantly absorbed by the other's nervous system and activities? If the activation of the mirror neurons also activated the motor neurons, the act would be carried out, which would result in the automatic imitation of other people's behaviour. Rizzolatti and Arbib (1998) conclude that the spinal cord provides a strong inhibitor that selectively blocks the motor neurons involved in the execution of the observed act. The workings of this neural mechanism are still somewhat unclear. There is, however, evidence that the maturation of certain areas in the prefrontal lobes leads to inhibitory mechanisms that curb this imitation tendency more and more.

Other people's moods and intentions

Other people's moods can be transferred through an unconscious motor imitation of their facial expressions, gestures, tone of voice, and other non-verbal indicators. Mirroring causes the other person's mood to be recreated in the observer's neural patterns via so-called sociobiological choreography. In a brief moment, an angry-looking face, for example, will lead to the tensing of tiny muscles—not enough for actual mirroring but enough to reflect the angry person's facial expression. Ekman (2003) has dedicated his research to experiments with mood changes in connection with the activation of certain facial muscles. If someone contracts the same facial muscles as another person, he or she senses the other's emotion. For example, when a mother sees her distressed child, she intuitively furrows her brow and turns her head, momentarily sharing the child's feeling of distress. She does not imitate the child completely. Her mirror neurons connect with the child and help her understand her child, which forms the basis for empathic attunement. The mirror neuron circuit is activated by external gestures, prosody, posture, etc., and is an intuitive way of sensing another's state (Cozolino, 2000). The link between emotional facial expressions and particular emotional states is active from birth, and imitating the care-givers' emotional facial expressions activates the infant's vitality affects. In this manner, the care-giver's mental state is communicated to the infant's state, and the infant thus takes part in the care-giver's subjective state (Beebe & Lachmann, 1988). The mirror neurons and their neural networks enable the infant to imitate, sense, and respond to the care-giver, which in turn gradually enables the child to form a theory of mind. Rizzolatti later explained that the mirror neuron system lets people comprehend another's mind, not through conceptual reasoning but through direct imitation: by feeling, not by thinking. Studies show that anxiety, tension, and stress reduce the activity of mirror neurons.

The ability to recognize and decode other people's intentions is crucial for adaptation and survival. An eighteen-month-old child is able to grasp the intention of an act without seeing the act performed fully. An experiment showed that if a child sees a person picking a piece of paper up from the floor with the intention of putting it in the bin but missing the goal because she "drops" the paper, the child will later be able to complete the task despite never seeing the person complete the task. When the person was replaced with a robot, the child did not react to the intention and would not complete the task at a later time. When humans are involved, the child will carry out the other person's presumed intent. Thus, the child acts not solely on the basis of observations. It appears that even very young children perceive that only humans, not robots, have intentions that are worth imitating and carrying out (Meltzoff, 1995; Meltzoff & Moore, 1999; Stern, 2004).

Imitation, protoconversations, and affect attunement

Humans are the most imitative species by far, and imitations and expressive movements occur soon after birth. At three weeks infants begin to imitate facial expressions. DeCasper and Fifer's (1980) and DeCasper and Spencer's (1986) studies demonstrate that even during the foetal stage the foetus turns towards the human voice and prefers the mother's voice. A newborn infant is prepared to enter into vocal communication, initially especially with the mother. Two-week-old infants are able to distinguish between different people's faces and voices and to relate face and voice to each other. They are often able to engage in active social communication and prefer human contact over other stimuli. Right from birth, the infant is able to display movements that are precisely and systematically synchronized with adult speech. Newborn infants are prepared to communicate with their care-giver and experience comfort or discomfort in relation to physical handling. Imitation requires that infants' sensations and perceptions of their care-giver are linked with their sense of their own movements and the position of their own body. When infant and care-giver imitate and mirror each other's behaviour, a process is initiated that later develops into so-called protoconversations, interactions that are well-organized in timing and affective modulation. The term proto-conversations was first used in 1975 by Mary Catherine Bateson, who described how 7–15-week-old children focused on their mother's face and voice and responded to her smiles and expressions in a mutually engaging manner. She used the term "proto" because she considered this language more primitive and pre-lingual (Meltzoff, 1985; Neisser, 1993; Stern, 1985, 2004; Trevarthen, 1989).

Infants only imitate their care-givers when they feel calm and secure. The imitation must be adapted to the infant's signs of interest and take place when the infant is ready for contact. There are big temperamental differences in infants' readiness to imitate. Infants have an innate communication repertoire and strive for what is biologically satisfying. Infants imitate movements that are close to their own spontaneous repertoire of expressions, and which are comprehensible and expectable. For example, a mother's repeated rhythmic movements and her consistent pulse coincide with a fundamental motivation for human contact. When a mother talks to her baby, her happy face is an exaggerated expression of love and kindness. Her voice is gentle and relaxed with a breathy quality, and she often speaks at a pitch around 300 Hz. Her hand movements are gentle, and her facial movements, vocalizations, and gestures are co-ordinated or synchronized. Her movements are regulated to optimize her communication with her child (Neisser, 1993).

Dyadic attunement

The transfer of affective information is enhanced through dyadic resonance. Affective arousal happens through shifts in energy and usually when an external sensory stimulation coincides with the endogenous rhythms of the organism itself. Synchronized moments require dyadic emotional regulation. Stern (1984, 1985) describes how dyadic regulation takes place through affect attunement, the behaviour that expresses a shared affective state without complete imitation of the exact behaviour. Affective attunement lets the partners communicate internal states. While imitation and protoconversation maintain the focus of attention on external behaviour, affectively attuned behaviour shifts the focus of attention to the quality of the shared emotion. Imitation and protoconversation show acts, attunement shows emotions. Attunement provides a sense of sharing internal experiences, which creates an experience of emotional connectedness.

Fonagy, Gergely, Jurist, and Target (2002) point out that there is a qualitative difference between regarding one's own reflection in a mirror and seeing a parent's expressive mirroring of one's own face. Children are unable to recognize themselves in a mirror until they are close to two years old. Regardless of how hard a care-giver tries to imitate the infant's state, she will never achieve a perfect imitation of facial expression and vocalization, which is important for the infant's ability to feel an independent individual in relation to the care-giver. Between two and six months old, infants respond communicatively by completing the care-giver's expression with an emotionally appropriate expression that goes beyond mere imitation. In order to perceive another person and respond appropriately, the infant has to be able to integrate the care-giver's emotional expression through the perception of her facial expression, vocalization, and touch. In order to be able to understand and empathize with other people's feelings later in life, the infant has to be able to imitate the care-giver's expression and achieve appropriate affect attunement with her through protoconversations. When care-giver and infant look at each other, it is usually the infant who looks away first. The infant initiates and disrupts some ninety-four per cent of all mutual gaze contact, while the mother typically maintains a stable gaze at the child.

Summary

In this chapter I have described how neurons connect in neural circuits through synchronicity and resonance. The human nervous system needs outside stimulation to develop, and deep-seated affective structures in the infant's brain develop through resonance with the care-giver's nervous system, an essential process for the ability to regulate physiobiological and psychobiological states. As mentioned earlier, the brain matures slowly, and the deep-seated structures in the brainstem mature before the areas in the prefrontal cortex. In the next three chapters, I use the triune model of the brain to describe the neural structures that are important for personality formation. I set out by looking at structures at the base of the nervous system, specifically structures in the brainstem and cerebellum, then move on to structures in the limbic system, and close with a look at neocortical structures.

CHAPTER SIX

The basic body-sensing and affect-regulating brain: brainstem and cerebellum

"The reticular formation was understood to constitute an activating system, which became known as the 'ascending reticular activating system'. The job of the system was to maintain the cerebral cortex in an awake and alert state ... The reticular formation exerted a powerful influence on virtually all the sectors of the nervous system located above it, but especially on the cerebral cortex ... Damage to the reticular formation would put the cerebral cortex to sleep, turn off the light on perception and thought, as it were, and preclude the execution of planned action"

(Damasio, 1999, p. 248)

"Those patterns correspond best to the tail of the process of consciousness ... (the reticular nuclei) are a part of the innate machinery with which the brain regulates homeostasis and are, in order to do so, the recipients of signals that represent the state of the organism moment by moment"

(*ibid.*, p. 251)

T he brainstem is a small region at the base of the central nervous system (see Figure 6.1) corresponding to the area that MacLean called the reptilian brain, or the protomental area. It is densely packed with nuclei and circuits that are involved in various vital functions. Most basic affect-regulating functions take place in the brainstem, which forms a very small part of the central nervous system. It is the brainstem that synthesizes most of the components in the affective system.

The most important function of the brainstem is to maintain breathing, heart rate, etc. The brainstem also contains the so-called reticular activation system, which serves to maintain the central nervous system in an aroused and alert state and regulate basic sensory functions. In addition to preserving physiological equilibrium and regulating sleep–wake states, the brainstem also contains structures that represent body states. Structures in this area are important for our spontaneous involvement with the world, and basic circuits controlling attention, alertness and sleep are regulated at this level (Damasio, 1999; Panksepp, 1998).

The brainstem and the core of the cerebellum are highly active from birth. The first affective self-regulation takes place at this primitive level, partly through the autonomic nervous system with sympathetic and parasympathetic activity. It is also at this level that most neurotransmitters are created and regulated. The three most important structures at this level are the reticular activation system, the cranial nerves, and the adjacent structure: the cerebellum. The reticular activation system and the cranial nerves extend throughout the brainstem and connect to the cerebellum (Figure 6.1).

Brainstem structures regulate motor, sensory, and emotional states.

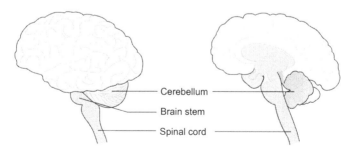

Figure 6.1.   Brain stem and cerebellum.

The brainstem is located at the end of the spinal cord and contains all vital, involuntary control centres, including a visual attention system, which animals use for catching a dancing mosquito, for example. This area also contains the startle centre, which enables the organism to respond instantly to a sudden move or sound. Even in a brain-dead person, parts of the brainstem may still be functioning. This part of the brain (together with the diencephalon) enables reflexive interactions that are also found in reptiles; for example, aggression, sexual behaviour, and the defence of territorial boundaries (Lewis, Amini, & Lannon, 2001). In this chapter, I shall focus on brainstem functions that play an important role in affect regulation.

The reticular activation system

The reticular activation system (Figure 6.2) is in charge of regulating our arousal level and alertness. Arousal and alertness depend on many complex factors, including the regulation of brain wave resonance, energy mobilization throughout the autonomic nervous system, heart rate, respiratory rate, blood pressure, etc. The reticular activation system consists of separate components, each with

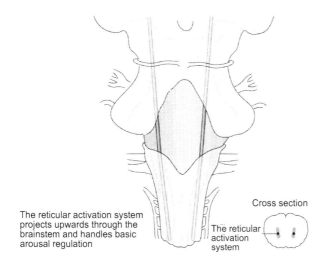

The reticular activation system projects upwards through the brainstem and handles basic arousal regulation

Cross section

The reticular activation system

Figure 6.2.   The reticular activation system.

their own biochemical properties (Goldberg, 2001). The axons in this area are highly branched-out, and on average the individual neurons connect to some 30,000 other neurons (Andresen & Tuxen, 1977–1980). It was Moruzzi and Magoun who identified the reticular activation system in 1949 and found that the area is in charge of basic self-regulation and contains structures that create certain neurotransmitters. These neurotransmitters project into the entire central nervous system and regulate neural activity. According to Luria (1973) the reticular activation system helps create harmony and balance, which is crucial for organized mental activity (Cicchetti & Tucker, 1994; Edelman & Tononi, 2000).

Moruzzi and Magoun found that stimulation to the upper section of the reticular activation system led to increased arousal and attention and desynchronized EEG activity. Stimulation of the lower section led to arousal inhibition. Even though the reticular activation system is no wider than a fingernail, it is able to regulate overall brain activity and inhibit arousal. The reticular activation system prevents sensory overload and is able to shut out incoming impulses. As the lower part of the brainstem regulates breathing by monitoring the consumption of oxygen and carbon dioxide in the bloodstream, there is reason to assume that breathing also helps control arousal regulation in the reticular activation system. Experiments with cats have shown that inhaling is associated with more neurons firing, while exhaling is associated with more neurons calming down. When breathing becomes calmer many neurons reduce their activation. The amygdala (see p. 131) in particular has a reduction in the number of neurons firing (Austin, 1998).

Our level of consciousness is controlled by reticular activation, and the area plays a key role in pain perception. Neocortical activity is co-ordinated and regulated by the reticular activation system, and the anatomy and chemistry of this part of the brainstem are established and differentiated during the foetal stage, long before the cortex is formed. The reticular activation system controls our focus of attention and flexibility of orientation. It directs the focus of the eyes towards interesting objects, co-ordinates stimuli, and regulates the rhythm and balance of attention, cognitive states, readiness to act, and environmental scanning (Cicchetti & Tucker, 1994; Trevarthen, 1989, 1990). In a comatose patient, the reticular system is still active, while the structures above it are inactive.

When the patient orientates his or her attention toward sources of light, this is often mistaken for a volitional act. In a manner of speaking, the reticular system can be said to act as the main circuit breaker of the brain.

The reticular activation system is affected by both internal and external sensory impressions, since practically all sensory nerve fibres pass through the brainstem. Areas in the cortex control the reticular system and act as a filter, so that the person does not respond to all outside disturbances but only to particularly relevant stimuli. Damage to the reticular system limits the arousal level, associated with symptoms of fatigue, incapacity, and lack of concentration, which makes all intellectually demanding activities impossible (Eriksson, 2001).

Research with infants has shown that immediately after birth the child has six levels of consciousness or arousal, probably controlled by the reticular activation system and connected to the previously mentioned frequencies of brain activity, alpha, beta, and gamma rhythms, etc. These are defined as calm waking state, active waking state, crying, drowsiness, calm sleep, and dream sleep (Brodén, 1991). Spontaneous smiles or spontaneous crying stem from brain structures that are situated deep in the brainstem structures. Both pleasure and distress are controlled by the brainstem in collaboration with other areas, including areas in the prefrontal cortex. The brainstem is activated when affects are triggered, and affects that are induced by brainstem structures are beyond volitional control. It is important to ensure adequate sensory stimulation in the early phases of the child's life to ensure the maturation of the reticular activation system and adequate regulation of arousal functions.

At birth, the reticular activation system is active and relies on physiobiological regulation to mature sufficiently. The character of care-giver–infant contacts has tremendous importance for this regulation. For the benefit of the interested reader, I now discuss some of the main structures in this system, a system that matures through early interaction, is involved in the regulation of some of the key neurotransmitters, and contains the basic structures for orientation and body representation. This section describes the main structures and the neurotransmitters they emit. Chapter Nine looks at the functions of the various neurotransmitters.

The basic structures

On either side of the brainstem is the *locus coeruleus*, which consists of neurons that contain noradrenalin. The area has projections to practically all brain regions and regulates the noradrenalin-based tonus and activity of many other neurons at every level of the central nervous system. This structure increases activity if a unit of information seems novel or potentially dangerous. Activity in this area reflects the degree of arousal and enables the organism to maintain attention on prioritized stimuli. Locus coeruleus co-ordi-nates cognitive processes with the sympathetic nervous system. Fear increases the activation potential of the locus coeruleus and, thus, the release of noradrenalin, which in turn increases heart rate, blood pressure, glucose metabolism, respiratory rate, and muscle tone. Regulating the respiratory rate, relaxing, and meditating seem to inhibit neuronal firing in this area. Locus coeruleus is connected to the sympathetic nervous system, consists of a mere 45,000 to 60,000 neurons, and is often referred to as the trauma centre of the brain (Allen, 2002).

Two other important areas are the ventral tegmental nucleus and substantia nigra, which both contain the neurotransmitter dopamine (Figure 6.3). Both areas ensure the supply of dopamine to the basal ganglia (see p. 126). Dopamine from the substantia nigra projects mainly to the basal ganglia areas that help the organ-ism execute motor patterns and involuntary movements. Dopa-mine from the ventral tegmental area mainly projects into areas in the basal ganglia, the limbic system, and the prefrontal cortex. The dopamine pathway from the ventral tegmental area is stimulated by positive facial expressions, among other things, and activates emotionally rewarding processes. In addition to dopamine it contains high concentrations of the body's own opioids (endoge-nous morphine) (Schore, 1994). These areas play a key role in stress management and have a significant influence on the regulation of arousal, affects, attention, the startle response, and sleep (Perry, 1990). Damage to the dopamine-producing neurons in the substan-tia nigra results in Parkinson's disease, which leads to motor dysfunctions (Bradley, 2000; Hansen, 2002).

The *raphe nuclei* (raphe means sleep) are located in the centre of the reticular activation system. They use the neurotransmitter sero-

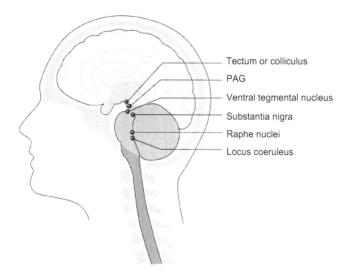

Figure 6.3.   The neurotransmitter-producing and basic orientation and body-representing structures.

tonin and are balanced through sleep–wake rhythms. The area projects neural connections to almost all areas of the central nervous system (Hansen, 2002).

PAG (periaqueductal grey matter) is located at the top of the brainstem and is an important but not very well-defined cluster of nuclei capable of modulating pain perception. This area is believed to release the body's own opioids. Activation of the PAG induces pleasant and unpleasant sensory experiences. Varying degrees of pleasure and unpleasure adjust the basis for the sensation of somatosensory pain, and the area registers both emotional and somatosensory discomfort. The area is also activated in fear reactions such as fight-or-flight behaviour, in immobilization states (freezing or "playing dead" response), in grief reactions, and in pleasure. PAG is involved in most affective processes (Damasio, 1999; Panksepp, 1998). Neuroanatomical studies of rat pups show that stimulation of the PAG inhibits the attachment cry, probably through an inhibitor triggered by systems within the PAG (Damasio, 2003; Hofer & Sullivan, 2001; LeDoux, 2001; Purves et al., 2001; Solms & Turnbull, 2002).

Tectum provides a primitive representation of the entire body; i.e., a combination of internal and external body sensations. This sensory integration provides a sensorimotor map of the body that activates basic action-generating mechanisms, such as approachment or avoidance behaviour, that are closely related to pleasure and unpleasure (Solms & Turnbull, 2002).

The *colliculus* areas process simple orientation responses and provide a sense of the body in the world. The areas provide a basic motor image of the body. In this area, visual, auditory, tactile, and other sensory stimuli come together through polymodal areas (Austin, 1998). The sensorimotor self-representation develops from the interaction of tectum, colliculus areas, and circuits in the PAG. The colliculus areas are closely connected to the premotor cortex, where motor plans and intentions arise.

The above-mentioned structures register changes in the body's internal environment, such as heart rate, blood pressure, etc.: the foundation of basic motivations and drives. Proprioceptive systems (from Latin: *proprius* = own, *capio* = capture, receive) provide a sense of the body's position in space. These sensations involve various modalities such as pressure/touch, warmth/cold, pain, and the kinaesthetic sense, which is based partly on one's sense of the static position of the limbs and partly on one's sense of the limbs in motion (Mathiesen, 2004). The proprioceptive sense is crucial for the affective sense of self. Most of the above-mentioned structures in the brainstem use individually specific signal substances, which are vital to affect regulation. In Chapter Nine, I discuss the importance of the main transmitters, the peptides and hormones.

The cranial nerves

At an early stage in evolution, the cranial nerves controlled body and self-regulating functions such as breathing, blood circulation, digestion, etc. In social animals the cranial nerves have developed ever more components that regulate communication and emotional attunement (Figure 6.4). The cranial nervous system is developed around the seventh foetal week, long before the neocortex has begun to form neurons. This part of the brainstem motivates selective attention, focusing, and motor functions (Trevarthen, 2004).

Darwin focused on facial expressions when he defined emotions, and he was of the opinion that facial expressions were under-

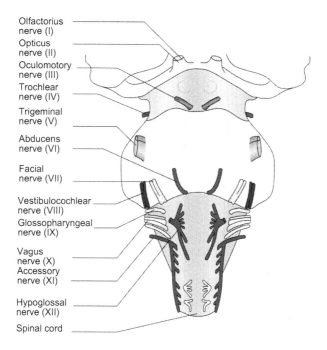

Figure 6.4.   The cranial nerves.

stood to mean the same in all cultures. He hypothesized that neural circuits connect facial expressions with activity in the brainstem and influence our breathing and heart rate. When an emotional state arises, the heart rate changes instantly, which in turn influences brain activity. Inspired by Darwin, Porges (1995, 1996, 1997) elaborated Darwin's emotional theory, and in this effort he focused on the cranial nerves. Porges points out that the autonomic nervous system and the brain–body link is transmitted through the tenth cranial nerve (the vagus nerve, which means the wandering nerve). Together, the fifth cranial nerve (the trigeminal nerve or triplet nerve), which is responsible for facial tactile sensations, and the seventh cranial nerve (the facial nerve), which controls the facial muscles, connect facial expressions with body sensations and enable humans to produce emotions and communicate them through facial expressions. This neuromuscular system is in charge of sensing and controlling all the small facial muscles.

Most of the time, facial muscles are controlled by unconscious mechanisms. The facial cranial nerves contribute to a sense of the facial muscles and play a role in the way we are affected by other people's facial expressions (cf. the previously mentioned mirror neurons). We form mirror images of other people's emotional expressions through our facial muscles (Damasio, 1999). Ekman (2003) found that true joy is only activated when muscles around the eyes are activated, and that certain facial expressions change our posture. Altering a facial expression to match a particular emotion causes physiological changes that accompany the emotion. "Much of the brain activity you find with genuine enjoyment occurs only if the muscle around the eye is engaged" (Goleman, 2003, p. 129).

The vagus nerve (the tenth cranial nerve) is the longest of the brain nerves, and it has a large supply area. It consists of a paired double nerve that projects from the skull through the jugular foramen and continues as two thick strands along the pharynx and oesophagus through the chest cavity and diaphragm to the abdomen. Along the way it sends out fibres to the organs, oesophagus, lungs, heart, gall bladder, stomach, intestines, liver, etc. The vagus nerve also consists of fibres that lead impulses from the organs to the parasympathetic centres in the brainstem, which triggers reflexes that regulate organ function. It is a part of the calming branch of the nervous system, the parasympathetic system within the autonomic nervous system. The vagus nerve is connected to the respiratory system, the heart, and the gastrointestinal system. The cranial nerves connect body and brain and enable us to sense emotions in the body, as when grief or pain "cuts like a knife". Its afferent (sensory) and efferent (motor) fibres provide a quick feedback system that manages the homoeostatic regulation of the physical and emotional state.

The autonomic nervous system

The autonomic nervous system is the branch of the nervous system that connects the central nervous system to internal organs, vessels, and sweat glands, and which regulates functions in these organ systems that are outside volitional control. The term does not describe a clearly defined area, neither anatomically nor functionally, but includes the neuron groups and fibre connections that regulate functions in all internal organs, the heart, blood vessels, glands and intestines. We have no conscious experience of activity in the autonomic nervous system, and we are unable to influence its functions deliberately (Brodal, 2000). It is a complicated system, which monitors and regulates the somatic state, and whose main function is to contribute to the body's homoeostasis. Without the autonomic nervous system, feelings could not be sensed, because feelings and assessments spring from the body. Feelings of pleasure and unpleasure are experienced through the autonomic nervous system and form the basis for sensations that affect our thinking and behaviour. The autonomic nervous system is the physical basis for sensing anything at all. It is the basis of instincts and drives, and it forms the "roots" of emotions. In jargon, the autonomic nervous system is sometimes referred to as "the four Fs": fighting, fleeing, feeding, and fucking (Eriksson, 2001; Schore, 2003b).

The hormonal (endocrine) system consists of hormone-producing glands such as the thyroid gland, the sexual glands, the adrenal glands, and the intestines. It communicates via neurochemicals. The autonomic nervous system, which communicates through neural impulses and the hormonal system, uses two different types of signals: a rapid, neural signal, and a slower, neurochemical signal.

As mentioned previously, the autonomic nervous system consists of two systems: the sympathetic and the parasympathetic nervous system (Table 6.1). The sympathetic nervous system controls the activation of the nervous system in response to threats and other forms of high energy mobilization. The parasympathetic

Table 6.1. Outline of the parasympathetic and the sympathetic nervous systems.

Parasympathetic activation	Sympathetic activation
Calming system	Activation system
Reduces heart activity	Responds to threats
Freezing/playing dead system	
Builds body energy and promotes cell growth	Increases heart rate and blood pressure
Relaxes the muscles	Increases muscle tone
Releases tears and salivation	Releases glucose and insulin
Increases digestive activity	Activates sexual behaviour

system is a vegetative system, which promotes the digestive process and reduces the heart rate, among other things (Brodal, 2000). The autonomic nervous system is regulated by reflexes, and the sympathetic and the parasympathetic nervous systems have opposite functions. Normally, the sympathetic and parasympathetic nervous systems fluctuate between predominantly sympathetic and predominantly parasympathetic activation, but in special cases both systems may be activated simultaneously; for example, when a person is driven to maximum activity levels, as is often the case in extraordinary states of consciousness or when the nervous system has been deeply traumatized over an extended period of time. Thus, certain environmental conditions may affect the specific balance between the two systems, but the balance of the autonomic nervous system is established before birth (d'Aquili & Newberg, 1999; Newberg, d'Aquili, & Rause, 2002).

The sympathetic nervous system

The sympathetic nervous system simulates the brainstem to release adrenalin and noradrenalin, and these substances in turn stimulate the glands that release glucose and insulin (Purves et al., 2001). The response of the sympathetic system is not an all-or-nothing response, and several distinct sympathetic reflexes are in play, depending on the energy charge that is needed. The sympathetic nervous system is activated by positive experiences; for example, when the hunter's heart rate increases as he nears his prey. It is also involved in sexual behaviour and in fear situations. Any situation that involves an element of survival will activate the sympathetic nervous system. Whether the situation concerns fear or readiness, the response is the same: the provision of high arousal. Physiologically, the sympathetic nervous system is expressed through an increase in heart rate, raised blood pressure, faster breathing, and increased muscle tone. The sympathetic nervous system is also referred to as the arousal system.

The parasympathetic nervous system

Parasympathetic activity dominates in calm and safe condition. It builds energy, unlike the sympathetic nervous system, which prepares the organism for fight-or-flight responses. Among other things, the parasympathetic system is involved in releasing tears and salivation and increasing digestive activity in the intestines. A drop in sympathetic activity lets blood vessels, skin, and the intestinal system expand, and relaxes the muscles. The parasympathetic system is in charge of preserving energy and for keeping the basic bodily functions in harmonious balance. It regulates sleep and relaxation and ensures that vital nutrients are transported throughout the body to promote cell growth. Because of its ability to promote a calming stabilization of the body's functions, it is called the calming system of the organism.

The centres of the parasympathetic nervous system are situated both above and below the sympathetic nervous system, and there are parasympathetic nerve fibres in several cranial nerves and spinal cord segments. Almost all organs receive fibres from both the sympathetic and the parasympathetic nervous systems, except the adrenal medulla, the sweat glands, and the blood vessels in the skin and muscles, which only receive fibres from the sympathetic system (Andresen & Tuxen, 1977–1980). Both the sympathetic and the parasympathetic systems play important roles in anchoring the emotions in the body. The parasympathetic nervous system is involved in our ability to perceive ourselves through bodily sensations.

The autonomic nervous system is characterized by a high degree of autonomy, and previously the autonomic nervous system was not believed to be susceptible to volitional control. However, recent research has shown that this part of the nervous system is more susceptible than previously assumed. For example, Uvnäs-Moberg (1998) has shown that vagus activity is increased when the skin is touched gently, or when there is light, pleasant stimulation, which implies a shift from sympathetic to parasympathetic activation, a reduction of blood pressure, and a general calming of the organism.

The enteric nervous system

The autonomic nervous system also includes the so-called enteric nervous system. Millions of neurons are located in the intestinal tract in order to control its many functions. Several studies suggest that the digestive system has its own local nervous system and its own reflex-controlled rules that operate independently of the sympathetic and the parasympathetic nervous system; many even talk about the enteric mini-brain. Researchers believe the enteric nervous system to be an evolutionary remnant from a time when the nervous system was regulated from the digestive system, prior to the development of the central nervous system. The enteric system consists of cells that release certain neurotransmitters, among other functions. The enteric nervous system maintains close communication with the sympathetic and parasympathetic nervous systems. The connection between the central nervous system and the enteric nervous system lets outside signals influence digestion, just as the enteric nervous system is able to affect the central nervous system via nervous reflexes and neurochemicals. The response of the digestive system to outside signals depends on a number of things, including the genetic make-up of the enteric nervous system; for example, different persons' digestive systems will respond differently to stress situations (Gershon, Kirchgessner, & Wade, 1994; Wood, 1994). No wonder, then, that our digestion is affected by our emotions, and that many emotions are sensed in the gut.

The vagus theories

In recent years, trauma research has been characterized by widespread debate about the basic foundation of our primary emotions. This has led to a number of different theories concerning the autonomic nervous system and vagus tone. In an extensive series of articles, professor of psychology Stephen W. Porges has described his so-called "polyvagal theory", which is applied by many American psychiatrists and neuropsychologists, including Bessel van der Kolk, Allan Schore, Daniel Siegel, and Robert Scaer. One of Porges' articles is mentioned in Antonio Damasio's latest book, *Looking for Spinoza* (2003). As a result of recent years' growing interest in the parasympathetic nervous system and in vagus tone as a psychophysiological indicator of emotional regulation, Theodore Beauchaine at Washington University has received economic support from the American National Research Service Award through the National Institute of Mental Health to assess, integrate, and clarify the area. Many neuropsychologists and neurobiologists find the theories on vagus tone, and especially Porges' polyvagal theory, speculative and controversial—more confusing than actually enlightening. My consultant for the Danish edition of this book, Professor of Neuroanatomy and Neurobiology Jens Zimmer Rasmussen, advised me to drop the vagus theories because he, too, considers them too speculative. He is particularly critical of Porges' hypotheses concerning the lateralization of the vagus nerve and its role in arousal regulation. However, the theories are used more and more in neuroaffective work, and they do offer important hypotheses concerning a possible understanding of basic affect regulation and, thus, basic psychological functions and dysfunctions in the autonomic regulation of the nervous system. After discussing the matter with Allan Schore, I therefore choose to present the theories here. In Schore's view, the parasympathetic nervous system has been neglected by both researchers and clinicians until now. Given this ongoing debate, I find it important to draw attention to the theories that exist about this complicated system, even if they may undergo extensive re-evaluation as we gain more insight into this deep-lying area of the brain.

The theory of diminished/increased vagus tone

As Fanselow and Lester (1988) described, the parasympathetic system in both animals and humans includes an evolutionarily developed "freeze" system, which is supposed to reduce the individual's risk of being spotted by a dangerous predator or at least make the predator lose interest. The freeze system prevented prey animals from moving and, thus, prevented triggering the attacking predator's hunting instinct. Freezing is an innate system that may be activated through the conditioned learning of stimuli associated with threats. Hofer (1970) noted that extended freeze reactions in connection with threats can be widely observed, from insects to humans. Physiologically, the freeze response reduces the heart rate and increases the breathing rate; however, the breathing is so shallow that it is barely audible. When the freeze mechanism fails to protect the prey from being spotted, and the predator is ready to strike there is a dramatic shift in behaviour. The prey tenses and gets ready for explosive behaviour, such as fighting, biting, clawing, etc., that might allow it to escape. If the prey is unable to flee, the freeze response will be re-activated, as the mouse does when the cat plays with it. During the freeze state the internal morphine system is released, probably to reduce the animal's pain during the death throes. How quickly the freeze response is activated depends on vagus nerve activation. When the vagus nerve is activated quickly, the stress response system is reduced, and the animal adopts the freeze response sooner, while a slower activation of the vagus nerve keeps the animal in the sympathetic fight-or-flight behaviour for longer.

Studies of the parasympathetic nervous system in infants reveal great individual differences in what it takes to activate the vagus nerve, and how quickly it happens. This can be observed through temperamental variation, social skills, attention skills, and aggressiveness. For example, newborn human infants with diminished vagus activation have increased stress responses when they are pricked in the heel for blood tests, and in nine-month-old infants diminished vagus activation predicts a vulnerable temperament. These infants startle easily, and their stress response is easily triggered. At a later time, diminished vagus response might have positive affective expressions, because these children are very sensitive in their responses to their environment. Infants who respond sensitively to their surroundings will be more sensitive to outside stimuli. In abused children, diminished vagus activity may lead to difficulties with affect regulation, depression, hyperactivity, etc., but in children raised in a safe and caring environment it could lead to involvement, empathy, joy, interest, and attunement with the environment. Increased vagus activity has been found in expressionless children who were raised by depressive mothers as well as in inhibited children who are withdrawn and fearful (Beauchaine, 2001).

The basic sensory experiences, affect regulation, stress management, etc., depend on parasympathetic and sympathetic activity. The parasympathetic and sympathetic nervous systems are fully developed at birth, and, as we shall see in the following section, Porges is convinced that the autonomic nervous system develops and matures through early care-giver–infant contact.

The polyvagal theory

As mentioned above, Stephen Porges (1995, 1996, 1997, 1998) wrote a series of articles describing his so-called polyvagal theory (Figure

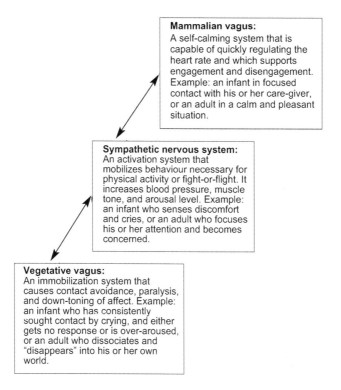

Figure 6.5.   Illustration of Porges' polyvagal theory.

6.5). In this theory, the autonomic nervous system is described on evolutionary terms, based partly on Darwin's theories. Porges says that when living beings were poikilothermic (cold-blooded) and had reduced mobility, their best chance of survival when faced with potential danger was immobilization. At this early time in evolution, a primitive parasympathetic system was activated, which caused the organism to "freeze". As reptiles became more mobile, the sympathetic nervous system developed to improve survival. The sympathetic nervous system inhibits gastrointestinal functions, increases the metabolism and oxygen absorption, and may also inhibit or terminate an immobilization state. This system was activated when it was necessary and possible to fight or flee. Mammals were now able to execute rapid shifts in their communication with the environment, while still maintaining attention. A further development in primates, and especially in humans, made it possible to signal moods through facial expressions and vocalization, i.e., to become socially involved.

In Porges' theory, the foundation is the vagus nerve, which consists of many fibrous bundles with different starting points in the brainstem. Like the two brain hemispheres, the vagus nerve is lateralized, and, according to Porges, functionally right-sided. In mammals, the motor fibres of the vagus nerve originate in two separate neuron groups in the brainstem. One group (the dorsal motor nucleus) is an evolutionarily older structure, which consists of a non-volitional orientation reflex. The other group (nucleus ambiguus) is mainly active in relation to heart rate regulation, and in mammals it has developed to include the capacity to maintain attention. It is through the latter group (the nucleus ambiguus) that we vocalize and connect facial expressions to bodily sensations. It enables us to engage in detailed information processing and to self-regulate in relation to changes in engagement with and attention of our environment.

The autonomic nervous system as a hierarchical and triune structure

According to the polyvagal theory, the autonomic nervous system self-regulates in relation to three different behavioural strategies that have evolved in different ways. The first stage is characterized by a primitive, unmyelinated, vegetative vagus system that supports digestion and responds to impulses by suppressing metabolic activity. This primitive vagus activation corresponds to immobilization behaviour. The second stage is characterized by the sympathetic nervous system, which increases metabolic activity and inhibits the influence of the primitive vagus system on the intestinal system. The sympathetic nervous system mobilizes behaviour that is necessary for energy mobilization, for example, fight-or-flight or hunting behaviour. The third stage is unique in mammals and is characterized by a myelinated mammalian vagus system, which is capable of quickly regulating the heart rate, and which supports engagement and disengagement with our surroundings. The myelinated vagus system arose and resides in the same location as the cranial nerves that control facial expressions, sucking, swallowing, breathing, and vocalization. Hence, this system is closely linked, for example, to the infant's imitation of the care-giver's facial expressions with a view to self-regulation. The response strategies are not an all-or-nothing system and may include temporary combinations with elements from all three systems.

The mammalian vagus system

One effect of the myelinated mammalian vagus system is that mammals are able to shut out irrelevant sounds, and infants are able to focus their attention; for example, to concentrate on the human voice. Porges believes that the mammalian vagus system allows care-giver and infant to engage in early interaction, and that it ensures that newborn infants get the protection, care, and attachment that they need during a vulnerable period. The system promotes the possibility of emotional attachment and the biochemical processes that are a prerequisite for development.

The mammalian vagus system evokes behaviour that is used to define emotions (including Darwin's "primary emotions") and regulates heart and lung functions. This vagus system arrived at a later stage in evolution, and in Porges' view it fosters early care-giver–infant interactions, forms the basis for the development of calming and prosocial behaviour, and has an inhibiting effect on sympathetic neural pathways to the heart. The neuroanatomical connection of the vagus nerve to the other cranial nerves means that the regulation of body functions is linked with facial expressions and vocalization and helps regulate social involvement.

The connection of the vagus nerve to the facial nerve has helped develop increased facial control, especially when the person is awake and considers the environment safe. The mammalian vagus system inhibits sympathetic connections to the heart and allows temporary energy mobilization without requiring sympathetic activation. In the face of a perceived threat, the mammalian vagus system is suppressed to make it easier for the sympathetic system to mobilize energy for fight-or-flight responses.

The vegetative vagus system

The primitive vegetative vagus system appears along with the orientation reflex. In case of oxygen deprivation, there is a radical reduction in heart rate and metabolism, which evokes the immobilization response. The immobilization response can be observed in newborn infants who are exposed to massive stress and is a well-known phenomenon in shock reactions. In videotapes of problematic infant–mother relations, this state is seen, for example, when the infant's crying makes the mothers sort of "freeze". The mother no longer seems to hear the infant's crying and appears unconcerned. When the infant has been crying (sympathetic activation) for some time, the infant, like the mother, "freezes", the crying subsides, and the infant becomes calm and motionless and develops a glassy, unfocused gaze. This reaction is seen in mammals when the attachment cry is futile, and the young animal goes quiet and passive. Bowlby pointed out that in English paediatric hospitals this "freeze" response in hospitalized infants was mistakenly considered a healthy response. One of the effects of his work was a change in practice in this area, so that children are now allowed to be with their parents when they are hospitalized.

The maturation of the hierarchical vagus system

Mammals have both the vegetative vagus system, sympathetic activation, and the mammalian vagus system at their disposal. Porges assumes that the autonomic system, like other brain areas, is hierarchical in structure, and that higher-order systems inhibit or control lower-order systems. When higher functions fail, lower functions increase their activity level. When all else fails, the nervous system seeks towards a lower system, which is adapted to lower levels of functioning (Porges, 1998). The vegetative vagus system and the sympathetic nervous system are active from birth, while the mammalian vagus system is activated during the first six weeks after birth. Prematurely born children often have inadequate regulation of their innate parasympathetic and sympathetic nervous system. Neonatal wards, for example, watch carefully for any bradycardia (when the heart rate is too slow) and apnoea (absence of respiratory functions) in premature infants. The newborn infant is regulated by unconscious, reflex-controlled functions from the primitive vagus system. The mammalian vagus system matures and is exercised during the first few months of life. Parasympathetic modulation continues to develop throughout the first year of life, and this may explain why the child's heart rate begins to decrease around the age of thirteen months. This is the time of maturation for regulatory functions in the prefrontal cortex that may help inhibit parasympathetic activity (Schore, 1994).

The vagal brake

Mammalian vagus activity is at its highest when the child is in situations that are unchallenging, and it goes away in case of panic or rage. Initially, infants have difficulty maintaining mammalian vagus activity, and they expend a great deal of energy on regulating the "vagal brake" by practising engagement with and withdrawal from their surroundings. In healthy infants, temporary behavioural states such as crying will make them withdraw and calm themselves down to re-establish the vagal brake. Infants with a well-developed mammalian vagus system are better able to self-regulate in relation to their environment. This is one of the things that the infants practise in their early contacts with the care-giver, which explains why it is necessary for infants to practise their arousal level by being in attuned contact and then withdrawing when even the tiniest increase in arousal would have made their nervous system break down. This training and expansion of the ability of the nervous system to handle ever higher levels of arousal are some of the skills that are trained in early "I'm going to come and get you" games. Here, care-giver and infant engage in joy-filled interaction where the child's arousal level gradually increases until the child disengages, recovers, and then returns to the joy-filled and exciting behaviour to have more arousal. The better the nervous system is at handling high arousal levels without disintegrating into increased sympathetic or vegetative parasympathetic activity, the more flexible and resilient the child will become.

The two theories on vagus activity have not yet been integrated, and, as I have mentioned, they remain speculative. Both theories assume that diminished vagus activation triggers the sympathetic nervous system and, thus, the stress activation system. In the next section I describe an aspect of adrenal gland function that plays a key role in stress management.

The adrenal glands—part of the body's stress response system

The adrenal glands consist of two hormone glands, each placed on top of a kidney and partially buried in the fatty tissue of the fibrous kidney capsule. They are the size of walnuts and weigh about 7 g each. In fact, an adrenal gland is a double gland, since it consists of two different kinds of tissue. The marrow (medulla) and the surface (cortex) are of different origin, and produce hormones with different tasks in the organism; their placement within one single organ is believed to be due to a coincidence.

The adrenal medulla is formed along with brain tissue, but takes a distinct path at an early stage in foetal development. It consists of glandular cells that were originally neurons, but which lost their nerve fibres, so instead of stimulating individual organs through nervous impulses, they affect the entire organism through hormones that are secreted into the bloodstream.

The adrenal medulla is part of the sympathetic nervous system and is not vital. The absence of the adrenal medulla would simply make the person less able to respond to peak stress loads. The adrenal cortex, however, is of vital importance. It produces hormones that activate enzyme production, and which are fundamental to many metabolic processes and to the body's immune system. In both sexes the adrenal cortex produces male and female sex hormones, so-called androgen and oestrogen, and so-called glucocorticoids (the name corticoids refers to their source in the adrenal cortex), which are essential for stress systems, especially the hormone cortisol (Andresen & Tuxen, 1977–1980).

The cerebellum

Over the past decade we have gained more insight into the function of the cerebellum. Until then, the opinion had been that the cerebellum merely regulated motor functions, but today the cerebellum is also believed to be involved in regulating emotional and cognitive functions and to have connections with circuits in the prefrontal cortex. Recent research suggests that the cerebellum is involved in all types of temporal processing and that it is a coordinating organ for motor functions as well as cognition and emotions. Thus, the cerebellum also manages the modulation and timing of affect regulation and language. Difficulty in stimulus regulation and temporal sequencing disturbs one's sense of rhythm and timing, the internal regulation is either absent or chaotic, and the person prefers stimuli that are recognizable and predictable (Cozolino, 2006; Diamond, 2000; Schacter, 1996).

The cerebellum is some 10 cm wide, and, like the cerebrum, it has two hemispheres, whose surface consists of a thin bark or cortex with underlying white matter (Andresen & Tuxen, 1977–1980). The cerebellum is active from birth, but it develops and myelinates very slowly and is susceptible to environmental factors (Figure 6.6).

The cerebellum registers body movements in relation to the surroundings; it regulates the control of fine motor functions and helps to co-ordinate rhythmic movements in the face, diaphragm, etc. The cerebellum adjusts motor movements to match the appropriate sequence in relation to sensory information, and damage to the cortex of the cerebellum is associated with timing issues (Andresen, 2002b), e.g., difficulties with learning to play a piano, plan action sequences, etc.

The ability to control crying and laughter results from co-operation between the brainstem and the cerebellum. The brainstem contains groups of nuclei and circuits that trigger laughter or crying through stimulation, and the cerebellum is able to modulate the intensity and duration of the components that make up crying and laughter. The cerebellum matures through stimulation acquired through primitive imprinting mechanisms (Damasio, 2003).

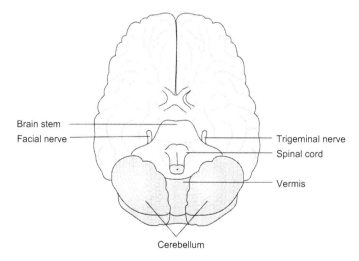

Figure 6.6.   The cerebellum and its location.

There is much to suggest that the cerebellar growth and maturation is stimulated throughout childhood, and certain areas take a long time to myelinate. The infant's nervous system is adapted to receive powerful physical stimulation, and, throughout much of human evolution, infants have spent much time being carried by their mothers as the mothers have bent down, turned around, run, climbed, etc. The infant needs to be held, touched, caressed, rocked, and carried in order to receive sufficient cerebellar stimulation, inadequate stimulation means that the cerebellum fails to mature sufficiently. Harlow's (1958, 1959) work with monkeys showed that monkeys became slightly less aggressive and less socially deviant when they were swung from side to side. This knowledge is reflected, for example, in treatment institutions for children with severe attachment disorders that deliberately apply methods to stimulate the cerebellum; for example, by placing the children in large swinging hammocks.

MacLean only associates the core of the cerebellum with the reptilian brain. He believes that the cerebellum, like the rest of the central nervous system, consists of three separate but deeply integrated levels. The core connects the right and left sides of the cerebellum; it is called the *vermis*. It wraps around the medulla in the mid-line between the two hemispheres and is one of the oldest evolutionary elements. Like other parts of the cerebellum, it co-ordinates emotional and motor functions, and studies by Chugani, Phelps, & Mazziotta (1987) showed that the vermis is active from birth. The area is closely connected to brainstem structures that modulate and regulate the locus coeruleus and the ventral tegmental nucleus in connection with the release of noradrenalin and dopamine. According to Teicher (2002), the vermis is highly sensitive to stressful experiences and to long-term environmental factors. For example, inadequate regulation of dopamine and nordrenalin may cause hyperkinetic disorders and attention disorders such as ADHD, and Teicher found diminished blood flow to the vermis in children who had been exposed to neglect or abuse.

The surface layer of the cerebellum, the cortex, develops along with the cerebral neocortex and is connected to areas that deal with language, memory, and reasoning in the prefrontal cortex (Cozolino, 2000). In the same way as balance requires the constant monitoring of posture and the inhibition of unnecessary and distracting movements, memory, attention, concentration, and language in their own way require a form of balance, and, like the prefrontal cortex, the cerebellum develops from the age of eight months until the age of approximately twenty-three years (Figure 6.7).

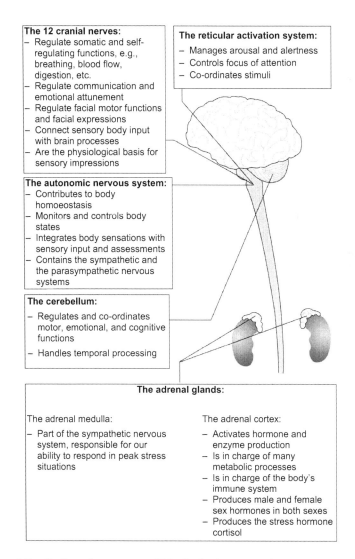

The 12 cranial nerves:
– Regulate somatic and self-regulating functions, e.g., breathing, blood flow, digestion, etc.
– Regulate communication and emotional attunement
– Regulate facial motor functions and facial expressions
– Connect sensory body input with brain processes
– Are the physiological basis for sensory impressions

The reticular activation system:
– Manages arousal and alertness
– Controls focus of attention
– Co-ordinates stimuli

The autonomic nervous system:
– Contributes to body homoeostasis
– Monitors and controls body states
– Integrates body sensations with sensory input and assessments
– Contains the sympathetic and the parasympathetic nervous systems

The cerebellum:
– Regulates and co-ordinates motor, emotional, and cognitive functions
– Handles temporal processing

The adrenal glands:

The adrenal medulla:
– Part of the sympathetic nervous system, responsible for our ability to respond in peak stress situations

The adrenal cortex:
– Activates hormone and enzyme production
– Is in charge of many metabolic processes
– Is in charge of the body's immune system
– Produces male and female sex hormones in both sexes
– Produces the stress hormone cortisol

Figure 6.7. Outline of structures within the brain stem and cerebellum.

Summary

In this chapter, I have described the most important structures at the lowest level of the triune brain. Buried deep and protected in the centre of the brain lies the brainstem, the circuit breaker of the nervous system. This structure is in charge of deeply instinctive, reflexive, and essentially sensory functions. In this area we find the reticular activation system, which is an arousal-regulating system that controls sleep and alertness. The brain's "chemical plant", which produces some of the most important affect-regulating neurotransmitters, and which enables motivation and emotions, is also located here. The twelve cranial nerves, which fine-tune, balance, and co-ordinate somatic and psychological processes and the regulation of the autonomic nervous system through vagus activity, are all involved in creating the foundation for the basic personality structure and basic affect regulation. In the next chapter, I turn to the top level of the reptilian brain: the diencephalon, and the next level in the triune brain: the palaeomammalian level—the area in charge of emotomentation.

CHAPTER SEVEN

The brain of motor systems and emotions: the diencephalon and the limbic system

> "Primate research demonstrates that social attachment is not only a psychological event: it is related to the development of core neurobiological functions in the primate brain . . . the limbic system controls the emotions that stimulate the behaviour necessary for self-preservation and survival of the species . . . the limbic system is also responsible for free-floating feelings of what is real, true, and meaningful"
>
> (van der Kolk, 1987, pp. 39–40)

W hen Paul MacLean developed his theory of the triune brain, he was inspired by an earlier neuroscientist, James Papez, who, in 1937, claimed that particular brain circuits were dedicated to emotional experiences and expressions. As early as the 1850s, neuroscientist Poul Broca had used the term "limbic lobe" to refer to a part of the cortex. He found that the area was clearly defined, and gave it the Latin designation limbus, which means ring, edge, or border. Papez was the first to consider whether the limbic lobe was related to emotions. Papez found that the removal of a large section of both temporal lobes in monkeys led to bizarre behaviour where the affected monkeys put objects into their mouths indiscriminately, were hyperactive and hypersexual, and sought to have physical contact with everybody. Even monkeys that had been hostile and frightening prior to the operation were tame immediately after the surgical procedure (Purves et al., 2001). Affects at the brainstem level, the lowest level of the triune brain, consist mainly of sensations that register comfort and discomfort. The top layer of the reptilian brain and the middle layer of the triune brain (i.e., the diencephalon and the limbic system) further process the affects and add subtlety, and at this level it is possible to distinguish between different emotional categories, for example fear, anger, joy, grief, etc. (Figure 7.1). In this chapter, I describe structures in the diencephalon and in the limbic system that are involved in regulating affect and adding subtlety. MacLean described the limbic system as the area of emotomentation.

The diencephalon

The diencephalon regulates homoeostatic functions such as body metabolism, hormone balances, and automated movements, while the limbic system deals with emotions, memory functions, and emotionally dictated behaviour. Signals from the sensory organs are collected in a relay station in the diencephalon, and from here they are conveyed to the limbic system and the neocortex. The neocortex sends signals back to the diencephalon and the limbic system, and thoughts, movements, emotions, and memory are connected. Most sensory input processing takes place outside the range of

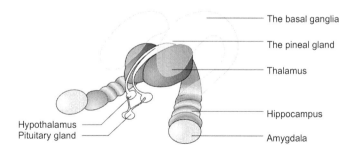

Figure 7.1.   The diencephalon and the limbic system.

attention, and only significant novel or threatening information is passed on to the neocortex for additional processing and attention. Much of the brain's self-regulation takes place in the diencephalon and in limbic structures that are implicit and unconscious. Thus, Freud's hypothesis that nine-tenths of what takes place in the nervous system is unconscious, while only one tenth is conscious, becomes relevant in this context.

The diencephalon is mainly made up of three structures: the thalamus, the hypothalamus, and the basal ganglia, all of which help to co-ordinate information from the brainstem. These three structures are all involved in regulating affects and motor functions at basic unconscious levels.

Thalamus

The *thalamus* (thalamus means bed) is an egg-shaped structure that acts as a sort of relay station, since all fibrous connections from the body and the sensory organs pass through it on their way to the cortex. It projects from the top of the brainstem and receives sensory impulses from the entire body, except for the olfactory pathways, and distributes them to various areas within the neocortex and the limbic system. It conveys information to the appropriate parts of the brain for further processing. Although it is often treated as a single structure, it is in fact a collection of many cellular structures.

The thalamus also integrates motor functions by distributing impulses from the cerebellum to a structure that co-ordinates automated movements (the basal ganglia), and to the motor cortex. The thalamus is involved in co-ordinating systems that are important in relation to orientation, behaviour and attention, and it is an area that, like the cerebellum, myelinates slowly. Much of the thalamus is closely connected to the prefrontal cortex. Due to its connections to the neocortex, the thalamus is often considered a precursor of the mammalian brain, because it contains, in a rudimentary form, most of the functions in the neocortex. In the precortical brain, the thalamus is believed to have been in charge of receiving and processing information from the outside world, while the basal ganglia handled motor behaviour and action (Goldberg, 2001).

It also enables the use of the senses, it is active both during sleep and in the waking state, and it constantly distributes signals to the cortex (thinking), the basal ganglia (automated movements), and the limbic system (memory and emotions). The thalamus enables co-ordination, regulation, and environmental interactions (Damasio, 1999; Trevarthen, 1989, 1990). Undoubtedly, the thalamus also functions as a sort of pacemaker that co-ordinates cortical rhythms. It regulates sensations stemming from the body and brain, creates temporal rhythm, and supports the establishment of memory tracks. The explanation for out-of-body experiences lies partly in the thalamus. When all the neural connections at the back of the thalamus dissociate at once, coherent proprioceptive sensation disappears, as this is the area that collects visual and auditory impressions, vestibular input, and other sensory impressions. The back of the thalamus is called the pulvinar (from Latin: pillow-shaped seat), and in humans it takes up about one quarter of the thalamus. This structure is essential for memory circuits, and the left-sided pulvinar is semi-specialized for language (Austin, 1998).

The basal ganglia

The *basal ganglia* are located towards the sides, deep inside the brain hemispheres (Figure 7.2). They organize instinctive motor skills and represent a basic source of will power. Activation of the basal ganglia also causes automatic excitement. Together with, among other structures, substantia nigra (black matter) in the brainstem, the basal ganglia adjust the arbitrary movements characterized as the extrapyramidal motor system. While the cerebellum creates

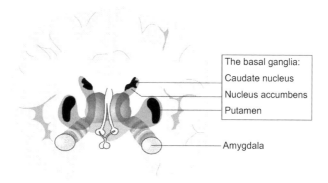

The basal ganglia:
Caudate nucleus
Nucleus accumbens
Putamen

Amygdala

Figure 7.2.   The basal ganglia.

temporal rhythm in our actions, the basal ganglia refine motor sequences and store them in organized motor programmes. We have long known that the basal ganglia co-ordinate motor behaviour, and recently it has been suggested that they also support a co-ordination of cognition and emotions. The basal ganglia filter both potential movement alternatives and the thoughts, ideas, and notions that reach the consciousness. Damage to the basal ganglia destroys habitual learning and disrupts the acquisition of motor and cognitive skills (Bradley, 2000; Mace, 2004; Schacter, 1996).

The basal ganglia consist of several structures. The most important in this context is called the striatum—which consists of *putamen* and *caudate nucleus*—and the *nucleus accumbens,* which is, in fact, located just below the basal ganglia. The basal ganglia are activated when presented with new stimuli or expectation-based rewards, e.g., food, and when they have previously experienced rewards in connection with the presented stimuli. While the putamen controls automatic movement, the caudate nucleus controls automatic thoughts and functions as a filter that regulates which thought products are to be acted out, and which are to be ignored. Caudate nucleus is a part of the brain's pleasure and reward system and is also associated with learning and attention. Feelings of love and devotion are associated with high activation levels in the caudate nucleus (Fisher, 2004). Stimulating the nucleus accumbens may lead to hyperactivity (Austin, 1998). Hypoactivity in the basal ganglia means that fewer thoughts reach consciousness, and thinking is impaired, while hyperactivity means that both good and bad notions make it through, and cognitive activity changes, frequently in a manic or paranoid direction. The caudate nucleus and nucleus accumbens receive input from the limbic system and release dopamine when neurons in the ventral tegmental nucleus are activated. Dopamine levels increase in response to natural rewards, for example food, water, and sexual stimuli (Bradley, 2000; Hansen, 2002; Purves et al., 2001; Scaer, 2001, Schore, 2003a).

The basal ganglia are closely connected to both the prefrontal cortex and the limbic system; they respond with motor activity to natural rewards and anxiety stimuli. When the nucleus accumbens receives input from limbic areas, emotions are linked with movements, which are controlled by the putamen (LeDoux, 2001). Disorders in the connections between the basal ganglia and the prefrontal cortex may cause attention disorders and hyperactivity. The basal ganglia appear to be involved in all forms of compulsory desire and dependency. There is increased activity in this area in connection with psychological disorders such as Tourette's syndrome and OCD (Goleman, 2003).

The hypothalamus

The *hypothalamus* is a small structure, which weighs only about 4 g. It is located below the thalamus, hence the name (see Figure 7.1). The driving force in the basic motivation system springs from the hypothalamus (Gade, 1997). Its role is to integrate autonomic, endocrine, and motor processes into behaviour that is appropriate in relation to the basic needs of the organism. Thus, while the thalamus monitors the outside world, the hypothalamus monitors internal states within the organism and helps keep them within adaptive and balanced levels (Brodal, 2000; Goldberg, 2001). It is involved in controlling the somatic balance of sex hormones, sleep, temperature, food intake, and thirst, among other things. Many complex actions, such as food intake and sexuality, are based on the regulation of internal needs that register in the hypothalamus, which in turn is connected to limbic and cortical structures. The hypothalamus is an important structure in relation to triggering basic affects such as rage and fear as well as positive affects such as pleasure and happiness (Newberg, d'Aquili, & Rause, 2002). It is essential for physiological reactions to emotional factors, i.e., psychosomatic reactions. It is connected to the pituitary gland through the pituitary stem, and certain neurons within the hypothalamus control pituitary hormone secretion. When it receives information of danger it releases stress hormones, which activate the sympathetic nervous system, among other things.

Certain areas within the hypothalamus contain sex hormone receptors; the central area of the hypothalamus is about two and a half times larger in men than in women, while individual cell groups are larger in women. This cell cluster is responsible for typical male sexual behaviour because it contains many receptors that are sensitive to male sex hormones (androgens).

The hypothalamus regulates the body's hormonal (endocrine) system, and it is the overriding and basic structure in relation to the regulation of the sympathetic and parasympathetic components of the autonomic nervous system. It receives information about the body's state and represents the somatic and autonomous components of emotional states (Schore, 2002).

The frontal hypothalamus is in charge of the instinctive triggering of sexual behaviour, dispassionate aggression, and "playing dead" behaviour. The outside part of the hypothalamus acts as an arousal-seeking system, and when this structure is stimulated the person feels that something interesting or exciting is happening. This part of the hypothalamus may be activated through self-stimulation, among other things; for example, by seeking out exciting states such as gambling or so-called "peak experiences". The inside of the hypothalamus is connected to a calming system (Panksepp, 1998; Schore, 1994). Stimulation of the back section of the hypothalamus will activate a high energy level with sympathetic activity. Strong stimulation causes fear and panic reactions. Simultaneous stimulation of the front part is calming and makes the above-mentioned reactions disappear. When normal stimulation in the frontal section of the hypothalamus is disrupted, a lab animal will become frenzied and hyperactive until it collapses with exhaustion. Stimulating the medial part of the hypothalamus causes violent fits of rage.

The hypothalamus has extensive connections to the limbic system, and it is through the hypothalamus that psychological processes, thoughts, and feelings are sensed in the body, partly through the autonomic nervous system. A relatively new hypothesis concerning the hypothalamus is that it contains many oscillating neurons. These neurons are involved in organizing the organism into a structure of rhythm and time, and they register when the production of sex hormones should take place, among other functions. Neurons in the frontal section of the hypothalamus are connected to the so-called suprachiasmatic nucleus, which is involved in regulating the circadian rhythm in relation to light and dark (Strogatz, 2003). Damage to the hypothalamus causes a deep comatose state. As part of childhood development, there is a maturation of circuit connections on a higher hierarchical brain level, which suppress the instinctive reactions of the hypothalamus through conditioned learning. Inhibitory stimuli reduce reflective behavioural responses and help the nervous system to teach us to civilize innate behaviours (Austin, 1998).

The limbic system

The limbic system is not clearly delineated. It is characterized by functional links with emotions and memory, and the system is often described as the "emotional brain". Parts of the limbic system function as an overall system for the autonomic nervous system and the hypothalamus, while other parts are more closely connected to the cerebral cortex. The limbic system forms the basis for our emotions. It is connected to the neocortex and collaborates with other structures on perceptual and cognitive processes. The limbic system is often called the "olfactory brain" because it is involved in olfactory perception (LeDoux, 1998).

The limbic structure is believed to have evolved as mammals became more closely attached to their offspring and the offspring reacted to separation with attachment behaviour. The limbic system is able to read signals from the outside world and combine them with body sensations. It adjusts information from external and internal stimuli and co-ordinates and fine-tunes the signals that the body emits to the surroundings. The limbic system rewards behaviour that is designed to maximize survival and keeps the organism away from situations that are threatening or unpleasant. It is able to adapt to a rapidly changing environment and organizes new learning. Limbic activity is an emotionally motivating structure, whose function is to filter what happens internally and externally. Until the prefrontal lobes are fully developed, the limbic system has substantial influence on children's behaviour. In regressive behaviour in both children and adults, the limbic system often takes over and overrides rational thinking, and the person acts on the basis of immediate impulses, for example, with instant gratification or unfettered fits of rage (Cicchetti & Tucker, 1994; Lewis, Amini, & Lannon, 2001; Schore, 2003a; van der Kolk, 2000; van der Kolk & McFarlane, 1996).

The limbic region interacts through a number of circuits that connect three main structures: the hypothalamus, the amygdala, and the hippocampus. The system is involved in increasing or reducing arousal and imbues perceptions with affective or emotional value (Bradley, 2000). When perceptions form circuits with the limbic system, the perceptions take on emotional meaning and achieve permanence in memory (Hansen, 2002). The limbic system has many receptors for the neurotransmitters that are produced in the brainstem, which means that experiences that are imbued with emotional value are easier to remember. The area consists of a large number of circuit connections; thus, emotions are not limited to one emotional circuit and have no single centre (Damasio, 1994).

Let us now look more specifically at the main structures in relation to affect regulation, motivation, and emotionality in the limbic system.

The amygdala

The amygdala is an evolutionarily old and relatively small brain structure that is named after its shape and size: amygdala is the Greek word for almond. It is situated above the brainstem at the base of the limbic system. It processes sensory impressions and is a crucial structure in the networks that regulate fear and aggression (see Figure 7.1). It develops during the foetal period and is functional from birth. Much suggests that during the first years of life the amygdala is of global importance for all emotional learning, and that it is the structure that enables us to sense emotional reactions intuitively. When the deep-lying areas in the prefrontal cortex mature and take over the regulation of the limbic structures, the amygdala's role is limited to that of "watchdog".

Fear is probably the oldest emotion of the limbic system, a further development of the startle reaction. All forms of anxiety reactions, panic, phobias, etc., are related to amygdala activation. The amygdala has a monitoring function and constantly scans for sensory stimuli throughout the brain, preparing the organism to act at the slightest sign of danger. It has reflexive reactions to sudden intense sensory impressions, which are rapidly assessed in relation to any threats, and it is activated through perceptions that appear frightening or scary. As a structure that registers fear it is involved in reactions related to fight-or-flight behaviour and freezing, and in the release of aggression (Damasio, 1994; LeDoux, 2001). Electric stimulation of the amygdala results in increased alertness, a quick scan of the surroundings, and increased heart rate, respiration, etc. (Newberg, d'Aquili, & Rause, 2002). There are different opinions as to whether the amygdala is involved in pleasure. Some researchers point out that pleasure circuits are activated without amygdala activation, while others point out that stimulation of the medial portion of the amygdala is capable of releasing religious experiences that trigger pleasure circuits, and that the amygdala has a large number of morphine receptors, capable of causing changes in consciousness (Cozolino, 2000; Panksepp, 1998). The disagreement probably stems from the fact that the amygdala is not clearly delineated but consists of at least fourteen anatomically distinct nucleus clusters, each with different functions (Kringelbach, 2004).

The border region between sensory impressions and analysis

The amygdala has access to practically all sensory information and receives information from the senses and changes in the body's physiology. It uses this information to determine rapidly whether a given situation is threatening enough to initiate a fight-or-flight reaction. It also has access to more refined and ordered information from later stages of processing; for example, in the prefrontal cortex, it receives a great deal of input from structures all over the brain, and it plays a key role in emotionally charged memories. It occupies a border region between primitive survival impulses from the hypothalamus and the thorough analyses of sensory impressions that are carried out in the neocortex, and it is unable to function without input from brainstem structures and the hypothalamus. The amygdala receives input from two sources: quick and rough input from the thalamus, and slower but more complete representations from the prefrontal cortex. The input that comes straight from the thalamus arrives sooner, which means that any emotional evaluation of sensory input precedes conscious emotional experiences. The circuits that travel via the direct pathway from thalamus to amygdala are primitive, and that might explain why emotions may be strong enough to overpower rational thinking. There are more neural pathways running from the amygdala to the prefrontal cortex than there are running in the opposite direction. Most of the time, signals go to the thalamus and on to the sensory processing areas of the neocortex, where the signals are combined to form the objects that we perceive. The signals are then conveyed from the prefrontal cortex to the amygdala, and an appropriate reaction is activated. Many emotional reactions are formed without any form of conscious or cognitive involvement.

Generalized anxiety detector

There is much to suggest that the amygdala is important in relation to learning to connect stimuli with primary systems of punishment and reward. It activates fight-or-flight behaviour, and if an incident is associated with a positive or a negative state it becomes easier to learn or remember (Carter, 1998; LeDoux, 2001; Perry, 1994). In post traumatic stress disorder (PTSD), phobias, and anxiety disorders, brainstem functions and amygdala have taken charge. Fear responses that have become conditioned by triggers such as sounds or light can be hard to extinguish. Even if the stimuli that are associated with the danger no longer exist, the amygdala still releases a fear reaction unless areas of the prefrontal cortex are able to inhibit the reaction. For example, the association of a sound (e.g., screeching brakes or clothes being torn), a smell (e.g., the smell of dewy grass), a movement (e.g., a threatening hand), or an observation (e.g., a particular constellation of stars) associated with a highly traumatic event may trigger a fear reaction independent of consciousness, over and over again. This reaction is seen in war veterans, victims of torture, and women who have been raped. A traumatized person's life can be impaired for years after the traumatic event due to the unconscious triggering of the link between a perception and a traumatic event. In other words, it does not take much to induce a retraumatizing reaction after a highly traumatic event. The extinction of fear conditioning appears to involve prefrontal regulation of the amygdala (Damasio, 1994; LeDoux, 1989, 1994, 1998). Fear is learnt by coupling a sensation, an emotion, a movement, or a thought with unpleasant stimuli such as pain, shock, shame, etc. The amygdala recognizes previous experiences, and for the rest of the person's life it is able to link a fear stimulus with anxiety or fear. The memory function of the amygdala is implicit, which means that it is not normally open to conscious processing.

The amygdala and kindling

The amygdala is a structure that is particularly sensitive to kindling. The term "kindling" comes from physics, but in biology it is often used to describe the way outside stimulation of a brain area gradually makes the area self-activating. Experiments with newborn rats showed that frequent, repeated electric stimulation at a particular frequency of particular brain structures triggered epileptic seizures, which eventually occurred spontaneously without outside stimulation. When the same experiments were carried out with adult rats, this kindling reaction did not occur. These studies showed that the amygdala is particularly sensitive to kindling and that the occurrence of heightened emotional responses such as anger, paranoia, panic anxiety, and nervousness may be explained by an over-activation of amygdala neurons. One might say that the amygdala is quick to learn but slow to forget. Learnt fear is resilient and has a tendency to return under stressful conditions (Scaer, 2001; Weiger & Bear, 1988).

Persons with double-sided damage to the amygdala are unable to recognize fearful facial expressions but have no problem recognizing angry facial expressions. Animals that have had their amygdala removed do not express fear, they lose their drive to compete and co-operate, and they no longer have any sense of their place in the social hierarchy. They do not form close social bonds and neglect and disregard their own offspring. They do not examine their surroundings or learn new reactions that might make them adapt their behaviour to others. In humans, amygdala damage makes it difficult to form an impression of trust levels, and feelings of anxiety are extinguished. Apparently the loss of the ability to experience and express anxiety makes us unable to register this emotion in others (Blair, 1999; Cozolino, 2000; Davidson, Putnam, & Larson, 2000; Gallese, 2001; LeDoux, 1998; Schore, 1994, 2003a). Persons who are prone to violent rages and unable to predict negative consequences of their anger seem to have damage that involves both the prefrontal cortex and the amygdala. Recent studies show that the amygdala can be severely shrunken in persons who are excessively aggressive (Goleman, 2003). The amygdala is able to promote as well as inhibit fear and aggression through its connections to the hypothalamus. Animals that have had their amygdala removed often have aggressive impulsive outbursts but show a reduction in overall aggressive behaviour. Damage to the amygdala reduced the startle response. Persons with amygdala damage become fearless and often bring themselves into dangerous situations. Similarly, they have a reduced ability to perceive fear or sadness in others.

Both an impaired and a hyperactive amygdala may lead to aggressive outbursts. Schore mentions (2003a) that there are two different forms of aggression: "cold blooded" and "warm-blooded". "Cold-blooded" aggression occurs, for example when a victim is attacked for no reason and killed in a dispassionate rage, while "warm-blooded" aggression occurs when a victim is attacked and perhaps killed after a major argument or brawl where both parties worked each other up. While "cold-blooded" rage may occur impulsively as well as planned but without any previous encounter with the victim, "warm-blooded" rage often builds up over a period of time against individuals that the aggressor already has an emotional involvement with. Thus, it might be hypothesized that the "cold-blooded" aggression occurs due to hypoactivation of the amygdala and is controlled by lower subcortical areas, for example the hypothalamus. This makes the reactions appear "reptilian" in character and controlled by the parasympathetic nervous system, which is related with hypoarousal—slow heart rate and low blood pressure. "Warm-blooded" aggression, on the other hand, is due to a hyperactive amygdala, which quickly activates the sympathetic nervous system and in turn triggers irritability and emotional and impulsive behaviour.

The hippocampus

Another important structure in the limbic system is the *hippocampus*, which is Greek for seahorse (see Figure 7.1). The structure gets its name from its appearance, and it is situated next to the amygdala. The hippocampus has extensive connections to the prefrontal cortex and is involved in learning and memory. It matures slowly, a few months after birth. Myelination of circuit connections between the prefrontal cortex and the hippocampus continues into puberty, and throughout the lifespan the hippocampus remains sensitive to oxygen deprivation (Cozolino, 2000). Damage to the hippocampus makes it difficult to remember recent events, as can be observed in patients with dementia, for example (Schacter, 1996). The hippocampus is vital to short-term memory and relates memories to time and place. It commits the spatial and temporal dimensions of experience to memory and categorizes and stores stimuli. Temporary amnesia, such as "Where am I?", "What day is today?" is associated with a dysfunction in the rear section of the hippocampus.

The hippocampus is especially associated with conscious (explicit) memory, and input from the amygdala is involved in activating the recognition of emotionally charged memory tracks (LeDoux, 1998). The hippocampus shapes spatial representations of the world and is important for so-called autobiographical memory, the ability to remember one's life story in a temporal context. Circuit connections between the hippocampus and the prefrontal cortex make it possible to establish complex memory tracks where many events are connected in relation to time and place (LeDoux, 1998; O'Keefe & Nadel, 1978).

Integration and discrimination

The hippocampus integrates information from many sensory modalities and creates representations that are independent of the original modality. That is how scents, sounds, and images merge into a global memory of a situation. Without this ability, memory tracks would be disjointed. The hippocampus is considered a super-convergence zone, able to convert unconscious (implicit) memory tracks into conscious (explicit) images or internal representations. It lets us retain information for short periods of time and supports the storage of memory material, but it does not hold permanent memories (Damasio, 1999). It is involved in the take-up and filtering of information throughout the brain (Damasio, 1999; LeDoux, 2001).

While the amygdala plays a key role in relation to the emotional and somatic organization of experiences, the hippocampus is an important structure in relation to conscious, logical, and social functions. The amygdala is involved in generalization, while the hippocampus is involved in discrimination or distinctions. For example, the amygdala releases fear at the sight of a spider, while the hippocampus enables the person to remember that the particular spider is neither poisonous nor dangerous, so there is no real cause for alarm. The hippocampus has a regulatory function, and its discrimination function enables it to regulate the arousal system.

The hippocampus is often described as the "diplomat", because it has a significant influence on amygdala activity and a regulatory effect on the thalamus. Together, the hippocampus and the thalamus are able to block sensory input from reaching certain neocortical areas. The hippocampus is also able to regulate arousal reactions triggered by the autonomic nervous system; for example, it can prevent an over-activation of arousal states. The hippocampus is also closely linked to the amygdala and the hypothalamus and balances arousal levels in these two areas. Unlike the amygdala and the hypothalamus, the hippocampus is unable to trigger emotions directly, but, due to its regulatory effect on other areas of the brain, it exercises great influence on the person's mental state (Newberg, d'Aquili, & Rause, 2002).

The hippocampus and sensitivity to stress

The hippocampus has many receptors for stress hormones, which makes it a fragile structure in connection with chronic stress and trauma. Excessive and chronic exposure to stress hormones will change synaptic formation and dendrite structures in the hippocampus and may eventually lead to hippocampal atrophy. A high activation level in the amygdala and the sympathetic nervous system may inhibit the function of the hippocampus. Impaired hippocampal function renders the nervous system incapable of putting things into a relevant and meaningful context, which is an additional stressor. When, for example, fear states are triggered very easily, the cause may be hippocampal dysfunction. Due to the close connections between the amygdala and hippocampus, damage to the hippocampus affects the amygdala and may cause the amygdala to respond rapidly to sensory stimuli, which disturbs affect regulation. Repeated or chronic stress seems to inhibit the development of neurons in the area of the hippocampus where new stem cells are developed, and atrophy in this area has been observed in connection with post traumatic stress disorder (Perry, 1994; Sapolsky, 1998; van der Kolk, 1996). There is much to suggest that traumatizing experiences early in life have a neurotoxic effect on the hippocampus and make the nervous system more vulnerable to future stressors due to a diminished hippocampus (Panksepp, 2005; Scaer, 2001).

Damage to the hippocampus leads to hypersensitivity to outside stimulation and makes the nervous system prone to activating highly emotional reactions very quickly; for example, an easily triggered anxiety can easily lead to a general sense of chaos and terror. One of the common characteristics in children who have been exposed to traumatic experiences early in life is a vulnerable nervous system that is prone to apprehension, so that even minor events will throw the nervous system into a state resembling chaos.

Emotions are one of the earliest means we have of learning about the state of the organism and learning to reorganize ourselves through our relations to others. There is a strong link between emotion and action. Sensorimotor and affective systems are co-ordinated in the limbic system and self-regulate in relation to interacting with the environment and securing survival (Gallese, 2001). Inadequate connections between the limbic system and overall structures in the prefrontal area lead to psychological disorders and reactions that may seem mysterious to our ordinary daytime consciousness (Table 7.1). For example, people who suffer from

Table 7.1.   Outline of the diencephalon and the limbic system.

Thalamus

Relay station that receives sensory impulses and distributes information
   to the appropriate parts of the brain
Integrates motor functions
Co-ordinates systems that are important in relation to orientation and
   behaviour
Enables the simultaneous use of the different senses
Co-ordinates and regulates interactions with the outside environment

Basal ganglia

Organize instinctive motor functions
Represent a basic source of willpower
Contain the pleasure and reward system
Adjust arbitrary movements
Refine motor sequences and store them in an organized motor
   programme
Probably co-ordinate cognition
Filter potential movement alternatives and thoughts
   Putamen
   Controls automatic movement
   Caudate nucleus
   Controls automatic thoughts and filters thought products that are
   to be converted to action
   Nucleus accumbens
   Receives input from the limbic system and releases dopamine

(*continued*)

Table 7.1. (*continued*)

Hypothalamus

Controls the autonomic nervous system
Controls the body's balance for, e.g., sex hormones
Regulates sleep-wake rhythm, temperature, hunger, and thirst
Triggers basic affects such as rage, fear, and joy
Releases stress hormones
Receives information about the body's state
Triggers dispassionate aggression and "playing dead" behaviour
Regulates the arousal and inhibitory (calming) system
Organizes a rhythm and time structure in relation to light and dark
The basis for instincts and drives

Amygdala

Monitoring function; scans for sensory stimuli
Prepares the organism for action on the basis of signs of potential danger
Relates stimuli with primary punishment and reward systems
Activates fight-or-flight behaviour
In charge of emotional and somatic organization of experience
In charge of generalizing experienced stimuli

Hippocampus

Makes it possible to remember sequences of events
Vital to short-term memory and relates memories to time and place
Commits spatial and temporal dimensions of experience to memory
Categorizes and stores incoming stimuli
Shapes spatial representations of the world
Makes it possible to remember one's life story in a time context
Integrates information from many sensory modalities
Converts unconscious (implicit) memory tracks to conscious (explicit)
    mental images
Makes it possible to maintain information for short periods of time
Influences the regulation of information take-up all over the brain
Structures conscious, logical, and social functions
In charge of discriminating experiences stimuli

panic anxiety often find it difficult to understand the source of their anxiety and are unable to inhibit their symptoms.

Summary

In this chapter, I have described the top level of the reptilian brain and the next level in the triune brain, the level of emotional mentalization. While the protomental functions in the brainstem consist of basic affect-regulating systems, the limbic level consists of areas that refine non-volitional motor functions and connect to areas that contain sophisticated emotional responses in connection with reward and punishment. This level refines and develops emotions and enables us to register a wealth of emotions such as joy, sadness, anxiety, grief, etc., and to make choices in various life situations. At this level, the nervous system is no longer at the mercy of primitive reflexes and instinctive acts. It becomes possible to make choices, and the environment takes on key importance for the reactivity of the nervous system. In the next chapter, I turn to the top level of the triune brain (cf. MacLean): the neomammalian level or the area of ratiomentation.

CHAPTER EIGHT

The brain of complex emotions, mentalization, abstraction, and reason: the parietal lobes and the prefrontal cortex

"Every task that calls for symbolic representation, strategy, planning, or problem-solving has its headquarters in the neocortical brain"

(Lewis, Amini, & Lannon, 2001, p. 29)

The human frontal lobes make up about one third of the neocortex and are the top hierarchical level in the triune brain. The back section of the frontal lobes is the motor cortex, which is able to exercise volitional control over muscle contractions. In front of this area is the premotor cortex, which co-ordinates the movements of individual muscle groups. The rest of the frontal lobes are called the prefrontal cortex, the area that generates impulses and plans for action sequences. This area is particularly well developed in primates, especially in humans. The human prefrontal cortex is about twice the size of that in other primates. In this chapter, I describe the structures that enable us to have complex emotions, delay gratification and responses, form symbols, and, in general, reflect on emotions and draw logical conclusions. The prefrontal cortex co-operates with the body-sensing areas within the parietal lobes, and together they account for much of what is defined as intelligence today.

The prefrontal cortex and the parietal lobes are situated in the neocortex. At the base of the prefrontal cortex, in the transition zone between the limbic system and the prefrontal cortex, lie a number of structures in charge of coordinating emotional, body-sensing, and rational structures (Figure 8.1). In the following review, we begin at the base and work our way up through the hierarchical structures.

Cingulate gyrus

The cingulate gyrus (from Latin: *cingulus* = belt, and Greek: *gyrus* = fold or ridge) is located on the inside of the cortex, wrapped around the corpus callosum. Some neurologists view this structure as part of the limbic system, while others consider it a paralimbic structure at the base of the neocortex. The cingulate gyrus perceives emotions, just as the visual cortex perceives visual impressions, and the area is a prerequisite for our ability to engage in human relations and to feel sympathy and empathy. The cingulate gyrus is a structure that not only directs one's attention towards outside stimuli, it also registers painful and other somatosensory signals arising inside the body. The area is activated both when we feel pain ourselves (including in the form of social rejection), and when we feel someone else's pain, regardless of whether this pain is physical or mental. While the insula (see p. 146) is involved in registering pain, the cingulate gyrus associates the pain with its qualitative

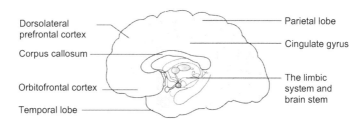

Figure 8.1.   Dorsolateral prefrontal cortex, orbitofrontal cortex, cingulate gyrus, and parietal lobes.

feeling. If the connection between insula and cingulate gyrus is destroyed, patients are still able to feel pain—but it does not hurt (Cozolino, 2006; Ramachandran, 2003). In a manner of speaking, the area is a "social attachment system" on top of the insula, which draws attention to physical injury. The insula enables us to be aware of physical injury, while the cingulate gyrus lets us attribute emotional aspects to the sensation of pain.

The structure is connected to the hippocampus, the amygdala, and the basal ganglia, and in humans the area has direct links to the frontal regions in both the right and left hemispheres. Stimulation of the area triggers what in infants would be called separation crying (LeDoux, 1998; Schore, 2001a). The cingulate gyrus induces emotional behaviour related to attachment and caring behaviour. The infant does not develop separation anxiety until the age of 6–8 months, when the cingulate gyrus area is activated. The structure enables us to direct our attention toward situations that feel particularly relevant.

In the 1950s, Stamm found that rat mothers with damage to the cingulate gyrus displayed distinct shortcomings in their maternal behaviour, including nesting, caring, and protection. Rat pups with similar damage did not produce separation cries and were unable to engage in play with other rats their age. The separation cry is probably the most primitive and basic mammalian vocalization, originally developed to allow the mother to stay in touch with her offspring. The cingulate gyrus has a high concentration of morphine receptors (opioids), and activation of the area offers a sense of safety and relatedness. The cingulate gyrus could be characterized as the youngest evolutionary part of the emotional system, and it enables maternal care, vocal communication to maintain contact with the attachment person, and play behaviour. When mammals began to live in families, they developed the most painful form of suffering: the pain related to separation or isolation from close relations, which we all know as the pain of losing someone dear to us— a function related to the cingulate gyrus (MacLean, 1985). In particular, the posterior cingulate gyrus regulates social behaviour, attachment behaviour, and our capacity for play. Damage to this part disrupts the drive to play and generate mental images, and attachment behaviour and caring behaviour disappear (Damasio, 1994; Joseph, 1993; van der Kolk, 1987).

The anterior cingulate gyrus plays an essential role when we have to act counter to innate or early acquired impulses. When an activity is being trained and has not yet become automated, the anterior cingulate gyrus is activated (Kandel, 2005). Choosing what to direct one's attention towards and what emotional meaning to attribute to it is controlled by this part of the cingulate gyrus. It is the energy source for both exterior actions (movement) and interior action (thinking), and it is involved in selective attention and volitional movements. It records whether stimuli come from the outside or the inside and enables us to focus on emotional content and pain perception. The area integrates the emotional quality stemming from deep-lying areas of the limbic system with normal attention, and it is hugely important for the integration of executive functions, our capacity for planning and structuring (LeDoux, 1998, 2001; Schore, 2003a; Tucker & Derryberry, 1992). The anterior part is activated by sad, fearful, and angry facial expressions, so damage to this section causes failure to recognize exactly these emotions. Double-sided damage to this area causes a lack of mental activity— no thoughts, no considerations (Blair, Morris, Frith, Perrett, & Dolan, 1999; Blair, Colledge, Murrary, & Mitchell, 2001; Damasio, 1999). The anterior cingulate gyrus contains spindle neurons (von Economo neurons). The body of the spindle cell is about four times larger than other neuronal bodies, and it has very long dendrites and axons, which increases the speed of transmission. The spindle cells are rich in receptors for the neurotransmitters serotonin, dopamine, and vasopressin and are also found in the orbitofrontal cortex (see p. 151). This type of cell is found only in higher primates and humans and is believed to be responsible for making social intuition limber. Spindle cells are experience-dependent in the sense that early neglect inhibits their development and organization (Cozolino, 2006).

The parietal lobes

The parietal lobes help to give us a sense of our own presence in the world and an internal subjective space. Much of this area is located in the diencephalon and the limbic system (hence, it is a bit of a stretch when we place the parietal lobes in the area of complex emotions and abstract thinking, since an equally big part is located in the subcortical areas). Association areas in this region process tactile and kinaesthetic information, such as sensing muscles and joints. The parietal lobes help us to locate our position in space and to co-ordinate and compare the sensed position with the outside world. The area helps us determine the location of objects in relation to the organism. The medial area processes movements, and damage to this area disrupts the ability to know the direction or the speed of a moving object (d'Aquili & Newberg, 1999; Ramachandran, 2003). Damage to the parietal lobes disrupts the person's sense of identity, the perception of who and where one is, and leads to body neglect and confabulations. Neglect involves being unaware of ones loss of function and, thus, of the impaired part of the body. A man who has neglect for his arm, for example, will feel and state that it is someone else's arm that is lying in bed next to him. Confabulation means that fantasy and reality are confused to form more or less bizarre tales; for example, when a child is unable to distinguish between actual experiences and imaginary ones and actually remembers something that never took place in real life. Confabulation often occurs in the case of simultaneous damage to the parietal and frontal lobes. The PTO area is the part of the cortex where sensory modalities come together and internal mental images have their sensory parallel. The connections between the parietal lobes and the frontal lobes account for much of human intelligence. Albert Einstein described often having visual and synaesthetic impressions when he was thinking. An autopsy of Einstein's brain showed that it was probably an expansion of the lower section of the parietal lobes (the angular gyrus) that made him so unique, not any characteristics concerning his frontal lobes, as many had previously thought (Goleman, 2003; Hansen, 2002). The angular gyrus is located between the parietal lobes and the other lobes, in other words the PTO area. It is a juncture where various sensory modalities merge to form abstract and metaphoric representations. The angular gyrus has gradually increased in size throughout evolution and has seen a colossal expansion in humans (Ramachandran, 2003).

The parietal lobe receives sensory input from all sensory modalities, especially auditory and visual material. This lets the organism generate a three-dimensional sensation of the body. There are two different orientation areas, one in each hemisphere. The left parietal lobe is in charge of generating a mental sensation of the physical body, while areas on the right side are related to the sensation of a body image. Like the thalamus, the right parietal lobe has areas that cause out-of-body experiences when they are stimulated (Ramachandran, 2003). Thus, the parietal lobes in the left hemisphere generate the brain's spatial sense of self, while the right parietal lobe generates a sense of the physical space for the self to inhabit (Schore, 1994).

Insula

The insula is closely connected to the frontal lobes and is located at the base of the parietal lobes (Figure 8.2). It is mostly known as an association area for the senses of hearing and equilibrium, among others. The insula consists of various areas that records visceral sensations and provides an intuitive sense of emotions. When the medial part of the insula is activated, pleasant feelings are generated through touch, and it is possible to sense a response to loving skin contact. The front part of the insula is activated by negative stimuli (Bartels & Zeki, 2004). It receives pain signal from the body's internal organs and from the skin. This is where unprocessed pain is perceived, while the cingulate gyrus (see p. 142) reacts emotionally to pain.

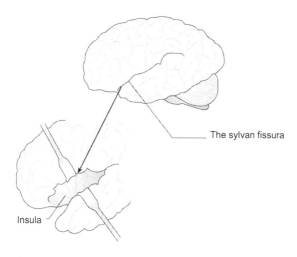

The sylvan fissura

Insula

Figure 8.2. The insula in the parietal lobes.

Damasio (2003) points out that the insula co-operates with the cingulate gyrus. Both the cingulate gyrus and the insula play important roles for mental involvement and provide ongoing information about the body's condition. The insula records changes in the autonomic nervous system, typically perceived as pleasure/unpleasure or physical comfort/discomfort. It is also in this area that pain impulses from the body's organs and internal parts are sensed, and where the organism becomes conscious of pain. The right hemispheric insula is dominant in relation to body experiences and integrates representations of the somatic state. Emotions are based on body sensations, and damage to the insula in the right hemisphere eliminates the awareness of one's own body states (one feels nothing). Emotions do not necessarily spring from current body states but may also be formed, once the prefrontal cortex is mature, through the recollection of representations of previously sensed states. For example, if one recalls an event, the incident will often be accompanied by an emotion or a sense of pleasure/unpleasure or a particular emotional quality that is accompanied by a bodily sensation (Damasio, 1994, 2003; Eriksson, 2001; O'Keefe & Nadel, 1978; Schore, 2001a). While the posterior parietal lobes register kinaesthetic aspects of facial and body movements and separate self from other, the insula integrates internal and external experiences by processing body states and integrating them with the areas that process motor functions and emotions. This integration allows for the connection of sensed body states and consciousness. The insula plays a key role in the development of the sensation of self and self awareness, which later enables the development of self insight (Cozolino, 2006).

Body experiences help to provide a basis for meaning and reasoning, and damage to the right-sided insula damages one's ability to comprehend another person's emotional state. The insula contributes to a sense of the somatic self and to intuitive sensations of self and others. Studies suggest that the insula contains mirror neurons and that the mirror systems are connected to the limbic region, which contributes to an immediate sense of the emotions of an observed other. One implication of the connections between the insula and the cingulate gyrus is that seeing a loved one experience pain causes one to feel the pain in one's own body. There is much to indicate that severe early neglect and inadequate support in verbalizing body sensations cause the insula, the limbic region, and the language areas to dissociate or to fail to develop adequate connections. Damasio (1994) believes that intuitive sensations are activated by implicit memories. The area is experience-dependent and affected by the early care-giver–infant relationship. The infant's ability to distinguish self-touching from being touched by others indicates that the insula is active from birth. The brain's ability to utilize body experiences and use them metaphorically is the foundation of imagination. Physical metaphors are generated through body experiences and movement and help enable cognitive reflection. Mental images and body sensations are building blocks for internal self-representations, which help generate capacities for mentalization and empathy. Both the parietal lobes and the prefrontal cortex are modelled by experience and are probably the brain regions that have the greatest plasticity. Without a sense of our own body we lose our sense of meaning, our capacity for abstract thinking, and our ability to relate to ethics, art, etc. (Cozolino, 2000; Schore, 1994).

The prefrontal cortex

The prefrontal cortex arose around the old limbic system and is a super-convergence zone, i.e., it consists almost exclusively of poly-modal areas, which renders it astoundingly complex. The prefrontal cortex is the most complex system in the brain, and it consists of a veritable symphony of perceptions from many sensory modalities, which enables abstract thinking. It is connected to all the reaction pathways available to the brain and converts signals from all sensory areas to images, thoughts, and body states, which are represented continuously. The area receives regulatory signals from neurotransmitters and hormones (Trevarthen, 1990).

The prefrontal cortex is crucial for maintaining emotional stability. The area helps ensure mental flexibility because it is capable of altering thoughts and actions on the basis of associative changes. It controls primitive behaviour and basic emotions by inhibiting impulses and overriding systems governed by reflexes and instincts. The many connections between the prefrontal cortex and the rest of the neocortex forms the basis for human imagination and for our ability to generate complex ideas based on a multi-modal system of sensations. The development of the prefrontal cortex has allowed humans to develop the capacity for self-reflection and to form a "theory of mind", i.e., a mentalization function and an internal ability to decode what is on another person's mind. This area enables us to go on mental journeys, including journeys into the future. The prefrontal cortex allows us to remember situations from our past, imagine the future, and integrate past, present, and future. It helps to provide a sense of one's particular subjective experience. It is this area that makes the human species unique, and it seems that individuals with damage to the deep-lying structures in the brainstem and limbic structures caused by massive early neglect fail to develop these mentalizing functions (Fonagy, 2003; Main, 1999; Schore, 2003a; Siegel, 1999).

Whenever a situation involves an element of choice, the decision-making process is governed by prefrontal calculations that include an assessment of the situation as well as desires, values, and assumptions about the consequences of acting. This is the "thinking brain", which enables us to generate long-term plans and strategic considerations (Gade, 1997). To a considerable extent, the prefrontal area is uniquely human, as it enables us to choose in the absence of one single correct solution. Damage to the outside part, the *dorsolateral prefrontal cortex*, causes cognitive dysfunctions and is closely related to the hippocampus, while damage to the deep-lying area called the *orbitofrontal cortex* causes emotional dysfunctions, as this part interacts with and is located close to the amygdala (LeDoux, 1998).

Prefrontal lobe functions do not mature until the infant is 8–12 months of age, and their inhibitory functions are internalized through culturally conditioned and socially transmitted behaviour. The neural circuits in the prefrontal cortex are plastic in nature. They are affected by experiences and learning processes and take a long time to mature. Not fully matured until the age of 20–25 years, the frontal lobes are the latest developing structure of the human brain (Goleman, 2003).

The prefrontal cortex is of great importance to affect regulation. The prefrontal cortex contains no primary sensory areas; its function is to control activity in other regions and to carry out associations of highly processed information from other neural systems.

For example, the circuits in the parietal areas combine visual impressions and motor functions, and the temporal lobes relate sensory information to emotions before the information reaches the prefrontal cortex (Nauta, 1971). It is in the prefrontal cortex that perceptions gain meaning, future can be predicted, and thoughts, feelings, and sensations can be selected for further consideration, while others, deemed less significant, are ignored. While the hippocampus, for example, is a key structure for recognition and short-term memory, functions in the prefrontal cortex are important as a working memory and in relation to recalling stored memory such as facts, rules, etc. There is a big difference between having to rely on certain stimuli, such as the smell of grandma's meat loaf, to be able to recall something, and being able to flip through a mental archive to recall memories, such as recalling meat loaf dinners at grandma's house. The ability to recall things deliberately makes our organism tremendously flexible.

Damage to the prefrontal cortex has derived effects throughout the brain, but, similarly, damage anywhere in the brain will affect the function of the prefrontal cortex. It is a control centre with a very complex set of neural connections running to and from other brain structures. As Goldberg (2001) points out, injury to the leader will disrupt the activity of many units, just as the functions of leadership will be disrupted if individual units are injured or if the lines of communication are cut off. For example, damage to the upper part of the brainstem, which disrupts projections to the pre-frontal cortex, a common feature in closed-head trauma, often leads to dysfunction of the orbitofrontal cortex. Damage to the prefrontal cortex does not cause the absence of conscious experiences, but the person will be constantly distracted by emotional and sensory impressions, fail to maintain focus, and have difficulty generating internal mental images. Such persons are trapped in the present, unable to shield themselves from the constant onslaught of sensory impressions and emotions. They are locked in a rigid and concrete way of thinking, often find it difficult to read social interactions, to recall the outcome of previous events, and to learn from experience. Alexander Luria called the prefrontal cortex the "organ of civilization", and even minor damage causes apathy, indifference, or behaviour bereft of social inhibition and responsibility. Brain scans show that certain criminals with a record of many violent acts have lower frontal lobe activity than normal and are unable to control their thoughts (Cozolino, 2000). Disorders in the prefrontal cortex are often associated with certain types of attention disorders.

The orbitofrontal cortex

The orbitofrontal cortex is located close to the limbic system and is called a paralimbic structure. The orbitofrontal cortex and the frontal cingulate gyrus are so close that they can be difficult to distinguish in practice. Therefore, some researchers consider the terms synonymous. The orbitofrontal cortex has unique and extensive connections with a large number of subcortical systems and represents the hierarchical top of the limbic system and the autonomic nervous system. Owing to its unique anatomical position between the cortex and the subcortex, it is able to adjust emotional responses and it is involved in integrating the body's internal state with the environment. Thus, it regulates both parasympathetic and sympathetic components and controls the activation of the vagus nerve in the brainstem. The area has close connections to the reticular activation system and plays an important role in arousal regulation. When the orbitofrontal cortex functions optimally, it is one of the few brain regions with knowledge of every single activity taking place at any given time within the organism (Damasio, 1994; Schore, 1994, 2003a). It is probably this structure that is able, through long-term meditation, to connect to structures that enable volitional control of functions that are involuntary in most people.

Medical science became aware of the orbitofrontal cortex after a dynamite accident in 1848, when the American railway worker Phineas Gage had a tampering iron blown through the deep-lying areas in his left-sided prefrontal cortex. Gage was a well-liked and respected man, but after the accident he began to display asocial behaviour. After the accident he became closely attached to objects and animals, and he was uninterested in, and incapable of considering, the future or making plans. He lost his sense of responsibility, and the decisions he made seemed arbitrary. He often made up outlandish stories that were without any basis in reality. Such behaviours are typical of dysfunctions of the orbitofrontal cortex

(Damasio, 1994). The role of the orbitofrontal cortex was not clear until the late 1940s when lobotomies were carried out to control extreme affective outbursts. Lobotomy severed the connection between subcortex and cortex in the orbitofrontal cortex, which led to a loss of emotions. Intelligence was unaffected, but the patients lost their personality and their ability to relate emotionally. Normal emotional responses were absent or "flat", there was no emotional depth, and the patients were unable to inhibit primitive needs, to process unconscious fantasies, and to symbolize (Karr-Morse & Wiley, 1997). In many respects, effects of damage to the orbito-frontal cortex are opposite to the effects of injuries to the dorsolat-eral prefrontal cortex. Damage to the orbitofrontal cortex leads to a lack of impulse control, a lack of emotional inhibition, and a drive for immediate gratification, and the affected person does not consider his or her actions wrong. The person is often boastful and immature and has a crude sense of humour. Damage to the dorso-lateral prefrontal cortex leads to flatness of emotions and a "loss" of personality.

The top level of emotional regulation

The orbitofrontal cortex is a super-convergence zone and receives multi-modal information from all sensory areas. It is involved in cross-modal association between stimuli from various sensory modalities and has extensive connections with areas in the visual association cortex, which combines representations of known faces and emotional expressions. Like the amygdala, the orbitofrontal cortex has special neurons that respond to facial expressions and gaze contact, and processing in the orbitofrontal cortex contributes to the experience of stimuli as familiar, meaningful, and personal (Blair, Morris, Frith, Perrett, & Dolan, 1999; Cozolino, 2000; LeDoux, 1998; Main, 1999, Schore, 1994).

Connections between the orbitofrontal cortex and the amygdala modulate behaviour through punishment and reward. The orbitofrontal cortex is involved in the pleasant qualities of social interaction, and, together with the frontal cingulate gyrus, the orbitofrontal cortex has the highest numbers of morphine-like receptors in the neocortex. The amygdala is in charge of relating stimuli to an emotional somatic state, while the orbitofrontal cortex determines whether the imagined stimuli trigger an emotional reaction. To some extent, the orbitofrontal cortex takes over control with the functions of the amygdala and generates a higher processing level and an expectation-based system, which is more flexible in its ability to co-ordinate external and internal stimuli and correct amygdala responses. The orbitofrontal cortex makes sense of the behavioural and unconscious reactions that have already been induced by the amygdala.

Impulse control

The orbitofrontal cortex is able to inhibit the activation of inappropriate acts. It suppresses oral tendencies and is involved in appetite regulation and the control of food intake. Owing to its direct link to the hypothalamus and the amygdala, it is able to regulate aggressive and sexual behaviour. This is the area responsible for inhibiting responses and deferring gratification, and it has a crucial function in affect regulation. When the orbitofrontal cortex fails to inhibit the subcortical structures, the result is uncontrollable impulsive outbursts that are inexplicable to the individual. The ability to inhibit distress is crucial to social interaction, and the ability to compromise is important for social harmony and equilibrium. This capacity depends on the ability to restrain distress—i.e., to control the impulse of frustration. The orbitofrontal cortex inhibits impulses from the amygdala and makes civilized discourse and conflict resolution possible (Goldberg, 2001).

Seeing a sad facial expression leads to heightened activity in the amygdala, while an angry facial expression increases activation of the orbitofrontal cortex and the cingulate gyrus, probably in order to suppress or inhibit behaviour and activate alternative behavioural responses that are more socially acceptable. Luria (1973) pointed out that it is the orbitofrontal cortex that enables self-control and the inhibition of affective outbursts. This structure incorporates social aspects of the personality structure and may be compared with the Freudian concept of moving from the pleasure principle to the reality principle. Mature orbitofrontal functions enable the organism to balance between internal needs and external reality, and the structure plays an important role for affect regulation, impulse control, and reality testing. Kaplan-Solms and

Solms (2002) found that a patient with damage to this area displayed free associations and expressed all her thoughts without any logical coherence. There did not seem to be an observing ego. She generalized present problems in relation to her overall history without distinguishing between past and present. Her reality testing was poor, because she was unable to inhibit her primary process thinking and convert it to secondary process thinking.

Object permanence

The orbitofrontal cortex is important for the generation of object permanence. Internalized internal representations are necessary for the ability to adapt one's behaviour by initiating certain responses and inhibiting others. The presence of this capacity indicates that the infant has acquired the ability to grasp the notion of object permanence in time and space and to invoke this knowledge at a later time when the object is not present. The development of object permanence begins at the age of 7½–12 months, and it marks a turning point in the development of the infant's memory functions. The orbitofrontal cortex makes it possible to modulate and manage strong affects and to process complex symbolic representations. For example, an infant who experiences negative emotions becomes able to generate a mental image of a comforting other. While it is an area buried deep inside the temporal lobe (the fusiform gyrus) that enables facial recognition, it is the orbitofrontal cortex that makes it possible to encode images of emotional facial expressions and internal mental representations, which in turn allows the child to modulate affective responses by maintaining an internal representation of the care-giver's response to an act (Davidson & Slagter, 2000; Goldman-Rakic, 1987a,b; Goldman-Rakic, Isseroff, Schwartz, & Bugbee, 1983; Luria, 1973; Schore, 1994, 2003b). The fusiform gyrus records "still" pictures of faces, while the sulcus temporalis superior (STS) integrates movements, facial expressions, mouth movements, and gaze direction. The STS is activated when someone witnesses other people's functional behaviour, and it is one of the areas that have been found to contain mirror neurons (Cozolino, 2006).

The orbitofrontal cortex is crucial for our ability to add an emotional dimension to rational thinking and for the link between mentalization and our emotions. It is our emotions that imbue our thoughts with meaning and make certain things seem more meaningful than others. The orbitofrontal cortex is often characterized as the thinking part of the emotional brain and is associated with preconsciousness. It inhibits stimuli from the subcortical areas and, for example, lets the infant react to situations on the basis of stored internal representations rather than acting directly on the information available in the environment.

The maturation of the orbitofrontal cortex

The orbitofrontal cortex is not "online" from birth, but during the first year of life the limbic circuits develop sequentially from the amygdala to the insula, on to the cingulate gyrus, and, eventually, to the orbitofrontal cortex (Schore, 2003b). The amygdala, which is active from birth, has a learning system that operates through early imprinting. The organic maturation of the orbitofrontal cortex seems to be dependent of the early imprinting of the amygdala, and without this imprinting the orbitofrontal cortex is unable to process emotions caused by imagined stimuli. The development of positive internal representations depends on early interactions with the care-giver.

The maturation of the orbitofrontal cortex is highly dependent on outside stimulation and requires that the care-giver is able to engage in a socialization process that involves inhibiting inappropriate behaviour in the child. The maturation of the orbitofrontal cortex around the age of twelve years triggers the shame reaction, a biological mechanism found in all highly advanced predator mammals that hunt and live in groups. The capacity for shame probably evolved as an effective socialization strategy. Children who have no shame reactions because the ability failed to develop due to general mental retardation or early emotional damage, or because the care-givers failed to exercise sufficient authority and inhibit inappropriate behaviour in the child, later develop difficulty with inhibiting responses and deferring gratification, while children who are locked into the shame reaction by the care-givers and humiliated eventually develop a deficient capacity for affect regulation as well as psychological disorders. A child's capacity for shame is vulnerable and needs to be adapted in a respectful manner to develop appropriately.

When the orbitofrontal cortex is fully mature, the processing of emotional stimuli takes place relatively independently of the amygdala, and emotional learning may take place through imagined experiences. Cortical inhibition of and control over subcortical structures are essential for affect regulation—the rapid mood changes and overwhelming emotions often displayed by young children illustrate what happens in the absence of this control. As the orbitofrontal cortex continues to develop, expanding and extending its fibres into the limbic system and into the brainstem, children develop a growing capacity for regulating their emotions and for finding ways to regulate their behaviour in relation to others. Initially, children rely on others for comfort, but they gradually develop the ability to self-regulate (Bechara, Damasio, & Damasio, 2003; Bradley, 2000).

Dysfunction of the orbitofrontal cortex

Like the hippocampus, the orbitofrontal cortex is an area sensitive to stress, and it has receptors that ward off excessive release of stress hormones (Damasio, 1994; LeDoux, 1998; Solms & Turnbull, 2002). Like the above-mentioned Phineas Gage, adults who suffer orbitofrontal damage appear normal and do not display any intellectual or perceptual difficulties. They are able to engage in conversation, and they remember experiences—as well as the rules that they violate on a daily basis. When confronted, they are aware that they have broken the rules. They are "flat" in relation to social emotions, and feelings of shame, sympathy, and guilt appear to have vanished. They are easily provoked, and there is no affect regulation or impulse inhibition, which leaves them unable to correct their own behaviour in relation to social situations. They have no empathy with the needs of others, no recognition of remorse or shame, and no sense of humour. Injury or dysfunctions of the orbitofrontal cortex makes it difficult to regulate arousal systems, partly because the amygdala is released from the restraint otherwise exercised by the orbitofrontal cortex, and this makes it difficult to extinguish anxiety-filled or aggressive impulses. Rodent experiments have shown that rats with damage to the orbitofrontal cortex continue to show fear reactions even when the danger is long gone, as can be observed in persons with panic/anxiety disorder (Damasio, 2003; Davidson, Putnam, & Larson, 2000).

Damage to the orbitofrontal cortex may also cause a series of temporally separate events to fuse into one. Internal impulses and desires may be acted out with no regard for the restrictions of external reality, which corresponds to the reaction mode of the young child. Children with damage to this area are rigid and inflexible, they have difficulty adapting their learning strategy, often show perseveration, and lack the ability to adjust their behaviour when there is a change in the rules. A person with damage to the orbitofrontal cortex is at the mercy of the external circumstances without any possibility of emotional self-regulation—a difficulty that is common in children who have been raised in chaotic homes. Apart from the lack of affect regulation, orbitofrontal dysfunctions may give rise to difficulties with distinguishing past from present and internal associations from events in the external reality. It becomes hard to tell actual experiences from imagined ones, and to sort out who said what and what happened in real life, as opposed to what took place only in one's imagination. The sense of time is lost, and it is difficult to tell whether something happened last week or over a year ago. The tendency to remember things that never actually happened is called confabulation; memory lapses are automatically resolved with made-up material, and fantasy mingles with fragments of real-life events, which are combined into fantastic stories (Hansen, 2002; Schore, 2003b). Children and adults with problems in this area often construct their reality based on their immediate situation, and they tend to lack integrity and adapt their behaviour and views to current company; others often consider them deceitful.

The orbitofrontal cortex is an important factor in our sense of identity; it is non-verbal and develops through patterns of affect regulation. It plays an important role in the exchange between the internal and the external environment and enables us to act on mental knowledge without having to think about it (Chugani, 1996; Damasio, 1994; Schore, 2003b). Partly overlapping and above the orbitofrontal cortex is an area called the *ventromedial prefrontal cortex*. The processing of emotional states takes place in the orbitofrontal cortex, while reflection on cognitive or perceptual states, e.g., the identification of other people's assumptions, is believed to be related to the ventromedial prefrontal cortex. The ability to predict and perceive other people's emotions and cognitive states is mediated through a collaboration involving the orbitofrontal and the ventro-medial prefrontal cortex.

The dorsolateral prefrontal cortex

The dorsolateral prefrontal cortex is located in the posterior and outside part of the prefrontal cortex. It is a relatively large area located just in front of the motor and premotor cortex. The dorso-lateral prefrontal cortex has strong neural connections to the pari-etal lobes and fewer to the limbic system (Austin, 1998). The dorsolateral prefrontal cortex is the ultimate structure for the co-ordination of information and reactions, for merging and directing emotional and mental impressions, and for planning action. It is this area that is able to maintain and manipulate mental images and to generate plans and imagine things. This area makes it possible to choose one strategy over another and to process a well-considered emotional response. One of its functions is to suppress or control emotions in order to handle a given situation more efficiently or to induce a new reaction if reassessment requires it.

The dorsolateral prefrontal cortex is an important structure in relation to the working memory, as it allows us to retain a piece of information long enough to manipulate it in our mind. The area enables us to organize and reorganize, and it contains the ability to resist diversions and the temptation of responding prematurely. This is where impulses or initial notions are inhibited when some other behaviour seems more appropriate. This part of the cortex has special connections to the motor cortex (Diamond, 2000).

Even though the dorsolateral prefrontal cortex and the orbitofrontal cortex are located side by side, they have different neural circuits, biochemistry, and functions. Both the dorsolateral cortex and the orbitofrontal cortex play important roles in inhibi-tion and control, but while the dorsolateral areas are more involved in conscious decision-making, decision-making in the orbitofrontal cortex is based more on affective information. While the orbito-frontal cortex is involved in implicit behaviour regulation, the dorsolateral prefrontal cortex is involved in the explicit regulation of behaviour. For example, in explicit behaviour regulation people may correct their behaviour to a certain extent once they realize that they have behaved inappropriately. The dorsolateral prefrontal cor-tex is activated when a person attempts through explicit, conscious consideration, with the use of language and the working memory, to find a new solution to an emotional problem, while the orbitofrontal cortex instead regulates emotions through social contexts, social rules, etc., that can not be verbalized or made explicit. The orbitofrontal cortex regulates emotional behaviour through its connections to the cingulate gyrus, the limbic system, and the autonomic nervous system, while the dorsolateral prefrontal cortex has strong connections to the association areas involved in sensory integration and intentional behaviour. The dorsolateral prefrontal cortex allows the person to be mentally present here and now as well as somewhere else simultaneously. We are present where our minds take us. When experiences are placed in a context of time and place, the dorsolateral prefrontal cortex and the hippocampus are activated (Bradley, 2000; Cozolino, 2000; van der Kolk, 2000; Wilson, O'Scalaidhe, & Goldman-Rakic, 1993). The dorsolateral prefrontal cortex is essential for our ability to recall memories and memory tracks. When stored information is needed, this brain region is in charge of activating relevant circuits that to retrieve the memory (the engram). Different stages of problem solving require different types of information, and the area has to be quick and flexible in activating relevant memories and letting go of currently irrelevant ones. It has to be able to switch between different cognitive tasks quickly and to work on several problems simultaneously. Information has to come into focus as needed, and the area must be able to switch quickly between relevant pieces of information (Goldberg, 2001).

Luria was one of the first to describe the difficulties that persons with prefrontal damage had in handling everyday life because they were unable to plan and organize actions in order to attain a goal. They had no problems in handling various cognitive and motor functions, but they were unable to apply these operations in a coherent manner. They were able to repeat a verbal instruction correctly, but could not use this information to carry out even the simplest tasks. This lack of planning often took a while to become apparent because the patients were able to imitate other people's actions, but left to themselves they failed to relate actions to adaptive goals (Schore, 2003b; Tucker & Derryberry, 1992).

Dysfunction in the dorsolateral prefrontal cortex is characterized by difficulty in relation to executive functions (the ability to articulate goals and to plan and execute necessary actions efficiently), while dysfunction in the orbitofrontal area has an emotional character. Damage to the dorsolateral prefrontal cortex makes it difficult to control and focus conscious attention, to carry out calculations, and to draw appropriate and logical conclusions. In the case of severe dysfunction, attention is free-floating and concentration is unattainable and disrupted by arbitrary irrelevant stimuli (Damasio, 1994). In early neurological literature, the dorsolateral syndrome was often referred to as pseudo-depression because extreme apathy and failure to initiate actions were common. A patient with a dorsolateral prefrontal injury is neither happy nor sad and seems indifferent even to pain. Damage to this area causes psychological rigidity and perseveration. This is often accompanied by a lack of awareness of, and insight into, one's own condition. This is characterized as anosognosia and is usually the effect of damage to the right hemisphere. In this case, the patient maintains that everything is fine (Goldberg, 2001).

The prefrontal cortex is the brain region that most distinctly separates man from other mammals (Table 8.1).

> We get upset at someone who meant to hurt us but not at someone who did it by accident. The rattlesnake never learns that you didn't mean to step on him—he will bite you regardless. This is where our social brain helps us. The prefrontal cortex gets intimately involved in the interpretation of social information. [Taylor, 2002, pp. 47–48]

Summary

In this chapter, I have discussed the main structures at the top level of the triune brain, the level of ratiomentation. This area is uniquely human in many ways, and it enables us to live in a world that has a past and a present and to mentalize and relate to other people's feelings and opinions. These brain structures allow us to reflect on ourselves, to delay responses, and to choose long-term strategies, even when they get in the way of our current short-term needs. This part of the nervous system offers countless possibilities for interpersonal communication through narratives and abstractions, which we can share in refined and sophisticated ways, for example, through artistic expressions. Unfortunately, this is also a vulnerable region, partly because it inhabits the top hierarchical level of the

Table 8.1.   Structures in the frontal and parietal lobes.

Cingulate gyrus:

Induces emotional behaviour related to attachment and caring
Induces separation anxiety and attachment behaviour
Induces play behaviour
Directs attention towards to situations that feel particularly relevant
Triggers feelings of safety and relatedness
Triggers separation pain
Enables us to act counter to innate or early acquired impules
Is the source of energy for both external action (movement) and internal
    action (thinking)
Is in charge of selective attention and volitional movements
Registers whether stimuli have an external or an internal source
Integrates executive functions—the capacity for planning and structuring
Is in charge of the recognition of sad, fearful, and angry facial
    expressions
Regulates social behaviour

The parietal lobe:

Maintains the sense of an internal subjective space
Creates a three-dimensional body sense
Processes tactile and kinaesthetic information such as sensing muscles
    and joints
Provides a sense of identity—who and where am I?
Enables us to distinguish between internal and external experiences
    (telling imaginary events from real life)
Combines sensory impressions with mental images

The insula:

Integrates representations of somatic states
Enables emotions through body sensations

The orbitofrontal cortex:

Regulates parasympathetic and sympathetic components
Controls vagary activation in the brain stem
Regulates arousal levels
Has connections to all brain regions and knowledge of all activity at all
    times throughout the organism
Receives multimodal information from all sensory areas
Combines representations of familiar faces and emotional expressions
Responds to facial expressions and gaze contact
Helps make stimuli seem familiar, meaningful, and personal
Enables the modulation of behaviour through punishment and reward
Is involved in pleasant qualities of social interactions
Links imagined stimuli with emotional reactions   (*continued*)

Table 8.1.   (continued)

The orbitofrontal cortex (continued):

Co-ordinates external and internal stimuli and makes sense of responses
   from the amygdala
Inhibits the activation of inappropriate actions (delayed response
function)
Suppresses oral tendencies
Is involved in appetite regulation and the control of food intake
Regulates aggression and sexual behaviour
Manages self-control and the restraint of affective outbursts
Enables object permanence
Attributes emotional value to rational thinking
Combines emotions and thoughts to form mentalization
Enables the distinction between past and present

The dorsolateral prefrontal cortex:

Directs emotional and mental impressions and plans actions (executive
   functions)
Retains mental images and manipulates them
Generates plans and mental images
Chooses between different strategies
Suppresses and controls inappropriate feelings
Induces new reactions through reassessment
Enables the working memory by retaining information in the mind
Processes conscious decision-making processes
Makes it possible to be mentally present in the here and now as well as
   somewhere else at the same time

brain. For example, severe affective disorders that have arisen in
deep-lying subcortical levels will often have a substantial impact on
our mentalization capacity.

   The previous three chapters have focused on various structures
within the triune brain, which we have studied in hierarchical
order. In the next two chapters we turn away from brain anatomy
and focus instead on what it is that enables these structures to co-
operate. The next chapter looks at the brain's neurochemistry or
messenger substances that help harmonize motor, motivational,
learning, and affective processes.

CHAPTER NINE

Neurotransmitters, peptides, and hormones: the messengers of the brain

"The neurochemical regulators of brains in higher animals have evolved to control and respond to social influences. In social mammals, brain development comes under control of signals that direct the motives of all individuals in a social group, with particularly strong effects on the young . . . In humans, this strategy is elaborated for the transmission of culture"

(Trevarthen, 1990, p. 341)

Any discussion of brain functions would be incomplete without a look at the messengers of the brain: the neurotransmitters. As mentioned in Chapter Three, the contact points between the neurons are called synapses. Neurons use chemical messengers, neurotransmitters, to jump the synaptic gap. In order for the electrical current to jump this gap, a chemical or electrical signal is released when the neuron fires. All neurons generate neurotransmitters, which are released from the neuronal terminals into the synapse. Catecholamines (see Table 9.1) are synthesized in the brainstem and distributed via modulator neurons throughout large parts of the cortex. This means that many of the neurons that produce and regulate arousal-regulating substances are located within the reticular activation system in the brainstem. Of the total number of neurons in the brain, less than one per cent produce catecholamines, but they are hugely important for the function of billions of neurons within the brain (Schore, 1994). They send out axons to thousands of structures on every level, and one single neuron is capable of projecting neural pathways from the brainstem all the way up to the prefrontal cortex (*ibid.*).

In the general debate, the neurotransmitters are most commonly mentioned in connection with psychoactive medication (for example Prozac, Ritalin, etc.), and much research in the pharmaceutical industry is aimed at influencing and regulating affective conditions by chemical means. To anyone outside the health professions, the explanations can be almost impossible to grasp, and in this chapter I attempt to describe the most common neurotransmitters in a way that, I hope, will make this knowledge somewhat more accessible and offer some insight into the ways that affective states are influenced by the distribution of biochemical substances.

Neurotransmitters, peptides, and hormones act as chemical substances throughout the brain and are transmitted through neuronal synapses (see Figures 3.5 and 3.6). The neurochemicals are vastly important to practically all the processes that take place within the organism. In relation to affects, these substances affect our moods, motivation, attention functions, etc. All neurotransmitters, peptides, and hormones have a synaptic language that transmits specific types of electric or chemical messages; some types inhibit, while others induce, certain tendencies in psychological behaviour. Most neurons contain different types of molecules, which means that they can be activated by different neurotransmitters. However, each neuron has one primary neurotransmitter. Neurotransmitters are neurochemicals that are released from neurons in the brainstem and released in the synapses. Hormones are neurochemicals that are transported via the bloodstream and released from the adrenocortical glands, the hypothalamus, the pituitary gland, the sexual organs, and other sources. Typically, they do not respond as quickly as the neurotransmitters. Peptides are made from amino acids and may function both as neurotransmitters and as hormones. Their function is to intensify and to modulate the effect of the neurotransmitters (Table 9.1).

Table 9.1.   The most widespread neurotransmitters, peptides, and hormones.

Neurotransmitters	Amino acids	
	Glutamate	
	GABA	
	Acetylcholine	
	Monoamines	
	Serotonin	
	Noradrenalin	
	Dopamine	Catecholamines
	Adrenalin	
Peptides	Opioids (beta endorphins and encephalins)	
	CRF (acts as a hormone in connection with stress activation)	
Hormones	Oxytocin	
	Vasopressin	
	Oestrogen	Sex hormones
	Testosterone	
	ACTH	
	(CRF)	Stress hormones
	Cortisol	

The release of peptides and neurotransmitters from the brain stem, among other places, alters the processes in numerous brain circuits and activates certain behavioural patterns Emotions are activated, among other things, by the release of neurochemicals and electric signals. The neural circuits of the neurotransmitters cause sensations that are, in fact, aspects of emotions. All neurotransmitter systems are present from birth, but they are not fully mature. Some of the systems do not mature completely until puberty (Benes, 1994). The effect of the transmitters seems to depend on the brain region where the substance is activated, which has been the source of some confusion. Neurotransmitters may have one effect in one part of the nervous system but quite another effect in another location. Similarly, the same neuron may respond differently and change chemically, so that even when it receives identical stimuli it may fire in different ways. Chemical signal substances may also act as modulators, i.e., not as primary inducers but as modifiers to the effect of the primary transmitter substance.

Neurons are constantly under the influence of thousands of other neurons, which links them in vast networks that form the basis for the workings of the brain. Brain activation and calming are determined by the neural symphony that is constantly switching on and off. It is the pattern of this neural symphony that determines a person's mental state rather than the particular neurochemicals and electrical signals (Gjærum & Ellertsen, 2002; LeDoux, 2001; Panksepp, 1998; Siegel, 2004).

Neurotransmitters may have an activating (excitatory) effect, which means that the neurons react quickly, or an inhibitory effect, which means that it becomes harder for the neuron to react. Activation and inhibition are the two basic processes in the brain, and it is the sum of excitatory and inhibitory effects reaching a neuron that determines its activity. Today, we know of hundreds of substances that serve as transmitters in the brain. The most widespread neurotransmitters are the rapidly reacting amino acids, which are capable of causing electrical change within milliseconds. Monoamines are another group of transmitters, which consists of better known substances such as acetylcholine, serotonin, dopamine, noradrenalin, and adrenalin. The neuropeptides include the body's opioid system (morphine-like substances), among others. As for the hormones, we will look at two categories in this context: sex hormones and stress hormones. The monoamines, neuropeptides, and hormones react slowly and have a relatively persistent and long-term effect (LeDoux, 2001).

Amino acid neurotransmitters

The amino acids include glutamate and gamma-aminobutyric acid (GABA), which are effective in some thirty per cent of the synapses in the brain. These two amino acids are involved in practically all brain processes, and it is difficult to study their functions specifically. Glutamate and GABA control all cognitive, emotional, and motivational functions and regulate each other.

Glutamate

Glutamate is an activating (excitatory) neurotransmitter with receptors throughout the brain. Glutamate is the neurotransmitter that enables neurons to activate simultaneously and thus connect in circuits. Glutamate helps the synapse react more rapidly next time it is activated, which is the basis of learning, long-term memory, and cognitive processes. Glutamate is probably involved in controlling every single thought, perception, and emotion in the brain. The ability to see, hear, remember, fear danger, and harbour desires is activated by glutamates (LeDoux, 2001; Panksepp, 1998; Schore, 2003a). An increase in glutamate causes animals to begin to vocalize with attachment cries if they are abandoned. A high level of glutamate probably maintains attention functions (Austin, 1998; Fisher, 2004).

Gamma-aminobutyric acid (GABA)

GABA is the most important inhibitory neurotransmitter. Unlike glutamate, GABA reduces the tendency of a given neuron to activate. Without the inhibitory capacity of GABA, neurons would be emitting signals constantly and eventually fire themselves to death. If GABA lost its ability to inhibit meaningless stimuli from firing, for example in the amygdala, non-threatening stimuli would constantly irritate the amygdala and make it respond. The function of GABA in the central nervous system is as widespread as that of glutamate, but while glutamate is distributed throughout the organism, GABA is only released in the brain. GABA is able to extinguish an action potential induced by glutamate, and a sedative such as Valium, for example, works by increasing the natural ability of GABA to regulate glutamate. All behaviour seems to involve GABA. GABA and glutamate act as yin and yang. GABA reduces primal separation anxiety and reduces dopamine and stress hormones (Austin, 1998).

Acetylcholine

Acetylcholine is neither an amino acid nor a monoamine. It is an excitatory substance that is involved in the control of muscle movements and heart rate and in connecting nerve fibres and muscle fibres. It supports the maintenance of attention, promotes arousal in the sensory systems, and affects activities related to cognition, learning, and memory. The facial cranial nerves, which control biting, sucking, chewing, and facial movements, have a high density of acetylcholine receptors, and acetylcholine acts to regulate alertness in the reticular activation system. Outbursts of anger appear to be controlled by glutamate and acetylcholine, among others.

Nicotine is believed to influence the production of acetylcholine, which implies that nicotine indirectly promotes memory, learning, and attention. Acetylcholine acts as an important transmitter throughout the parasympathetic nervous system, but acetylcholine receptors are also found in the nerve terminals of the sympathetic nervous system and in the sweat glands (Panksepp, 1998; Purves et al., 2001). Acetylcholine was the first neurotransmitter to be identified some seventy-five years ago, and we continue to learn about new areas of influence. In addition to the functions already mentioned, acetylcholine controls both the quantity and quality of our levels of consciousness. If insufficient acetylcholine is released we have difficulty maintaining attention and thinking clearly (Austin, 1998).

Monoamines

Along with acetylcholine, the monoamines noradrenalin, serotonin, and dopamine are produced in the brainstem, especially in the reticular activation system, and they exert great influence over large areas of the central nervous system. Noradrenalin can be converted to adrenalin by a minor chemical change, but adrenalin is not a very widespread neurotransmitter. The monoamines are necessary for neural activity throughout the central nervous system and play a key part in regulating and developing brain circuits in interaction with environmental stimulation. The monoamines are essential for all the processes that are important for motivational and emotional processes, and monoaminergic receptors are found throughout most of the brain (Figure 9.1).

The neural structure determines the character of a function, while substances based on monoamines determine co-ordination and arousal levels. The balance between monoamines is regulated through early life experiences but is also related to our genetic material. For example, the internal and external stimuli involved in causing monoamine arousal make it possible to initiate the imprinting process that triggers the attachment process (LeDoux, 2001;

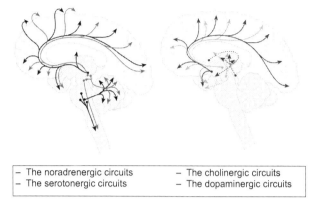

| – The noradrenergic circuits | – The cholinergic circuits |
| – The serotonergic circuits | – The dopaminergic circuits |

Figure 9.1.   The monoaminergic circuits.

Panksepp, 1998; Schore, 1994). Cloninger has proposed what he calls a biosocial personality theory organized around a model with three axes representing the three main neurotransmitters: serotonin, noradrenalin, and dopamine. The serotonin axis involves avoidance of pain or reduction of vulnerability in the face of rejection. The dopamine axis regulates reward-seeking behaviour, while the noradrenalin axis regulates reward dependency to prevent us from becoming too dependent on pleasurable stimuli (Johnson, 2004).

In the following sections, I discuss the functions of the four monoamine-based substances in relation to arousal, motivation, and emotions.

Serotonin

Serotonin is one of the best known neurotransmitters because of its presence in anti-depressants such as Prozac. The popular anti-depressants increase the level of accessible serotonin in the synapses and neural networks, thus causing a higher degree of activation in the serotonin-based networks. Serotonin-producing neurons are clustered in specific brainstem areas (the raphe nuclei) and distributed throughout most of the basal ganglia, the limbic system, and the neocortex. Serotonin contributes to all aspects of behaviour and cognition and stabilizes perceptual and cognitive information. Its receptors are especially concentrated in the amygdala and the orbitofrontal cortex. In primates, serotonin inhibits aggressive behaviour and promotes social behaviour. Serotonin modulates the responsiveness and arousal of noradrenalin, and it activates GABA to inhibit firing neurons.

If serotonin levels are too low, the organism becomes unable to modulate arousal. Low levels of serotonin may reduce investigative behaviour and lead to aggressiveness, impulsivity, suicide attempts, sleep deprivation, and inward aggression. Thus, serotonin has an inhibitory function that suppresses behaviour. Activities such as food intake, play, and sexual behaviour are reduced when serotonin levels are increased. Raised serotonin levels may result in rigidity or compulsive conditions. In addition to its inhibitory function, serotonin channels information and helps lessen the impression of incoming information. A temporary drop in serotonin levels allows us to have new insights and ideas, while a lasting reduction may lead to a sense of incoherence and mania. The amygdala is balanced by serotonin; among other things, this increases the release of GABA, which diminishes the intensity of the startle response and of impulsive behaviour. Serotonin is associated with social trust and a sense of relatedness (Bradley, 2000; Hansen, 2002; Panksepp, 1998).

In Chapter Two, I mentioned that Suomi discovered a connection between diminished serotonin levels and the position of higher primates in the social hierarchy. Monkeys with a short allele for serotonin were hot-tempered, and instead of engaging in play they went wild and engaged in destructive play. The outcome was conditioned by the environment they were raised in, and the monkey only displayed impulsive aggressiveness if it had suffered neglect or abuse or been raised by monkeys its own age. Serotonin levels change in connection with caring and grief in both humans and animals. Animals exposed to repeated shocking experiences develop reduced serotonin levels (Suomi, 1991, 1997, 2000; Suomi & Levin, 1998; Taylor, 2002; van der Kolk, 1996).

The effect of serotonin can only be understood in relation to noradrenalin. While serotonin modulates impulsive behaviour on a neocortical level, noradrenalin makes the organism respond to danger. Normally, the serotonin level is higher during sleep and drops during the waking state, while the opposite is true for noradrenalin. The balance between serotonin and noradrenalin is the key to stable affect regulation. Raised noradrenalin levels and reduced serotonin levels caused by early environmental experiences may

lead to impulsive behaviour later in life. Low levels of both noradrenalin and serotonin may lead to hypoarousal and the resulting
desire to engage in risky behaviour in order to achieve arousal.

Serotonin levels depend both on environmental experiences and
on the ability of the nervous system to synthesize serotonin from
the amino acid tryptophan, which exists in regular food items.
Serotonin synthesis depends on the availability of tryptophan, and
limiting tryptophan in the diet may reduce serotonin and lead to
aggressiveness (Davidson, Putnam, & Larson, 2000). Serotonin is
closely related to melatonin, which is produced in the pineal gland.
In most mammals, melatonin is released as it gets dark, and the
animal or person prepares to sleep. Melatonin synchronizes the
circadian rhythms, regulates growth processes, and is effective in
inducing sleep. Tryptophan is an important amino acid for the
production of both serotonin and melatonin (Joseph, 1996; Karr-
Morse & Wiley, 1997).

Noradrenalin

Noradrenalin is distributed throughout most of the central nervous
system and is almost always inhibitory. The hypothalamus has a
high concentration of noradrenalin, and the substance is released in
the presence of potentially dangerous, painful, or stress-filled stimuli. Noradrenalin triggers fight-or-flight behaviour, maintains high
signal levels, a high arousal level, alertness, attention, and efficient
information processing. It exerts global control over brain activity
and is involved in powerfully emotional events. Noradrenalin
tones down background noise and reduces neural activity in the
neocortex that is irrelevant to a particular task. For example, when
the impala on the savannah picks up a sound and stops to locate
potential dangers, noradrenalin is released. While acetylcholine is
the "gate keeper" that controls the information flow in relation to
incoming sensory signals, raised noradrenalin activity enhances the
ability to process the information that is already entering the
neocortex (Panksepp, 1998).

Noradrenalin is essential for our understanding of stress and
trauma. A raised level of noradrenalin results in anxiety, irritability,
alertness, quick temper, and defensiveness. When we concentrate
on a task, or when we are under stress, our noradrenalin level is

high. Noradrenalin enhances memory tracks in connection with stress-filled and traumatic events, even when it is only released in moderate quantities, while highly raised levels have the opposite effect. Both adrenalin and noradrenalin prepare the organism for high levels of activity in relation to survival behaviour, which may be triggered by threats, surprise, or joy. Adrenalin mobilizes the glucose metabolism, which in turn raises the blood sugar, expands the blood vessels in the muscles, and increases heart rate and blood pressure, but it usually leaves the body again quickly (Cozolino, 2000; Scaer, 2001).

Neurophysiologists have considered the biological basis for cautious, but not necessarily shy, children. They have considered whether these children have raised noradrenalin levels, causing them to be at a constant level of alertness that makes them respond more rapidly to even very small changes. On the other hand, it has also been considered whether extrovert children have low levels of noradrenalin, making them need a higher degree of stimulation to activate their response to environmental stimuli, such as parental prohibitions (Karr-Morse & Wiley, 1997). At this time, our knowledge of the sources of temperamental differences is rather limited, and the matter is likely to prove extremely complex.

Dopamine

Dopamine co-ordinates many different functions in the cortex. The basal ganglia have many dopamine receptors, and when these areas are activated by dopamine the motor regions become highly activated and initiate movements. The dopamine system plays a key role in relation to reward behaviour, inquisitiveness, and positive emotions. Thus, dopamine helps foster a positive and interested involvement with the world, is vital to physical motivation, and is strongly activated in the face of moderate stress. Optimum dopamine levels make the basal ganglia work efficiently, while excessive activation (as in amphetamine or cocaine abuse) may cause delusions, illusions, hyperactivity, aggression, and psychotic behaviour. All forms of compulsive behaviour, such as compulsive gambling, excessive eating, etc., involve problems with dopamine concentration. Persons with a strong inclination towards high-risk behaviour have a high concentration of a particular type of dopamine receptors. Impaired of dopamine function leads to shaking and the inability to initiate volitional movements (Parkinson's disease), and a low level of dopamine is often associated with feelings of meaninglessness, low drive, unpleasure, lack of motivation, and withdrawal (Carter, 1998; Goldberg, 2001; LeDoux, 2001; Tucker & Derryberry, 1992).

Dopamine levels rise in response to natural rewards such as food, water, and sexual stimulation, and in pleasant emotional arousal states. Disorders in the dopamine circuits lead to a loss of pleasure, wishes, motivation, and joy. The dopamine system activates stimulus-seeking, inquisitiveness, and interest, and, with sufficiently complex functions in the neocortex, also the motivation to solve complex issues. Dopamine is the main inducer of feelings of involvement and excitement and provides the impulse for being active and engaged, whether expressed as food-seeking for survival, excessive shopping, or engagement in cognitive pursuits. Without dopamine, only the very strongest emotional stimulation would lead to action. A balanced dopamine level plays an important role for the pleasant feelings that arise in connection with rewards, and deprivation may affect dopamine concentration and consequently brain development and plasticity. Animals that are chronically treated with a drug that breaks down dopamine soon begin to display fear and aggressiveness (Goleman, 2003; Panksepp, 1998). The infatuation phase in a love relationship is characterized by raised dopamine levels, which leads to increased energy, hyperactivity, insomnia, loss of appetite, etc. The delay or absence of an expected reward triggers the production of dopamine, and the sense of expectation grows. When a puppy is moved away from its mother, it begins to energetically and tirelessly scratch, bark, and try to find a way to be reunited with the mother. This protest reaction may be related with raised levels of dopamine and noradrenalin. An increase in these two substances, which stimulate the central nervous system, increases alertness and makes the puppy search and call for help. A rise in the level of dopamine leads to a drop in the level of serotonin (Fisher, 2004).

Dopamine is an important chemical from birth. It regulates the growth of nerve fibres, not least in the prefrontal regions. Schore (1994) has pointed out that parents who meet their child with joy and interest generate a sympathetic arousal state in the infant's nervous system, which promotes attachment formation. Positive affect attunement with the child triggers the dopamine system, which stimulates the reward centres in the brain through the opioid system. According to Schore (*ibid.*), dopamine reaches its maximum concentration level in the prefrontal cortex sooner than noradrenalin. Pleasure activation at an early stage in infancy is important for the development of the nervous system, and infants who do not experience pleasant caring events develop deficiencies in the balancing of the nervous system, partly due to insufficient dopamine activation.

The neuropeptides

Neuropeptides are neurochemicals that act either as transmitters or as hormones. Neuropeptides can be inhibitory as well as excitatory, and the brain contains at least 100 different kinds. Neuropeptides may react as neurotransmitters in one region and as hormones in another. Many have specific control over basic psychological functions such as appetite, stress, separation anxiety, etc. The neuropeptide system includes the endogenous opioid system and the stress response system corticotropin-releasing factor (CRF), among other components. CRF is described in the section on hormones, because the substance is usually characterized as a hormone. The opioid and CRF systems have a sort of yin-yang function in relation to each other. CRF activates stress responses, while the opioid system releases anti-stress responses and has a generally calming influence on negative arousal. The opioids modulate the activity of monoamines and are involved in regulating pain, joy, and reward responses, among other things (Panksepp, 1998; Purves et al., 2001).

The opioids—the body's morphine system

Opioids are compounds (e.g., heroin or morphine) that are able to attach to the opioid receptors that are found in the central nervous system, among other places, where they have an analgesic or pain reducing effect. The endogenous opioids include endorphins and encephalins, which reduce stress and provide a sense of overwhelming calm. The endorphins deliver their substance to the primitive brain regions, while the other opioid system, the encephalins, is more widely distributed in cortical and subcortical structures. The basal ganglia in particular contain high levels of encephalins. Opioids have a short-term effect because they are quickly broken down by enzymes. The endorphins, however, tend to last slightly longer than the encephalins. There are many opioid receptors in the vicinity of the amygdala and the orbitofrontal cortex (Austin, 1998). Opioids are able to extinguish aggressive tendencies, and raised levels may lead to a tendency to allow oneself to be oppressed in the social hierarchy. Pleasure is nature's way of letting the brain know that the current experience is a good and useful event that supports the survival of the organism. For example, sexual rewards or sugary substances such as sweets or chocolate may trigger the release of opioids. The opioid system is involved in the pleasant feeling stemming from maternal care and other social interactions. In animals, the opioid system is active when the animals play with each other and engage in close bonding. Panksepp (1998) imagines a neural parallel between the dynamics of opiate dependency and the dynamics of close relational bonds and attachment, and he speculates that the pleasure of positive interactions with others is related to the opioid system. Opioids have an anti-aggressive function and an important inhibitory effect on separation stress. The opioid system is also activated by stress or pain, acting to alter the person's mood and pain perception (Panksepp, 1998).

The opioids activate the dopamine system and produce pleasant activity, for example during social exchanges. Among other things, they are triggered by positive facial expressions: for example, in the parents. High opioid levels lead to a sense of safety, while low levels stimulate approachment behaviour and a search for care and safety. The opioids are important for the emergence of early attachment experiences and encourage the child to seek safety and comfort (Cozolino, 2000; Schore, 1994).

The opioids have a direct influence on the stress hormones, reducing their impact. When animals are socially isolated, their opioid levels drop; when they reunite with their kind, their levels go back to normal and they may experience a sense of euphoria. The limbic brain has more opioid receptors than any other brain region. Separation studies have shown that when the mother is removed from her young, their separation cries are triggered instantly, but if they are given just a tiny dose of morphine, without being sedated, the protest stops immediately (Taylor, 2002).

Opioids are released in the case of fear or pain. The substance veils the feeling of pain involved in traumatic experiences, and memory is impaired, especially when one is unable to affect the outcome of a dangerous situation. Opioids may reduce pain and reduce states of panic and chaos, but are only released after long-term exposure to severe stress. Self-harming behaviour may be related to the opioid system, since the exposure to excessive pain or exhaustion activates the opioid system (van der Kolk & McFarlane, 1996). For example, a young woman with anorexia who had self-inflicted burn injuries and deep, bleeding cuts explained that the self-harming behaviour gave her an instant sense of control, and that she felt great satisfaction, pleasure, and relief when she inflicted pain on herself. She stated that it was far easier for her to handle tangible physical pain than vague psychological pain. She did, however, feel trapped in a vicious cycle because she had to inflict growing levels of pain in order to feel the relief, which caused a deep sense of guilt. The opioids cause feelings of joy, euphoria, and pleasure, while dopamine causes feelings of expectation, of looking forward to something. The opioids are released, for example, when one listens to one's favourite music and is overwhelmed with feelings of pleasure.

As mentioned earlier, the neuropeptides may react either as neurotransmitters or as hormones. Hormones are often transported through the blood vessels, and typically do not react as quickly as the neurotransmitters, but, like the other modulators, they are able to alter the effects of glutamate and GABA. In the following sections, I discuss the main hormone categories in relation to our affects: sex and stress hormones.

Hormones

Hormones are released from organs such as the adrenal glands, the hypothalamus, the pituitary gland, and the sexual organs. There are many different hormones, and, in relation to the sex hormones, I shall be discussing vasopressin, oxytocin, androgens (including testosterone), oestrogens, progesterone, and prolactin. The stress hormones activate stress responses and include CRF, adrenocorticotrophic hormone (ACTH), and cortisol, among others. The stress hormones help the organism mobilize the necessary energy to handle a stressful situation (van der Kolk & McFarlane 1996).

Vasopressin

Both oxytocin and vasopressin are synthesized in the hypothalamus and resemble each other in chemical structure. In mammals, both hormones are involved in reproductive behaviour (LeDoux, 2001). While oxytocin promotes typically feminine behaviour such as calmness and caring, vasopressin promotes typically male sexual behaviour and aggressive assertiveness. Vasopressin exists in both sexes, but males have far more receptors for vasopressin than females. Vasopressin is especially important in relation to male courtship behaviour, territorial behaviour, and aggressive behaviour among males, but it may also provide energy for aggressive aspects of female behaviour. While oxytocin triggers attachment behaviour in females, vasopressin triggers attachment behaviour in males (Panksepp, 1998; Porges, 2001; Schore 2003a; Taylor 2002).

   Vasopressin has other functions besides that of a sex hormone, as it is related to the stress response system. Vasopressin raises blood pressure, partly by stimulating sympathetic functions that increase the release of the stress hormone CRF in situations that are perceived as unsafe or challenging. When the sympathetic nervous system is activated, a message is sent to the kidneys to reabsorb water, which is partly achieved through the release of vasopressin; this reduces urine secretion. Children who are bedwetters are often prescribed a drug containing vasopressin in order to reduce their urine secretion at night.

Oxytocin

Oxytocin is produced in the hypothalamus, the ovaries, and the testicles and is believed to be a mutation of vasopressin. Oxytocin is released from the sexual and reproductive organs and, for example, floods the brain during an orgasm and in the final stages of giving birth.

Oxytocin produces a warm, light, loving feeling, which encourages attachment in couples, and it helps to create the calm needed to engage in social interactions and attachment formation. Oxytocin supports the formation of attachment bonds between mother and child and in friendships, love relations, and social preferences among adults. Oxytocin triggers self-calming behaviour by lowering activity in the sympathetic nervous system and activating the parasympathetic nervous system. It is a calming and anti-aggressive hormone, and women have far more oxytocin receptors than men. In both male and female rats, oxytocin has a physiological anti-stress effect. If rats are injected with oxytocin for a period of five days, their blood pressure and stress hormone levels drop (Uvnäs-Moberg, 1998).

Oxytocin is released, for example, when a woman is in labour or when she breast-feeds, and it promotes maternal behaviour. The infant's vagus nerve is activated when the infant sucks on the nipple, and this increases the infant's uptake of nourishment in the gastrointestinal tract. Soothing stimulation such as touching and warmth raises the oxytocin level. In animals, oxytocin has a calming effect in both mother and offspring and reduces anxiety in the offspring (Taylor, 2002). When a mother soothes and comforts her child, she is regulating the child's oxytocin level, because the oxytocin is released as a result of sensory stimuli such as facial expressions and vocalization that express warmth and safe familiarity. When children are nursing, they not only receive milk from the mother but also warmth and touching. Oxytocin supports the initiation of maternal behaviour, but if, for example, the mother has suffered severe neglect as a child or is living under extremely stress-filled circumstances, the oxytocin activation will be insufficient to trigger and maintain her maternal care. Environmentally responsive factors have a greater influence on her behaviour than oxytocin, since no hormone is able to block socially acquired behaviour.

Uvnäs-Moberg (1997a,b, 1998) has presented the theory that oxytocin release may be caused by internal mental images or thoughts that arise through the prefrontal cortex, and which relate to situations that have previously led to the release of oxytocin, i.e., thoughts about situations that were previously perceived as positive.

Oxytocin and the opioid system are closely related, and oxytocin might, for example, increase the sensitivity of the opioid system. While oxytocin triggers the need for social attachment, the opioids release the pleasant feeling of relatedness with the care-giver or partner. Oxytocin, vasopressin, and the opioids form the physiological basis for the formation and maintenance of social attachments in mammals. Friendships are apparently cemented by the same chemical system that originally helped foster maternal care and attachment behaviour. The hippocampus, which enables conscious memory storage, has many oxytocin and vasopressin receptors. The same brain chemistry that supports friendship bonds and sexual behaviour apparently helps create memory consolidation concerning these experiences. Oxytocin and the opioid system are essential in creating pleasure and family values and may help reduce irritation and aggressiveness (Panksepp, 1998; Taylor, 2002).

Experiments with prairie voles showed that if the release of oxytocin is blocked in the female immediately prior to mating, she mates without subsequently bonding with her sex partner. Thus, the failure to release oxytocin disrupts attachment but not sexual behaviour. If vasopressin is blocked in the male prairie vole just before mating, the male will fail to form an attachment with the female and protect her from the aggression of other male prairie voles. Thus, the failure to release vasopressin blocks attachment but not sexual or aggressive responses. Sex and attachment are triggered by different neurochemicals (Damasio, 2003). These experiments were carried out by Insel and Young (2001), who pointed out that it is the release of vasopressin in the male prairie voles that makes them engage in close monogamous relationships. Similarly, they found both oxytocin and dopamine receptors in the nucleus accumbens in the basal ganglia of these monogamous prairie voles, i.e., close to the reward circuits of the brain. In humans, too, oxytocin receptors are often located close to dopamine receptors (Fisher, 2004; Johnson, 2004).

While vasopressin and oxytocin are important for sexual behaviour, the sex hormones testosterone, oestrogen, progesterone, and prolactin are important for our reproductive capacity and the development of sexual organs. Oestrogen is also important for the production of oxytocin, while testosterone is important for vasopressin production.

Sex hormones

Testosterone, oestrogen, and prolactin

The adrenal cortex is a vital organ that produces hormones that activate cellular enzyme production, and that are of fundamental importance for many metabolic processes and for the body's immune system. In both sexes, the adrenal cortex produces small amounts of both male and female sex hormones (androgens and oestrogens). The sex hormones are also produced in the sexual organs and, to a smaller extent, in the hypothalamus. The androgens are used, among other things, for the production of testosterone, a male sex hormone that triggers the fight response. There is evidence that physical aggression as a response to stress is more common in males than in females due to the higher levels of testosterone in males (Panksepp, 1998).

In women, the behavioural effect of sex hormones is much more subtle and complex than in men. For example, the removal of the ovaries, the main sources of oestrogens and progesterone, does not have a major effect on the woman's sex drive. However, the sex drive does disappear if the adrenal glands are removed. The adrenal glands release large quantities of androgens (including testosterone), which is the sex hormone that appears to account for both men's and women's sex drive (LeVay, 1993).

Prolactin is a hormone that ensures lactation, and, together with oestrogen, this hormone also stimulates maternal behaviour. Prolactin is released in the pituitary gland, and female rats that have had their pituitary glands removed show no maternal behaviour until they have received a dose of prolactin. Prolactin affects the front part of the hypothalamus, and when prolactin is injected directly into this area, mice, for example, immediately begin to nest and display maternal behaviour (LeVay, 1993). Both dopamine and noradrenalin might stimulate the release of testosterone and stimulate the interest in sex (Fisher, 2004).

Testosterone has a powerful impact on many different neurochemical systems. Testosterone triggers the fight response in certain contexts and is associated with positive qualities such as strength, dominance, competitiveness, social assertiveness, and physical strength. Testosterone is associated with aggression, but not with the impulsive, destructive form of aggression. Men with high levels of testosterone are normally able to inhibit their aggressive impulses in a socially acceptable manner, probably due to the inhibitory function of serotonin. Testosterone increases muscle mass in adults; this is why some athletes abuse anabolic steroids, which contain testosterone among other substances (Panksepp, 1998; Taylor, 2002).

Stress suppresses the level of sex hormones in the bloodstream. For example, stress suppresses the production of oestrogen and inhibits reproduction. In the following section, I review the stress response hormones that, as one of their functions, have to support the regulation of the autonomic nervous system.

Stress hormones

Acute stress activates the sympathetic nervous system, partly through the release of noradrenalin and adrenalin. Raised levels of noradrenalin and adrenalin cause reactions in the form of irritability, arousal, and the startle response (Perry, 1994).

Acute stress also activates the release of three other hormones: ACTH, CRF, and cortisol (glucocorticoids). Cortisol is used, for example, in the synthetically manufactured cortisone gel that is used in acute cases of eczema, but which has a harmful and destructive effect on the immune system if used on a long-term basis.

Corticotropin-releasing factor (CRF) and adrenocorticotrophic hormone (ACTH)

CRF plays an important role in all forms of stress response and is an activating neurotransmitter that is synthesized in the hypothalamus, largely in the same location as the encephalins. ACTH (which is also known as corticotropin) is released from the hypothalamus and the pituitary gland. In negatively charged information the hypothalamus controls the release of ACTH from the anterior pituitary gland. When CRF and ACTH are emitted into the bloodstream, cortisol is released from the adrenal glands, which reduces investigative behaviour and causes defensive withdrawal. CRF activates the sympathetic nervous system, which is followed by an increase in heart rate and blood pressure and the inhibition of digestive functions. Negatively charged information increases the release of CRF, ACTH, and opioids from the pituitary gland and the hypothalamus. ACTH increases attention and motivation if the person is bored or exhausted. CRF increases arousal and may cause tearfulness (Uvnäs-Moberg, 1997a,b, 1998).

Tactile stimulation and experiences with caring primary caregivers cause permanent modifications of CRF levels. Rodent experiments have shown that extended separation from the mother during the first two weeks of a rat pup's life causes the pup to produce increased quantities of CRF and ACTH when exposed to stressful experiences later in life, compared with rats that had not been separated from their mother (Hofer, 1984).

CRF and opioids have a yin-yang function. In negative arousal, CRF activates a stress response, while the opioids induce anti-stress responses and calming. Opioids and CRF are only represented in specific subcortical brain regions and have limited representation in the neocortex (Panksepp, 1998).

Cortisol

In connection with a stress reaction, CRF is released instantly, the ACTH level takes about fifteen seconds to rise, while it takes several minutes before cortisol is released into the bloodstream. When a stressful event is over it takes hardly any time before the levels of CRF and ACTH are down again, while it may take an hour before the cortisol is out of the bloodstream. The function of cortisol is to extinguish reactions that were induced as part of the stress response, and in this sense it acts essentially as an anti-stress hormone. Cortisol does not induce the stress response; it is a hormone that ensures the overcoming of the stress response. Cortisol prepares the organism for the next stressful experience in addition to helping it overcome the present stressful state. Experiments with rodents at the bottom rung of their social hierarchy have shown that animals that attempt to address social challenges have low levels of cortisol and a highly activated sympathetic nervous system, while animals that appear to have given up trying to fight their way up the ladder have high levels of cortisol. Studies of depression in humans have shown that half the patients release large quantities of cortisol (Sapolsky, 1998). Cortisol reduces the levels of serotonin and noradrenalin, which disrupts the mood balance and disturbs the sense of wellbeing (Wilson, 1980).

Cortisol is produced in the adrenal cortex, and the concentration of cortisol in the bloodstream varies throughout the day. Cortisol is not only produced at times of stress. The basic level changes throughout the circadian cycle, and the cortisol level is highest in the morning and lowest in the evening. From an evolutionary point of view it would seem that the purpose of a high morning level is to motivate the organism to look for food and new experiences. The rhythm is managed by ACTH, which stimulates the cells in the adrenal cortex. Cortisol is conveyed via the bloodstream to certain organs and eventually reaches the saliva glands; hence, the level of cortisol can be measured through the secretion of saliva.

Cortisol, the hypothalamus, and the pituitary gland

The hypothalamus and the pituitary gland react to diminishing cortisol concentration by releasing CRF and ACTH. Any form of stress, for example a fever, pain, psychological stress, etc., will lead to an increased release of cortisol, which strengthens the ability of the organism to neutralize harmful effects and return to normal conditions. In the long term, however, a chronically raised cortisol level inhibits the immune response and reduces the body's resistance to infection. Cortisol gives the body a boost of energy to recover after stressful situations, but raised levels over extended periods of time increase the likelihood of stomach ulcers, cardiovascular diseases, and other harmful conditions. Emotionally, chronically raised cortisol levels cause attention disorders, problems with short-term memory, and difficulty with self-regulation because cortisol maintains the organism in a state of sympathetic activation, comparable with the symptoms of long-term and chronic stress (Andresen & Tuxen, 1977–1980; Hansen, 2002; Kalin, 1999).

Cortisol and the hippocampus

The hippocampus is highly sensitive to cortisol and has more cortisol receptors than any other brain region. The hippocampus probably has to be sensitive to stressful experiences in order to recall previous experiences in the face of danger. A high level of cortisol in the hippocampus facilitates neural activation, but when the level of cortisol remains high for more than thirty minutes, the uptake of glucose in the hippocampus begins to be impaired, about twenty-five per cent less glucose is metabolized, and the energy supply to the hippocampus is reduced. If the stress level is maintained for a longer period of time, the cortisol begins to destroy neurons, and memory problems begin to occur. Experiments with rats have shown that after a few weeks of chronic stress, which exposed the rats to excessive quantities of cortisol, the neurons in the hippocampus begin to shrink and die (atrophy). Fortunately, it appears that the neurons are able to rebuild their connections once the stressful period is over.

As mentioned in the section on stem cell research (Chapter Four), the hippocampus is one of the areas capable of reproducing neurons. The production of stem cells is induced with all new learning, but is reduced when the organism is under stress. Possibly, cell death can cause the hippocampus to shrink as a result of chronically raised cortisol levels. Depression is often associated with raised cortisol levels, a diminished hippocampus, and memory problems. Similarly, prefrontal areas have many cortisol receptors, which are affected when the level of cortisol is chronically raised; this may explain the cognitive changes seen in connection with depression and other disorders. The level of cortisol is raised in connection with many psychiatric disorders, and raised levels increase the intensity of anxiety reactions (LeDoux, 1998, 2001).

Cortisol and attachment

Studies of rodents have shown that early experiences can alter the balance of cortisol levels permanently, and that these animals will over-react to stress responses for the rest of their life. Early stress experiences have probably led to damage in particular areas of the hippocampus, which makes the hippocampus less efficient when a special effort is required (LeDoux, 2001; Panksepp, 1998; Scaer, 2001; van der Kolk & McFarlane, 1996). When rat pups are separated from their mothers they are exposed to separation stress; this raises the cortisol level, which drops back down when the pups are reunited with their mothers. Dopamine is activated by positive stimuli and inhibits cortisol receptors. Children with an insecure attachment to their care-givers have a chronically raised level of cortisol, which probably reflects the child's lack of positive stimuli and inadequate adaptive strategies. Thus, there is a connection between cortisol and social skills. Children who have a secure attachment to their caregivers have raised cortisol levels in stressful situations but use approachment strategies in those situations; in the long term this makes them more competent. When the child experiences a high degree of control in a challenging or stressful situation, the event is not always experienced as stressful. It is the experience or perception of stress that determines the stress level and thus the amount of cortisol released. Coping strategies or a sense of control reduces the experiences of stress and therefore quickly brings the cortisol level back to normal (Gunnar & Barr, 1998; Gunnar et al., 1989; Schore, 2003a). Socially isolated individuals usually have few coping strategies for engaging in social relationships, and they are often found to have raised cortisol levels and a highly active sympathetic nervous system. Social support seems to offer protection not just for humans but for all mammals (Sapolsky, 1998).

Children with a reactive temperament who have difficulty with self-regulating have also been found to have raised levels of cortisol. A study of pre-school children found that children who are often rejected by other children have raised levels of cortisol. Another study, which involved forty-eight institutionalized Romanian orphans, showed that, apart from lacking care, these children had not established a circadian rhythm. Normally developed children have a raised level of cortisol in the morning and follow a circadian rhythm. The institutionalized Romanian orphans had low cortisol levels in the morning, and then the level rose slightly towards noon but dropped again during the afternoon and evening. The children who were adopted were re-tested two to three years after adoption. The re-test found that children who had been adopted before the age of four months had a normal cortisol profile, while the slightly older children had still not established a cortisol rhythm. The children with the highest cortisol levels were the ones who had lived under severely deprived circumstances during the first twenty months of their life (Gunnar, 2001; Gunnar & Cheatham, 2003).

The growth hormone GHRH (growth hormone-releasing hormone) and GH (growth hormone)

In deprived children we find not only an increase in cortisol but also often impaired growth, which may be at least partly due to an inhibition of the growth hormones that are normally released in response to environmental stimulation.

Growth hormone GH is produced in the anterior pituitary gland, and the release is controlled by the hypothalamus through GHRH. During infancy, the level of maternal care is crucial for the release of growth hormones and for the infant's sensitivity to their effect (Schore, 1994). In his study of rat pups, Myron Hofer (1984) found that growth hormones are stimulated when the rat pup is actively touched. If an infant rat pup is separated from its mother, there is an immediate drop in the level of growth hormone; if the pup is in contact with a sedated mother, the growth hormone level is also reduced. When the mother's licking is mimicked, the level goes back to normal. The same experiment was carried out with premature babies in a neonatal ward; the study showed that the infants' production of growth hormones rose drastically once the staff began to stimulate the babies through touch. They developed faster and were discharged almost a week earlier than the premature babies who had not received this stimulation. Several months later, the difference was still evident (Field et al., 1986).

Summary

The biochemical processes in the nervous system are tremendously complicated, and in this chapter I have attempted to make this "landscape" a little easier to grasp. I have chosen to focus on the main neurotransmitters, neuropeptides, and hormones in relation to affect regulation. Although the neurochemical systems are innate and biological in nature, they are dependent on, and susceptible to, the adequacy of environmental stimulation. In this area, too, nature and nurture are inseparably intertwined. The balance of neurochemical substances in the organism is a delicate matter, and imbalances during the foetal period or in early infancy are likely to have grave effects on our ability to achieve affect regulation. Neurotransmitters work through the structures and circuits of the brain. As I have mentioned earlier, the personality is shaped by the unique way in which the nervous system wires itself up in circuits. In the next chapter, we turn to some of the circuits that are activated by the neurochemicals in the brain and lead to emotions of joy, grief, anger, etc.

CHAPTER TEN

The affect-regulating system
of the brain

"There are hundreds of functionally specialized ... areas,
each containing tens of thousands of neuronal groups ...
These millions of neuronal groups are linked by a huge set
of convergent or divergent, reciprocally organized connections that make them all hang together in a single, tight
meshwork while they still maintain their local functional
specificity. The result is a three-dimensional tangle ... Any
perturbation in one part of the meshwork may be felt rapidly
everywhere else"

(Edelman & Tononi, 2000, p. 44)

E
motions arise in many interconnected brain systems with
specific properties. When mammals began to appreciate
social support, emotions became closely linked with various
forms of vocalization. The fear and rage systems developed as the
organism sought to cope with dangerous situations that posed a
threat to survival. Attachment feelings and separation pain developed as mammals developed a need for social support and when
the offspring began to be born without the ability to survive without the caring and support of the adult animals. A panic system

emerged to provide a sensitive emotional barometer that would engage the full attention of the care-givers. If the social contact was lost, the organism experienced a painful feeling of separation and the animal cried out in protest in an attempt to regain the vital contact and care (Panksepp, 1998).

Six-month-old babies begin to vocalize sad and angry sounds of protestation in order to get attention when they are abandoned; this is usually characterized as separation anxiety. Separation anxiety forms part of the basis for attachment theories. The separation cry is believed to spring from primitive pain mechanisms, and the panic circuit is one of the key forces in constructing attachment behaviour. When these circuits are activated, animals seek to reunite, which is the basis for their ability to care for each other. The sense of having a secure base triggers inquisitiveness and playful-ness in the child, which promotes the construction of social struc-tures, helps the child to acquire social skills, and produces pleasure. In humans, the play instinct is developed and modified by higher cognitive brain regions, while in lower mammals the play has the character of simple rough and tumble play. Separation pain mech-anisms, attachment, and affective exchanges appear to be essential conditions for laughter, and both play and laughter serve as social attachment functions.

One of the features that make the brain so immensely compli-cated is that there is no one brain centre that is in charge of any one function. Instead, functions are handled by brain circuits. As early as in the 1930s, Jackson argued that the organization of complex mental processes had to be understood through the notion of neural circuits—a line of thinking that was later followed up by Luria. Jackson believed that mental processes had to be organized in a system of concertedly working zones, each filling its role in a complex functional system that may be located in separate and often far-flung areas (Schore, 2003a). No psychological process can be explained on the basis of one particular brain region or circuit. All processes interact. For example, there is no centre in the brain for specific emotions that does not interact massively with other functions; there are, however, circuits that are crucial for speci-fic emotions (Panksepp, 1998). What makes every brain unique is not the size of the various centres or the number of neurons or synapses, but the different and unique ways in which the neurons are wired and connected; this is the source of every unique personality.

Many brain circuits have specialized functions, for example, language, vision, etc. Other circuits are diffuse and serve to modulate particular conditions, such as states of arousal, moods, and motivation. Approximately one third of all neural networks consist of these diffuse connections, which distribute neurotransmitters over large brain areas. The production and distribution of neurotransmitters, peptides, and hormones are affected by the current interaction between the organism and its environment. Innate circuits are related to the survival of the organism, and these circuits are constantly kept up to date on activities throughout the brain, also in the later developed areas (Damasio, 1994; Trevarthen, 1990). For example, locus coeruleus (see Figures 6.3 and 9.1) consists of only a few thousand neurons in the brainstem that send out a net of tiny fibres to the neocortex, the hippocampus, the basal ganglia, and the cerebellum, among others, thus influencing billions of synapses by altering their strength. The connections between the hypothalamus, the amygdala, the hippocampus, and the prefrontal structures are wired to activate each other. Neurons never operate in isolation but are always organized in clusters or circuits (Edelman & Tononi, 2000; LeDoux, 1993, Mesulam, 1985) (Figure 10.1).

Papez was the first to define an emotional neural circuit. He found that the cingulate gyrus, the hippocampus, and the hypothalamus were connected to the thalamus, and that this circuit was important for the control of emotional expressions. Today, this circuit is known to include parts of the prefrontal cortex, the basal ganglia, and the amygdala (Purves et al., 2001).

Any mental function is a result of a diversity of contributions from different brain regions with varying levels of complexity within the central nervous system. The location of a specific injury may be hard to determine, and Goldberg (2001) mentions a case concerning a patient whose brain damage was diagnosed as an injury in the reticular activation system, which had severed the connections to the frontal lobes. The reticular activation system increases arousal, and the injury led to disruptions of functions in the orbitofrontal cortex, among other places. Every night, the patient in question would lay out the same clothes for the

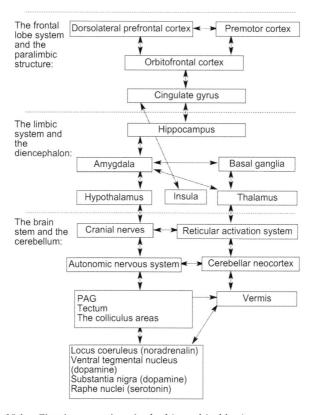

Figure 10.1.   Circuit connections in the hierarchical brain.

following day, regardless of the season: for example, he would wear his sheepskin jacket even on a sweltering July day. He spent most of the time in his apartment and liked to play simple card games with others. When he won he clapped his hands with joy, and when he lost he threw temper tantrums. He would cheat when he got the chance. His moods oscillated between euphoria and superficial rage. He would compete with his children for his wife's attention, and his way of thinking was astoundingly concrete. In this chapter, I shall discuss the main affect regulation circuits in the brain, with the limited knowledge we still have of this area, in order to give an impression of the contributions made by structures on different levels to various emotional categories or forms of cognition.

Pleasure and reward systems

Mike is twelve months old, and for a few months now he has been able to get around on his own, first by crawling, now by walking. He seems fascinated with everything he sees and often gazes up at his parents with a delighted look as he walks around. His pleasure is so contagious and intense that he often makes his mother and father laugh.

In 1954, James Olds and Peter Milner discovered that activating electrodes in the pathways that connect the brainstem and the limbic system in rat brains led to so much pleasure that the rats soon learned to trigger the stimulation themselves. When the rats were given a choice between food and self-stimulation, they would choose self-stimulation until several of them collapsed with exhaustion. It was later discovered that self-stimulation depends on the dopamine pathways that connect the ventral tegmental nucleus, the caudate nucleus, and the nucleus accumbens in the basal ganglia (Figure 10.2). This path consists of the so-called mesocortical dopamine system (Gade, 1997; Goldberg, 2001).

Pleasure creates expectations and directs behaviour towards positive rewards from the surroundings. All learning that is related to the activation of motivation, the pleasure of mastering a skill, and positive expectations is related to activity in the dopamine circuit. Pleasure and expectation are activated at an early stage in life and play a key role in brain development. For example, what drives the infant forward towards the next zone of development is the parents' pleasure and excitement when the child is on the verge

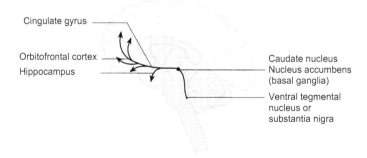

Figure 10.2.   The pleasure and reward circuit.

of reaching a new stage in developmental progress. The dopamine circuit induces investigative and inquisitive behaviour and promotes attachment functions; for example, the circuit is activated by the happy look on the care-giver's face. The dopamine system facilitates the establishment of social structures and helps the child to acquire social skills. When children play, their dopamine and opioid circuits are activated, and play helps mature the neocortex. The orbito-prefrontal cortex regulates excitement and other positive emotional states (Panksepp, 1998; Schore, 1994).

The purpose of natural rewards is to make the organism stop what it is doing and turn towards the reward. Rewards such as food, caresses, sexual activity, and novel stimuli are called primary inducers, while the stimuli that are related to the primary inducers through learning are called secondary inducers; for example, the expectation of ice cream upon hearing the jingle from the ice-cream van. The purpose of primary and secondary inducers is to maintain a goal for the given behaviour, and it is accompanied by a sense of pleasure. The dopamine circuit is only activated when the reward is unpredictable, and it marks an event as good in relation to expectations. It increases neuronal activation, thus creating a tendency towards persistent attention, which is probably the purpose of the dopamine system. There are close anatomical connections between the dopamine-based reward system, the basal ganglia, the amygdala, the hippocampus, the cingulate gyrus, and the orbitofrontal cortex, but the precise function of these connections is still somewhat unclear. Dopamine is energizing and co-ordinates functions within many higher brain regions. Through the connection of the dopamine circuit to the nucleus accumbens in the basal ganglia, the medial section of the amygdala, the hippocampus, and the orbitofrontal cortex, dopamine plays a key role for the way the organism selects actions in connection with primary and secondary inducers. Hippocampal activation makes it possible to control behaviour on the basis of spatial and directional dimensions in order to get at "the good stuff". For example, one needs to know where one is, where to go, and how to navigate in order to reach one's goal. The orbitofrontal cortex plays an important role for the production of secondary inducers, i.e., for the modification of the primary inducers, and it is therefore involved when external conditions change (Gade, 1997; LeDoux, 2001).

According to Panksepp (1998) the pleasure circuit is connected to play behaviour. The dopamine circuit lets people and animals act with regularity and efficiency in their daily routines, and this circuit seems to be the main source of the sense of involvement and excitement, both in relation to searching for material resources that our body needs for survival, and in relation to searching for the cognitive interests that provide positive existential meaning in our lives. The dopamine circuit organizes behaviour by activating or inhibiting motor routines. It is, in fact, bereft of cognitive content, but it helps to maintain the perception of causal connections concerning the world and it is involved in creating ideas and imagination. The dopamine circuits spark states of eagerness, and if the brain's dopamine circuit is destroyed, our desires and strives disappear. If the dopamine circuit is over-activated and isolated from other circuits, our sense of reality is violated, the circuit reacts independently of the inhibitory structures in the neocortex, and the organism seeks immediate gratification and creates unrealistic, arbitrary ideas about the way the world relates to internal events within the organism (Panksepp, 1998). For example, psychological disorders related to manic activity or compulsive gambling are probably related to an isolated and strengthened dopamine circuit.

Aggression systems

As Mike crawls on the living room floor, he sometimes grabs hold of things that he is not supposed to touch, for example, an electric plug, and which he is prepared to put in his mouth—something that his parents immediately intervene to prevent. This makes him furious; he cries, screams, and pushes his parents away and tries hard to get at the forbidden object.

In addressing aggression, we must distinguish between aggression, rage, and anger. By aggression, I mean a state where even small impulses may lead to violent acts directed at oneself or others. By anger, I mean a strong feeling of dissatisfaction, usually expressed in speech or action. Rage is an affect that combines anger and aggression. Aggression may arise without anger, and anger does not necessarily lead to aggression, particularly not in mature individuals who are able to control their basic impulses. Infants typically experience rage when they are frustrated; for example, if their freedom is restricted because they are being held, or if they fail to receive expected rewards. Reward systems left unsatisfied may spark the rage circuit (Figure 10.3).

In mammals, the aggression circuit may be activated by many different causes and display as fear-induced aggression, maternal aggression, irritation aggression, sex-related aggression, territorial aggression, hunting aggression, etc. The aggression circuit is connected to the amygdala and the hypothalamus and projects to the periaqueductal grey (PAG) in the brainstem (see also Figures 6.3 and 7.1). Affective rage is induced in the hypothalamus and activates the sympathetic nervous system, which in turn increases the anxiety capacity and suppresses parasympathetic activity.

So-called "cold-blooded" and "warm-blooded" forms of aggression are probably characterized by different circuitries. "Warm-blooded" aggression is induced by an activation of the amygdala and the medial part of the hypothalamus. Activation of the medial part of the hypothalamus activates the sympathetic nervous system. "Cold-blooded" aggression is activated in the most lateral part of the hypothalamus, which induces parasympathetic activation. The amygdala is probably closely connected to the medial part of the hypothalamus, while the instrumental aggressiveness that is triggered by the lateral part is less closely connected to the amygdala (Panksepp, 1998; Schore, 2001b).

In the amygdala, fear and rage are both clearly separate systems and intimately related. From an evolutionary point of view, it

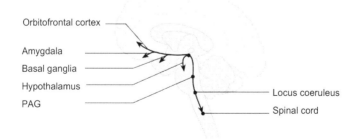

Figure 10.3.   The aggression circuit.

makes sense for fear and rage circuits to be intimately related, since one of the functions of anger is to provoke fear in the adversary, and one of the functions of fear is to reduce the effect of other individuals' anger. The function of the amygdala is to induce fight-or-flight actions or to engage the freeze response, both of which are response systems that activate either fear or defensive rage.

When the amygdala is activated, the release of dopamine is inhibited, and noradrenalin production is activated. This activates the sympathetic nervous system, causing alertness and preparing the fight-or-flight response. Frequent activation of the noradrenalin system results in chronic alertness, which disrupts sleep, appetite, and sexual activity (Bradley, 2000; Cozolino, 2000).

Human brains appear to be evolutionarily prepared to blame others for the emotions aroused, and the prefrontal cortex refines this aggressiveness. Damage to the orbitofrontal cortex causes insufficient impulse inhibition from the subcortical areas and leads to aggressive behaviour that ignores social rules. The orbitofrontal cortex exercises inhibitory control over the hypothalamic areas that trigger aggression and fear (Schore, 1994).

Fear and anxiety systems

> One day, as Mike and his dad are taking a walk, they suddenly see a large, barking German Shepherd dog running towards them. At first, Mike is startled, then he is afraid. He cries, becomes hysterical, and wants his dad to pick him up and keep him safe. Dad picks him up, and Mike hides his face against his father's chest. After this incident Mike reacts with anxiety every time he visits the parents' friends, who have a dog.

The distinction between fear and anxiety is normally said to be that fear has a visible, causative factor, while anxiety conditions are induced without any external trigger factors. For example, a person may be afraid of spiders but feel anxious without knowing why. Anxiety states are a reflection of the brain's fear system (LeDoux, 1998).

The fear and anxiety systems may be activated by external as well as internal events. Organic conditions such as heart problems or epileptic seizures are often related to a form of free-flowing anxiety, where the person is unaware what it is that he or she is afraid of. External stimuli that have posed a constant threat throughout our evolutionary history are also believed to act as unconditional triggers of the fear system. One example of this is separation anxiety. Specific individual fear phenomena are also learned or acquired through individual experiences that are assessed as being unsafe or dangerous. For example, the brain is predisposed to relate a frightened or angry facial expression with fear, and internal stimuli such as conscious or unconscious memory tracks from previous events may trigger the fear system (Figure 10.4).

The general fear system runs from the amygdala through the hypothalamus and PAG in the brainstem and continues down to the autonomous and behavioural components in the spinal cord, among other places, which control the physiological symptoms such as increased heart rate, raised blood pressure, the startle response, and respiratory functions. Neuronal nuclei in the amygdala decode the emotional patterns in facial expressions and pass on the information.

Some emotional reactions may be formed without any conscious or cognitive involvement. The evolutionary advantage of this must be that dangerous situations often do not leave any time to pause and consider. The construction of the emotional system means that we are affected emotionally before we engage in any explicit or conscious assessment of the stimulus that we are reacting to. The amygdala is connected to the hypothalamus and the basal ganglia,

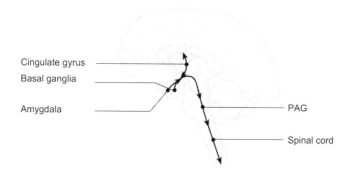

Figure 10.4.   The fear and anxiety circuit.

which enables the organism to activate actions very rapidly (Goleman, 1997; LeDoux, 1998, 2001; van der Kolk, 1996). This is a benefit in acute emergencies; if one is in an accident, for instance. For example, I was riding my bicycle when a passing car hit an object on the road that was deflected up and into the spokes of my bicycle. This sent me flying over the handlebars, and I managed to register that for a split second my consciousness was alert but "blank", i.e., without thoughts, visual impressions, body sensations, or emotions. Afterwards, I was startled but unharmed. I had broken my fall with my arms, so my face was unharmed, and I had curled up into a ball so that the softer parts of my body were protected. The survival benefits of this response pattern are substantial, because the close connection between the amygdala and the basal ganglia enables the organism to respond quickly to danger that requires immediate action.

The two amygdala circuits

LeDoux (1998) has pointed out that there are two connections that transfer information to the amygdala. One is a crude but fast and direct pathway that goes straight to the amygdala, and which is able to produce fear responses independent of the cortex. The other is a slower but more refined circuit that contains complete representations from the neocortical areas. The cruder circuit allows for rapid response independent of the neocortex and it has direct access to the medial part of the amygdala, which is connected to brainstem areas that activate autonomous responses. The crude circuit is capable of activating the fear system without any involvement of higher cortical processes: that is to say, without thinking, reasoning, etc. This circuit has a head start on the more refined circuit. In a rat brain, a crude signal takes about twelve milliseconds to reach the amygdala, while it takes about twice as long when the signal has to go through the neocortex. Even if the crude circuit cannot tell the amygdala exactly what is going on, it is able to trigger a rapid signal, a warning that something dangerous is happening. The amygdala has already induced a reaction, for example, a defence against an attacking tiger, before the cortex catches on. The connections that convey information from the cortex to the amygdala are much weaker than the connections that run in the opposite direction. This may explain why emotional information invades our mind so easily, while it is difficult to gain conscious control over our emotions (LeDoux, 1998).

Chronic anxiety states, panic attacks, etc., probably arise when subcortical networks are activated independently of higher cognitive functions and there is an imbalance between the crude and the refined circuits. Amygdala kindling (early external stimulation that has made the amygdala self-activating) may have a long-term effect and cause chronic anxiety conditions. For example, a child who has early experiences of frightening, incomprehensible, and uncontrollable arguments between adults may later react with anxiety when hearing others engaging in loud arguments. Stimulation of the amygdala, the hypothalamus, and the PAG trigger mechanical fear responses. Panic attacks occur, among other things, due to the activation of the suffocation alarm system in the brainstem, which is activated when the respiratory system fails to maintain a steady rhythmic pattern (Panksepp, 1998). When breathing resumes a rhythmic pattern the panic dissipates.

The fear that is activated in separation anxiety has specific pathways and is probably activated through the posterior part of the cingulate gyrus, ending, like the other fear circuits, in the PAG in the brainstem (see Figure 10.4). This system activates feelings of loneliness and grief and may also trigger a panic attack. Separation anxiety is closely linked to the attachment system, which is integrated with the pleasure circuit that is activated when we are together with attachment figures.

Systems that inhibit fear and aggression

One day Mike, now eighteen months old, takes a stranglehold on the family cat, and later that day the neighbour's dog sneaks into the family's garden while no one else is around. When Mike's mother sees what he is doing to the cat she shouts and runs towards him in a threatening manner. Mike is startled; he quickly lets go of the cat, runs away, and hides in some bushes. When the neighbour's dog comes into the garden Mike is startled, but he quickly realizes that there are no adults around to help him out of this situation. He stands very still, eyes to the ground, trying to avoid the dog's attention. When he sees his mother, he runs to her and begins to cry.

The dorsolateral prefrontal cortex, the orbitofrontal cortex, and the anterior cingulate gyrus are all connected. The anterior cingulate gyrus is involved in resolving motivational conflicts and is essential for our ability to overcome an emotional state such as fear, due to its key role in enabling us to act counter to innate or early acquired impulses. For example, a fear response that is activated in the amygdala soon monopolizes our consciousness unless the front portion of the cingulate gyrus manages to inhibit this impulse (LeDoux, 2001).

The orbitofrontal cortex also has powerful connections to the amygdala and brainstem areas capable of inhibiting and regulating fear responses (Figure 10.5). The prefrontal areas are able to inhibit the amygdala functions to such a degree that it becomes difficult to express fear and aggression at all. If the orbitofrontal cortex is damaged or immature, impulses from the amygdala are not inhibited, which makes it take considerably longer to extinguish fear conditioning. In the above example, Mike has access to self-regulation strategies that he can use when exposed to stimuli that make him scared or angry because he is able to inhibit his subcortical impulses. The maturation of the orbitofrontal cortex inhibits unconscious impulses induced by the amygdala (Davidson, Marshall, Tomarken, & Henriques, 2000; LeDoux, 2001).

Primary and secondary inducers

The connections between the amygdala and the orbitofrontal cortex are important structures in relation to assessment and

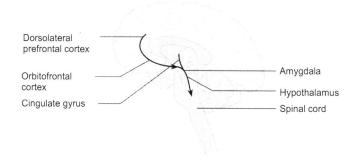

Figure 10.5.   The fear and aggression-inhibiting circuit.

decision-making. Both the amygdala and the orbitofrontal cortex link external sensory information with internal sensations and release somatic or emotional states, but they do this on different levels, thus contributing with different states in the process. Bechara, Damasio, and Damasio (2003) point out that somatic reactions can be triggered by the activation of both primary and secondary inducers.

The amygdala is an important structure for triggering primary inducers. It is activated both by innate unconditioned stimuli, for example, the startle response, and by acquired conditioned emotional stimuli, for example, a fear of dogs. The primary inducers are triggered via the amygdala's connections to the brainstem, PAG, and hypothalamus.

The orbitofrontal cortex triggers an emotional reaction on the basis of mental images of perceptions, called secondary inducers. Secondary inducers are activated by the recognition or recall of personal or hypothetical emotional events. For example, when a somatic condition is triggered on the basis of the recognition or recall of an emotional event, such as mental images of a snake or the loss of a large sum of money, secondary inducers are activated. Secondary inducers can only develop when the system of primary inducers is intact; an intact amygdala function is a prerequisite for the normal development of the orbitofrontal cortex and, hence, for the development of secondary inducers. When the orbitofrontal cortex is matured, it processes the activation of somatic states via secondary inducers, and the function of the orbitofrontal cortex is then less dependent on the amygdala.

The infant is dependent on appropriate amygdala function to be able to relate the observation of someone else's fear, sadness, or anger with a somatic state. This learning process is necessary for the development of the orbitofrontal cortex, which in turn enables the child to form mental images on the basis of body sensations and emotions. The organic maturation of the orbitofrontal cortex relies on the amygdala. When the circuitry connecting the amygdala and the orbitofrontal cortex is fully developed, the orbitofrontal cortex is apparently able to function relatively independently of the amygdala and interact with the hypothalamus and other structures. Understanding the notion of consequences in the form of punishment and reward requires co-operation between the hypothalamus, amygdala, and orbitofrontal cortex. This circuitry is crucial for the ability of mental images to activate somatic sensations, i.e., the body-based sense of fear, anger, shame, etc. When the orbitofrontal cortex is matured, this structure is able to inhibit anxiety impulses from the amygdala via secondary inducers. For example, when a primary inducer triggers a fearful reaction, this impulse may be inhibited by the recall of situations that suggest that the situation does not imply any real danger (Bechara, Damasio, & Damasio, 2003). Thus, one might imagine that before the maturation of the orbitofrontal cortex around the age of 8–12 months, the amygdala has a global influence on affective sensations through primary inducers while the maturation of the orbitofrontal cortex restricts the function of the amygdala, which turns the amygdala into a sort of "internal watchdog" that relates to fear stimuli.

Hyperactivation and deactivation of primary inducers

Threatening stimuli always activate the amygdala, and the amygdala response is inhibited by the orbitofrontal cortex. Damage to the orbitofrontal cortex makes it difficult to extinguish inappropriate behaviour and to recognize angry expressions. Perceptions of sad and fearful facial expressions activate structures within the amygdala, while the perception of angry facial expressions activates structures in the orbitofrontal cortex. Sad, fearful, and angry facial expressions all activate the anterior cingulate gyrus. Seeing a sad or fearful facial expression activates the amygdala, and this is associated with social discomfort. Seeing an angry facial expression activates the orbitofrontal cortex and encourages one to abandon one's current behaviour as quickly as possible (Blair, Morris, Frith, Perrett, & Dolan, 1999).

If the amygdala function is exposed to chronic over-stimulation, for example through massive neglect, the primary inducers are deactivated, and it is then only possible to relate to punishment and rewards on a higher mental level, without the activation of somatic reactions. This fosters a calculating and unfeeling behaviour because one is unable to "feel" one's own emotions or those of others on a sensory level. For example, a young seventeen-year-old male who had been raised in one of London's deprived neighbourhoods was arrested after a long series of thefts and because he had repeatedly threatened an elderly woman with a knife. He considered his actions lesser offences, and, when he was arrested, he demanded, in a provoking manner, to see the arresting officer's ID. On the day of his arraignment hearing, he expressed great frustration because he had to take a day off from his new job in a local supermarket. When he received his sentence and was placed in an institution for juvenile delinquents, he appeared confused, surprised, and hurt. When his lighter, keys, and knife were taken away from him, he cried (Gerhardt, 2004).

Aggression-inhibitory mechanism

Most social animals possess an aggression-inhibitory mechanism that makes the weaker animal submit to the stronger. Certain features help to end an aggressive attack; for example, an aggressive dog will stop its attack once the counterpart bares its neck. The evolutionary roots of the aggression-inhibitory mechanism probably have to do with controlling aggression, and sad facial expressions may act as a human submission response. Sad and angry facial expressions regulate social interactions. Sad facial expressions inhibit the counterpart's potential aggressive behaviour and induce prosocial behaviour (provided the amygdala function is intact), while an angry expression from the counterpart stops ongoing behaviour (provided the orbitofrontal cortex is intact) in situations where social rules or expectations are violated. The orbitofrontal cortex is able to end ongoing behaviour (Blair, Colledge, Murray, & Mitchell, 2001; Blair, Morris, Frith, Perrett, & Dolan, 1999).

As an aspect of the aggression-inhibitory system, all highly advanced herd predator animals have evolved to possess a biological mechanism that quickly socializes the young into the herd so that they can adapt and adjust to the other members. In humans this mechanism is defined as shame.

The shame system

Mike is still eighteen months old, and, in more and more incidents, he insists on having things his way, even when this is at odds with what his parents want. One day he has taken his mother's make-up purse and is smearing nail polish and lipstick on the table. Mike's mother is angry and frustrated and scolds him severely. Mike can tell from his mother's face that she is angry and upset, and he immediately stops what he is doing. He averts his eyes because it makes him uncomfortable to meet her gaze; he cries and runs away. Mike's mother finds him curled up and upset in his room. At first he wants nothing to do with her, but, after a while, he cautiously ventures out and wants to sit on her lap and be comforted.

The shame system is not active from birth but is activated as the child becomes more mobile and development makes it necessary to restrict the child's behaviour. This happens in connection with the maturation of the orbitofrontal cortex, and shame does not occur in humans below the age of twelve months or so.

The orbitofrontal cortex forms circuits with the dopamine-releasing areas in the brainstem, and, at the age of twelve months, the child's immediate sensations of pleasure and inquisitiveness reach a peak. The orbitofrontal cortex continues to develop, while the dorsolateral prefrontal cortex becomes more active. At this point, the prefrontal areas connect to brainstem areas that release noradrenalin. The noradrenalin-based circuit is the physiological basis for anxiety, and what inhibits anxiety is the connection between the amygdala and the orbitofrontal and dorsolateral prefrontal cortices. Stimulating the prefrontal noradrenalin inhibitory circuits results in behavioural calming (Figure 10.6).

Around the age of 12–14 months, when the orbitofrontal cortex and the dorsolateral cortex have developed sufficiently, the dopamine- and noradrenalin-based circuits will be in competition, and

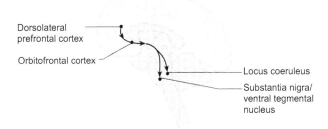

Figure 10.6. The shame circuit.

noradrenalin-based inhibition also affects the maturation of the prefrontal areas. From the age of 14–18 months, the two circuits begin to be able to carry out self-regulatory functions. The dopamine system is an expectation-based motivation system, while noradrenalin delays responses through its connections to the dorsolateral cortex. The dopamine circuit regulates positive emotions (reward behaviour), while the noradrenalin-based circuit regulates negative emotions (punishment behaviour). When both systems are activated at the same time, the result is a shame reaction. This reaction must be modulated through parental responses to prevent the child from getting stuck in the shame reaction, which the child perceives as humiliating and degrading (Schore, 1994, 2003a). Schore (1994) calls the ongoing development of the child's nervous system through shame regulation "narcissistic deflation affect". In the above example, Mike takes great pleasure in playing with his mother's make-up purse (dopamine activation). When his mother yells at him, the feeling of pleasure is disrupted immediately (noradrenalin activation). Mike is kept in an unpleasant state of conflicting emotions that make him both unhappy and angry. This mutual activation of dopamine and noradrenalin exerts a strong pressure on the nervous system, which Mike ought not to remain under for long. His mother's comforting actions balances the dopamine and noradrenalin circuits, and this helps Mike to learn strategies for self-calming and for abandoning pleasant behaviour. He also learns how friendships can be repaired.

Schore (2003b) suggests that the establishment of a superego structure is related to the inhibitory (noradrenalin-based) impulses, which are controlled by prefrontal limbic circuits.

The stress systems: sympathetic adrenomedullary (SAM) and hypothalamic–pituitary–adrenal (HPA)

When Mike is four years old, he and his family move to another part of the country and his maternal grandmother suddenly dies. Mike's mother is grieving, and Mike is left more to himself emotionally. He joins a new kindergarten, which is complicated since he is teased because he speaks with a different dialect. Mike develops sleep problems, he has frequent nightmares, he is easily irritated, and everything seems to cause him frustration. He hits the other children, and his pre-school teachers express great concern when they speak with his parents.

The ability of the nervous system to manage stress is crucial for its flexibility. A nervous system that has difficulty regulating high arousal levels is more prone to disintegration, and the person is more likely to wind up in situations where he or she is exposed to high levels of stress, which cause maladaptive behaviour.

The organism has two stress response systems, both related to sympathetic activation. One system is called the sympathetic adrenomedullary system (SAM), the other is the the hypothalamic–pituitary–adrenal system (HPA system).

Stimulation of the amygdala activates the sympathetic nervous system, which prepares the organism for actions that aim, among other things, at making the threat go away.

The SAM system is regulated by the stress hormone CRF, which, among other things, induces the release of noradrenalin and adren-alin, which in turn activates the sympathetic nervous system and makes energy more easily accessible to the vital organs. The SAM system is activated by the startle response, among other things; it responds quickly but does not stay active for long, and the organ-ism can return to normal without any release of cortisol. The SAM system activates faster than the HPA system. It is a simple system, the precursor of the far more complex HPA system, which we will look at in the following section (Schore, 2003a).

One has no doubt when one is startled, for example, and the SAM system engages. The HPA response, on the other hand, is less obvious. The HPA response is activated in connection with anxiety, apprehension, or a sense of impending danger. HPA activation inhibits body activities that are not essential for maintaining the body in a state of arousal and mental alertness (Taylor, 2002). The HPA system is activated by cortisol, which extinguishes sympa-thetic activation by inhibiting the release of CRF, mainly through receptors in the hippocampus and hypothalamus. Cortisol is only released several minutes or hours after the event and has a much longer-lasting effect on the organs; when stress becomes chronic, these effects have a negative impact on the organism. This is not an all-or-nothing system, and the more severe the stressor is perceived to be, the larger are the quantities of neurochemicals that are released (Figure 10.7).

When the amygdala registers danger, the information is passed on to the hypothalamus, which releases CRF and ACTH; this passes the information on to the pituitary gland, which responds by releasing additional ACTH. This hormone flows into the adrenal glands, which release cortisol. The cortisol binds to receptors in the hippocampus, amygdala, and prefrontal cortex, among other places. The hippocampal receptors form a control system that regulates adrenalin levels, among other things. When a sufficient number of receptors in the hippocampus have connected with cortisol, the hippocampus sends signals to the hypothalamus to stop the release of CRF. In this way, the hippocampus regulates the stress response that began in the amygdala. The connection between cortisol and the hippocampus is intensely complex, and both excessive and deficient quantities of cortisol are believed to be able to cause apoptosis in the hippocampus. Apoptosis is not a threat as long as the

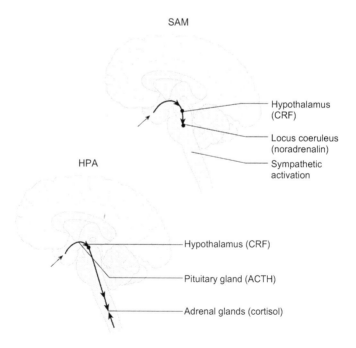

Figure 10.7.   SAM and HPA circuits.

reaction is not chronic, and it is probably an adaptive and reversible response serving to temporarily prevent synaptic hyperactivation. When the stress system is chronically activated, receptors are reduced through apoptosis in the hippocampus, which results in fewer cortisol receptors. With fewer receptors for the cortisol to bind to, the hippocampus has difficulty regulating the HPA system. The hippocampus is less able to "extinguish" a stress response, and even mild stressors may produce extended cortisol activation. In stressful situations, a flexible nervous system is able to balance itself with a rapid neurochemical response at the right time in order to avoid widespread disruption (LeDoux, 2001; Sapolsky, 1998; Schore, 2003a; Yehuda, 1997).

The protest and despair phases

When young animals are separated from their mother, they initiate intense vocalization, which helps the parents find their offspring again. After a while, the animal stops screaming and goes into a behaviourally inhibitory phase of despair, probably to preserve energy and prevent the helpless organism from being spotted by predators or leaving a safe place. The protest phase of the separation vocalization creates the conditions for the subsequent despair phase. These observations formed part of the basis for John Bowlby's attachment theory. During the protest phase, the CRF hormone is activated, and in the subsequent despair phase, the noradrenalin-based system is reduced, partly due to the release of cortisol. Both deficient and excessive levels of activity in the HPA system can be harmful to the organism. Ideally, the level of cortisol should stay within normal levels and be self-regulatory. In some forms of depression and post traumatic stress disorder the HPA system is dysregulated (Panksepp, 1998; Sapolsky, 1998). Half of all depressed adults have chronically raised levels of cortisol, and dysfunction of the orbitofrontal cortex might cause dysregulation of the HPA system because the reparative functions in connection with self-comforting, for example, are insufficient. In an unstable nervous system with a dysfunctional orbitofrontal cortex, even slight stressors can easily lead to intensely stressful states, perceived as sudden shifts from a positive to a negative affective state (Schore, 1994; 2001b).

Newborn rat pups that are separated from their mother for extended periods of time are more timid and have a higher and more enduring HPA response to stressors than rat pups that were only separated from their mothers for brief periods of time. In rat pups that were only briefly separated from their mother, cortisol levels return to normal more rapidly than in rat pups that were never separated from their mother. In nature, parents often have to abandon their offspring for brief periods of time in order to find food. These brief absences appear to organize and enhance maternal behaviour, and the mother licks the pups more. The brief absences make the nervous system more resilient in relation to stress management.

Developing stress tolerance

Anatomical and molecular studies of rat pups show that when the mothers lick and nurse their pups, these two actions regulate the activity of the HPA system independently of each other. The regulatory effect is established within the first few days of life and continues throughout the nursing period. The licking behaviour and the nursing regulate the nervous system and develop additional cortisol receptors, capable of inhibiting the release of stress hormones, which lets the rat pups recover more quickly from stressful states. Thus, qualitative differences in early mother–infant interactions may have a long-term effect on the HPA response, also in relation to stress management in adults (Hofer & Sullivan, 2001).

There is considerable evidence that the critical period for balancing the cortisol level in humans coincides with the development of attachment behaviour when the infant is 6–12 months old. Sensitive and accommodating caring seem to act as a "buffer" for hyperactivation of the HPA system, but it is still unclear whether an early activation of the HPA system has any long-term effect in humans. Infants are probably able to organize and reorganize their HPA system, provided the caring deficiencies were relatively mild, while there is considerable evidence to suggest that intense and chronic neglect does have a long-term effect on the nervous system and, thus, more severe ramifications. The longer a child has been exposed to severe neglect, the less able the HPA system is to return to normal levels, even when the setting is changed (Gunnar & Cheatham, 2003).

Severe chronic negative influences, as for children exposed to early emotional damage in the form of abuse, neglect, and deprivation, activate the HPA systems and increase the production of cortisol. Chronically raised cortisol levels are particularly harmful to a developing nervous system, and gradually, as a physiological protection mechanism or as a sign of psychological habituation, the nervous system reacts by reducing the production of cortisol. The sympathetic nervous system increases the production of noradrenalin, and a state of hyperarousal occurs, which involves anxiety, irritation, aggression, and a low stress tolerance with reduced impulse control. The parasympathetic system responds by increasing opioid levels; this has a soothing effect but may result in dissociation phenomena (Gjærum & Ellertsen, 2002). As mentioned in Chapter Six, the parasympathetic and sympathetic systems regulate reciprocally, but chronic and long-term increase in cortisol may disrupt the balance between parasympathetic and sympathetic activation, and even a slight stressor may cause simultaneous activation of the two systems, which is probably characteristic of sociopathic behaviour. Sociopaths respond quickly to irritation, for example, when they cannot have things their way, or when they are addressed in ways that they find inappropriate. This activates impulsive aggressive behaviour characterized by extreme vengefulness that is out of order with the actual gravity of the incident and completely lacking in acknowledgement of, or sympathy with, the person who is the target of this behaviour.

Affect-motor systems

When Mike is five years old, he begins to develop twitches and make clicking sounds, and he constantly wants to wash his hands. He feels that his fingers are dirty, and he is worried about germs. The parents realize that Mike still feels under pressure in kindergarten, and he receives psychological support to overcome his symptoms. He receives emotional support and help with verbalizing difficult feelings and experiences. He also learns techniques that give him volitional control over his symptoms when they emerge, and his parents manage to resolve the problems that have put him under pressure in the kinder-garten for a long time.

Emotions and motor behaviour are closely intertwined, and sensory impressions, perception, affects, and motor functions are inseparable. In 1893, William James said,

> what kind of an emotion of fear would be left if the feeling neither of quickened heart-beats nor of shallow breathing, neither of trem-bling lips nor of weakened limbs, neither of goose-flesh nor of visceral stirrings, were present, it is quite impossible for me to think . . . I say that for us emotion dissociated from all bodily feeling is inconceivable. [James, 1878–1899, pp. 355–356]

Different circuits connect volitional and non-volitional actions. In this context, we distinguish between the extrapyramidal circuit, which is the non-volitional system, and the pyramidal system, which is a volitional system (Hansen 2002; Purves et al., 2001). The non-volitional extrapyramidal system consists mainly of connec-tions between brainstem structures and the basal ganglia. The voli-tional pyramidal system consists of some one million axons running from the motor regions in the neocortex to the basal ganglia, among other structures, through a wide bundle of path-ways (the internal capsule) (Figure 10.8). About two thirds of the motor cortex is devoted to controlling muscle groups that operate fingers and facial expressions. It takes an intact pyramidal pathway system to carry out volitional fine motor movements such as acquired finger movements and facial expressions.

Studies concerning facial expressions have shown that a forced smile produced through the volitional control of facial muscles acti-vates a different set of neural circuits than a spontaneous emotional smile. The volitional motor circuit consists of a pyramidal pathway projecting from the premotor cortex in the frontal lobes, which allows detailed volitional control of facial muscles. In the extrapyra-midal system, the basal ganglia play a key role, and this system involves emotional aspects that are outside volitional control. The spontaneous smile connects in circuits with the basal ganglia, limbic structures, and the brainstem, which controls the facial muscles through the cranial nerves. Emotional and motivational

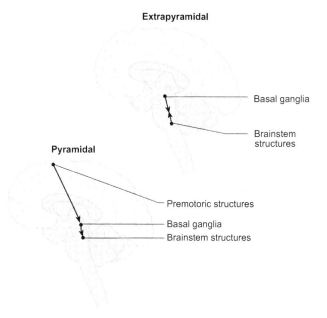

Figure 10.8.   The extrapyramidal and pyramidal circuits.

processes that are controlled by the limbic system take place through facial motor expressions that are outside volitional control (Hansen, 2002; Purves et al., 2001).

The basal ganglia co-ordinate motor behaviour with motivation, emotion, and cognition, and plan movements. The amygdala has access to non-volitional motor behaviour and may initiate the motor system without any influence from the prefrontal cortex. An area in the basal ganglia called the striatum controls automatic, non-volitional movements and thinking and receives input from the prefrontal cortex and from limbic structures. It is connected to the motor cortex, and hyperactivation of this pathway is likely to be associated with behavioural hyperactivity, involuntary movements, attention disorders, and physical outbursts, as seen, for example, in Tourette's syndrome. The amygdala and basal ganglia are closely connected, and there is reason to assume that involuntary movements and outbursts, hyperactivity, and compulsive ideas may be related to anxiety and anger, since amygdala activation in connection with anxiety and fear reactions causes the basal ganglia to induce motor activity through the non-volitional (extrapyramidal) and unconscious system. The dopamine circuit induces inquisitive behaviour and maintains attention focus. It activates the basal ganglia, which in turn activate the prefrontal cortex. The circuitry connecting the basal ganglia and the prefrontal cortex is believed to be essential for maintaining attention focus, and dopamine deficiency is believed to be a factor in attention disorders (Carter, 1998; Tucker & Derryberry, 1992).

Executive systems

At eight years of age, Mike has left his difficulties behind him. He is able to maintain attention and is praised for his ability to plan and strategize and for being considerate of others. He is well liked for his ability to help resolve conflicts, and he is always a source of good ideas when he plays with others. He is good at balancing the fulfilment of the other children's wishes and the fulfilment of his own, and he is considered a smart and resourceful boy.

Executive functions (planning, judgement, flexibility, goal attainment, etc.) are distributed over a number of areas in the prefrontal cortex and are mainly controlled by the dorsolateral prefrontal cortex. The dorsolateral prefrontal cortex is connected to the orbitofrontal cortex, the parietal lobes, and the frontal cingulate gyrus in an integrated system, which is an important part of a volitional network that makes executive functions possible. It is involved in selective attention, and it allocates mental resources, is involved in decision-making and volitional control of movements, and resolves conflicts between competing stimuli (LeDoux, 2001) (Figure 10.9).

The areas in charge of executive control are the last areas in the human brain to mature. They form a circuit characterized by a high degree of plasticity, which has development potential throughout the lifespan and the potential for developing wisdom. Executive networks combine sensory, motor, and emotional information and form plans, actions, thoughts, and fantasies. They enable us to work towards the integration of neural networks based on volitional control. The executive brain is only involved in more basic functions when the incoming stimuli are novel, or when a problem arises (Cozolino, 2000).

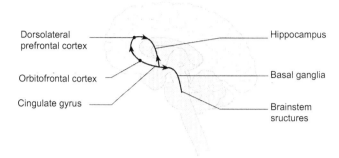

Dorsolateral prefrontal cortex

Hippocampus

Orbitofrontal cortex

Basal ganglia

Cingulate gyrus

Brainstem sructures

Figure 10.9.   The executive circuit.

The prefrontal cortex adapts thinking and behaviour to match the current reality by structuring and reflecting, and it balances internal needs with external reality through control and affect-inhibition. The prefrontal cortex is connected to the dopamine-producing areas in the brainstem and to the motivation and reward systems in the basal ganglia. In the prefrontal cortex, dopamine-based circuits are activated to encourage inquisitiveness and pleasure-filled behaviour, while noradrenalin-based circuits inhibit this activity. The opposite mechanism between pleasure-filled excitement and inhibition helps create a rapid regulation of arousal levels. The balance between dopamine- and noradrenalin-based impulses in the prefrontal cortex maintains the attention function (Schore, 2003a,b).

The connections of the orbitofrontal cortex to the motor systems organize actions, its connections to the limbic structures imbue mental representations with emotional value, and its connection to the brainstem modulates the level of activity. The overall control that the orbitofrontal cortex exercises over the sympathetic and parasympathetic branches of the autonomic nervous system determines the inhibitory or excitatory autonomic balance in the prefrontal system that regulates emotional responses, and which makes adaptation possible. Functions in the orbitofrontal cortex enable the organism to regulate and adapt responses to internal body states in relation to changes in the external environment. This circuit between the prefrontal cortex and the limbic system is specialized for processing the social intentions of others and self-regulating accordingly. The integration of this vast neural hierarchical circuit, managed by the highest hierarchical levels of the brain, enables efficient executive functioning (Schore, 2003a; Tucker & Derryberry, 1992).

Attention disorders are often discussed as a homogeneous issue. But attention disorders may spring from any level in the hierarchical brain. Luria (1973) distinguished between two attention systems: a reflex-based system that developed early, and that lay outside volitional control, and a later emerging, volitional system. The orbitofrontal cortex represents pre-consciousness and controls or inhibits impulses and attention that are outside volitional control, while the dorsolateral prefrontal cortex is a conscious and volitional system, capable of devising plans and strategies (Smith, 2001). In all likelihood, there are many levels of attention control at brainstem, limbic, and prefrontal levels. For example, deficient regulation of the autonomic nervous system on brainstem level may cause diffuse attention disorders, where the nervous system has trouble with basic affect regulation and with focusing, while amygdala activation on a limbic level may cause a more tension-filled condition because the organism concentrates on fear stimuli. Attention disorders on a prefrontal cortical level make it difficult to inhibit impulses stemming from the subcortical structures, and it may be difficult to maintain concentration for long, for example if one is reading something boring.

Cognitive systems

Among other things, cognition consists of making selections from a wealth of sensory information, which certain neural structures must process for meaning and relevance. Perceptions of sensory information are processed and analysed in the association areas. The cognitive systems are hard to describe and consist of complex functions that draw on many different brain structures. The cognitive functions include our ability to think, interpret, and analyse the world, and they make thoughts and emotions unique to every single person. Cognitive phenomena can be divided into various categories.

Newberg, d'Aquili, and Rause (2002) divide cognition into seven different functions, which usually operate in complex harmony: the *holistic function* enables the organism to view the world as a whole and is probably based on activity in the parietal areas of the right hemisphere. The *reductionist function* is based in the analytical left brain hemisphere and lets the organism view the whole divided into its single parts. The *abstract function* probably arises in the parietal lobes in the left brain hemisphere and enables the formation of general concepts, such as the ability to recognize a German Shepherd or a dachshund based on a single conceptual category. The *abstraction function* enables the brain to discover connections between two separate facts. The *quantitative function* includes our grasp of mathematics and contains more basic survival functions such as the assessment of time and distance, the numerical sense, and the ability to arrange objects or sequences in numerical order. The *cause-and-effect function* enables the brain to interpret a fact based on sequences of cause and effect. The *two-sided function* organizes reality by making it possible to reduce even the most complicated relations to simple elements. For example, persons with severe damage to the deepest-lying areas of the parietal lobes lose their ability to name the opposite of an object or a word. The *existential function* offers a sense of existence or reality. This function is probably linked to the sensory association areas and the limbic system, since sensations and emotions are an important part of the sense that experiences are real.

Summary

The brain can be divided into a large number of different circuits, and in this chapter I have only included integrative circuits that are essential for the understanding of our emotions, i.e., systems related to pleasure, aggression, fear, affect-inhibitory mechanisms, affective motor systems, executive functions, and various forms of cognition. Research into the neural networks of the brain is still in its early stages, and we must presume that coming years will provide important new insights into the various affective circuits. Hence, this chapter is only an introduction to an area that will probably continue to develop in the years to come.

Neurotransmitters and hormones are essential for brain functions, and in the next chapter I describe the influence of sex hormones on various brain structures. We will also look at the foundation of sexual identity, which is laid at an early stage in the foetal period and later interacts closely with the environment.

CHAPTER ELEVEN

Girls, boys, men, and women: the impact of sex hormones and environment on differences between the sexes

"One might speculate that the contribution of genetic influences, relative levels of estrogen and testosterone, or differences in interaction with the maternal caregiver based on gender expectations from the moment of birth could contribute to gender specific vulnerability"

(Scaer, 2001, p. 91)

For many thousands of years, people lived in relatively small hunter-gatherer societies, where the division of tasks between the sexes was clear, as, in fact, it continues to be in most modern societies. The men hunted the big game, which often required them to travel long distances, and they were responsible for defending the group against predators and enemies. Usually, the men produced the weapons. The women probably gathered food close to the dwelling, prepared the food, took care of clothing, and cared for the children. This specialization placed different evolutionary pressures on men and women. Men had to be able to navigate over long distances and tell different routes apart. They needed target-shooting skills for killing their prey. Women had to be able to navigate short distances and needed fine motor skills. They had to be able to direct their attention towards many things at the same time (multi-tasking) and had to master emotional communication and verbalization with their babies (Kimura, 1999a).

The sex differences have evolved along with the brain structures. People are born with a set of sex-specific, biopsychological conditions that have to be fitted into human culture. Sex characteristics play out in close interaction between heredity and environment, and for sex characteristics, as for many other human aspects, a person's innate sex-specific potential can only really unfold through culture (Michael & Zumpe, 1998) (Figure 11.1).

Typically masculine and feminine features hold different advantages. The typically masculine features offer advantages in the form of systems thinking and the ability to produce and use tools. Systems thinking lets the person quickly construct a mental map of an area, and, in the social arena, the masculine systems thinking brain lets the person attain, maintain, and improve a social position through hierarchies of power. The typically feminine brain offers other advantages, including empathy. Empathy provides the basis for good communication skills and awareness of other people's feelings. Good empathy skills make it far easier to be aware of a child's needs and feelings and to understand what goes on in a child's mind (Baron-Cohen, 2003).

Sex hormones play an important role in regulating neural structures and their function. We still only have limited knowledge about the neurobiological basis for sex differences and about the impact of environmental interactions on sexually specific behaviour. Sexual

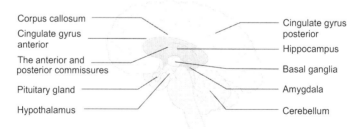

Figure 11.1.   Brain structures which have an importance for sexual organization.

identity and masculine/feminine self-esteem are strongly influenced by early interactions with care-givers, and it is only during the past ten years that we have begun to gain greater insight into the role of sex hormones.

There is much disagreement about sexually specific anatomical differences in the brain, except for the hypothalamus, which shows a distinct differentiation. Several writers, among them Cameron (2001), have pointed out that mammals have minor sex differences in brain structure in the hypothalamus, amygdala, hippocampus, basal ganglia, cerebellum, and various areas of the prefrontal cortex, and that there is a structural asymmetry in the corpus callosum and anterior commissures (see Figure 11.1).

There are indications that early childhood conditions may have a modulating effect on sex differences in brain structures (Cameron, 2001), but we are still far from a full understanding of sex differences, and many research findings are mutually contradictory. In this chapter, I describe some of the best known findings and discuss the connection between genetically determined sex differences and the impact of the environment, both during the foetal period and later in life. In order to shed light on the connection between hereditary and environmental factors, I first describe the sexual specialization that takes place during the foetal stage and the ways in which the X and Y chromosomes manifest their influence.

Sex selection during the foetal period

Our basic psychosexual development is genetically determined, and physical differences in male and female anatomy are usually apparent from birth. The most obvious anatomical distinction is the development of the genitalia, which are related to sexual reproduction, and to differences in instinctive behaviour. As mentioned previously, the genes contain twenty-three pairs of chromosomes, and males and females have twenty-two pairs in common. Therefore, males and females have far more similarities than differences. The female genome consists of two X chromosomes, while the male genome consists of an X and a Y chromosome. This leads to the development of, respectively, male and female gonads, which determine the production of oestrogens and androgens (Solms & Turnbull 2002; Trevarthen, 1990).

Early foetal development leads to the production of the early stages of gonads. The foetal organs that produce gametes are called gonads, and these are identical in boys and girls until the sixth foetal week, at which time the Y chromosome is activated. The activation of the Y chromosome induces the production of a protein called TDF (testis-determining factor), which in turn induces the production of testosterone. TDF affects genetic transcription, which means that an organ that would otherwise have become an ovary instead develops into a testicle. The presence of testosterone creates the basis for the male body, but oestrogen is important for a fully developed male phenotype. At an early foetal stage, the production of androgens (male sex hormones), including testosterone, leads to the development of biological sex differences. In the absence of testosterone the foetus becomes a girl, so, until the sixth foetal week, any foetus is, in principle, a girl. Boys develop testicles, and this causes the production of large quantities of testosterone, which in turn activates a large number of testosterone receptors, but women also have testosterone receptors.

Foetuses with XX chromosomes produce no TDF and hence hardly any testosterone. The neutral gametes create the basis for the ovaries. Thus, the development of the female phenotype depends on the absence of androgens in early development and the presence of oestrogens. It would be wrong to think of oestrogens as female and androgens as male, since both males and females synthesize both oestrogens and androgens, and in both sexes oestrogens are the effective trigger. Sexual identity is determined by the neural receptors that are available to bind oestrogens and androgens when they go into circulation. The brain has receptors for all sexually specific hormones, but females and males have different distributions of receptor types. For example, there are many more oestrogen receptors in the female hypothalamus than in the male (Purves et al., 2001).

Children with two X chromosomes, who are genetically girls, may develop masculine features due to an innate imbalance in the production of sex hormones, which causes them to store large quantities of androgens. The external male features may change as the result of early hormone treatment, so that the girls have a

normal sexual development, but the effects of the hormones in relation to their sexual identity is not going to change. The foetal stage
is critical for the distribution of androgens and oestrogens. Girls
who are treated for this hormonal imbalance later tend to be boyish
in their choice of games, and they do better in tasks that require
spatial perception skills (Tetzchner, 2002). Experiments with rats
have shown that exposure to testosterone at an early foetal stage
increases the likelihood of the development of masculine sexual
behaviour. There is some evidence that the exposure to sex
hormones at an early stage in brain development may have a lasting organizing effect on neural activity and the behaviour of the
central nervous system throughout the lifespan (Cameron, 2001;
Tetzchner, 2002).

Maternal stress and demasculinization

In animals, exposure to stress during pregnancy prevents the
normal masculinization of the brain. If testosterone is released too
early, before the receptors are prepared to receive the message,
normal masculine development is hampered. The activation of
sexually specific hormones is determined by complex chemical processes that are susceptible to environmental manipulation. In 1980,
Ward and Weisz found that male rats born to mothers under stress
became demasculinized. The exposure to stress did not have to be
particularly long-term or particularly severe. A stressful period
during the last part of pregnancy was found to have the greatest
effect. Their research also showed that when the female offspring of
these stressed mothers reproduced as adults, they too would have
demasculinized offspring, even though they themselves had not
been exposed to stress during pregnancy. Pregnant rats who
received sedatives had male foetuses with chronically low levels of
testosterone, which led to demasculinized and typically feminine
sexual behaviour. If pregnant rats are exposed to stress, for example by living in overcrowded cages or being exposed to unpredictable electric shocks, twelve per cent of the male rats display
feminine sexual behaviour from birth (Geschwind & Galaburda,
1987; LeVay, 1993; Solms & Turnbull, 2002). Thus, the production of
sex hormones during the foetal period has a significant impact on
the development of sexual identity.

The development of sexual characteristics in infancy

The sex-specific organization of the brain is also influenced by the infant's environment after birth, as the activity of sex hormones interacts with the infant's environment, and the genome encounters the environment through interactive experiences that set off hormone secretion. Primate studies have shown that the development of sexual organs is a separate issue from the development of sex-specific behaviour. Genome and environment interact through experiences after birth, and the infant's sexual identity is established during the first two years of life. Neural sex differences depend on the early childhood environment, and affective stimulation permanently shapes the psychological sex (Goy, Bercovitch, & McBriar, 1988; Schore, 1994).

The maturation of brain circuits after birth is affected by the level of sex hormones in infancy, which produces a permanent sex difference in brain structures and functions. The genetic differences between males and females are minimal, but the psychological effects of these tiny differences are multiplied throughout development. Children with an innate temperament that makes them active and extrovert encounter a different response than children who are calm and passive. Girls and boys often evoke different types of response from their care-givers and other primary relationships due to typically girlish or boyish behaviour. Additionally, adults' expectations and derived responses are affected by their presumptions concerning the infant's sex, for example, based on the colour of the child's clothes. The different reactions serve to further differentiate the original behaviour. Even though innate differences are minimal, they soon become self-increasing (Solms & Turnbull, 2002).

As previously mentioned, one standard method for determining the influence of innate factors is to record a particular behaviour in monozygotic twins who have been raised separately. Studies showed a concordance of around fifty per cent (the same as for schizophrenia) among male homosexuals and thirty per cent among female homosexuals, while the frequency in the general population is around ten per cent or less (LeVay, 1993; Solms & Turnbull, 2002). Thus, if one monozygotic twin is homosexual, the likelihood that the other twin also develops homosexuality is far greater than the random factor in the general population, but we still do not know how much should be attributed to foetal influences, and how much should be chalked up to heredity.

Tiny differences in relevant brain structures during the foetal period trigger significant differences in sexual identity and behaviour. Differences in hormone secretion make difference; for example, low levels of circulating androgens in infant boys can lead to a relatively feminine brain, while high levels of circulating androgens in infant girls can lead to a relatively masculine brain in terms of genotype. The environment has substantial impact on the development of the phenotype, which has been shown, for example, in studies of children born as hermaphrodites, but at the same time there is no doubt that sex hormones have an effect on neurological organization at the foetal stage that affects behaviour. Animal studies have provided considerable evidence of the environmental impact on sexual identity and behaviour, both at the foetal stage and during the first years of life.

During the first two years of life, sex hormones influence the number of dopamine receptors, and dopamine is also involved in activating the sex hormones. Dopamine secretion is activated through pleasant interactions between care-giver and child, which in turn affect the activation of sex hormones. Oestrogen increases the sensitivity of certain dopamine receptors and creates a sexual difference in the amount of dopamine released, which leads to the creation of feminine or masculine dopamine-based circuits (Schore, 1994). Perhaps the lack of pleasant interactions early in life may explain why children who have suffered massive early neglect sometimes have difficulty with their sexual identity development.

We distinguish between genital sexual development and the development of sexual identity. Sexual identity refers to the sense of identifying with one's sex. At certain developmental stages the production of sex hormones rises dramatically. During these activation periods, the brain has the highest sensitivity to hormonal changes. Around the fourteenth foetal week, the testosterone level in the male foetus is the same as in an adult man. Later in pregnancy the level drops; it rises again just before birth, then drops after a while and stays low until pre-puberty. The critical period for sexual differentiation is from around the sixth week of pregnancy until the child is about eighteen months old. At this time there are many circulating sex hormones, which organize and have permanent effects on feminization and masculinization. If the same hormones are introduced at later developmental stages they fail to have any effect (Geschwind & Galaburda, 1987; Hines, 1982; LeVay, 1993).

Exposing boys to testosterone before and immediately after birth leads to a masculinization of certain types of brain tissue and a defeminization of other types, because sexually specific tissue types have different critical periods. In primates and humans the sexual differentiation takes place over an extended period of time before and after birth (Cameron, 2001). The amount of circulating oestrogen and androgen both prior to birth and during the first eighteen months of infancy, when the orbitofrontal cortex develops, has an irreversible effect on the sexual specialization of brain structures.

Sexual identity formation

While the sexual identity begins to develop at an early stage in the foetal period, the sensory system that causes sensitivity in the sexual organs does not develop until the age of eighteen months. At this time, children begin to enjoy stimulating themselves sexually. It is also at this time that children begin to be interested in and enjoy the opposite sex, which further helps to shape their sexual identity (Hadley, 1992). The interest in the sexual organs and the development of sensitivity in the sexual organs arise simultaneously and just after the development of shame, and the parents' response to their child's emerging sexuality and sexual feelings has a considerable impact on the pleasure or shame that children relate to their sexual identity. The activity of sex hormones is basic to children's early sexual behaviour and their motivation to explore their sex organs, but, from the age of eighteen months, there is a dramatic increase in genital excitement, and shame is an important factor in regulating the sexual urges.

Parental reactions to a child's sexual behaviour are imprinted in the prefrontal areas, and children form internal representations of themselves as sexual beings in interaction with their environment. The orbitofrontal system stores representations that integrate external environmental responses, including mental images of the parents' expressive facial expressions in response to the child's sexual behaviour; for example, in relation to the child's internal feeling of pleasant sexual arousal. The orbitofrontal cortex is the overall regulator of sex hormones because of this area's close connections to the hypothalamus, and the store of male or female internal representations in the orbitofrontal cortex is involved in regulating sexual behaviour (Schore, 1994).

During the first eighteen months of life, the circulating sex hormones influence the development of neural circuits in the limbic and orbitofrontal regions. The quality of the relationship with the care-giver influences the level of circulating sexual steroids and is involved in developing sexual differences in affect regulation. During the development period for sexual identity, children begin to develop triangular friendships and become more active in their search for contact with other adults and children (Bentzen, 2005; Schore, 1994).

Sex hormones and puberty

From 6–18 months of age, the production of sex hormones gradually drops to a dormant level, where it remains until pre-puberty. The hypothalamus, pituitary gland, and gonads are fully functioning throughout childhood, but after the age of eighteen months the hypothalamus becomes sensitive to the inhibitory effect of the sex hormones, and only tiny amounts of hormones are released from the gonads (Andresen & Tuxen, 1977–1980). The production of sex hormones picks up again well before puberty, i.e., around the age of ten years for girls and eleven years for boys. The production of sex hormones is triggered by GnRH (gonadotrophin-releasing hormone) (Spear, 2000). The pituitary gland and hypothalamus form a self-regulating system that maintains a particular concentration of sex hormones in the bloodstream. The hypothalamus produces GnRH, which makes the pituitary gland release its general sex hormones (gonadotrophins), which stimulate testicles and ovaries to release testosterone and oestrogen. Until puberty, the testosterone level is approximately three times higher in boys than in girls. During puberty, the boys' testosterone level rises until it is about fifteen times higher than the girls'. Girls produce about twice as much oestrogen as boys until puberty, and about eight times as much after (Stein, 1987). The sex hormones stimulate neurons to increase the number of synaptic connections (Purves et al., 2001).

Giedd and colleagues (1999) have shown that there is a general increase in sprouting and pruning in the grey matter during puberty, especially in the parietal and frontal lobes. The increase in grey matter in the prefrontal cortex peaks at an age of approximately eleven years in girls and twelve years in boys, and lasts until the age of twenty-two years. The same process begins in the temporal lobes around the age of sixteen years. It is not yet known whether the increase in grey matter is due to an increase in neuronal size or in the branching of dendrites and axons.

The corpus callosum, anterior and posterior commissures, and cerebellum also change during childhood and youth, both in size and shape. During puberty, there is an increase in synaptic connections in the corpus callosum and anterior and posterior commissures, which means a far greater transfer of information between the two hemispheres. The cerebellum is only fully myelinated at the age of twenty-two years, so the ability to balance various affective and cognitive processes and to navigate in a complex social life is a slowly developing facility.

The increase in brain activity during puberty is evident in the cerebellum, hypothalamus, amygdala, hippocampus, orbitofrontal cortex, and dorsolateral cortex (see Figure 11.1), and there appears to be a difference as to which areas are increased in girls and boys, respectively (Sowell & Jernigan, 1998).

Much of the brain's volume comes from myelin, and it is still uncertain how much of the change in brain structures stems from an increase in myelination. If the increase in grey matter is due to a new wave of over-production of synapses in puberty, the increased production of sex hormones in puberty may prove to imply a new critical development phase when teenage activities provide direction for the ongoing development of cortical organization. The increased secretion of sex hormones probably has an organizing effect on brain structures and, thus, on feminine and masculine behaviour (Giedd, 2002, Sowell & Jernigan, 1998).

The impact of sex hormones on behaviour

In addition to their influence on sexual/reproductive behaviour and on sexual identity, sex hormones also play a role in the development of aggression and other typically male and female behaviour. For example, testosterone in the amygdala has been found to trigger rough and tumble play in young male animals.

Generally, men are physically stronger, more socially assertive, more dominant, and more competitive than women, while women are more nurturing and more socially motivated. In men, the amygdala areas that induce aggression circuits, among other things, are denser and more active, while the cingulate gyri, which trigger caring, social, and emotional circuits, are more concentrated and active in women (Panksepp, 1998). Girls who have been exposed to increased quantities of testosterone as foetuses, due to a hormonal disorder, become fiercer and more aggressive and have the same toy preferences as boys (Kimura, 1999a,b; LeVay, 1993).

Children with a low foetal testosterone level display more gaze contact and a larger vocabulary at the age of 12–24 months. Studies by Lutchmaya and Baron-Cohen found that girls as young as 1–2 years have more gaze contact with their mothers than boys do, and at the age of four years the girls do considerably better in a "theory of mind" test than same-age boys (Baron-Cohen, 2003; Lutchmaya & Baron-Cohen 2002; Lutchmaya, Baron-Cohen, & Raggatt, 2002).

There are indications that women and men develop lateralized functions at different stages. Women and men use different strategies to navigate in unfamiliar surroundings. Men typically look for holistic geometric features and on average complete this sort of task faster than women. Women draw on large or recognizable individual features and take longer to grasp the big picture. Women in general have better language skills, both in terms of articulation, speed, and grammar. Men are generally better at tasks that require spatial and mechanical abilities and mathematical reasoning.

Boys and girls who are exposed to traumatic experiences or neglect have different reactions, partly due to the impact of sex hormones. Thus, boys are more likely to have hyperarousal disorders in the form of impulsive, aggressive behaviour and attention and conduct disorders (ADHD), while girls are more like to react with hypoarousal disorders in the form of anxiety, panic attacks, and dysphoria. Boys or men are often more likely to react with a sympathetic fight-or-flight pattern, while girls or women are more prone to a parasympathetic freeze response. Biological research has found that in animal species where the male is more than twenty per cent larger than the female, females respond by freezing when attacked by males, probably because this offers far better survival chances. Before puberty, about three times as many girls as boys are referred for psychiatric treatment, but when the children reach adolescence the ratio changes, so that referrals involve about twice as many young women as young men. The explanation for this change in distribution is probably that the boys typically act out, which makes their difficulties very obvious, while the girls adapt and disguise their problems. When the girls reach puberty, their problems become visible through psychological reactions that are often related to self-harming behaviour and psychological pain.

Men identify more frequently with the aggressor, while women are more likely to identify with the victim. Thus, boys or men tend to project more and blame society or other individuals for their acting out, while girls or women tend to be introjective and blame themselves for traumatic actions and to display a behaviour characterized by guilt and shame. Women who have been exposed to traumatic events in childhood are more likely than men to assume a role of helplessness and to form attachments with violent, domineering men. This reaction pattern is probably related to the fact that oestrogen triggers oxytocin, which activates the parasympathetic system, while testosterone triggers vasopressin, which activates the sympathetic nervous system (Perry, 1994, Perry, Pollard, Blakely, Baker, & Vigilante, 1995; Scaer, 2001; Schore, 2002).

As described earlier, men and women produce both "male" and "female" sex hormones. Sexual differences are the result of different ratios of these hormones. The sex hormones play a key role in neurological development and the organization of neural circuits, and they are important throughout childhood and adulthood in relation to activating specific behaviour. Sex hormones are not just important in relation to reproduction, they also determine all the features that makes an individual masculine or feminine (Cameron, 2001; Kimura, 1987).

Sex and neurological organization

Sex hormones probably influence the anatomical structure of the brain. There seems to be evidence that the brain has a somewhat different organization in men and women, but so far, the findings are uncertain and somewhat contradictory. Comparisons of brains from women and men of similar body weight and height show that men's brains weigh about 100 g more than female brains. A Danish study (described in Kimura, 1999b) showed that men had approximately four billion more cortical neurons than women. Apart from brain size, many structural features appear to be sexually differentiated.

The biggest subcortical difference between women and men has been found in the anatomy and chemistry of the hypothalamus. The medial area of the hypothalamus is approximately three times larger in men than in women, while individual hypothalamus cell clusters are larger in women. This difference is probably due to the organizing effect of the sex hormones. Castration of male rodents just after birth, not later than the seventh day, will shrink the volume of the medial part of the hypothalamus down to female size. Oestrogen treatment of female rats causes changes in the medial part of the hypothalamus, including an increase in oxytocin (Cameron, 2001; Solms & Turnbull, 2002).

The medial area of the amygdala is receptive to sex hormones, and high concentrations of androgen and oestrogen receptors have also been found in the brainstem, especially in the PAG, which controls male and female sexual reflexes. Thus, there are minute anatomical and neurochemical differences between men and women in these areas, which probably affect the management of fear and aggression (Panksepp, 1998).

The hippocampus is larger in male rats and voles, but this anatomical differentiation has not been found in humans (Kimura, 1999b). The inner part of the parietal lobes is different in men and women, which probably reflects different perceptions of body sensations.

During the foetal period, boys appear to have a slightly larger cortex in the right hemisphere than in the left, while girls have equally sized hemispheres. In male rats, the posterior cortex is thicker in the right hemisphere than in the left. Early changes in sex hormone levels may cause changes in the distribution of thickness. This difference in volume has also been found in human foetuses but not in adults. If this difference were to be found in men, it might help explain men's superior visuospatial abilities, which rely especially on functions in the right hemisphere (Gesch-wind & Galaburda, 1987; Kimura, 1987, 1999b)

Generally, men's brains are believed to be more functionally asymmetrical than women's brains. Women are generally better at co-ordinating left and right hemisphere, and many scientists believe women have better interhemispheric integration due to the larger fibrous connections in the corpus callosum and anterior and posterior commissures, which will be discussed in the next chapter. While the anterior commissures, which connect the deep-lying subcortical areas, are believed to be larger in women, the corpus callosum, which connects the right and left neocortical regions, has a different shape in female than in male brains, and a particular area in the corpus callosum called the splenium is believed to be larger in women than in men (Kimura, 1999b; LeVay, 1993).

A study where men and women were asked to think of sad, dysphoric experiences, such as thoughts concerning the death of a loved one, found increased blood supply to the orbitofrontal cortex. When the women thought of sad situations, the orbitofrontal cortex in both hemispheres was activated, while men only showed activation in the left hemisphere. In the study, more women than men became tearful. Women had greater activity in affect-regulating structures than men, especially in the right hemisphere. This might suggest that sexually specific differences in circuitry between the limbic system, prefrontal cortex, corpus callosum, and anterior/ posterior commissures relate to different ways of processing emotional material, but a great deal of research is still needed before we can accurately describe the structural and functional differences between men's and women's brains (Kimura, 1999a; Purves et al., 2001; Siegel, 1999; Schore, 2003b; Tetzchner, 2002).

The impact of sex hormones on parenting

Sex hormones are important for maternal and paternal behaviour. Evolution has not left nurturing and attachment up to chance or social learning. Nurturing love is triggered by brain systems that facilitate parental attachment, while erotic love undoubtedly springs from brain systems that produce a search for sexual partners. Nurturing love is mainly based on oxytocin and opioids, while erotic love relations are mainly based on dopamine (Panksepp, 1998).

Oestrogen levels rise during pregnancy, and these high levels are believed to help induce intense maternal behaviour after birth. The continuation of this behaviour requires experience with parenting. A few days of interaction between rat pups and their mothers after birth serve to establish maternal behaviour. If the rat pups are removed for three to four days, the maternal behaviour resurfaces instantly upon reunion, but longer periods of separation render the mother indifferent to her offspring (Anders, 1989).

In humans, too, psychobiological and sex-hormonal factors affect novice parents' sensitivity and capacity for parenting in one form or another. Human parenting behaviour is not exclusively innate, and some parenting tasks will be different or non-existent during certain historical eras or in certain cultures (Stern, 1995).

Maternal and paternal behaviour

Mothers and fathers have different roles in shaping the child's development. The father often brings a different sort of dynamic to the relationship than the one that exists between mother and child. Parents provide different kinds of care, and children clearly benefit from the combination. Brazelton (1992) notes that observations of brief sequences of an infant's arm and leg movements reveal whether an infant is with his or her mother or father. From the outset, fathers interact differently with their children than mothers do. When the mother hums and vocalizes as she wraps her arms gently and carefully around her infant in a flowing pattern, the infant moves his or her arms and legs calmly towards her. Fathers "push" more, and their behaviour with the infant encourages play behaviour more. Fathers' behaviour intensify the infant's mood and arousal, and the infant's arm and leg movements show more lively gesturing with quick and energetic movements. These differences in parenting style often continue throughout childhood. Mothers continue to offer protection, while fathers often hold their infants in a way that lets them see what is going on in the world around them.

Generally, fathers appear to be more controlling, while mothers tend to let the infant control the interaction to a higher degree. The father often takes more risks, such as throwing the infant into the air, etc. The father's interactions invite risk-taking and independency, while the mother's behaviour encourages intimacy, protection, and emotional subtlety. Mothers tend to be more verbal, while fathers are typically more physical and encourage rougher play, especially with their sons. Rough-housing lets children practise important skills in handling their aggression; for example, when children play too roughly or get too excited, fathers will typically intervene and stop the inappropriate behaviour. The child's main attachment is often with the mother, but in families where the mother is absent, sick, or unavailable, a secure attachment with the father can compensate for an insecure or non-existent relationship with the mother. Normally, the father responds just as much to infants' crying and attention needs as the mother, and fatherhood may be more variable and flexible and less biologically determined than motherhood (Karr-Morse & Wiley, 1997; Taylor, 2002).

Primate studies have found that the father's role develops the young monkey's ability to move outside the mother's reach, and fathers appear to have an ability that enables them to offer their sons and daughters something that the mother cannot provide. Fathers often act as role models for their sons, and the sons are able to imitate them, compete with them, and admire them. A boy's relationship with his father is essential, and boys who do not have such a relationship often yearn for it. The quality of the father's relationship with his son has a deep influence on the boy's identity development and sense of himself (Sroufe, Cooper, & Deltart, 1992).

Summary

Apparently, there are only minute anatomical and genetic differences between girls and boys, women and men, but, through the XX or XY chromosome, sexual characteristics are built into every single cell. The production of sex hormones in the early foetal stages has substantial impact on the development of masculine and feminine behaviour. Sex selection is determined when the egg and sperm cell merge, but the delicate balance between nature and nurture in connection with the release of sex hormones, sexual identity, and sexual self-esteem is struck in a close and indivisible interaction. Because the neuroanatomical differences between women's and men's brains are so small, and because the average variation is so big, we still have a long way to go before we have enough information to offer a convincing definition of neuro-anatomical sexual differences. In the next chapter, I will discuss theories and hypotheses concerning the two brain hemispheres and hemispheric lateralization.

CHAPTER TWELVE

The lateralized brain: right and left hemisphere

"The distribution of white matter to grey is not even throughout the brain—the right hemisphere has relatively more white matter, while the left has more grey. This microscopic distinction is significant because it means that the axons in the right brain are longer than in the left and this means they connect neurons that are, on average, further away from each other . . . this suggests that the right brain is better equipped than the left to draw on several different brain modules at the same time . . . The left brain, in contrast, is more densely woven. The close-packed, tightly connected neurons are better equipped to do intense, detailed work that depends on close and quick cooperation between similarly dedicated brain cells.

(Carter, 1998, p. 38)

The human brain is not only hierarchical in nature, it is also characterized by functional asymmetry. All motor pathways from the central nervous system that continue down the spinal cord must cross the mid-line in the brainstem, which means that the right brain hemisphere controls the left side of the body, and vice versa. The hemispheric asymmetry develops at an early foetal stage, long before the differentiation of the neocortex, and the cortical asymmetry between left and right hemisphere springs from the modulation of functions all the way from the reticular activation system, which is similarly lateralized (divided into a left and right hemisphere). All structures (except for the pineal gland) occur in both brain hemispheres. Similarly, as mentioned in the previous chapter, the two hemispheres are connected on different levels by the corpus callosum, which connects the hemispheres on the neocortical level, and the anterior and posterior commissures, which connect the hemispheres on a subcortical level. Even the two hemispheres of the cerebellum are connected (Porges, 1995; Siegel, 1999; Trevarthen, 1990).

For many years the left brain hemisphere was referred to as the dominant hemisphere because it was in charge of analytical, detailed, problem-solving thinking, and the function of the right hemisphere has long been unclear. It is the general view that the complex functions of the brain are made possible by the integration of two hemispheres that complement each other, and which cannot exist without each other's functions (Figure 12.1).

So far, research into the function and importance of the two hemispheres has failed to provide clear-cut answers. The two hemispheres are almost identical physiologically, and only minor, subtle anatomical differences have been found. In terms of psychological

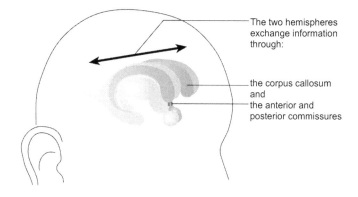

The two hemispheres exchange information through:

the corpus callosum and the anterior and posterior commissures

Figure 12.1.   The inter-hemispheric connection: the corpus callosum and the anterior and posterior commissures.

functioning, however, the two hemispheres are radically different. This is not true, however, for all parts of the two hemispheres. The primary cortical zones, for example, are completely symmetrical, while the association cortex is completely asymmetrical. There is probably no single factor that distinguishes the functions of the two hemispheres, and the functional difference between the hemispheres seems to be based on multiple factors (Solms & Turnbull, 2002).

In this chapter, I will review some aspects of lateralization and its importance for certain functions. The lateralization of the brain is an area of particular theoretical dispute, and much of the theory in the area is speculative in nature. It is, however, indisputable that the brain is lateralized, and hopefully, future research will be able to provide a clearer picture of the relationship between neurophysiological differences and function.

History

As early as 1904, it was clear that the brain is not only lateralized on the neocortical level but also on a deeper level, in brainstem functions. The limbic system is also lateralized, and in the human brain emotional facial expressions are processed in the right hemisphere. Recent neurophysiological research shows that hemispheric lateralization is not just found in primate brains but is also a feature of lower mammals, fish, reptiles, birds, etc. The evolutionary advantage of brain lateralization has long been the topic of speculation, and today it is generally believed that lateralization has developed in order to make room for new skills without the loss of existing skills. Lateralization makes room for additional skills because functions can be divided between the right and left hemisphere, and the two hemispheres are free to specialize in different functions (Gazzaniga, 1999; Geschwind & Galaburda, 1987; Schore, 2003b).

Some functions have had to give way to new ones. For example, the expansion of the parietal and frontal lobes probably took place at the cost of the visual cortex. A look at the skulls of some of the prehistoric humans who lived some two million years ago reveals that their skulls were constructed to accommodate a much larger visual cortex than is found in modern man. In particular, the frontal motor areas in the left hemisphere expanded at this time, while there are no major changes in the corresponding areas in the right hemisphere. This development probably took place in order to accommodate language, since this is the region where we find the neural roots of language (Gazzaniga, 1999; Hansen, 2002).

Hemispheric asymmetry

The hemispheres are capable of functioning independently of each other, and the right and left hemispheres probably have very different forms of consciousness. However, the hemispheres require mutual functional integration to function in everyday life. Parts of the somatosensory cortex in the right hemisphere are more closely integrated with functions in the deeper parts of the subcortical layers than is the case for the left hemisphere, and they have better access to body-sensing structures (Damasio, 2003). Body responses such as changes in the internal organs, e.g., the digestive tract, heart, or lungs mainly register in the hypothalamus, orbitofrontal cortex, and related areas in the right hemisphere, while the reward and arousal circuits and value systems are located in both hemispheres. Thus, it is the totality of the brain's structures and circuitry that creates the basis of a perceived self. Emotions are related to assessment and arousal mechanisms in both hemispheres and influence all aspects of cognition, from perception to rational decision-making (Siegel, 1999).

Right and left hemispheres develop at different growth rates, and the adult left hemisphere is capable of differentiating, analysing, and sequencing, while the right hemisphere is spatial, holistic, and integrative (Thatcher, 1997). Paul MacLean suggested that the "emotional" brain, corresponding to the right hemisphere, and the "verbal" brain, corresponding to the left, function in parallel but different ways and are not necessarily able to communicate with each other (Mathiesen, 2004). Numerous studies by Robert Sperry and Michael Gazzaniga have found that the right and left hemispheres have different cognitive and emotional perspectives on the world. Studies have also found that verbalization can cause as much confusion and distortion as clarification, unless it is deeply integrated with the right hemisphere.

Gazzaniga and Sperry carried out experiments where the subjects were either injected with an anaesthetic (sodium amytal), which could be quickly absorbed into one hemisphere, or had undergone a surgical procedure that severed their corpus callosum (split-brain patients) as a means of handling epilepsy. This allowed the researchers to separate left and right hemispheric functions and test the capacity of each hemisphere individually. They found that subjects expressed themselves in different emotional terms, depending on whether they expressed themselves through their left or right hemisphere, or whether they had access to both at the same time. They found that the right hemisphere remembers species-specific facial expressions, prosody, and gestures. The right hemisphere is able to synthesize and create a holistic view of social situations. It responds to emotional stimuli that are not necessarily conscious and to stimuli that have emerged on the basis of mental images and thoughts. Gazzaniga, LeDoux, and Wilson (1977) found that the left hemisphere formulates explanations for experiences, even when there is no information available from the right hemisphere. While verbal material is stored in the left hemisphere, visual material to a much higher degree is stored in the right hemisphere.

The right hemisphere perceives messages through facial expressions and prosody, and this is the hemisphere that expresses and registers the primary emotions that were originally described by Darwin. Emotional processing, in all likelihood, takes place in both hemispheres. The right hemisphere is incapable of logical conclusions, it thinks in concrete terms, and it is not creative. The logical, detail-focused, and linguistic left hemisphere is important for human creativity and technology. The left hemisphere is important for our ability to formulate social information that can be transferred from person to person (Siegel, 1999).

While the right hemisphere regulates intense emotional processes and non-verbal primary emotions, the left regulates verbal social emotions, and it intensifies positive and inhibits negative emotional behaviour. The cortex of the left hemisphere is able to inhibit emotional expressions that spring from the limbic areas of the right hemisphere (Davidson & Hugdahl, 1995; Schore, 2003a). The right hemisphere achieves basic mastery of a new repertoire more quickly, while the left hemisphere makes it possible, through practice, to refine the repertoire and accomplish a more perfect performance. At the level of the frontal lobes, the left hemisphere specializes in sequential organizing, while the right hemisphere specializes in processing novel stimuli that disrupt sequential organized behaviour. The different characteristics of the left and right hemisphere result in different self-regulation strategies (Dawson, 1994; Goldberg, 2001, Tucker & Williamson, 1984).

Patients with right-hemispheric epilepsy in the limbic system are excessively emotional, and this abnormal limbic influence appears to inhibit right-hemispheric cognition. Patients with left-sided temporal lobe epilepsy show a preoccupation with mystical ideas, including intellectual and religious themes, which are reproduced verbally through the language area of the left hemisphere. Unconscious perception mainly activates the right-sided amygdala, while conscious perceptions mainly activate the left-sided amygdala (Cicchetti & Tucker, 1994; Hansen, 2002).

The right hemisphere

The right hemisphere is more hierarchically integrated than the left, and it is dominant in the processing of emotional information (Luria, 1973). The frontal lobes in the right hemisphere are connected to the body-sensing structures, including the autonomic nervous system, which controls parasympathetic and sympathetic responses (see Figure 6.5). The primary emotions are experienced instantly and intensely in the right hemisphere and arise in the right side of the brainstem, partly through the vagus nerve (see Figure 6.4). The representation of internal states in the organism probably occurs through right hemisphere processes (Cozolino, 2000; Damasio, 1994; Gazzaniga, 1999; Porges, 1995, 2001).

The insula (see Figure 8.2) in the right-hemispheric parietal lobes integrates body sensations through signals from both the left and right side of the body, which enables us to perceive our organism as a whole. Representations of current body states are shaped by these body sensations, which form the basis for our ability to sense ourselves. The recognition of emotions through facial expressions requires the activation of areas in the parietal cortex as well as the somatosensory cortex in the right hemisphere. Simulating another person's facial expression enables us to recognize the person's emotional state. It is the right hemisphere that enables us to intuit and to have the sense of feeling something deep inside the body (Damasio, 1994, 1999, 2003; Schore, 2003b) (Table 12.1).

Functions in the right hemisphere let us quickly grasp the essence and emotional content of a situation. Since the right hemisphere often does not have language functions, many persons with a dysfunctional left hemisphere can only express themselves nonverbally, either by sketching or pointing. The right hemisphere processes information holistically and grasps facial expressions in less than thirty milliseconds, i.e., long before the emotional information can be perceived consciously. This means that we have already received a great deal of social and emotional information

Table 12.1.   Overview of functions in the left and right hemispheres.

Left hemisphere	Right hemisphere
Differentiates, analyses, and sequences	Has better access to body-sensing structures
Creates explanations of experiences	Is spatial, holistic, and integrative
Stores verbal material	Remembers species-specific facial expressions, prosody, and gestures
Is logical and focused on details	Stores visual material
Is able to verbalize	Creates prosody
Is creative and technological	Thinks holistically
Articulates social information	Forms an overview of social situations
Regulates verbal social emotions	Responds to emotional stimuli
Integrates body sensations	Perceives messages through facial expressions and prosody
Intensifies positive emotional behaviour and inhibits negative emotional behaviour	Expresses and registers primary emotions
Inhibits emotional expressions that spring from the limbic areas in the right hemisphere	Regulates intense emotional processes

unconsciously before we become aware of it consciously. The right hemisphere enables us to create mental images of others, which lets us understand other people's emotions and feel sympathy and empathy (Schore, 2003b).

Patients with right-sided brain damage have difficulty with tasks that require them to think about spatial relations (visuospatial skills), they have difficulty maintaining eye contact, and their prosody and facial expressions are strikingly sparse. They often have attention disorders, probably because their attention is maintained through emotional control and by focusing on stimuli that are considered important (Hansen, 2002; Siegel, 1999). Right-sided brain damage in the cingulate gyrus and orbitofrontal cortex (see Figure 8.1) renders the person unable to interpret emotional facial expressions and causes them to be strikingly indifferent. Functions in the right hemisphere enable us to remember events of an emotional nature without the active involvement of the left hemisphere, while functions in the left hemisphere enable us to verbalize moods. Structures in the right hemisphere enable us to register emotions, such as getting upset, exhausted, angry, or happy, and in many ways the right hemisphere is a primitive and egocentric hemisphere. Damage to the parietal lobes in the right hemisphere makes it difficult to maintain the distinction between self and other and to separate one's own needs from those of others (Solms & Turnbull, 2002; van der Kolk, 1987, 2000).

The orbitofrontal cortex in the right hemisphere is dominant with regard to processing, expressing, and regulating emotional information. It is involved in storing emotional facial expressions and mental images, which is the basis for our ability to form internal mental representations of others. Dysfunction in the right-sided orbitofrontal cortex causes poor body sensations and a poor sense of identity. This poor sense of identity leads to a poor capacity for emotional mentalization, i.e., the ability to reflect on one's own and other people's emotional states (Schore, 2003a,b). Kaplan-Solms and Solms (2002) point out that damage to the right-hemispheric areas that integrate the prefrontal cortex, limbic regions, diencephalon, and brainstem structures leads to far more severe disorders concerning personality, emotions, and motivation than damage to the same areas in the left hemisphere. These areas in the right hemisphere involve a much higher degree of self-organization. Patients with disorders in the right hemisphere accept their condition intellectually but are indifferent towards it.

The left hemisphere

The left hemisphere consists of structures specialized in language production, cognitive analysis, logical conclusions, and the perception of details. These structures enable us to look for causal explanations to events and to use rational reasoning to conclude relationships of cause and effect, often on the basis of limited information. The left hemisphere enables us to process details step by step and to integrate individual elements into meaningful entities. Activity in the left hemisphere explains why a particular response is displayed. Structures within the right hemisphere are responsible for enabling a person to gain implicit insight into the underlying motive for a though or action, and if the connection to the left hemisphere is severed the information remains unconscious. Structures in the left hemisphere enable the person to develop a form of reflective consciousness. Gazzaniga carried out experiments where he instructed a subject with an active right hemisphere to wave. He then deactivated the person's right hemisphere, activated the left, and asked the subject why he was waving. The subject said that he did this because he had seen an acquaintance. Sperry presented pornographic pictures to a patient who had a deactivated left hemisphere. The patient blushed and giggled but was unable to account for her embarrassment (described in Solms and Turnbull, 2002, p. 82). When a picture is presented to the right hemisphere, it often sparks a powerful emotional response, but when the picture is presented to the left hemisphere, the person instead searches for a logical reason for these emotions. When a split-brain patient is presented with a picture of Hitler, his facial expression may express anger or disgust. When asked to explain this emotion, he often constructs replies that are unrelated to the picture of Hitler; for example, that he was thinking of something that made him angry (Hansen, 2002; LeDoux, 1998; Newberg, d'Aquili, & Rause, 2002; Solms & Turnbull, 2002).

Persons with a deactivated right hemisphere and a highly activated left hemisphere are social and construct stories, but do not reveal their deep emotional secrets. They seek to construct explanations for the information they are receiving, but they lack the ability to process their current context. Their conclusions are often based on selected details that do not necessarily make any rational sense. Often, an explanation is reduced to a convenient logical conclusion without any emotional or contextual substance. Structures in the left hemisphere process information in a linear, sequential, and linguistic manner, and connections in the left hemisphere are not as closely linked with body functions as the connections in the right hemisphere. The left hemisphere fills in gaps as the person engages in guesswork to offer explanations. This corresponds to the replies offered by children when they are unable to explain why they did something that adults consider unacceptable or inappropriate. With a highly activated left hemisphere, the person looks for logical answers without worrying about the correctness of the answer. The left hemisphere lets us interpret and synthesize available information and produce coherent stories; this corresponds to the conscious social self, i.e., the person we believe we are. The left hemisphere contains functions that enable us to think and express ourselves through language, and it lets us express a "social self" that is based on other people's expectations of our behaviour. The left hemisphere represents the conscious reflective self, which is not always in accordance with the unconscious or non-verbal sides of the personality (Cozolino, 2000; Panksepp, 1998).

"False" memories are a left-hemisphere phenomenon. MRI scans have shown that both the left and right hemisphere are activated when test subjects recall a "false" memory, while a "true" memory initially only activates the right hemisphere. Based on functions in the left hemisphere, the person is able to offer an interpretation that is not necessarily correct, and this produces false feedback. When the left hemisphere is involved, the person looks for the meaning of an event and for a particular order or reason, even when none exists; in this process, the person tends to overgeneralize and construct a potential past instead of the actual past. When the left hemisphere is active, finding meaning becomes more important than finding the truth (Gazzaniga, 1999).

Intuitive thinking is probably lateralized on the right side and matures before language. The "social self" is constructed in the left hemisphere and interprets information, including information that comes from the right hemisphere. The left hemisphere plays an important role in communicating emotions that relate rigidly to social rules. Two-year-old children, for example, have already learned to display facial expressions that do not reflect their actual emotions, and they begin to be able to inhibit emotional expressions through the dorsolateral cortex—a function that continues to develop well into adulthood. If children spend a great deal of time being "socially correct", their authentic or intuitive emotions will be inhibited, which means that reasoning becomes separated from primary emotional experiences (Hansen, 2002; Schore, 2001a).

The left hemisphere receives less input from the body than the right, but is capable of using abstract manipulation of linguistic representations. Humans are able to reflect verbally on their past and present and to formulate plans for the future. This capacity lets us create new combinations of everything in the world. Research by Davidson and Irwin (1999) found that the left prefrontal area regulates neural pathways in the lower regions of the brain that determine the duration of time needed to recover from unpleasant impressions. The more left-sided prefrontal activity there was in relation to right-sided prefrontal activity, the better the person's ability to develop cognitive strategies for regulating emotions and recovering and to quickly restore cortisol levels to normal.

Language functions

The left hemisphere has an essential function in relation to social communication, and it is through the language functions that our human potential is most fully expressed.

In most people, the language functions are located in the left hemisphere, especially in Broca's and Wernicke's areas (Figure 12.2). In right-handed people the language functions are always located in the left hemisphere, while the same is true for sixty per cent of left-handed people. In some left-handed persons, the language functions are represented in both hemispheres (Geschwind & Galaburda, 1987). Wernicke's area is a part of the sensory association cortex, and its location allows it to synthesize information from many modalities. Wernicke's area produces symbolic and content-related representations of language and sends information to the nearby premotor region, Broca's area, which forms the basis

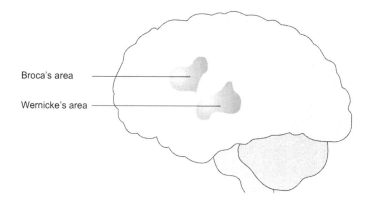

Broca's area

Wernicke's area

Figure 12.2.   Broca's and Wernicke's areas.

for language articulation and controls the articulation system in the mouth and throat.

The meaningful content, which is integrated in Wernicke's area, is quickly translated into sound, which, after a learning process, can be re-symbolized and transferred to reading and writing. The desire to communicate verbally in the first place depends on activation in the anterior cingulate gyrus, which also controls the arousal of social motivation. Language is a social act that is made possible by Wernicke's and Broca's areas. Wernicke's area enables very rapid language processing, perhaps based on what one expects to hear rather than what is actually said (Cozolino, 2000; Trevarthen, 1990).

As mentioned previously, Wernicke's and Broca's areas are located in the left hemisphere, while the corresponding areas on the right side handle prosody and gestures. The right-hemispheric area corresponding to Wernicke's area enables the interpretation of the emotional tone of language, while the area corresponding to Broca's area enables the expression of emotional meaning and affective nuances in linguistic form. Without the functions in the right hemisphere the language becomes "flat" and expressionless. Studies with split-brain patients have found that the right hemisphere is capable of producing simple words such as mum, dad, yes, no, good, etc. The right hemisphere is involved in the earliest manifestations of verbal affect-regulating social communication, and early protoconversations and pre-verbal utterances are probably produced through the right hemisphere. The left dorsolateral prefrontal cortex is not activated until language becomes automated and speech is fluent (Panksepp, 1998; Schore, 1994).

Language development

Language lets us reflect on past and present and enables us to consider and plan for the future. Language enables novel combinations of thoughts and unique form of communication with our surroundings. The co-operation between the logical, linear, and detail-focused linguistic left hemisphere and the holistic, emotional right hemisphere is crucial for all forms of creativity. Language makes it possible to communicate in a way that lets us combine thoughts and transfer social information in an abstract form. Abstract manipulation of linguistic representations enables us to transfer experiences of far greater complexity than any other animal (Cozolino 2000). "Language may not be the source of the self, but it is certainly the source of the 'I' " (Damasio, 1994, p. 243).

Newborn infants are sensitive to the human voice, and even in the womb the foetus becomes familiar with certain aspects of the mother's voice and prefers her voice immediately after birth. At a very early stage, infants co-ordinate their movements temporally and spatially with language sounds. Motor co-ordination integrates with language sounds in the left hemisphere (Trevarthen, 1990). Infants have an innate disposition for acquiring a language, but which language they learn is culturally determined. Language sounds integrate already at the foetal stage, and language development develops from inarticulate sounds over babbling to protoconversation and eventually fluency, provided the child has received linguistic stimulation from birth. Young children's thoughts are not ordered in coherent words and sentences until the left hemisphere is sufficiently mature.

If the infant is deprived of hearing the sound of speech and fails to receive lingual stimulation, language development is severely affected. In Los Angeles in 1970, authorities discovered the girl Genie, who from birth had been locked in an empty room with minimal human contact. When she was found at the age of thirteen years, the only words she was able to mutter were "stop" and "no more". When she received help with language learning, her vocabulary increased drastically, but she never acquired the rules of grammar. Brain scans revealed that only her right hemisphere was activated when she spoke. The language areas in her left hemisphere were reduced in size, probably due to lack of stimulation, and when she was presented with spoken words other brain areas would compensate but never adequately (Rymer, 1993).

Children's language develops rapidly once they have developed object permanence and the delayed response function that requires the maturation of the orbitofrontal cortex. Children gradually internalize what their parents say, partly through "inner speech", and through this approach the parents' external prohibitions are partly internalized and converted to internal inhibitions. Studies found that when 3–4-year-old children were left alone with a bowl of sweets and told that they would receive a reward if they did not eat from the bowl while the parents were gone, the children spoke out loud, repeating the parents' admonition, and they had great difficulty complying. Not until the age of 5–6 years are children able to comply by means of inner speech. At first, the children repeat what was said (parrot-like), then the behaviour gradually becomes internalized, and action is translated to thought. Thus, language becomes a powerful instrument for self-regulation on a cortical level. Through the ability to link prohibition with language, children develop their ability to self-regulate through language. For example, patients with frontal lobe injuries often dissociate knowing and doing. The patient may be asked to stand up but remains seated despite answering in the affirmative. When this is pointed out to the patient, he or she confirms the request but still does not carry it out. Due to this dysfunction the person has lost the ability to self-regulate behaviour verbally (Solms & Turnbull, 2002). Children who have been exposed to severe neglect show a similar inability to self-regulate on the basis of verbal instructions. The children have no problem comprehending the message, but apparently the verbal information in the left hemisphere fails to integrate with the affect-inhibitory structures in the right hemisphere.

The integration of right and left-sided functions is necessary for the nervous system to act as one entity. The personality can only express its full potential when both the right and the left hemispheres are intact and clearly connected through the corpus callosum and the anterior and posterior commissures.

Interhemispheric integration: corpus callosum
and the anterior and posterior commissures

The hemispheres are separate entities, but they are functionally integrated through the corpus callosum and the anterior and posterior commissures. This combined structure is the bridge that connects the cortical areas in the right and the left hemisphere. The corpus callosum connects the hemispheres on a neocortical level, while the anterior and posterior commissures connect the subcortical areas. The combined structure consists of some 200 million nerve fibres. The number of nerve fibres in this structure is at its highest at the time of birth. About nine tenths disappear during the first year of life just after the cortical cellular synaptogenesis followed by myelination. Much communication is based on this cross-hemispheric link, which myelinates very slowly and is not fully developed until around twelve years of age (Panksepp, 1998; Trevarthen, 1990).

Young children have difficulty communicating information between the two hemispheres. As one consequence of this, both hemispheres store memories that cannot be shared with the other hemisphere. Confabulation in children may be seen as a reflection of immature interhemispheric integration. The left hemisphere attempts to form an opinion of events in the right hemisphere, but the inadequate transmission between the two hemispheres leaves the left hemisphere to fill in the gaps with assumptions. Thus, when four-year-old Peter has hit his four-year-old playmate in the head with his toy shovel, and his mother asks why, Peter probably starts his sentence by saying, "It's because . . .," although the ensuing explanation may have little or no relation to the actual reason. The right hemisphere is unable to describe the event verbally, and instead it is lived out emotionally and behaviourally without any intervention from the left hemisphere. Patients with damaged interhemispheric integration mix fanciful stories and interpretations in order to explain and make sense of their right hemisphere perceptions (Joseph, 1993; Siegel, 1999).

Maturation of the right and left hemisphere

The right and left hemisphere develop at different rates; the right hemisphere matures earlier than the left, which has significant impact on childhood emotional development.

The brain's asymmetry occurs in the middle of the foetal period, and as early as around the twenty-fifth foetal week the right hemisphere has a more developed surface structure than the left; a difference that is maintained until the left hemisphere begins its growth spurt. The growth spurt of the right hemisphere lasts until the age of twenty-four months, while the growth spurt of the left hemisphere does not begin until around the age of eighteen months. Even though the left hemisphere begins its growth spurt around the age of eighteen months, the right side is dominant during the first thirty-six months of life. An expansion of connections in the left hemisphere does not occur until the child is between eighteen months and three years old, and language acquisition accelerates (Thatcher, Walker, & Guidice, 1987). Subsequently, dominance alternates between the right and left hemisphere, which allows for the ongoing reorganization of emotional and interpretative processes in both hemispheres throughout the lifespan. The right hemisphere is closely connected to the autonomic and limbic arousal systems that are necessary for processing social, emotional, and body information. Due to the earlier maturation of the right hemisphere, children are able to interpret the emotional content of facial expressions at a young age. After the first year of life, the left hemisphere becomes more active and develops at a faster rate. Towards the end of the third year of life, the connection between the two hemispheres is sufficiently developed to transmit information between the two hemispheres in an adequate manner, and language begins to gain emotional meaning. After the age of four years, children are able to describe their internal states and impulses. In particular, the linguistic analytical processing approach of the left hemisphere becomes more dominant in the child's life (Schore, 2003a,b Stern, 1985).

The right hemisphere dominates until the child develops motor and language functions, so the close emotional contact between care-giver and infant has particular influence on the development of the right hemisphere. This contact facilitates the infant's ability to self-regulate emotionally and maintain attention on relevant information. Changes in brain maturation with the switch from right-hemispheric to left-hemispheric dominance probably reflects a switch from the dependency of close emotional attention (right-hemispheric dominance) to increased cognitive, linguistic, and motor control and increasingly autonomous self-regulatory skills (left-hemispheric dominance). Thus, when inquisitiveness and motor skills enable the child to move away from the care-giver, this reflects a switch from right- to left-hemispheric dominance; the maturation of basic emotional skills is complete, and the child's development now revolves more around cognitive, linguistic, and motor skills.

The development of attunement and regulation mechanisms

The early growth of the orbitofrontal cortex is particularly pronounced in the right hemisphere and plays a key role for the self-regulatory systems. Owing to its extensive and close connections to the limbic system and the autonomic nervous system, the orbitofrontal cortex in the right hemisphere acts to inhibit and control intense emotional arousal, which, among other things, gives this area access to cortical control over facial expressions. This cortical control makes it possible to carry out conscious volitional adaptations of emotional expressions in a social context. Brainstem structures, the insula, and the orbitofrontal cortex in the right hemisphere integrate body sensations, emotions, and mental images, and this forms the basis for entering into a field of resonance with another person's internal states and developing an understanding of the other's mind. The early care-giver–infant relationship stimulates the infant to enter into a field of resonance with the care-giver through imitation, protoconversation, and affect attunement—functions that are related to the right hemisphere, and that develop attachment patterns. Once the infant is able to engage in joint attention, again it is areas in the right hemisphere that are activated (Schore, 1994, 2001a; Tucker, 1992). The ability to enter into a field of resonance with another person's internal states and achieve joint attention is essential throughout life for engaging in close relationships with others. Among other aspects, our personality consists of internal representations of our attachment relations and of the coping strategies and affect regulation skills that we have developed in these interactions (Schore, 1994, 2001a).

The right hemisphere is dominant during the first three years of life, so an infant who suffers severe emotional deprivation or abuse during this period will be at risk of developing functional disorders in the structural components of the right hemisphere, which will affect the child's body sensations, synchronization capacity, and affect regulation. Non-verbal communication, facial expressions, prosody, and emotional attunement are all functions that can be disrupted in the early dyad. When these functions are disrupted, the infant has difficulty achieving emotional attunement, accomplishing affect regulation through language, and developing mentalization and reflective functions. The integration of the two hemispheres through the corpus callosum and anterior and posterior commissures is impaired. The ability to put oneself in someone else's place emotionally and mentalizing the other person's situation requires co-ordination between the two hemispheres and a combination of the right-hemispheric capacity for emotional processing and the left-hemispheric capacity for interpretation and social understanding (Siegel, 1999). Teicher (2002) and Teicher and colleagues (1997) found that children who had suffered massive neglect had diminished blood flow through the corpus callosum

Schore (1994) states that shame, which is a biological regulation mechanism, develops through functions in the right hemisphere, while the next step in shame development, guilt, is a phenomenon of the left hemisphere. In some psychological and behavioural disorders the shame–guilt reaction is out of balance; reactions may be exaggerated, as in affect-inhibiting conditions such as neurotic disorders, or they may be subdued or absent, as in psychopathy. Furthermore, it is important to distinguish between children who fail to develop shame, for example, children who have suffered early emotional frustration, children who develop shame but not guilt, for example, children with severe narcissistic disorders who have not been supported through shame regulation, and children who are able to feel both shame and guilt and who are, for example, excessively adaptive. Well-integrated children often have well-balanced shame–guilt reactions.

Positive and negative emotions

Left and right hemisphere functions are very different, and according to some researchers the two hemispheres also have basically different moods, with the right hemisphere being more active in negative emotions and the left being more active in positive emotions. Goldberg (2001) points out that the left frontal lobe typically has more dopamine pathways, while the right typically has more noradrenalin pathways.

Davidson and colleagues (Davidson, 1995; Davidson & Fox, 1982; Davidson & Hugdahl, 1995) have pointed out that the left hemisphere is generally more socially communicative and "happier", while the right hemisphere is the one that records intense negative emotions. This affective hemispheric distinction probably springs from the two hemispheres' different approaches to emotional messages from subcortical circuits. Davidson and colleagues (*ibid.*) mention that it was an amazing discovery to find that positive emotions in connection with EEG measurements are related to arousal in frontal areas in the left side, while negative moods, such as sadness, anxiety, and apprehension, are related to frontal arousal in the right hemisphere. This distinction is also seen in the resting EEG pattern in individuals with different temperaments. Persons who tend to be depressive have a higher degree of right-sided frontal arousal than people who are generally more positive. In younger children, this form of asymmetry is also found in the difference between extrovert and inhibited individuals. Inhibited children display right frontal lobe activation and diminished left-sided activation, while inquisitive, adventurous children show heightened left-sided frontal activation. Left-sided frontal activation is related to inquisitive investigative behaviour and social interaction, while reduced left-sided activation is related to withdrawal, negative affects, and timidity. Inhibited and uninhibited children have different approachment patterns, which is associated with different degrees of left-sided activation. Impaired activation of the right frontal lobe leads to impulsivity and hyperactivity. Studies have found that at ten months of age, the brain is lateralized for positive and negative affect. Even at this early stage, the aspects of the infant's personality that have to do with inquisitive, investigative behaviour versus inhibited behaviour are apparent and influence the way the infant relates to the environment and to subsequent relationships (Davidson, 1995; Davidson & Fox, 1982, 1989; Davidson & Slagter, 2000; Davidson, Ekman, Saron, Senulis, & Friesen, 1990; Panksepp, 1998; Siegel, 1999). Differences between right and left hemispheric activation have also been found to be related to relationship experiences and not just innate differences. The degree of activity in the two hemispheres might change over time due to changes in relational experiences (Glaser, 2004).

Damage to the left frontal region typically result in apathy or euphoria; damage to the right frontal region generally result in depression or feelings of catastrophe (Dawson, 1994). The closer to the mid-line the left hemispheric damage is, the more severe are the depressive symptoms. Persons who develop manic behaviour following a brain injury often have damage to the right hemisphere. Fear and loathing are associated with right-sided activation in frontal and temporal areas, while pleasure is associated with activation of the left temporal region. However, when pleasure is not related to approachment behaviour there is no activation of the left hemisphere. This has led Davidson and colleagues (1990) to state that it is not negative or positive feelings that activate the right or left hemisphere but rather approach or withdrawal behaviour (Davidson, 1995; Davidson, Ekman, Saron, Senulis, & Friesen, 1990).

Explanations for hemispheric differentiation of positive and negative reactions have been the topic of some dispute. Fox (1994) has proposed a model that associates right-sided frontal activation with control over negative affects, while left-sided frontal activation is associated with control over positive affects. Schore (2001a,b), however, seems to disagree with this view and states that the right hemisphere plays a key role in the unconscious evaluation of both positive and negative emotional stimuli. He points out that the ability to produce and maintain positive auto-regulating representations depends on efficient activity in the right hemisphere. Cozolino (2000) has proposed that the left hemisphere may interpret emotional moods from the right hemisphere, acting as the "secretary of the self". It attempts to put experiences in a positive light; it is social in nature and adjusts a story to make it presentable to others in an acceptable and positive way. If the left hemisphere "translator" does not do its job well enough, for example, if it is under-activated or dysfunctional, the person becomes pessimistic and depressed. An adequately developed interhemispheric link will convey information from the right to the left hemisphere. If one shows a toddler an interesting toy while the child's arms are restrained, the child's face will show signs of anger in response to the situation. The left hemisphere is activated as the child attempts

to overcome the obstacle and reach the exciting toy. Even if a problem is frustrating, resolving it may still be associated with pleasure.
When Buddhists with a long history of meditative practice underwent fMRI scans while meditating on a mantra concerning compassion, the scans showed particularly intense activation of the left
prefrontal cortex in exactly the area that previous research had
identified as the area for positive emotions such as happiness,
enthusiasm, joy, high energy, and arousal (Davidson, 1995; Goleman, 2003).

Patients with severe damage to the right hemisphere become
inappropriately optimistic and may seem emotionally unaffected;
faced, for example, with terrible suffering they often maintain their
optimistic outlook and display inappropriate cheerfulness. In
extreme cases they completely refuse to acknowledge their condition. The left hemisphere is satisfied with "laughing in the face of
adversity"; it often perceives ordinary situations as funny and
grasps humour and "twisted" logic. Injury to the left prefrontal
cortex results in a loss of positive emotions, which causes feelings
of sadness and a negative outlook (Purves et al., 2001).

As demonstrated by this brief discussion, there is considerable
dispute about the link between positive and negative emotions and
the right and left hemisphere, and future research will probably be
able to sum up this debate and offer a more consistent understanding. In the next section, I describe the influence of lateralization on
consciousness, although the concept of consciousness is not defined
until Chapter Fourteen.

Lateralization and consciousness

The dorsolateral prefrontal cortex has different representations in
the two hemispheres, and the forms of consciousness in the two
hemispheres are qualitatively different. Mostly, the two hemispheres represent a well-integrated network that triggers various
neural groups across the hemispheric connections. The basic form
of consciousness in the left hemisphere is a verbal representation of
thoughts. The basic form of consciousness in the right hemisphere
consists of sensations and mental images. Facial recognition, for
example, mainly takes place in the right hemisphere and is based

on presentations of other people's emotional states. The form of consciousness found in the right hemisphere is filled with mental images of the world, perceptions of other people's emotions, body sensations, holistic patterns, and intuitive insights that are often non-verbal. The form of consciousness that is characteristic of the left hemisphere handles the world in abstract and lingual terms that are often independent of emotional content. Patients with a severed link between the two hemispheres perceive the ego as left-hemispheric, while the right hemisphere is associated with an outside force that may seem self-alien. When these patients are controlled by their right hemisphere, they appear to be subject to someone else's will, a will outside their control, which corresponds to the explanations often offered by children after massive impulsive outbursts. Impulsive outbursts are probably a combination of several powerful arousal states in deep-lying subcortical layers that can neither be inhibited nor verbalized (Cozolino, 2000; Siegel, 1999).

The left and right cortices process two different types of representations or forms of consciousness, and if the integration function is not optimal, the two hemispheres may dissociate. Early emotional experiences stored in the right hemisphere, for example of a threatening or stressful nature, may be unknown to the left hemisphere. Dissociated experiences stored before the growth spurt of the left hemisphere tend to remain non-symbolized and beyond language. These experiences exist as a separate reality that cannot be verbalized, and which consequently cannot be shared with others. If the right and left hemispheres are not integrated they work from two different perspectives. For example, on the basis of activity in the left hemisphere a person may work with cognitive aspects and make an effort to carry out a task, while simultaneous activity in the right hemisphere makes the person frustrated over emotional aspects of the task. Any form of psychological disorder includes disorders both in hierarchical and lateral (interhemispheric) integration. Integration of brain systems is crucial for the development of appropriate brain functions and identity, and all forms of psychotherapy essentially aim to integrate and reintegrate neural circuits (Bentzen & Hart, 2005; Cozolino, 2000; Schore 2001a).

Lateralization and trauma or neglect

In 1997, Teicher (2002) studied thirty children and young people, half of whom were psychiatric patients with a childhood history of physical or sexual abuse, and half of whom were a control group consisting of individuals with normal mental functioning. In the control group, the left cortex was more developed than the right, while in the psychiatric patients the right cortex had the same degree of development as in the control group, while their left cortex was distinctly smaller. When the psychiatric patients recalled neutral events, they displayed activation of the left hemisphere, while memories of traumatic experiences were associated with right-sided activation. In the control group, both types of memories activated both hemispheres. This might suggest that traumatized children lack interhemispheric integration. Their corpus callosum was therefore also studied, and the medial section was found to be significantly smaller than in the control group. Studies involving patients with post traumatic stress disorder (PTSD) who had been traumatized as children found a narrowing of the interhemispheric structure that encumbered transmission between the hemispheres. PTSD patients often have difficulty putting their emotions into words (alexithymia) and have problems with abstract and symbolic thinking (van der Kolk, 2000).

Long-term traumatization affects the integration between the two hemispheres, and the right hemisphere gains in influence, while activity in Broca's area and in the left prefrontal cortex is reduced. This intensifies emotions, but the emotions are beyond words. Children in this situation are unable to articulate or symbolize the psychological pain resulting from the traumatic experiences. The behaviour of traumatized children often involves a higher degree of emotionality with more emotional arousal and more negative feelings such as anxiety, sadness, and aggression, which they fail to understand or verbalize. Traumatized patients often experience depersonalization and have a sense that their own self is unreal. The surroundings also appear alien and strange, an experience that is often accompanied by a sense of being separated from one's body. In neurological terms this reflects a neural dissociation on a hierarchical level as well as on a lateral level. The depersonalization and the self-alien feelings correspond to the type of experiences found in patients with a severed interhemispheric link (Gjærum & Ellertsen, 2002).

The lack of interhemispheric integration probably means that right hemisphere processes are dissociated from consciousness. For children who have been exposed to massive neglect and traumatic experiences, this dissociation may offer some protection against feelings of terror and loss of control. Dissociation functionally isolates anatomically dispersed processes by blocking neural circuits between hierarchical structures as well as between the two hemispheres. Just as unconscious recall can be isolated from conscious recall, right and left hemisphere functions can be divided so that one hemisphere comes to dominate the other (Siegel, 1999).

Children with early emotional damage may express dissociation by developing isolated motor and cognitive functions that are not connected with the emotional areas. It should be noted here that the research literature does not distinguish between dissociation and inadequate maturation of neural circuits. It might be relevant to study whether lack of stimulation, as in severe deprivation, causes inadequate integration of neural circuitry, and whether hyperactivation, for example, through traumatic events, causes previously integrated neural connections to separate. It might also be relevant to study whether different intervention options are available for under-stimulation and dissociation, respectively. Whether the child has been exposed to deprivation or traumatization, the consequences for the child's personality seem to be the same. Even children of normal intelligence become unable to develop their "theory of mind" or mentalization capacity because they are cut off from integrating their cognition emotionally. This becomes particularly apparent in children with early emotional damage when they reach an age at which most other children are able to reflect on their own and others' feelings. For example, the twelve-year-old boy Matt, who suffered early emotional frustration, feels that he never does anything wrong, and that it is unfortunate when others make him upset because it makes him stay upset for the rest of the day. He is good friends with all the boys in his class, but he is not going to miss anyone when he moves away from town. He is particularly fond of one of his classmates because he does not annoy him, but he is also happy to be with others, as long as they do not annoy him. He states that nothing ever worries him. Matt's teachers describe Matt as a boy with good motor skills who is good at sports; he is also good at language tasks, but not at linguistic analyses that require empathy. He often has a cheeky or flippant attitude towards the teachers, something that he is unaware of; he adapts to whatever classmates he is with; he does not understand why friends fall out sometimes. At other times, he adjusts and adapts his external behaviour without having an opinion of his own or considering the relevance of his behaviour.

The development of a mentalization capacity requires that nonverbal internal representations with emotional content from the right hemisphere are able to connect with an interpretative and analysing part, which is located in the left hemisphere. Both hemispheres are necessary for appropriate processing and self-reflection and involved in forming narratives and life stories. Sharing mental knowledge and experiences with each other requires the involvement of both hemispheres (Cozolino, 2000).

Summary

As explained above, human consciousness relies on the harmonious integration of both hemispheres, and the complex structures give the hemispheres different consciousness qualities. For example, the human need to tell stories does not stem from the right hemisphere but from the left, which seeks to integrate with and absorb information from the right hemisphere when the brain system is internally connected and integrated (Newberg, d'Aquili, & Rause, 2002; Siegel, 2004).

In this chapter, I have discussed various aspects of brain lateralization and the modest anatomical but substantial behavioural differences between the two hemispheres. Neither hemisphere is dominant in relation to the other. They handle different functions, and their mutual synchronicity is one of the features that shape our personality and enable us to develop the capacities for empathy, mentalization, and symbolic and abstract thinking. In the next chapter, I turn to the function that enables all learning, and that enables us to relate to our past and future. The memory functions are diverse and express themselves in a multitude of ways, from primitive imprinting to sophisticated recall of semantic and autobiographical material. Without the sophisticated memory functions, we would not have been able to achieve the high mental levels that have allowed us to build a viable modern democratic society.

CHAPTER THIRTEEN

Memory and its impact on the formation of personality and mentalization

"What has happened to us in the past determines what we take out of our daily encounters in life; memories are records of how we have experienced events, not replicas of the events themselves. Experiences are encoded by brain networks whose connections had already been shaped by previous encounters with the world. This pre-existing knowledge powerfully influences how we encode and store new memories, thus contributing to the nature, texture, and quality of what we will recall of the moment"

(Schacter, 1996, p. 6)

M emory is a complicated concept that covers several separate processes and systems. Each system relies on a particular constellation of neural networks that each plays a specific role. Memory involves more than simply remembering the past. It also involves implicit or unconscious memory, which is essential for our ability to handle many different tasks. There are many different memory systems, each handling different memory functions. Like the different emotional systems, the different memory systems are located in different brain regions. The memory systems are complex, and our understanding of them relies on a wide range of theoretical perspectives, which makes it exceedingly difficult to form a general understanding. Personality formation and the potential for continued development rely completely on stored complex memory information and memory chains that can be recognized and drawn into conscious awareness as the situation requires.

A basic aspect of all memory is that it does not consist of literal recordings of reality. We do not store raw images, but rather the sensory impressions, meanings, and emotions related to the experience in question. Among other things, memory is related to our endeavour to make sense of experiences. We strive to construct something meaningful out of an experience, and events in the past determine the particular selection of experiences we store from the present. Our earlier encounters with the world have considerable influence on the way that new memories are transformed and stored and, thus, on what we recall. Our experiences are reconstructed by a brain that is different from the brain that shaped the memory in the first place. "Learning and memory . . . fill in the details of who we are as we become a unique person" (LeDoux, 2001, p. 134). Some memory systems are functional right before birth or soon after, while others take some time to become functional.

Our personality, sense of identity, and sense of self are inseparably intertwined. Sensing oneself requires a subjective experience of remembering the past. What separates interaction from relation is a form of historical continuity. One prerequisite for having this sense of historical continuity is a memory capacity (Stern, 1985).

In this chapter, I aim to order, categorize, and describe the basic and predominant theories concerning memory and to explain memory functions in relation to the triune brain model in order to demonstrate how various memory function present at different mental organization levels in the hierarchical structure of the brain.

The multiple memory systems

As mentioned above, memory covers many concepts and types; the most important of them are illustrated in Figure 13.1.

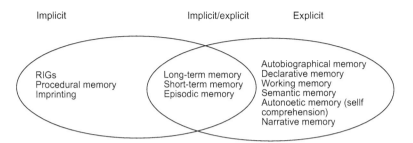

Figure 13.1.   The multiple memory systems.

The memory system that is accessible to our consciousness is called explicit or declarative memory. All other forms of memory are implicit or unconscious memory. Explicit memory consists of conscious reflections, while implicit memory exists outside the reflective consciousness without necessarily repressing it. As shown in Figure 13.1, explicit memory is divided into autobiographical, semantic, declarative, and working memory. Implicit memory is divided into representations of interactions that have been generalized (RIGs), procedural memory, and imprinting. In addition, memory is characterized as long-term, short-term, or episodic memory, which can be either explicit or implicit.

The implicit and explicit memory systems consist of two different structures. Because the implicit memory system becomes functional before the explicit, they are often described as, respectively, early and late emerging memory systems. We know that persons with damage to the hippocampus lose the ability to create new explicit memory tracks, but remain capable of implicit learning. In a case story from the beginning of the twentieth century, a young woman was hospitalized with severe amnesia, which meant that at every consultation her doctor had to introduce himself to her anew, as if they had never met before. One day the doctor concealed a thumb tack in his hand when he shook the young woman's hand, and the woman responded to the pain. The next time the doctor showed up, although she still did not recognize him, she refused to shake his hand. She said that she found the thought highly repulsive although she did not know why (Kringelbach, 2004). Damage to the organs that involve implicit memory, for example the amygdala, does not prevent continued learning about facts and events, but it does destroy the ability to incorporate implicit knowledge. Damage to the amygdala, among other areas, will have severe ramifications and may be severely disabling emotionally, especially if the damage occurs early in life. Matt (the case story mentioned in Chapter Twelve), who had suffered early emotional frustration, is unable to integrate emotional events in his memory. He has no problems in storing general learning, but it is extremely difficult for him to integrate the kind of knowledge that he needs to understand his own and other persons' emotions.

Explicit and implicit memory relates to different structures. For example, implicit memory relates to structures such as the hippocampus and thus shapes the organization of explicit memory. As in the example with the woman who refused to shake the doctor's hand although she did not know why, implicit and explicit memory may be dissociated, and this phenomenon of dissociation is probably also involved in repression where someone has no explicit recollection of an event but acts and reacts as if he or she did (Kandel & Hawkins, 1999). Conditioned anxiety responses involve implicit processes that are independent of conscious awareness. When implicit learning is complete, the stimulus in question does not have to be perceived consciously in order to trigger the conditioned emotional response: a sound or a sight that reminds a person of a traumatic event may trigger anxiety even if the person does not consciously associate the sound or the sight with the event.

Implicit memory

The implicit memory system is a learning system that does not require a consciously reflective focus of attention during encoding. The implicit memory system may be activated by sensory and motor systems and can be observed in practically all living beings. In implicit memory, the nervous system is affected independently of any conscious involvement. Implicit memory reflects automatic thoughts and actions that are not necessarily based on explicit knowledge. Implicit memory plays an important role in personality characteristics, such as someone's way of walking, talking, and smiling. The implicit memory system is active during the foetal period, and newborn infants will turn towards sound stimuli that have been learned during gestation. A child who has been scared by a loud noise associated with a particular toy will react with discomfort when presented with the same toy in the future (Siegel, 1999).

Implicit memories are perceived as sensations, feelings, or intuition. Sometimes the implicit memory system intuitively captures the essence of a complex issue that the logical brain fails to resolve. Experience formation often takes place implicitly without any conscious decision to acquire a particular skill or insight. For example, older people are often able to predict the weather without knowing what specific conditions these predictions are based upon. From decades of generalizations about cloud and wind conditions their nervous system has learned what precedes certain weather conditions. When confronted with repetitive experiences, the brain unconsciously deduces the underlying rules of the experiences, and implicit knowledge occurs without any focus on learning. Implicit memory has no sensation of self, time, or recall.

Explicit memory

Explicit memory actually just means memories that are remembered consciously, and which are potentially present when needed. Explicit memory works as an extension of the implicit memory system and relies on it to work (LeDoux, 1998).

Explicit memories may be sensory, motor, cognitive, or linguistic. Words and visual images are often the key to explicit memories. Explicit memory lets us store information about a particular event that took place at a particular time and place. The explicit learning system is quick, and sometimes only needs one learning attempt, unlike implicit learning, which accumulates knowledge through a repetition of numerous experiments. The encoding process in the explicit memory system requires directed attention to activate the hippocampus. Excessive activation, as in the case of anxiety, or inadequate activation, as in the case of sleepiness, has negative effects on attention and learning (Kandel & Hawkins, 1999).

Much of our knowledge of explicit memory comes from the patient HM, who, in 1953, had both his temporal lobes surgically removed, including both hippocampi, as an attempt to treat severe epileptic seizures. The operation appeared successful, as the epileptic seizures disappeared. It turned out, however, that HM had lost the ability to form explicit, declarative memories. Forty years after the operation, HM could not remember where he lived and did not know his own age or history. HM was able to retain information for a few seconds (i.e., his short-term memory was intact), and he was able to recall memories that had been stored prior to the surgery. He was able to improve his performance through training; for example, he was able to copy patterns and improve the outcome by repeating the task. Researchers do not agree whether it is the hippocampus alone that enables us to transfer information from short-term to long-term memory. For example, Kringelbach (2004) points out that another part of the temporal lobe cortex is also crucial for correct transfer and consolidation. However, Zola-Morgan, Squire, Rempel, Clower, and Amaral (1992) say that there is sufficient evidence that limited damage to the hippocampus alone can impair memory functions.

Long-term memory

Long-term memory consists of memories that last hours, days, or years, in some cases a lifetime. Stored memories do not necessarily last forever, since long-term memories that are not used may gradually fade away. This is what happens when someone returns after twenty years or so to a city where they once lived, and discover that they are no longer able to find their way around, although the area has hardly changed at all.

Long-term memory integrates separate association chains, which become linked and form memory units that are constantly reorganized. This consolidation process probably relies on REM-sleep (dream sleep), which is believed to play a key role in storing the essence of personally significant experiences and activities from the day gone by. Very few stored memory tracks are transferred to long-term memory to undergo long-term consolidation (Siegel, 1999).

Experiments with HM taught the researchers that the brain system that involves the shaping of new long-term memories is different from the system that stores old long-term memories. HM had no problem recalling memories from the time before the operation, but after the procedure he was unable to move information from his short-term memory into his long-term memory. Long-term memory involves two stages, an encoding phase, which requires hippocampal function, and a subsequent stage where one is able to recall the experiences, probably through the prefrontal cortex. Hippocampus is a necessary element in the formation of long-term memories, but once consolidation has taken place, memory is independent of the hippocampus (Damasio, 1994; LeDoux, 1998). Loss of long-term memory is associated with horrendous human loss, as we see it, for example, in the late stages of Alzheimer's disease. One patient with Alzheimer's disease put it this way: "I am floating down an unknown river, every new situation is impossible to predict, anything can happen, and I am only able to relate to the present itself" (Lautrop, 2002).

Long-term memory is important for our ability to remember our history, and, as such, it is the structure for our sense of identity. It provides the sense of being oneself and having historical continuity. Our short-term memory and our working memory, however, are essential structures for conscious learning, for example when we memorize something or try to grasp the text in this book.

Long-term potentiation and Hebb's axiom

Regardless of what mental organization level a given memory system is located on, it appears to be the same neural basis that enables both learning and memory. Memory is based on changes in neural patterns and activities that can only occur when the brain is in use. The brain alters its neural activity in response to changes, and information is stored throughout the brain. Memory phenomena are created when synaptic connections between simultaneously firing neurons are strengthened. Structural changes at the synaptic level are based on experience, and experience helps determine the strength of neural cooperation and, in some cases, survival. Our short-term or working memory seems to have a passing neurochemically modifying effect on synapses, while long-term memory is based on more or less permanent structural synaptic changes (Mathiesen, 2004).

As previously mentioned, the brain consists of a mesh of neural nets that fire in countless different ways and patterns throughout the brain. Memories are created when temporarily connected activity occurs in separate neuron groups. When a neuron fires, the adjacent neuron is activated, and when the adjacent neuron has been activated once, any new stimulation will make it increasingly receptive. The more frequently a pattern is activated the greater is the chance that it will activate at a later time. Life consists of a myriad of visual impressions, sounds, actions, and words that are analysed in the nervous system and picked up by neuron groups that offer a coherent experience of an event. These patterns of connections have the potential to enter into our field of attention and contribute with the explicit memory of something under the right circumstances, but most of the time most of them lie dormant (Schacter, 1996).

As mentioned in Chapter Two, in 1949 Hebb developed his theory, which was later synthesized into Hebb's axiom, that neurons that "fire together wire together". Synaptic connections are altered and strengthened both through the formation of new neural connections and through the modification of existing neural circuits. Bliss and Lomo (1973) later identified the mechanism that forms the basis for Hebb's axiom. They called the mechanism "long-term potentiation", which involves the neurotransmitter glutamate among other elements. Long-term potentiation takes place on the background of theta wave activity in the brain, and three to four weeks after the stimulation occurred, the connection remains visibly strengthened (Austin, 1998). Long-term potentiation is the neural basis for all existing memory systems.

Neural circuits connect into networks, which enhances the possibility that a given memory track activates many other memory tracks when it is recognized or recalled. What is stored is the likelihood that particular neurons will fire in a particular neural pattern. In the recognition or recall process, neuron groups fire synchronously in a chain reaction. Neurons in different areas develop stronger mutual connections, and the new connections "store" the event, which Hebb called an engram, the neurological term for what memory scientists call schemata. Millions of engrams have the potential to step into the field of attention. Only a fragment of the original experience is needed to trigger the recognition or recall of the entire episode. The neural networks combine information in the present with patterns stored in the past, and the resulting mix is what the network "remembers". For example, a repeat visit to Vietnam will produce very different memories for a Vietnam veteran and for a tourist, and the memories they each take with them will also be very different. Neurons rearrange themselves over time and create new connections. Memory studies with rats have shown that new learning causes synaptic reorganization. This principle applies to all learning and memory (Karr-Morse & Wiley, 1997; LeDoux, 1998, 2001; Schacter, 1996; Siegel, 1999).

Conditioning, deconditioning, extinction, habituation, and sensitization

The brain has billions of neurons, which connect with billions of neural circuits, and every synaptic juncture has the potential to enter into a memory. The capacity of the human brain is infinite. Memories are groups of neurons firing together in the same pattern every time they are reactivated. This was how Ivan Pavlov's experiments with conditioned responses worked. Pavlov found that certain unconditioned reflexes, such as the secretion of saliva, can become conditioned through habituation. Through experiments with dogs, he discovered that once the dogs had learned to relate a signal, like the ringing of a bell, with a reward such as a tasty snack, they would begin to salivate as soon as they heard the signal, the sound of the bell. It took time, patience, and a consistently conditioned response to get the dogs to associate the external stimulus, the sound of the bell, with a subsequent reward, but once the dogs had acquired the conditioned behaviour it was very difficult to extinguish. Therefore, Pavlov experimented with deconditioning, the extinction of previously conditioned behaviour. For example, if for an extended period of time he rang the bell without giving the dogs their snack, the salivation response would eventually disappear. In relation to the reorganization of neural structures there is a mechanism that weakens synaptic connections. It is a sort of long-term fading, which probably sets in when a neuron fires without activating the adjacent neuron. Memory tracks are weakened when firing neurons fail to activate adjacent neurons. As important as memory is, forgetting is equally essential, lest the brain fill up with all sorts of useless information (Kandel & Hawkins, 1999).

In one case, Pavlov found a more drastic mechanism for deconditioning. In 1924 Leningrad was flooded, and the surge of the floodwaters came close to drowning many of Pavlov's dogs in their cages. The frightened dogs paddled for dear life and were rescued in the nick of time. Subsequently, many of the dogs developed shock reactions akin to PTSD reactions in humans. Before the flooding, Pavlov had trained the dogs to acquire certain conditioned behaviour patterns. After the flooding, he found that the dogs that displayed shock reaction patterns no longer remembered the conditioned behaviour patterns—the patterns had been extinguished (Austin, 1998).

From the moment of birth, many of the infant's functions consist of unconditioned reflexes that gradually become conditioned under the influence of life events. Some behavioural features are hard to unlearn, partly because they have become habituated and sensitized during early sensitive or critical phases and have become intricately interwoven with the architecture of the brain. Conditioning, and probably all sorts of associative learning, evolved to enable animals to learn to distinguish between events that coincide often as opposed to more rarely. The brain developed a simple mechanism for predicting frequent occurrences. This has significant survival value in terms of recognizing and warding off danger, finding food, and avoiding tainted or toxic foods (Austin, 1998; Kandel, 2005).

The simplest form of learning is habituation, which consists in reducing the response to a repetition of the same stimuli. For example, the first time we hear a sound we pay attention to it, and the sympathetic nervous system is activated. If the same sound is repeated, one soon learns to recognize the sound, and the attention and body reactions gradually fade away. Habituation consists in recognizing and ignoring stimuli that have lost their novelty or meaning. Sensitization is the opposite of habituation. It is a process during which one learns to increase a response as the result of new stimuli. For example, sensitization leads to the awareness of stimuli that may lead to painful or dangerous consequences (Kandel, 2005).

To protect itself from being flooded with stimuli, the brain does not encode all information. A selection takes place, based partly on prior knowledge. One only remembers what is encoded, and what is encoded depends on one's temperament, previous experiences, knowledge, and needs. Different people may have very different recollections of the same event (Purves et al., 2001).

In the next section, we look at the way memory collects in schema-based memory units or general mentalized representations.

Schema-based memory and RIGs

As early as the 1930s, Bartlett (1932) was aware that memory collects in expectation-based entities, which he called schema-based memory. Both Bartlett and memory scientist Edelman have pointed out that the experience of remembering takes place in the present, not in the past. Memory fragments are recognized, recalled, and combined on the basis of the current context. The current moment sets off perceptions, sensations, and feelings, which together activate many different memory networks. The combination of the current context and previous experiences determines which fragments are recalled and recognized at any given moment (Stern, 1995).

To some extent, the present is determined by the past, but the way our memory works means that the past is also constantly being reconstructed by the present. All acts of recognition and recall involve a reorganization that reconstructs the past (Piaget, 1973). From the moment of birth, the brain is busy creating multi-modal models of the world. Our mental models are influenced by our encounters with the world, and this helps the central nervous system build expectation-based systems. Deviations from the recognizable are studied, which gradually makes the environment increasingly predictable. The brain is constantly scanning its surroundings to prepare for what may happen next. Generalizations form the basis for mental models that help the infant translate experiences that take place in the present by comparing them with the past. Children are constantly seeking to form expectations about what will happen in the immediate future. Every single day offers opportunities for new learning, as present experiences integrate with previous experiences and are interwoven with an expected future. Thus, our memory is constantly changing. For example, memories of clear, individual childhood experiences probably never offer a completely reliable reflection of the actual chain or character of events (Siegel, 1999). A neuropsychologist and colleague once explained how he had recalled a clear memory from his childhood and mentioned it to his brother some thirty years after the event. He remembered that their father had caught him when he fell off a horse and kept him from getting hurt. When he told his brother of the episode, the brother began to laugh; he told him that he also remembered the episode, but that in his recollection he was the one who fell off the horse!

New memories are inevitably coloured by old memories, and distortions of an event are a common occurrence. For example, the occipital lobes are involved in both visual mental images and visual sensory impressions. Frequently imagining an event may make it seem as if the event actually took place, because imagined images are generated by the same neural machinery that is involved in the perception of actual events. Recalling actual events, however, simultaneously activates structures in the brainstem.

Bartlett pointed out that memory fragments are reconstructed through recognition and recall processes, and that previous experiences change in relation to later interpretations. The past is constantly rewritten and updated to match our current view of the present. Memories offer more than just a frozen image of the past. Remembered events are often reconstructed, and gaps are filled in an attempt to make the past fit the present. The remembered past is constructed and reconstructed to fit our notions of the present (Gleitman, 1995; van der Kolk, 1987).

Stern says that right from birth, perhaps even during the foetal period, memory consists of episodic events that are indivisible entities of perceptions, affects, and actions. Repeating an episode many times results in generalized episodes or generalized memory. Generalized memory implies an expectation concerning the way that a situation is likely to develop from one moment to the next. The generalized memory gives us a sense of self-permanence. The impressions and experience of the primary care-giver are interwoven, ordered, and combined to form the basic memory units that Stern calls RIGs (representations of interactions that have been generalized). The repetitive nature of many events means that they are likely to form the basis of representations. The child remembers these representations as prototypical situations, such as being put to bed, being at a birthday party, etc. In the care-giver–infant interaction the infant is constantly creating RIGs on the basis of interactions with the care-giver, generalizing the way in which she holds the child, comforts it, speaks to it, changes the nappy, etc. (Nelson & Gruendel, 1981; Stern, 1989).

RIGs are flexible structures that represent an average of many specific experiences. An RIG is something that never happened in exactly that way, but that nevertheless does not involve anything that did not take place at some time or other. If an episode proves to be different from previous episodes, the RIG will change, i.e., the RIGs are continually updated on the basis of current experiences. The more previous experiences the RIG is based on, the smaller is the influence of any specific episode. RIGs are a sort of working model that changes as new experiences are incorporated, and others are extinguished (Stern, 1985).

We derive psychological meaning and coherence from experiences that consist of many different forms of impression that are processed in different brain structures. The coordination and integration of processes at lower levels leads to the emergence of a more global mental event. Events and emotions are connected on the basis of individual events, they are stored, and on a higher level they assume another sense or meaning. Even young infants are able to form primitive RIGs on the basis of interaction events, and, as the brain matures and the networks are expanded with the addition of the cortical areas, fantasies, memories, and narratives develop, and the RIGs gradually change.

Schema-based memory and RIGs are what shape the internal images or representations that help to form our self-perception. Our memory is expectation-based and needs certain experiential patterns to repeat themselves in order to form internal representations of them. Children who are raised in a chaotic and disorganized environment fail to receive stimulation through these experiential patterns, and this has severe consequences for their developing nervous system. These children will have difficulty forming stable internal representations to facilitate the development of self-regulatory skills, and their nervous system does not have the opportunity to integrate sufficiently with higher cortical functions, as we saw in the example with Matt in Chapter Twelve.

Memory and internal representations

The encoding of specific memories of actual experiences begins as early as the foetal stage, and the repetition of similar experiences allows the organism begin to generalize and, subsequently, to react on the basis of these expectations. Expectation-based behaviour is frequent, even in lower species of animals. The nervous system seeks to organize or synchronize according to the rhythm of the surroundings by identifying patterns and looking for recognizable features, a process that helps to mature the nervous system. Gradually, the recognizable features merge to form generalized patterns or representations.

The generalized representations contain interaction patterns, which in humans are constructed through the contact between care-giver and infant. During their first six months of life, infants form representations of repeated moments of social interaction. The interaction patterns contain the infants' internal representations of their own arousal and capacity for self-regulation as the interaction unfolds. For example, when they begin to smile at the care-giver around the age of two months, they experience their own motor acts through the smile and the related arm or leg movements. They receive feedback from the care-giver and experience an emotional quality, such as pleasure. At the same time, the infant sees the care-giver's face, as she engages and returns the gaze, and expects her face to open up into a smile if this is the usual consequence. These repeated interactive moments contain many features from the two individuals. Infants recognize and remember the patterns from repeated experiences, and the repeated experiences organize the infant's nervous system. The generalized representations arise through the dynamic interaction from moment to moment. When experiences are repeated sufficiently often, infants distil a proto-typical constellation out of the many individual moments. These moments merge into generalized acts between infant and care-giver and lead to the formation of internal representations (Beebe & Lachmann, 2002; Stern, 1989). The generalized acts embedded in the care-giver–infant relationship explain the personality formation on the basis of internal representations that spring from the mutual attachment. In other words, our personality is formed by our partic-ipation in each other's nervous systems.

Internal representations are constructed on the basis of interac-tion experiences with others and stem from experiences of being with others. For example, when young children imitate others, they form a representation of the feelings they have when they are together with the other. Stern points out that representations are about doing and being, and that the infant's impressions of the caregiver are woven together, arranged, and merged (Stern, 1985). The impressions that arise have their counterparts in the neural circuits. Our lived relational experiences are successively incorporated throughout the development of the nervous system and gradually shape our personality. Relational experiences are incorporated into the neural circuits and reorganized on an ongoing basis.

Implicit information about close relationships lies outside language and is not normally translated into a linguistic form. Internal representations are constructions created through the interaction of the infant's nervous systems with external care-givers, and they consist of more than just internalized objects. It is implicit relational knowledge, imprinted into the neural circuits, that constructs the internal representations, and which develops through a jointly constructed regulation pattern. The internal representations become increasingly integrated into the nervous system and become part of the infant's verbal self-experience as language develops (Lyons-Ruth, 1998).

The developmental psychology of memory

The memory systems develop gradually as the structures of the nervous system mature. Some memory systems are functional from birth or shortly thereafter, while others develop later.

The child's earliest memory system organizes around motor and sensory patterns at brainstem level. Infants remember the relationship between their own behaviour and the surroundings, and they remember what felt pleasant or unpleasant. The internal representations at this level consist of the movements, acts, and gestures that occur in interactions with the care-giver (Beebe & Lachmann, 2002; DeCasper & Carstens, 1980; DeCasper & Fifer, 1980; DeCasper & Spencer, 1986).

Brainstem structures are active from birth, and the amygdala is also believed to develop early and to have largely reached its final shape at the time of birth, unlike the hippocampus, which probably matures gradually. Until the hippocampus matures, the role of the amygdala is to create an intuitive emotional sense of adaptation and misattunement between infant and parents. The hippocampus enables the child to organize experiences in a temporal and spatial context, and while this structure is still immature, experiences are stored in brainstem structures and in the amygdala as crude nonverbal emotional templates. When emotional memories stored in brainstem structures and the amygdala are evoked later in life, they will not be available as specific events with a temporal and spatial aspect, and there are no narratives and thoughts to explain the response.

There is a likely to be a connection between the development of the prefrontal areas, the cingulate gyrus, and the hippocampus on the one hand and the development of explicit memory on the other. Separation anxiety relies on the ability to recall separation episodes and to maintain representations of non-present persons—in other words, object permanence. These abilities are not present until the age of 7–8 months. Before that time, infants are unable to form explicit memories about time, place, and specific events. They are capable of acquiring skills, but not of establishing memories concerning specific events, and have no access to information about where and when a key event took place (Table 13.1). Events influence the child as implicit, non-verbal templates, unrelated to time and place, and although the child is unable to recall individual events, these events are nevertheless important for the development of an early self-experience. Most of the internal representations that create the basis for our self-experience are implicit and stem from countless micro-interactions with the environment. From the foetal stage and early infancy, events are imprinted into the nervous system and form the basis for the development of personality.

Infants under the age of eight months do not respond to the difference between familiar and novel objects, but react with conditioned behaviour when they hear, for example, a sound that is associated with a pleasant or unpleasant experience. Piaget noted that when 8–9-month-old infants had to find objects that they first saw being hidden in one place, then in another, they looked where they first saw the object being hidden. This development probably reflects the emerging maturation of the hippocampus. For example, the memory system in seven-month-old infants is not sufficiently developed to allow them to remember their mother's disappearance. At the age of 9–10 months, the infant begins to be able to

Table 13.1.   Scematic outline of memory development.

0–8 months. Structures involved in memory:

Brain stem and amgdala. Imprinting, which consists of movements, actions, mimicry, and gestures

8–12 months. Structures involved in memory:

Hippocampus in co-operation with other parts of the limbic system. The infant is able to form explicit memories about time, place, and specific events based on recognition. Development of object permanence.

12–18 months. Structures involved in memory:

Orbitofrontal cortex and large parts of the neocortex. The child begins to be able to recall events.

18 months–2 years. Structures involved in memory:

Further maturation of the hippocampus and orbitofrontal cortex in interaction with the emergence of cognitive abilities, for example language, strategies, etc. The infant becomes able to talk about memories from daily events and remember experiences from the past. The infant also begins to be able to recognize him/herself.

2–4 years. Structures involved in memory

Broca's and Wernicke's areas.
The child is able to talk about previous events.

remember her disappearance, but the system is still sensitive, which is one of the things that make the peek-a-boo game fun. At the age of twelve months, the child is able to remember where objects are hidden, even when there is a longer interval between hiding and recovering the object (Schacter, 1996; Schacter & Moscovitch, 1984).

With the development of the orbitofrontal cortex, the infant begins to be able to maintain object permanence in time and space. Before the maturation of the orbitofrontal cortex, the infant has depended on the care-giver's presence in order for the internal representations of her to be activated. The development of the orbitofrontal cortex now enables the infant to maintain stored information about internalized representations that may influence behaviour and to induce certain responses and inhibit others. The internal representations of an external object, for example the mother, who constantly responds to the infant's impulses in a stimulating fashion, is stored in memory and may modulate impulses in the future, even when she is not absent. The presence of object permanence indicates that an object exists permanently in time and space in the infant's mental world. This skill emerges around the age of 7½–12 months, a period that also marks a turning point in the infant's memory development (Rovee-Collier & Fagen, 1981; Schacter & Moscovitch, 1984; Stern, 1985).

Childhood amnesia

Early childhood amnesia has been the object of a fair amount of research. Piaget was one of the first to describe the importance of distinguishing between recognition and recall in memory research. Recognition, he stated, develops at an early age and is found in organisms far down on the phylogenetic scale, while recall requires symbolic functions that only develop in humans around the age of 1½–2 years. Piaget (1973) believed that memories that fail to be integrated on a semantic/linguistic level tend to organize on a more primitive level, for example, through visual imagery or somatic sensations. When recall memory begins to function, the subjective experience will be social, regardless of whether the child is alone or not. After this age, infants engage in interactions with care-givers some of the time, and with their internal representations almost all the time (Stern, 1985). At this time, the infant's mental life begins to take on greater importance. It becomes possible to form mental images about others who are not present, and these others can take on great importance whether they are present or not. However isolated a person may be, a major part of our personality consists of internal representations that are present whether or not we are together with others. Our thoughts about other people mean that relationships have become an integrated part of our nervous system. At times, the various internal representations co-exist harmoniously, at other times, they are dissociated and hostile towards each other; the latter is often the case in individuals with a critical and judgemental superego structure, which acts disparagingly towards other aspects of the personality.

The technical memory skills undergo considerable change after the first two years of life, probably due to the development of the prefrontal cortex and cognitive abilities such as language, self-comprehension, expansion of general knowledge and strategies, etc.

Around two years of age, the child is able to talk about memories of daily events and remember experiences from the past. This probably reflects a further maturation of the hippocampus and orbitofrontal cortex. At this age, children develop more complex representations of themselves in the world and begin to recognize themselves. For example, at this time children realize that when they see a red speck on their nose in the mirror, the speck is on their own nose not on the mirror image (Schacter & Moscovitch, 1984; Siegel, 1999).

A one-year-old infant is pleased when he or she opens the door and sees grandmother outside, even if it has been a long time since her last visit. Seeing grandmother sparks implicit memory tracks that enable the infant to recognize her with ease. At the age of one year, the infant uses image symbols to store information, while a two-year-old child has begun to use language, which provides an entirely new symbol and memory system. Around their second birthday, children are able to talk about previous events and gradually develop their mental imagery. Around this time they begin to be able to remember specific experiences from the past, and as the prefrontal cortex continues to develop, this ability becomes more and more complex and sophisticated. As previously mentioned, the prefrontal cortex continues to develop well into adolescence, and the mentalizing capacity and ability for self-reflection is not fully developed until the age of 20–25 years (Siegel, 1999; van der Kolk, 1987).

Generalized and expectation-based schemata

Children gradually form an extensive store of RIGs for various events, and an activated RIG contains an amalgam of typical sequences and specific events. A child's first RIGs include individual interaction routines that involve the child, such as eating, going to the nursery, visiting grandmother, etc. Autobiographical memories in chronologically ordered sequences of important events do not occur until the age of 3–4 years. Organizing mundane events is a key element in the child's acquisition of social and cultural understanding. When 3–8-year-olds describe a sequence of events, their stories do not reflect what happened on any particular occasion, but rather what normally happens. The immature memory system seeks to co-ordinate knowledge that is based on separate experiences. When the working memory becomes sufficiently developed, children become better at applying strategies that help them recall individual episodes. Children under the age of seven years only apply this type of strategies to a limited extent (Nelson, 1984, 1996).

Memory tracks need strengthening, and only acquire permanence after sufficient and repeated experiences. Childhood is a period when children have to learn to recognize situations that later evolve into expectation-based schemata, the very thing that shapes a child's self in the world. As the child grows older, patterns emerge through narratives where the child shares experiences about the past with parents and others, and this becomes the basis for autobiographical memory (Nelson, 1996). Children who are not stimulated through their care-givers' tales of previous events in their life will fail to create their self-narrative and become "ahistorical". This can have serious consequences for the child's self-comprehension and inner sense of continuity and coherence. Mentally, the child will find it difficult to relate current events to previous events.

It is necessary to distinguish between self-experience and self-comprehension. An infant takes the care-giver's behaviour for granted, and the care-giver–infant interaction is imprinted into the infant's nervous system. Interaction experiences are stored implicitly and experienced as "self". Self-comprehension, on the other hand, depends on what is remembered and recalled about the past. This memory system relies on the accessibility of appropriate recall tracks, and if the nervous system fails to match experiences with dormant memories, much of the past will be placed beyond sensory access. Self-experience is different from self-comprehension—the two concepts rely on different structures that develop at very different times. Self-experience is related to early imprinting and the experience of object permanence, while self-comprehension is related to so-called autobiographical memory, which is discussed later in this chapter.

In this section, I have described how the memory systems are activated in the course of the development process, but the infant's arousal regulation has considerable influence on memory functions. Our autonomic nervous system and reticular activation system are important for memory, as arousal can both facilitate and hamper the processes of encoding and storage. For example, a chronically heightened stress level may restrict the storage process, and in the next section I review the link between arousal and memory.

Arousal and memory

Events that are perceived as highly emotional are categorized as particularly important and thus become easier to remember in the future. If events are overwhelming and characterized by extreme anxiety, a number of factors, including the release of cortisol, inhibit hippocampal processing of the explicit memory. When hippocampal function is inhibited, the implicit memory system is active during the storage process, while explicit processing is hampered. Thus, implicit elements of major—and perhaps minor—traumatic events may continue to shape the individual's life without the person's conscious awareness. In the case of extreme stress, memories will be stored only in the amygdala, not in the hippocampus. As a consequence, memory tracks have a more primitive and somatic quality and are less accessible to limbic and frontal control. In the absence of inhibition from the prefrontal cortex, stress responses are activated rapidly and are outside volitional control (Siegel, 1999; van der Kolk, 1994).

Rats that are injected with a stress-related hormone immediately after learning a task increase their memory capacity. Heightened arousal is accompanied by the release of noradrenalin, which contributes to memory consolidation, and heightened arousal at the time of memory processing therefore has a positive effect on memory storage. If the state of heightened arousal is chronic, memory function in the hippocampus is inhibited, partly due to the release of cortisol, and explicit memory is weakened. People who have been exposed to long-term and repeated severe trauma, for example patients with post traumatic stress disorder (PTSD), are often unable to verbalize events and, consequently, unable to orientate themselves in time and place, partly due to the impaired hippocampus function and failure to activate the language areas (Broca's area) in the left hemisphere. Children who have been exposed to massive stress-related experiences often show reactions akin to those of PTSD patients (Schacter, 1996; van der Kolk, 1994, 1996).

The many different memory structures are closely interwoven. Over time, researchers have studied different aspects of memory, and in the following I discuss the most widely known memory systems in order to establish a sort of "map" of the placement of the different memory structures within the brain. This discussion will be based on MacLean's triune model of the brain.

Memory and the hierarchical brain

In the hierarchical brain, each layer is involved in different aspects of the memory function. The reptilian brain contains both genetic and instinctive memory tracks developed through evolutionary processes and conditioned learning on a sensorimotor level. In the palaeomammalian brain, emotional and motor aspects are added to memory, and conditioned learning is coordinated with emotional categories and non-volitional acts. Both the instinctive and the emotional system are non-verbal and unconscious. The neomammalian brain processes and controls networks in charge of explicit memory; many of these functions are also unconscious. The implicit memory systems are crucial for the acquisition of sensory, motor, and emotional networks and for explicit memory (Figure 13.2).

Memory is stored in different structures, depending on what it is that is learnt and remembered. For example, the amygdala and basal ganglia enable emotional memory, while the cerebellum, basal ganglia, and motor cortex enable behavioural memory, etc. Somatosensory (body) memory is linked through circuits with the autonomic nervous system, hypothalamus, amygdala, cingulate gyrus, parietal lobes, and orbitofrontal cortex, and the more connected the systems are to structures at the top rungs of the hierarchy, the more advanced, symbolized, and volitional they become. Memory systems connect both hierarchically and across the two hemispheres through top-down and bottom-up processes. Just as implicit memory can activate the amygdala without activating explicit memory,

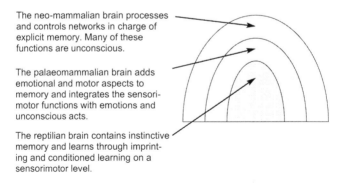

The neo-mammalian brain processes and controls networks in charge of explicit memory. Many of these functions are unconscious.

The palaeomammalian brain adds emotional and motor aspects to memory and integrates the sensorimotor functions with emotions and unconscious acts.

The reptilian brain contains instinctive memory and learns through imprinting and conditioned learning on a sensorimotor level.

Figure 13.2.   The triune brain with memory functions.

conscious memory tracks may activate anxiety because there are connections from explicit memory to the amygdala (LeDoux, 1998).

In the following, I look at each of the mental levels of organization in relation to the memory functions. We begin at the base with protomentation in the reptilian brain, and then move up through emotomentation at the palaeomammalian level to ratiomentation at the neomammalian level.

The level of protomentation

At the level of protomentation, all memory functions consist of implicit memories. The most basic and primitive form of memory exists in all nervous systems and is called imprinting memory.

Imprinting memory

Imprinting takes place in primitive neural circuits and is often a rigid system that resists change. Through studies of goslings, animal behaviourist Konrad Lorenz showed that newly hatched goslings will form an attachment to the first large moving object that they see and hear—an attachment that lasts the rest of their lives. He found that geese imprint an attachment figure during a limited period right after hatching. When the geese are sexually mature, they get together with geese that they were exposed to during this early period of imprinting. In geese, the early environment shapes and imprints the neural networks, which means that later in life they seek out what they recognize from earlier experiences. Even though the attachment systems of primates and humans are far more flexible than in geese, we, too, have an imprinting system that is located deep in the subcortical structures—a system characterized by some rigidity. The imprinting process that forms the basis for the attachment process involves an early and largely irreversible branding of previous experiences into a developing nervous system (Bowlby, 1969; Cozolino, 2000; Lewis, Amini, & Lannon, 2001).

Highly intensive events help "drive" the imprinting process. Imprinting is induced through behavioural synchronization between care-giver and infant, which activates polymodal areas, i.e., areas capable of transferring the sensation of a sound to the sensation of an emotion. As a natural process, stimulation from a familiar, safe care-giver strengthens the imprinting process. Imprinting memory is a biologically prepared learning system that requires minimal stimulation and training, and responses to stimuli are quickly incorporated (Petrovitch & Gewirtz, 1985).

Procedural memory

Procedural memory (also referred to as non-declarative memory) is a part of implicit memory, and like imprinting it refers to auto-mated functions. Procedural memory carries out behavioural tasks on the basis of instincts and early acquired knowledge, without the person having any knowledge of the "how" and "when" of this earlier learning. Automated tasks no longer need brain capacity from higher-order functions to be carried out. This memory system is mainly subcortical and is functional already at the foetal stage (DeCasper & Fifer, 1980).

Procedural representations are rule-based and do not have to be encoded symbolically; this includes knowledge about how to ride a bicycle, play the piano, etc. Procedural memories are stored in different locations at a protomental level. For example, motor learn-ing of the "how to ride a bicycle"-type and certain habitual patterns are stored in the cerebellum and basal ganglia. Motor learning such as facial expressions is also stored in the cerebellum and connects to the reflex system through the cranial nerves and autonomic nervous system. In order for memory to function normally, many different memory layers must be connected and co-ordinated. Here, the thalamus is essential. It does not store memories but provides the connections. Damage to the thalamus causes different levels of autobiographical knowledge to be torn apart, like a Second World War soldier who is unaware that the war is over (Scaer, 2001; Schacter, 1996).

The cerebellum controls the precision and timing of movements, emotions, etc., and is able to change as a result of experience. Many memories are tied to muscle patterns and their co-ordination. During the first months of life sensory, perceptual, bodily, and emotional memory combine through the polymodal networks.

These networks make it possible, for example, to connect the sight of mum and dad with raised arms, a smile, and a good feeling. During the first years of life somatic, sensory, motor, and emotional experiences sculpt the neural networks, which provides the basis for the infant's ability to sense a physical self (Cozolino, 2000; LeDoux, 2001; Stern, 1985).

An important part of procedural memory is implicit knowledge about how to interact with others. Thus, procedural memory contains knowledge about how to get attention, express affects, engage in social interactions with others, etc. Much of this memory system consists of so-called implicit relational knowledge, i.e., knowledge concerning how to engage in interactions with others and about what feels pleasant or unpleasant (Lyons-Ruth, 1998).

Memory functions on a protomental level connect with the emotional level, which helps give memories their emotional value, connects memories in time and place, and makes explicit memory possible. In the next section, we examine functions at the emotional level that aim, among other things, to balance and co-ordinate primitive procedural and imprinting memory functions at the protomental level with the sophisticated memory functions at the prefrontal level.

The level of emotomentation

The hippocampus enables us to learn facts and events. In the mature brain, the amygdala, hippocampus, and prefrontal areas form circuits and interact closely. When information is recognized or recalled, the amygdala determines whether the information is emotionally important. The limbic system ensures a quick and precise reaction to environmental stimuli. The emotional memory system co-operates with sensorimotor experiences through the autonomic nervous system, where, for example, a sense of danger activates the amygdala. Without the emotional arousal that is evoked through the implicit memory system, the explicit memory would be emotionally "flat". It is the current emotional arousal that imbues the explicit memory with its emotional charge. Explicit memories of emotional experiences, emotional arousal, and logical conclusions come together in the working memory, and together they create a sense of and a motivation for appropriate action (LeDoux, 1998).

Implicit memory is often less "forgetful" than explicit memory, and may activate the amygdala without activating explicit memory tracks. For example, implicit experiences of fear may be imprinted in the amygdala in ways that affect the nervous system for life. Throughout evolution, the nervous system has developed to utilize survival experiences from encounters with an adversary to increase survival chances in future incidents. Imprinting of fear circuits in the amygdala, however, is not always helpful, and in some cases there is a high price to pay for an efficient fear system. Anxiety conditioning can be extremely hard to extinguish, and anxiety-related psychological symptoms are extremely common. A fragment of an implicit memory, for example, an arm movement in connection with the experience of being hit, may set off an anxiety reaction because the amygdala is activated without an explicit memory of the event. Conditioning can only be extinguished and inhibited by neural mechanisms in the prefrontal cortex, but if, for example, the orbitofrontal cortex fails to inhibit the amygdala impulses, the emotional memories are actualized over and over again. The emotional reaction becomes incomprehensible, and the person may be emotionally upset without knowing why. Early exposure to traumatic events is imprinted into the implicit nervous system. For example, when an infant senses an unpleasant event, this sensation is matched with previously stored memory tracks. If the sensation is unfamiliar, or if it is related to previous threatening experiences, an alarm response from the amygdala is induced in a process that is outside the prefrontal cortex. Traumatic memories may create indelible emotional memory tracks and become part of the basis for anxiety disorders (LeDoux, 1998; Perry, 1999a,b).

Even though the hippocampus has relatively little to do with emotions, it is an important structure in the regulation of emotions, including the regulation of anxiety. The hippocampus provides the transition between implicit and explicit memory. Implicit memory systems are not processed in the hippocampus. For example, persons with damage to the hippocampus will not remember that they have heard an unpleasant sound, although their skin response is activated as a result of exposure to the sound. The hippocampus receives input from the amygdala and from the highest neocortical levels, among other structures. The hippocampus directs the storage process concerning explicit memories. New information only remains in the hippocampus for a few weeks or months, and the information is then transferred to relevant areas in the neocortex where it is stored on a more permanent basis (Hansen, 2002; LeDoux, 1998, 2001).

Memory is hemisphere-specific—damage to the left hippocampus causes difficulties with remembering verbal information, while damage to the right hemisphere causes problems with remembering visual designs and spatial localization. Adults with damage to the hippocampus display some of the characteristics seen in younger children. A dysfunctional hippocampus causes the person to lose his or her bearings concerning the time and place of events (Nadel & Zola-Morgan, 1984; Schacter, 1996).

The hippocampus integrates information, creates a sense of internal coherence, and shapes explicit memories. Due to its close connections to the amygdala it is involved in making body sensations and intuitive knowledge explicit. The hippocampus and neocortex enable us to establish complex memory tracks where many events are connected in time and place (Damasio, 1994; LeDoux, 1998, 2001; O'Keefe & Nadel, 1978). The top tier of the hierarchical brain contains the uniquely human and sophisticated memory functions. In the next section, I describe the memory functions that rely on structures in the prefrontal cortex.

The level of ratiomentation

At the prefrontal level, memory functions are sophisticated and diverse, and here language plays a key role and integrates with the memory systems. The hippocampus and prefrontal cortex are involved in two different types of recall processes. Associative recall or recognition relies on the hippocampus and is an automatic recall process. Recognition occurs when a memory track is automatically activated by a stimulus, for example when one hears a tune that reminds one of . . ., etc. Non-associated recall consists of strategic recall, which implies a slow and laborious search for a particular memory, like looking for a particular piece in a jigsaw puzzle. This process relies on activity in the prefrontal cortex. Without the prefrontal cortex, one can only wait for a suitable memory track to come along and connect with an important memory track in store. Encoding in the prefrontal cortex requires attention and focus and the simultaneous activation of implicit and explicit memory systems and dorsolateral prefrontal structures. Recall is experienced as a sense of remembering something right now (Schacter, 1996).

The memory functions that develop on the basis of structures in the prefrontal cortex are well researched and include, among other structures, short-term memory, working memory, and executive functions. These three structures rely on functions in the dorsolateral prefrontal cortex and are able to function far removed from the more emotional structures.

Short-term memory, long-term memory, working memory, and executive functions

While long-term memory consists of memories that last hours, days, or years, the short-term memory consists of memories that last a few seconds or minutes, and which retain small amounts of information for brief periods of time. What we are aware of here and now is what occupies the short-term memory. What enters the short-term memory may enter the long-term memory. The short-term memory is important for our ability to retain small amounts of information, while we need the working memory to be able to both retain and manipulate information. For example, we need the short-term memory to be able to reproduce a meaningless list of numbers, while it takes working memory to be able to reproduce it backwards. The working memory processes information that comes from the senses or from the long-term memory. The main component of the working memory is the central executive function. The central executive function consists of planning and control functions, control of behaviour and actions, judgment, flexibility, goal attainment, etc.

The working memory is normally defined as a temporary storage mechanism that lets various sorts of information be retained, compared, contrasted, etc. (Gjærum & Ellertsen, 2002). In the early 1970s, Allan Baddeley pioneered research into the working memory and executive functions. He believed that the working memory is used in all active thought processes relating to comprehension, learning, and reasoning. The executive functions handle the overall co-ordination of activities in the working memory, for example, by determining what specialized systems to hold in attention at a given time. The executive functions blend information and push it into and out of the working memory, moving it to and from different memory networks. The working memory only holds a limited amount of information at any given time but is able to hold any type of information. The working memory provides tremendous flexibility and makes it possible to combine countless different modalities, thought fragments, logical conclusions, etc. There is no sharp distinction between memory and thought. The central executive functions coordinate information from a number of sources, direct the ability to focus and shift attention, organize incoming material, recall memories, and combine recalled information. They receive information from many memory stores, for example from visuospatial areas containing images, from auditory areas containing acoustic and speech information, etc. (Baddeley, 1986).

The working memory is not merely a product of what is taking place in the present. It relies on experiences and previous knowledge, i.e., information stored in the long-term memory. The executive process determines what information is activated in the long-term memory and maintained in the short-term memory.

The working memory, which is located in the prefrontal cortex, has reasoning and symbolizing functions at its disposal. It directs volitional behaviour towards a goal and is able to connect with the implicit memory system. The working memory is a mental process that is activated when one says or thinks something. It enables reflection on thoughts that arise here and now and connects with recalled memories. In attention disorders, the working memory is out of order and incapable of handling large amounts of information over long periods of time. Research lends support to this hypothesis through MRI-images of children with attention disorders. These images have shown disorders in the dorsolateral prefrontal cortex, which is considered one of the main structures in relation to the working memory (Goldman-Rakic, 1999; LeDoux, 2001; Main, 1999; Siegel, 1999).

The working memory is one of the brain's most sophisticated capacities and involves all aspects of thinking and problem solving. It enables the simultaneous retention of different options and thought processes. One's attention may slip for a moment and then be recaptured and redirected to the original topic. The working memory is crucial for our ability to lead a conversation, and the working memory is required to bring material into consciousness from pre-consciousness (Goldman-Rakic, 1999).

Thinking, planning, problem solving, weighing pros and cons, etc., are all processes that activate the dorsolateral prefrontal cortex and, thus, the working memory. Thoughts require internal mental representations, which consist of signs and symbols that represent something else, just like a map, which symbolizes the landscape without being identical to it. Some internal mental representations are in the form of images, while others are abstract and symbolic, and much of our knowledge is based on mental images. However, the link between mental images and thoughts require circuit connections between the visual cortex, the orbitofrontal cortex, the dorsolateral prefrontal cortex, and structures in the parietal cortex (Gleitman, 1995). The dorsolateral prefrontal cortex lets us select and search for the information needed to manage a given task. The engram is activated and retained until the task requires a new engram, which is quickly and efficiently brought "online" while the old engram is abandoned.

A concept that is often mentioned in connection with memory studies is declarative memory functions, a concept that resembles the short-term memory and the working memory which in many ways.

Declarative memory

The declarative memory system corresponds to what is commonly referred to as memory in laymen's terms, and it incorporates aspects of time and place. The declarative system is the "knowing system", which stores specific facts and events. This memory includes the recall of objects, persons, names, places, events, etc., and everything that can be expressed explicitly.

Declarative memory lets us represent objects in space and time, which in an evolutionary context enables us to find food caches or recall where an enemy might be lurking. This presupposes a memory of time and place as well as object permanence, in other words an intact hippocampus and orbitofrontal structure. Declarative memory is often defined as a memory structure that not only recognizes but is also able to recall. "As rememberers, we can free ourselves from the immediate constraints of time and space, reexperiencing the past and projecting ourselves into the future at will" (Schacter, 1996, p. 17).

Declarative memory is commonly divided into a semantic memory and an episodic and autobiographical memory. Semantic memory includes general knowledge, for example the name of the capital of Denmark, while episodic memory is self-experienced knowledge.

Thus, the episodic and autobiographical memory is related to the emotional structures.

Semantic memory

Semantic memory is the learning of impersonal knowledge, such as facts or word meanings. Semantic memory consists of associations and concepts that are basic for our general knowledge of the world, and which are not linked with any particular time and place. Semantic recognition is believed to mainly involve the activation of the hippocampus and dorsolateral prefrontal cortex in the left hemisphere. Episodic and autobiographical memory on the other hand involves a higher degree of activation in the hippocampus and orbitofrontal cortex in the right hemisphere (Siegel, 1999).

Episodic and autobiographical memory

Episodic memory is a particularly subjective aspect of explicit memory. It was described by Tulving in 1972. Episodic memory contains an experience tied to a time and place as well as a self-reference where one perceives oneself as a participant in the episode (Olson & Strauss, 1984). Normally, the terms episodic and autobiographical memory are used synonymously, but Siegel (2004) proposes a distinction between the two concepts. According to Siegel's view, episodic memory contains self-reference and develops in connection with semantic memory from around the age of eighteen months, while autobiographical memory does not develop until the age of 4–5 years, and in addition to the self-reference it also involves a sensation of the episodic memory in time and place. Most of us, for example, have difficulty recalling life events that predate the age of 4–5 years. Episodic memory includes everything that can be related to specific previous events. Personal knowledge is stored in long-term memory and shapes life stories and personal myths. Autobiographies offer a sense of narrative continuity. They tie the past, present and future together and create a sense of authenticity and the recognition of events as self-experienced, which is associated with the sense of a personal identity (Schacter, 1996; Siegel, 1999).

Although semantic episodic and autobiographical memory systems have much in common and can be recalled explicitly through language, drawings, etc., they still appear to be triggered by different mechanisms. As previously mentioned, the autobiographical memory includes more than just the recall of representations from the past; it also involves a structure of time and place. For example, young children as well as adults who have suffered massive neglect in childhood often display an inability to recognize or recall specific events or relations, which are instead described in general terms. For example, a young child will often be able to describe how mum usually behaves when she is angry, but is unable to describe any specific incident. Autobiographical memory organizes sequentially in time and place and is a prerequisite for emotional regulation and self-identity. Autobiographical memory requires the ability to recall and is associated with activation of the prefrontal cortex in the right hemisphere (Main, 1999). Autobiographical memory develops at the age of 4–5 years, but scientists believe that the autobiographical memory has an extension that is related to additional maturation and expansion of the prefrontal cortex. This system has been called autonoetic (self-comprehending) memory.

Autonoetic (self-comprehending) memory

The memory structures within the prefrontal cortex relate to our awareness of ourselves as persons with a history and a future, which enables us to go on mental journeys in a self-reflecting way

(Gardiner, 2000). While the autobiographical memory is a structure that enables us to recall earlier life events in a time and place context, the autonoetic memory enables us to go on mental journeys in the past, present and future (Siegel, 1999, 2004).

At an early age, our memories of life events become intertwined with verbal stories, and already at the age of 2–3 years the narrative memory develops, which becomes crucial to higher consciousness and mentalization.

Narrative memory

Narrative memory refers to the storing of experiences in a story-like narrative form, and requires that circuits in many neural structures activate simultaneously. Narrative memory requires a high degree of integration of multiple neural networks concerning cognitive, emotional, and behavioural functions. Narrative memory lets us integrate emotional and neural circuits to achieve personal development. Narrative construction is an important process across cultures, and families relate to each other through stories of their daily life. In describing daily experiences with their parents, children create stories about themselves. Narratives are an important means for organizing events and achieving coherence between episodic personal memory and language (Cozolino, 2006; Siegel, 1999).

The maturation of the prefrontal cortex enables recall and the blending of previously acquired knowledge with later acquired knowledge. These narratives are very influential for recall memory. For example, it can be difficult to distinguish between real and false memories in children if the false memories are corroborated by persons close to the child. In the recall process, interpretation affects what is recalled. What is remembered is affected by the child's context. When adults ask young children about events, it is the adults who provide structure and coherence for the child's story. For infants under two years of age, it is the adults who relate the events while the child confirms, denies, and repeats what the adult says. For example, when two-year-old Mike comes back from a visit to the zoo with his parents, they want to talk about what animals they saw. At this age, Mike is not very good at recalling events, so his parents ask him whether he has seen a monkey, a lion, etc., and Mike either confirms or denies.

Gradually, the child is able to contribute more, but it is only after the age of three years that the child begins to initiate stories about events that took place and is able to construct reasonably coherent stories. The narrative construction that the child co-creates with the adult provides the child with a model for the presentation of events. New experiences integrate with the child's current development stage and previous experiences. Thus, through the narrative process, the child draws implicit and explicit conclusions that go beyond the information that was originally provided (Kagan, 1990, 1994; Tetzchner, 2000). For example, now that Mike is three, he will be able to relate his experiences at the zoo independently. The way he constructs his story will resemble the structure of his parents' questions. He includes the same elements that the parents included, describing the monkeys, the lions, etc., and links it with self-experiences.

The narrative memory system is based on internal representations that we share with ourselves or each other. Internal representations are implicit and non-verbal, and are based on perceived experiences in interaction with others. Narrative memory is conscious, verbal storytelling. It is social in nature and created through other people's stories. The drama of life often unfolds more through stories than through actual events. The past is constructed through subjective, possibly embellished, stories. Like all human stories, our episodic or autobiographical memory consists of elements of truth, experiences one wishes one had had, and elements that aim to either please the audience or put the storyteller in a better light. Our history books are full of embellished stories about our past.

The mentalization capacity is closely linked to language. The ability to verbalize enables one to reflect on one's life story and change a future outcome. Narratives and stories help us to organize our experiences. From the time the child is about 2½ years old, the parents co-create and co-organize the child's self-story together with the child by constructing narratives through many daily conversations. Language plays a crucial role in the development of higher consciousness and mentalization. For example, Mike's parents will often verbalize to Mike what they are doing together, which helps him organize and relate his non-verbal impressions of an experience with a narrative. In any form of therapeutic work with children, it is important to verbalize what is going on in the interaction between therapist and child in order to facilitate the integration of affective structures with the symbolizing verbal and narrative structures.

Narrative memory consists of the stories of internal representations. Verbal reproduction links non-verbal internal representations with a larger context. In neurophysiological terms, the right hemisphere co-ordinates the internal representations with the left hemisphere. The narratives never quite match the internal representations. The internal representations are implicit and non-verbal and consist of experienced events. The narratives are explicit, verbal, and social, and they are constructed by the storyteller as the story is told. There may be varying degrees of harmony between internal representations. For example, one may have a positive, idealized narrative image of one's mother as a safe, stable, and warm attachment figure, but closer inspection may reveal that the implicit internal representations are, in fact, much less positive and mixed with ambivalent expectations and emotions. Clinical practice devotes much time to bringing these two models into closer harmony (Stern, 1989). Through the process of psychotherapy, the memory system is able to restructure narratives, which creates new experiences that can have a positive and integrative influence on the nervous system. Narrative memory is formed at a high level in the brain's hierarchical structure and may contain many different internal representations. Renewed assessment and evaluation of childhood experiences from an adult point of view may offer new approaches to understanding one's own story and history. For example, sixteen-year-old Sara talked about the way her life changed when she was four years old. From being doted on as her mother's favourite little girl, she was suddenly put down and scolded and no longer felt her mother's love. From this day on, Sara felt wrong and guilty; she hated herself and had many explanations concerning how she herself had caused this change in her mother's behaviour. During the process of psychotherapy she realized that her mother's behaviour probably stemmed from the divorce from the girl's father and the serious alcohol abuse that followed. When Sara realized that her mother's altered behaviour had nothing to do with her but was due to severe circumstances that she had no influence on, her self-hatred and feelings of guilt were diminished.

There have been a number of examples that the re-assessment of childhood experiences in connection with therapy has caused so-called "false memories". The schema-based human memory system does not match the requirements of a court of law, because memory is not based on objective truth. In psychotherapy, the plasticity of memory helps to change neural systems. Narrative memory may contain memories that were not a part of the person's direct experiences but are elements of family stories, myths, secrets, etc. In the creative narrative process surrounding events, narratives are able to regulate and alter experiences, which is an important element in both children's and adults' ability to regulate daily experiences.

Confabulation

Damage to the prefrontal cortex may make it impossible to remember the source of one's knowledge (lack of source memory) and may also lead to confabulation (the recall of events that never actually took place). Confabulation contains elements of actual memories, but the memory gaps are filled in with made-up material, and fantasy and reality are interwoven to form bizarre tales. Source memory helps distinguish actual experiences from imagined ones, and links experiences in time. Persons with prefrontal damage are not characterized by memory difficulties but rather by difficulty remembering whether something actually took place. Loose associations are associated with arbitrary stimuli and memory fragments that are not rooted in time and place. Often, the result is a messy and confusing life story. Pre-school children may have difficulty with source memory because the prefrontal cortex develops at a very slow rate. Children's performance in cognitive tests often resembles the performance of adults with frontal lobe damage (Hansen, 2002; Schacter, 1996). Children with attachment disorder are often accused of lying. Twelve-year-old Toby is characterized as a liar by his foster parents because his statements are often self-aggrandizing, and, according to his own descriptions, there is no limit to what he can do. Even when the foster father and Tobias together have ascertained that he is not, for example, able to pick up a telephone pole, Tobias later insisted on his omnipotence. He often tells dramatic stories where he himself is blameless, although in fact he is often involved in fist-fights and stealing. Children with attachment disorder probably have the same difficulty as younger children in distinguishing real events from imagined ones due to an inadequately matured orbitofrontal cortex.

Summary

The integration between the various memory structures on the various mental levels of organization is what integrates the personality, and in ideal circumstances the memory systems combine to form a harmonious symphony. As Schacter (1996) points out, "Our memories are the fragile but powerful products of what we recall from the past, believe about the present, and imagine about the future" (p. 308).

In a way, memory functions are the "glue" that keeps our personality together. It is a large and complex area, partly due to the many different and complicated human memory functions. The diversity of the memory functions enables a number of self-functions, and that is the topic of the final chapter of this book.

CHAPTER FOURTEEN

The foundation of personality: self and consciousness

"The core of the self is thus nonverbal and unconscious, and it lies in patterns of affect regulation. This structural development allows for an internal sense of security and resilience that comes from the intuitive knowledge that one can regulate the flows and shifts of one's bodily-based emotional states either by one's own coping capacities or within a relationship with caring others . . . The activities of the 'self-correcting' orbitofrontal system are central to self-regulation, the ability to flexibly regulate emotional states through interactions with other humans"

(Schore, 2001a, p. 38)

I t is impossible to reach a consensus on the nature and definition of the self. Nevertheless, most of us have a very real sense of self. In this context, "self" means a social formation of internal organizations that grew out of childhood relational experiences and the experience of self in interactions with others. The self is able to develop throughout the lifespan and to reorganize on the basis of new experiences and relational experiences.

There is no central location in the brain for self or consciousness. Self or consciousness is a cluster of qualities that are related through brain-body circuits in motor and mental systems that engage with the environment. In this chapter, I examine the many views of self and consciousness from a neuro-affective perspective that connects the neural level with brain maturation and the importance of interactions viewed within the framework of the hierarchical, triune brain. But first, I want to focus on the concepts of self and consciousness.

The concepts of self and consciousness

Self, personality, temperament, consciousness, and awareness are independent concepts, but in many contexts they are confused with one another. Just as the concept of self, for example, is hard to define, it is also exceedingly difficult to define consciousness, and the concepts of awareness and consciousness are often confused. Awareness has to do with a mental focus on an experience or an object. Overall consciousness often refers to a process of being aware of being aware, or what might be called meta-awareness, or meta-consciousness. In laymen's terms, consciousness usually refers to what is held in the working memory. What we are conscious of is what the working memory is dealing with, which can be related to the explicit domain of the sense of knowing.

In the implicit domain there is no "conscious" processing during encoding or recognition. This domain is related to brain structures, many of which are in place from birth and remain accessible throughout life. Our implicit structures permeate and shape the construction of the self and remain an important part of the self throughout our lives. Reflective consciousness, on the other hand, is a part of the explicit system and relies on mental focus and meta-consciousness. Reflective consciousness consists of both implicit and explicit memory. The explicit structures form only a small part of the activity of the self; the vast majority of perception, abstract cognition, emotional processes, memory, and social interactions takes place largely without explicit involvement and have considerable influence on behaviour, emotions, and thoughts.

Implicit knowledge is not conscious, but it is not repressed either. The unconscious, in a psychoanalytical sense, presupposes a defence barrier: The dynamic unconscious is not conscious because the repression mechanism actively keeps the forbidden content from entering the consciousness. A simple and broad definition of resistance would be anything that obstructs a person's access to non-conscious material. In a psychoanalytical sense, resistance and defence are largely one and the same, since both obstruct the dynamic non-conscious from becoming conscious. Implicit know-ledge is not dynamic unconscious and is not kept away from the consciousness by means of resistance or defences. The implicitly regulated memory systems and representations constantly help form transfer relations, and they are the basis of explicit conscious-ness (Stern, 2004). In some of Freud's last works, he uses the term unconscious in three different ways: as the dynamic unconscious that requires a defence mechanism; as the unconscious part of the ego, which is about habits, perceptual and motor skills, and which is a part of procedural memory; and, third, as the pre-conscious, which refers to all mental activities that may become elements that enter the field of awareness (Kandel, 2005).

Temperament is often confused with personality, but the two are not the same. Personality consists of a combination of temperament and experience, especially experience related to habitual behaviour, psychological coping strategies, and notions about oneself and others. The temperament forms the basis for self-development and characterizes the child's basic levels of affect and arousal. Temperament can be defined as innate variations in emotional, motor, self-regulatory, and attention functions (Karr-Morse & Wiley, 1997; Rothbart & Bates, 1998).

The most basic forms of consciousness at the lowest hierarchical levels of the brain are under strict genetic control, although these levels are also subject to some environmental regulation. The forms of consciousness that are placed on higher hierarchical levels, for example in the neocortex, and which support the development of autobiographical memory, among other things, are under less gene-tic control but nevertheless develop and mature on the basis of innate biology (Damasio, 1999). The deep roots of self-consciousness are found in brain activities that maintain a relatively stable body state on an ongoing and unconscious basis. This consciousness is the implicit precursor of all other levels of self-consciousness. Self-consciousness lets us connect our internal life and self-regulating processes with mental images of the outside world; it begins as a sense of what happens when one sees, hears, or touches something. The newborn infant has no internal organization of expectations, and extended self-consciousness unfolds slowly through the child's interactions with the environment. This form of consciousness essentially requires activity in the neocortex and connections to the mid-brain and limbic system. The infant carries the seeds of self-consciousness, but self-consciousness only unfolds and organizes in the dyadic system between infant and care-giver (Damasio, 1999; Sroufe, 1989a).

Despite the many explanatory models for consciousness, the subjective experience of consciousness cannot be described or explained. For example, it is difficult to theorize about the way something feels, and a relevant question would be whether we will ever be able to capture the concept of consciousness. This difficulty has been referred to as the "qualia problem". The crux of the problem is the difficulty of explaining how neural structure can provide an experience of, say, the redness of the colour red, or the taste of coffee or red wine. These are hugely different ways of describing the world (Ramachandran, 2003). Stern (1985) explains that the sense of self is not a cognitive construction but an experiential integration that is established between the ages of two and seven months. Philosopher Frank Jackson described the dilemma through a mental experiment: he imagined that a female neurophysiologist in the twenty-third century was the leading expert on brain processes concerning colour vision. The woman had lived her entire life in a black and white room and had never seen colours. She knew everything worth knowing about the physical processes in the brain required to produce colour vision, but never learned what it is like to experience colours (Chalmers, 1999). There are facts about conscious experiences that cannot be deduced from physical data on brain function. The way in which we sense our own self and our own consciousness or the experience, for example, of experiencing a work of art, could never be described in scientific terms. Experientially orientated *vs.* scientific levels of description are worlds apart, and that gap can probably never be bridged.

As early as 1895, Freud said that conscious and unconscious forms of processing are reflections of the neural architecture of the brain and the nervous system (Freud, 1954), and there is no doubt that an understanding of the neural structures and the hierarchical brain offers an impression of various levels of consciousness. However, the Dalai Lama for one has stated that it is difficult to capture the self in a neural explanatory model:

> There is no reason to believe that the very subtlest state—called "innate mind", the very essential nature of awareness itself—would have neural correlates, because it is not physical, not contingent upon the brain. But for all other mental processes that manifest throughout the course of a human life, it is certainly possible. [Goleman, 2003, p. 206]

Even though the concepts of self and consciousness are difficult to grasp, it is still relevant to consider the processes from the perspective of psychological and neurological explanatory models. In the following we will consider the relationship between brain circuits and consciousness.

Processes of consciousness and neural circuits

Processes of consciousness only occur when neural activity occurs simultaneously among neuron groups in different structures through reentry or feedback processes. They occur in the circuit connections between brain regions at many levels and in many structures. As previously mentioned, there is no one area in the brain that handles conscious experiences.

We constantly carry out unconscious routines in order to give our consciousness room to execute tasks that are necessary for conscious planning, structuring, or processing. It takes practice to master a task, and the execution becomes increasingly automated as learning progresses. The number of brain regions involved in the execution of a task continues to shrink. Explicit or conscious control is only necessary in so far as choices or planning is involved. Thus, it is only the last level of control or analysis that is accessible to the reflective consciousness, while all other processes take place automatically (Edelman & Tononi, 2000).

The self is made up of many relatively separate but interdependent neural systems that work as a coherent self-system. When the nervous system loses this ability, various self states may conflict, which leads to a sense of chaos or lack of internal harmony. This occurs, for example, when one fails to control and comprehend one's own impulsive acts or when one judges one's own thoughts or behaviour. Achieving future emotional flexibility depends on the ability of the self to integrate a sense of coherence between various self states over time. When the co-ordination and integration of brain circuits are not well established, the brain is unable to pull itself together into a coherent system, and parts of the brain will dissociate (Edelman & Tononi, 2000; Siegel, 1999); this is characteristic, for example, of psychological disorders.

The neural networks that organize functions of consciousness are shaped by previous experiences. Even from a young age we form defence mechanisms that lead our emotions and thoughts away from situations that involve discomfort. For example, stimuli that trigger anxiety signals lead us to avoid situations that cause discomfort. Subcortical processing organizes the experience before it reaches higher consciousness. Because the organization of neural processing mainly takes place on a subcortical level, there may be perceptual distortions and misrepresentations. Much psychotherapy is about discovering, understanding, and correcting the content of implicit or unconscious organizations (Cozolino, 2000). For example, eight-year-old Lena went into therapy to try to verbalize her experiences in connection with being placed in a foster family after a dramatic scene where the police came to pick up her and her sister. Every time she reached the end of the session she began to get nervous and speak hectically. When her foster mother came to pick her up, she rushed out the door without saying goodbye. Only once she was able to talk about the difference between final goodbyes and temporary goodbyes with an assurance that the therapy sessions involved temporary goodbyes, was Lena able to say goodbye in a relevant way.

It is probably the re-entry or feedback process that forms the neural basis for consciousness. The various forms of consciousness develop gradually as the child develops, and in the following I describe this maturation process and the emergence of the self.

*The maturation process of consciousness
and the emergence of the self*

The consciousness systems are subject to the particular organization
of the brain, which implies that systems that mature later are
dependent on previously developed systems. Consciousness forms
grow increasingly complex as processing moves up the hierarchical
levels of the brain, and the ability of various brain regions to integrate various kinds of information helps to expand the field of
consciousness. The capacity for consciousness is genetically determined, but culture affects the development of consciousness. As
previously discussed, the structural organization of the brain
reflects its history.

We maintain a sense of an inner core and of self-constancy even
though our personalities change over time. Under normal circumstances, a person will have the sense of remaining the same, regardless of personality developments, which must imply that the brain
system consists of a structural entity that is invariable, and thus
able to maintain a sense of continuity over long periods of time.
Continuity is a requirement for maintaining a sense of self. Neurons
are not replaced, but change with learning. Life experiences cause
neurons to change their patterns and interconnections, and no
single component remains the same for very long. Most of the cells
and tissue that the organism contains today are not the same as they
were years ago; what remains the same is the blueprint of the
brain's structure (Damasio, 1999).

At an early stage, infants sense that a given affect belongs to
them, not to the person who triggered it. The internal experience
of emotional states evoked through countless previous situations
causes a self-sense of what one is like and what one may feel, which
gradually becomes independent of the other's presence. Infants
soon learn to distinguish self from other, but during the first year of
life they are egocentric and fail to draw a clear line between self and
other or between their own actions and the actions of others. This
lack of distinction forms the basis for projection and introjection.
When two-year-old John hurts himself by bumping into the edge of
the table, he rarely thinks that he is stupid—instead the table is
stupid for being in the way. When John is a little older, he may feel
guilty when he witnesses an event in which he himself is blameless:

for example, when he sees his big brother dip into the "off-limits" jar of sweets.

The experiences that the child has with another person form internal representations that eventually contribute to releasing the self. Through their internal representations, infants gradually form a representation of their own self as an objective entity that can be perceived from the outside as well as sensed subjectively from the inside (Damasio, 1999; Stern, 1977, 1985). As children grow older, they will have to adapt to various social situations and roles, for example, in relation to teachers, siblings, and friends, and this requires a high degree of flexibility in self organization.

The development of a sense of self

Personality consists of many different levels, and through his work with infants, Daniel Stern (1985) has developed a model for the human sense of self, which he divides into a number of structures or organizations. Stern believes that self development takes place in leaps, and that a new sense of self is a new way of organizing subjective experiences that revolve around experiences of self with others. Senses of self are always established in interaction with others, and they form the basis of what happens to the self when it is together with another. Stern talks about five senses of self: the emergent self, the core self, the intersubjective self, the verbal self, and the narrative self (Figure 14.1). The self develops through attention patterns that only occur in connection with the infant's actions or mental processes. A consistent attention pattern is a form of organizing subjective experience.

The emergent self

The emergent self is formed on the basis of the senses of self arising from the physiological rhythm with the care-giver. The first structural form has to do with the body and is initially based on body sensations in the form of experiences of intensity and duration. Through these body sensations, infants gradually begin to sense their own existence and boundaries. The interaction is about modulating affects and achieving balance through comfort and

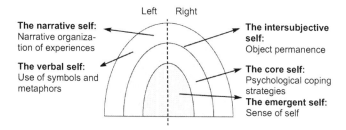

Figure 14.1.   The triune brain with the different senses of self according to Stern.

soothing. It is aimed at helping the infant handle the transitions between different states, an early form of physiological affect-regulation. The polymodal perception enables the infant to perceive sensory wholes and relations and to translate impressions from one sense into another sense and store them across the senses. The experiential world is coloured by the emotions that are aroused, which help the infant navigate in the world. The emergent self is formed within the first two months of life, and with it the infant begins to sense meaning and coherence on a sensory level. The sensory organization and polymodal perception create the basis for enabling the infant to engage in social interactions immediately after birth. The interaction between infant and care-giver at this level is about creating rhythm and modulating affects.

The core self

The core self emerges at the age of 2–6-months. At this time, the infant begins to sense a boundary between self and environment and develop a sense of having needs that do not belong to anyone else. Infants begin to develop their first psychological coping strategies. Until the age of two months, infants have been imitating others' bodily expressions with small variations, and, although imitation continues to be important, they now begin to choose independent actions, i.e., they begin to apply protoconversation in response to communication. At this age, all the basic non-verbal elements of human interaction appear. Infants begin to develop a variety of interaction experiences with different care-givers, and they are able to adapt to various social situations and explore new relationships.

The intersubjective self

The intersubjective self is formed during the 7–15-month span. At the beginning of this period, infants learn that affect regulation depends on others, and they begin to develop an internal sense that experiences of being with others belong to them, and they are now able to achieve affect attunement with others. At this level, the sense of self is related to subjective and mental experiences. Halfway through this period, infants develop a deepened understanding of cause and effect, the ability to predict events, and an understanding that persons and objects have permanence. They are able to decode the care-giver's subtle moods, regulate along with her, and instantly put themselves in her place. At this stage, infants come to understand that they have a mental life with emotions, motives, and intentions, and that others do, too. They see that others have their own internal mental world. They understand that experiences can be shared with others, and they begin to point while looking at the parents.

The verbal self

The verbal self develops from the age of fifteen months. This sense of self is related to linguistic meaning and context and involves the ability to reflect on oneself, communicate about oneself to others, and use symbols and metaphors. Language development is anchored in dialogue and personal experience, and words gain meaning through concrete interaction experiences. The verbal self is also called the symbolic self, and the ability to use symbols enables self-reflection. At the age of 2–3 years, language becomes an important part of the child's way of communicating, and this has a radical influence on social interactions and conceptual thinking. What is conceptualized through language can reshape subjective and emotional experiences and cause the child to lose his or her sense of the original emotional experience. The perceiving self and the verbal self can at times be very far apart. For example, the therapeutic process often seeks to link the emotions and sensations of essential care-givers with the thoughts and articulated perceptions concerning these emotions and sensations.

The narrative self

The narrative self emerges around the age of 3–3½ years, and at this level the sense of self has to do with creating meaning and coherence on the basis of an autobiography, i.e., telling one's own story in one's own words. This organizational level serves to structure experiences that may in themselves be incoherent or chaotic. The autobiography is based on the parents' presentation of reality, and children are able to see themselves from the parents' perspective (Stern, 1985).

Stern does not address any additional senses of self, but throughout childhood and adolescence and later in life, our senses of self continue to change, partly due to additional maturation of the prefrontal cortex and age-related changes in the nervous system. Stern points out that the different levels of self sense are not replaced by increasingly mature levels, but become subordinate to them. That is to say that all the levels of self sense remain represented in the brain. Like the memory functions, the successive levels of self sense and layers of consciousness grow increasingly sophisticated, and at the level of rational mentalization, consciousness reaches its final, specifically human form. In the following, I describe the forms of consciousness at each level of mentalization in the triune brain.

Representations of consciousness at the level of protomentation

The basic sensory structures and the sense of being and existence are located in the brainstem and form the basis of consciousness— the physiological foundation of personality. In evolutionary terms, this form of consciousness is ancient and is found in many species of animals. It comes from brainstem functions that regulate the body state, and which are shared by almost all mammals. Primitive self-representation consists of neural networks that are able to control a primitive attention focus, and it is linked to body sensations and the motor system, which presupposes the ability to sense the body as a coherent whole (Panksepp, 1998). These basic brain functions control arousal, sensory stimulation, motor tone, and simple orientation responses. They create behavioural coherence and body consciousness and form the basis for developing sophisticated executive functions.

The most basic form of consciousness, which relates to the sense of one's own and others' existence, is located near the mid-line of the brain. The deeper consciousness structures integrate with the sympathetic and parasympathetic components of the autonomic nervous system, which supports Freud's idea of a system of drives, which he believed were embedded in our genetic material and present at birth (Damasio, 1999; Schore, 2003b) (Figure 14.2).

The reticular activation system is related to the basic level of attention and forms the "tail" of the consciousness process. The trigeminal nerve (fifth cranial nerve) provides the organism with tactile information and processes body stimuli concerning sensory impressions, temperature, and pain and helps control the facial muscles. The vagus nerve (tenth cranial nerve) is also a main co-ordinator of emotional responses. Brain damage at this level jeopardizes the very foundation of consciousness, since the organism no longer knows what is going on because it is unable to feel sensory changes. The production of chemical substances in the brainstem and hypothalamus is induced when the organism is affected by internal or external stimuli. The release of neurotransmitters and hormones changes the processes in countless brain circuits and triggers certain behavioural patterns. Damage to the brainstem and

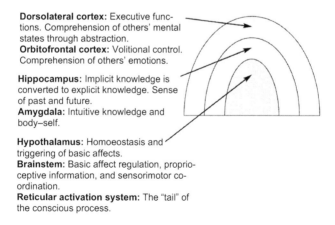

Figure 14.2.   The triune brain with representations of consciousness.

hypothalamus causes major disorders of consciousness and often leads to coma. Damage to the thalamus and the cingulate gyrus area disturbs higher forms of consciousness, as is the case in severe mental retardation, while damage to the hippocampus and pre-frontal areas reduces the working memory and the autobiographical memory, the highest form of consciousness, as in individuals suffering from severe dementia. The brainstem is crucial for maintaining life, and it is the anchor of the self or personality (Damasio, 1999; Purves et al., 2001).

Vitality affects and somatic markers

As described in Chapter Ten, William James described as early as the 1880s that emotions are often followed by bodily responses such as a pounding heart, sweating, muscle tension, etc. He believed that emotions are perceived through sensory body responses. Different emotions feel different because they are accompanied by different body responses and sensations. Fear feels different from anger and love, because it has a different physiological signature. Body responses provide feedback for the brain, not just in the form of body sensations, which are a part of the felt response, but also in the form of hormones, which influence synaptic activity (James, 1878–1899; LeDoux, 1998, 2001).

Thus, pleasant and unpleasant feelings both cause body sensations and trigger neurotransmitters and hormones. This process is implicit and helps shape what Stern (1985) calls vitality affects. These arise as an effect of encounters with other people, and, as described in Chapter Five, they are elusive qualities that can best be captured through dynamic, kinaesthetic expressions such as surging, fading, fleeting, explosive, etc. The vitality affects come from the brainstem and hypothalamus level, and may be activated with or without explicit attention. Intuitive sensations have a somatic representation and are triggered by certain stimuli. Intuition has a considerable influence on decision-making processes and usually lies outside the focus of attention (Damasio, 2003; Siegel, 1999; Stern, 1985).

Emotional and social learning is possible because the nervous system implicitly evokes an autonomic reaction that resembles the other person's emotion. Damasio calls these body sensations or "somatic markers" (Damasio, 1994). The internal representations created in the orbitofrontal cortex connect with the body sensing structures through the autonomic nervous system. The combination of internal representations and somatic markers leads to the formation of mental theories about one's own and others' functioning. The somatic markers render the decision-making processes more precise because decisions hinge on what feels intuitively right, and they mix with the mental processes in the orbitofrontal cortex, among other places. The normal, functional sense of identity is anchored in the body, and only the somatic markers can confirm what feels right or wrong. "On a mental level anything can be right, because it is possible to imagine anything," (Sørensen, 1996, p. 75, translated for this book). It is probably a failure to register the somatic markers and to integrate emotional and reasoning structures that leads children with attachment disorder to construct stories that others perceive as deceitful, and that causes severe disturbances in their capacity for empathy and their sense of their own needs.

A positive somatic marker triggered by a mental image of a good future outcome may form the basis for tolerating discomfort in order to achieve something that is potentially better. This enables people to tolerate suffering in order to reach a positive outcome; in childhood development this is described as the transition from the pleasure principle to the reality principle. Most somatic markers are formed during childhood and may be triggered by implicit knowledge, independent of the explicit structures. Certain stimuli are associated with somatic states, and the adaptation of somatic indicators requires both a "normal" brain and a "normal" culture. If either brain or culture is deficient from the child's birth, the somatic markers will not develop adaptively (Damasio, 1994). For example, children with autism will not utilize their somatic markers in a relational context due to severe innate communications disorders, and children with attachment disorder fail to link their somatic markers due to early, massive environmentally responsive disturbances.

An emotion is a snapshot of a part of a body landscape. The basic affects arise through brainstem structures that depict and integrate signals from the body and project to the limbic system and the neocortex. Body states make it possible to feel painful or pleasant sensations, and without them we would not be able to sense suffering, yearning, love, etc. "The soul breathes through the body, and suffering, whether it starts in the skin or in a mental image, happens in the flesh" (Damasio, 1994, p. xvii).

Forms of consciousness that represent at the brainstem and hypothalamus level develop so-called somatic consciousness, while the next mental level of organization is emotional consciousness.

Consciousness representations at the level of emotomentation

Emotions play an important role for the process of consciousness. The absence of emotions spells the end for motivation, and there would be little to talk about, take pleasure in, be surprised by, or saddened by. Emotions direct the flow of energy and imbue information processing and internal representations with emotional meaning. The primitive amygdala core is as distant from the prefrontal functions as can be imagined, and it is closely related to the hypothalamus and the autonomic nervous system. Together, these structures form the "body ego", or the level of intuitive knowledge. Explicit consciousness has little control over emotions, but emotions may overwhelm and claim the focus of attention. Connections from the emotional systems to the cognitive systems are more powerful than the connections that run from the cognitive systems to the emotional systems. Emotions are highly motivating for future behaviour and plot the course for our actions, now and in the future. Psychological disorders usually arise on the basis of breakdowns in the emotional systems, as is apparent, for example, in the case of bipolar disorder. Personality disorders involve difficulty with self-regulation at the level of affects/emotions (Damasio, 1998; LeDoux, 1998; Schore, 2003b). Emotions are triggered by other people's moods, and it is possible to activate certain feelings by deliberately changing one's facial expression. The brain activity induced by genuine joy only occurs when the muscles around the eyes are activated, and if one alters one's facial expression and body posture, one's emotions change as well. The face is one means of activating an emotion; it is partially under volitional control, but the expressions that activate the emotive system are usually involuntary (Ekman, 2003; Goleman, 2003). When emotions are activated, the arousal level in the reticular activation system is intensified. The presence of emotions implies a greater likelihood of a co-ordinated learning process that involves many brain structures. The emotional systems support the co-ordination and integration of neural circuits and a "fusing" of the self. The hippocampus integrates information and creates a sense of internal coherence.

The most frequent forms of dissociation are dissociations of explicit and implicit consciousness. For example, the amygdala may learn fear responses independently of the prefrontal cortex if the cognitive and emotional systems are not adequately connected, which leads to anxiety states that cannot be inhibited by the prefrontal areas. Synaptic connections may dissociate both horizontally (between the hemispheres), vertically (between the hierarchical structures), and between rear and front. Information must pass both bottom-up and top-down, across the hemispheres, and back to front and vice versa in order to achieve coherence, and when the three systems resonate, the limbic system works within an integrated circuit capable of rapid and flexible handling of the new demands made by both the internal and the external world (Schore, 2003b).

Basic emotions

The limbic system is located between the primitive sensorimotor level and the highly processed cognitive level. The sensorimotor level contributes with arousal and somatic markers, while cognitive processes enable psychological events to take place in time and place on a highly processed level. Emotions may be triggered in response to rich cognitive decisions through the interaction with higher brain regions, but they may also be triggered through connections to the body sensing systems. The limbic structures grow increasingly complex as they rise up the hierarchy. They change from being vitality affects and somatic markers, connected to brainstem structures, as in vague sensations of pleasure or unpleasure, to being basic emotions springing from the deep-seated limbic structures, as in a vague sense of joy or sadness, and eventually become subjective states springing from connections between the limbic system and the neocortex, as when a message or a thought triggers a state of excitement, compassion, etc. In the next section, I describe consciousness representations at the rational level of consciousness.

Consciousness representations at the level of ratiomentation

Higher cognitive skills evolved at a much later time than the emotions and are probably not yet fully integrated with the rest of the brain. The integration of emotions and extended cognition enables explicit consciousness of emotional states as well as reflections and flexibility in interactions with the environment (Damasio, 1994; LeDoux, 2001).

Extended consciousness

One way to illustrate the transition between the limbic and the prefrontal consciousness representation is by means of Freud's theory of primary and secondary process thinking. Primary process thinking is the form of fantasy thinking where "primitive" needs are expressed, and where children do not distinguish between logical coherence, external reality, and internal needs. Secondary process thinking inhibits the "primitive" needs and creates the basis for rational notions and reality testing. As the orbitofrontal cortex develops, the mental organization changes, and children begin to relate to actual circumstances in the external world. This mental organization level does not deal simply with emotional aspects in the form of pleasure and unpleasure but also with what is true and false, real and unreal, even if what happens is not pleasant. At this stage, we see the emergence of the ability to decide whether thoughts, notions, or ideas are in accordance with reality. Thus, it is social relations that create the basis for secondary process thinking and make it possible to relate to realistic assessments (Benjamin, 1996). Extended consciousness goes beyond the lower forms of consciousness that exist in a here-and-now state. The working memory lets us maintain experiences long enough to manipulate them, which opens the possibility of making choices, developing creativity and mental skills, feeling guilt, and having a conscience—and of repression.

Extended consciousness enables the capacity for self-reflection and for understanding other people's emotions, and it makes it possible to negotiate a complex social world effectively. The orbitofrontal cortex enables our extended consciousness to control the tyranny of emotions, and the dorsolateral prefrontal cortex makes it possible to reflect and plan—to act rationally. Reason is highly informed by emotional content. The executive functions play a crucial role in co-ordinating mental processes and strategic plans, and enable us to stage a flexible effort to reach our goals. The role of the emotion system is to distinguish between what feels good and pleasant *vs.* what feels bad and should be avoided. The emotions play a key role in cognitive processing, but extended consciousness may control the emotions adaptively. Extended consciousness enables us to adapt emotions and, to some extent, to control them (Damasio, 1994; Siegel, 1999).

As mentioned in the previous section, our emotions inform our rational thinking, and there are more bottom-up connections from the limbic system to the prefrontal cortex than there are top-down connections running in the opposite direction. When the nervous system is not well-integrated or when the emotional pressures are high, it can be difficult to maintain rational control, and one may be emotionally overwhelmed, which happens all the time when some-one acts in the grip of anger, grief, or elation. We all have different nervous systems. Some have an explosive and extrovert tempera-ment and have difficulty controlling their impulses, while others have been through dramatic and traumatic experiences that have left them prone to being emotionally overwhelmed. Others again are able to inhibit their emotional impulses; this is often a healthy reaction, but if the prefrontal inhibition is very pronounced it may lead to neurotic states.

When extended consciousness is integrated with lower forms of consciousness, it offers protection. For example, when fear sensa-tions are triggered the organism may either react instinctively, with-out volitional control, or on the basis of experiences resulting from cognitive processing. Will-power means the ability to choose in accordance with long-term outcomes, and, thanks to the expansion of the prefrontal cortex, humans are able to act in ways that run counter to biology or culture. When the nervous system functions coherently, the orbitofrontal cortex makes it possible to switch seamlessly from one state of functional organization to another, for example, between different forms of information processing and emotional states. The prefrontal cortex processes and stores cognitive, interactive representations, and through its connections to the subcortical systems it changes the physiological, homoeostatic states, depending on mental representations. The internal representations have encoded strategies for affect regulation and expectations of future interactions (Damasio, 1994).

Mentalization

The prefrontal cortex makes it possible to be psychobiologically attuned, to empathize, and to understand the mental life of others. This ability is necessary for engaging in satisfactory interactions with others (Hofer, 1990; Schore, 2003a,b). Our identity is a social construct, and interactions with others are essential. One becomes aware of one's own internal states when one realizes that other persons' states may be both similar to, and different from, one's own. Experiences can also be shared with different sides of one's own personality. There are many different context-dependent personalities within one and the same personality, all mutually interacting, communicating, and observing each other, both inside and outside the explicit consciousness. "In psychoanalytic terms, the observing ego witnesses the experiencing ego, or the supergo watches and judges the experiencing ego" (Stern, 2004, p. 129).

The multi-modal association cortex, which is able to construct ideas by integrating information from the different senses, is closely connected to the emotions and to the brain's highest level of neural symbolization. The prefrontal cortex enables us to have expectations and to predict events. The prefrontal cortex possesses the highest form of consciousness and helps to provide us with a coherent life story and sense of self. This form of consciousness lets the self produce explanations for its behaviour on the basis of its self-image, previous experiences, and expectations of the future. Our senses of self develop gradually through the construction of an autobiographical memory based on years of experiences that is constantly re-modulated implicitly as well as explicitly. The executive functions and the ability to focus one's attention on certain representations are mainly conditioned by functions in the dorsolateral prefrontal cortex. The dorsolateral area connects thought products, manipulates them, and puts them together in new ways. The dorsolateral region is well-developed in humans; it is related to our sense of identity and is the prerequisite of intelligence (Damasio, 1999; LeDoux, 1998; Siegel, 1999).

Our sense of identity consists of memories that contain thoughts, feelings, and sensory impressions woven into the narratives that we tell about ourselves, and that are ultimately created through culture. In many ways, human consciousness is a story that has already been written. The narrative or story springs from infants' relations with their care-givers and from the way in which the brain organizes and processes information. The combination of these factors creates narratives and a sense of identity, which may either promote or damage our mental health (Bruner, 1990; Cozolino, 2000; Miller & Sperry, 1988; Nelson, 1993).

In order to develop, the nervous system needs constant environmental influences capable of destabilizing old states and striking new balances between continuity and flexibility. Through their care-givers' regulation patterns, infants develop their own patterns of self-regulation, and this enables the nervous system to strive for ever higher levels of complexity. The prefrontal cortex enables us to process and engage in complex thought patterns, but it is no easy task to control the subcortical systems that form the basis for needs, motivation, and emotional reactions. Doing the right thing is not always as simple as knowing what the right thing is. For better and for worse, the explicit consciousness tries to dictate whom we are and how we should act, but it does not always succeed. Synaptic connections keep the self together for most of us, most of the time. At times, thoughts, emotions, and motives dissociate, and the self begins to disintegrate, which results in psychological disorders.

Insight and wisdom have to do with the capacity for mentalization in relation to deep sensations, emotions, cognitive strategies, and behaviour. This form of consciousness is different from person to person, and in its noblest form it relies on the capacity for introspection and self-reflection. The capacity for mentalization is closely associated with self development and can only develop when the basic structures and neural circuits at the levels of proto-mentation and emotomentation have matured. For example, children and adults who have suffered severe neglect often fail to develop mentalizing skills. The mentalization capacity develops children's capacity for affect regulation on a sophisticated level, and the mentalization capacity is crucial for a psychological sense of self on a higher level (Fonagy et al. 2002; Fonagy, Gergely, Jurist, & Target, 1995; LeDoux, 2001).

Whom we are is not synonymous with whom we think we are. Whom we are is a much more basic part of our personality and is better able to predict our behaviour than the ego reflecting upon itself (Davidson, 2002).

Summary

Personality and self structures are created in a historical context through relational experiences throughout the lifespan. The basic structures of self-sense are founded early in infancy, and new self-representations gradually develop and reorganize the original ones. Brain organization relies on genetic structures for this maturation to take place and for innate dispositions to interact with the environment. The nervous system needs stimulation to mature; inadequate stimulation in early childhood results in neural damage. In order for the nervous system to achieve reflective and extended levels of consciousness, the neural circuits must be coherently organized.

Epilogue

I n this book, I have taken the first tentative steps towards an integration of neurophysiological knowledge and theories from developmental psychology concerning the formation of relations. The journey is long, and we are still only in the early stages. I hope that it is a journey that will continue for many years to come, and that may develop and unite the various psychiatric and psychological disciplines. This integration would enable us to locate personality disorders far more precisely and offer far more accurate interventions. Combining the various bodies of theory would enable a far more appropriate discussion of the relationship between psychological development and brain organization on the different levels of mental organization.

Psychologists have often considered the brain a mysterious, impermeable, incomprehensible organ, impossible to grasp in connection with personality formation and emotions. My hope with this book is to help to make the structure of the nervous system appear somewhat less mysterious, although I do admit that the brain is complex, and the topic is not easily accessible.

In my opinion, psychology has reached a stage when it would be fruitful for us to engage in closer dialogue with other branches of science in order to develop new theoretical understandings. A dialogue between neurophysiology and developmental psychology may, in time, have a considerable impact on psychology, for, by integrating psychodynamic and neuroaffective theories, we would be able to construct a neuro-affective developmental psychology that would combine scientific "hard-wired" data with a theory founded in psychodynamics to incorporate the best from both areas. Among other outcomes, this might provide the evidence for the huge importance of early experiences and intervention for personality formation. A dialogue between the two bodies of theory would allow us to develop specific common knowledge that would offer significant benefits for assessment and intervention in relation to a wide range of psychological disorders.

I believe that the neuro-affective perspective may lead to a reassessment of psychological concepts in psychodynamic thinking—for example, there is no core self buried deep inside our nervous system. Similarly, the theory would be able to offer a more sophisticated view of various psychological disorders, such as ADHD and depression. The brain is so complex that psychological disorders never have just one cause, and symptoms may be related to several different structures on different hierarchical levels of the brain.

Previously, there has been little focus on the dynamic interaction between brain development and the importance of relationships and attachment for this development process. The human brain is designed to engage in social interactions with its environment, and if the nervous system fails to receive stimuli that are relevant for personality formation, the person's unique human potential will fail to unfold properly.

This book is intended as a foundation for, or an introduction to, an understanding of the brain structures involved in personality formation. It is my hope that the book might offer a basic understanding of the emotional structures of the nervous system, which, in evolutionary terms, have become anchored in a hierarchical and non-linear organization, and I hope that this introduction might make it far easier to navigate in the emotional universe of the brain.

> . . . any psychological theory must, in addition to meeting the demands made by natural science, fulfil another major obligation.

It must explain to us the things that we know, in the most puzzling fashion, through our "consciousness"; and since this consciousness knows nothing of what we have so far been assuming—quantities of energy and neurons—our theory must also explain to us this lack of knowledge. [Freud, 1954, p. 369]

Glossary

Acetylcholine: A neurotransmitter involved in nerves that control muscle movements and heart rate. Acetylcholine is excitatory and supports the maintenance of attention, arousal, in the sensory systems.

ACTH (adrenocorticotrophic hormone): ACTH (also known as corticotropin) is released from the pituitary gland and plays a key role in all types of stress response. Negatively charged information increases the release of ACTH, among other substances, from the pituitary gland.

Adrenal cortex: Vital part of the adrenal glands; produces hormones that activate enzyme production and are fundamental for a wide range of metabolic processes and for the body's immune system. In both males and females, the adrenal cortex produces androgens and oestrogens.

Adrenal medulla: The central core of the adrenal glands, which are a part of the sympathetic nervous system. From here adrenalin and noradrenalin are released into the bloodstream.

Adrenalin: A hormone released by the adrenal medulla. Somewhat similar to noradrenalin, but exists only in limited quantities. Adrenalin causes the mobilization of glucose metabolism, which in turn raises the blood sugar, expands the vessels in the muscles and raises the heart rate and blood pressure.

Afferent: Conveying or moving inward, towards the cell core.

Amygdala (from Greek, means almond): A relatively small structure in the temporal lobe in the limbic system. Plays an important role in emotional learning, fight-or-flight responses, and the anxiety response.

Androgens: The male sex hormones. Androgens are produced in large quantities in males and in smaller quantities in females. The male sexual organs produce large quantities of androgens, including testosterone, which triggers the fight response.

Anterior: Situated toward the front.

Anterior cingulate gyrus: The front part of the cingulate gyrus, which is necessary for the ability to act counter to innate or early acquired impulses. Emotionally related movement is controlled from here, and the area is involved in selective attention and volitional movements.

Apoptosis: Programmed cell death.

Arousal: Energy level; alertness.

Association cortex: The parts of the cortex that are not involved in primary sensory or motor processing.

Atrophy: The physical loss of cell tissue, usually due to inadequate use, for example, muscular atrophy following paralysis.

Autobiographical memory: Part of the explicit/declarative memory system that includes self-experienced knowledge.

Autonoetic memory (autonoetic = self-knowing): A memory structure that is located in the prefrontal cortex, and which is associated with a person's awareness of him/herself as a person with a history and a future.

Autonomic nervous system: Nerve fibres running to and from the body's organs. Consists of a sympathetic and a parasympathetic division, both of which are controlled mainly by the brainstem and the hypothalamus. The autonomic nervous system monitors and regulates the body's endocrine state and has nervous connections to almost all internal organs.

Axons: Nerve fibres that lead signals away from the cell body to other cells.

Basal ganglia: Located off to the sides, deep inside the hemisphere and consist of the corpus striatum (putamen and caudate nucleus) and the nucleus accumbens, among other components. The basal ganglia organize instinctive motor skills and represent a basic source of will-power. Known as a component of the extrapyramidal motor system.

Bilateral: Having two sides.

Brainstem: The part of the central nervous system that is located between the mid-brain (mesencephalon) and the spinal cord. Controls vital body functions.

Broca's area: A frontal area, typically in the left hemisphere, which forms the basis for the production of speech sounds. The area forms the basis for linguistic articulation and controls the articulatory system in the mouth and throat.

Catecholamines: A category of substances that include an amino acid group. Examples of this category are adrenalin, noradrenalin, and dopamine.

Caudate nucleus: Part of the basal ganglia that deals with aspects of automatic thinking.

Central nervous system (CNS): The brain and spinal cord.

Cerebellum: An independent structure that is located at the top of the brainstem and is constructed of two hemispheres. It is involved in regulating motor, emotional, and cognitive functions.

Cerebral cortex: The cerebral cortex is the outside layer that forms the surface of the cerebrum.

Cerebrum: Latin for "brain".

Cingulate gyrus: Part of the cortex in the medial part of the brain. Divided into the anterior (towards the front) and posterior (towards the back). This area perceives emotions and induces emotional behaviour related to attachment and caring behaviour.

Circadian cells: Endogenous "clocks" or chronometers.

Colliculus areas: Structure located within the brainstem that processes simple orientation responses and provides a sense of "being". The area is important for eye movements and auditory impulses.

Commissures, anterior/posterior: Structures involved in connecting the right and left hemispheres on a subcortical level. These structures may connect perceptual information as well as inhibit or induce cortical neural activity across the hemispheres.

Confabulation: Fantasy and reality mixed up in bizarre tales.

Corpus callosum: Structure that provides the functional connection between the right and left hemisphere on a neocortical level.

Cortex: Latin for bark. The grey matter of the brain.

Cortisol: An adrenocortical hormone that plays an important role in stress responses. It enhances the ability of the organism to neutralize harmful stress effects. Cortisol is released during stress states through the activation of CRF and ACTH.

Cranial nerves: Twelve paired brain nerves, ten of which project from the brainstem.

CRF (corticotropin-releasing factor): CRF plays an important role in all forms of stress responses; it is an activating neurotransmitter that is synthesized in the hypothalamus. CRF activates the sympathetic nervous system, which raises heart rate and blood pressure and inhibits of digestive functions.

Declarative memory: What is commonly referred to as "memory" in everyday language; it incorporates aspects of time and place, stores specific facts and events, and includes everything that can be expressed explicitly.

Dendrites: Receive incoming information from other neurons.

Dopamine: A neurotransmitter that coordinates various cortical functions. For example, dopamine plays an important role in relation to reward behaviour, inquisitiveness, and positive emotions.

Dorsolateral prefrontal cortex: Part of the cerebral cortex in the frontal lobe. This area coordinates information and reactions, combines and directs mental impressions, and plans actions.

EEG (electroencephalography): Measures electric activity through electrodes attached to the scalp. An EEG measures the overall neuronal activity over a large area of the cortex. Measurements of the distribution and dissipation of electric potentials make it possible to roughly estimate which cortical areas the potential is coming from.

Efferent: Leading or moving outward from something.

Embryo: A foetus during the first three months of gestation

Encephalins: Peptide with pain-reducing (analgesic) effect that stimulates the opioid receptors.

Endocrine system: The hormone-producing glands in the body, for example the thyroid gland, the sexual glands, and the adrenal glands.

Engram: Interconnected neurons in different areas.

Enteric nervous system: Neurons that are interconnected in their own local nervous system, and which control the gastrointestinal system. Closely connected to the sympathetic and the parasympathetic nervous system.

Epigenetic: Genetic expression (phenotype) determined by indirect influences from non-genetic factors, for example environmentally responsive factors.

Episodic memory: A part of the explicit/declarative memory system, which includes self-experienced knowledge.

Excitatory: Activating.

Executive functions: Control functions for planning and directing behaviour and actions, judgment, flexibility, goal attainment, etc.

Explicit memory: Memories that are remembered consciously, and which are potentially available when needed.

Facial nerve: (Seventh cranial nerve) Controls all the small facial muscles.

fMRI-scan (functional magnetic resonance imaging): While MRI-scans are like still photos, fMRI-scans are more like video recordings. It is a technically difficult process, and the slightest movement of the head may produce pseudo-activity.

Frontal lobe: This part of the cerebrum includes the motor cortex, the premotor cortex, and the prefrontal cortex. It induces commands for actions, inhibits impulses, makes choices, and forms impulses and plans for action sequences.

GABA (gamma-aminobutyric acid): An amino acid. The most prevalent inhibitory neurotransmitter. It reacts rapidly and can be found almost everywhere throughout the central nervous system.

Gamete: Sperm cells in the male, egg cells in the female. They each carry only half the full number of chromosomes (in humans, twenty-three).

Genotype: An individual's genetic makeup or predisposition for a given quality.

GH (growth hormone): A growth hormone that is produced in the anterior pituitary gland. The release of this hormone is controlled by the hypothalamus through the hormone GHRH.

GHRH (growth hormone—releasing hormone): A release hormone in the hypothalamus that triggers the release of the growth hormone, GH.

Glial cells: A certain type of support cells in the central nervous system. Glia is Greek and means glue. These cells are necessary for maintaining homoeostasis in the neuronal environment and for reparation processes after damage. They are also responsible for insulating nerve fibres to achieve higher transmissions speeds.

Glucocorticoids: Adrenocortical hormones. The most important hormone in this category is cortisol.

Glutamate: An amino acid. The most prevalent stimulating neuro-transmitter in the central nervous system.

GnRH (gonadotrophin—releasing hormone): A hormone that triggers the production of sex hormones. GnRH is produced in the hypothalamus and causes the pituitary gland to release its generic sex hormones (gonadotrophins).

Gonadotrophins: Generic sexual hormones that stimulate the testicles and ovaries into releasing testosterone and oestrogen.

Grey matter: The parts of the central nervous system that are rich in neurons, for example the neocortex, basal ganglia, and other essential regions of the brain.

Gyrus: Raised fold of tissue in the cortex (plural = gyri).

Hippocampus (Greek for seahorse): The hippocampus is an older part of the cortex, which belongs to the limbic system. It is located in the temporal lobe and is vital for short-term memory. It relates memories with time and place, provides a sense of space/direction, and balances emotional impulses.

Homoeostasis: Maintenance of a dynamic, stable state by means of internal regulation processes that counteract external disturbances of equilibrium.

Hormones: Neurochemicals which are transported into the system via the bloodstream and lymph paths. Hormones are released from endocrine glands, including the adrenal glands, the hypothalamus, the pituitary gland, and the sexual organs, and they affect those cells in the body that have specific receptors for the individual hormones. Typical hormones include the sex hormones oxytocin, vasopressin, testosterone, and oestrogen, and the stress hormones, including the glucocorticoids (cortisol).

HPA-system, the (hypothalamic–pituitary–adrenal system): One of the two stress response systems of the organism that are related to sympathetic activation. The HPA system is activated by cortisol.

Hypothalamus: A small component of the brain, which is located just under the thalamus. Its role is to coordinate autonomous, endocrine, and motor processes into behaviour that is appropriate in relation to the immediate needs of the organism.

Implicit memory: This form of memory operates outside the reflective consciousness and is divided into procedural memory, imprinting, and RIGs. It is activated through sensory and motor systems, among others.

Imprinting: Imprinting is a primitive memory system that activates primitive neural circuits. Imprinting memory provides a quick and permanent form of learning, which occurs in response to early experiences.

Inferior: Located near to the base or bottom.

Insula: Structure located deep inside the lateral sulcus that separates the parietal and temporal lobes. Registers pain stimuli and integrates various sensory modalities, such as taste and scent. It also registers signals from the vestibular system and other proprioceptors.

Lateral: Located away from the central area.

Lateralization: Functions that are situated in one of the two hemispheres.

Limbic system: A common term for structures inside the hemispheres below the corpus callosum that process and deal with motivation, emotions, memory functions, and behaviour dictated by emotions.

Locus coeruleus: An important component in the network of the reticular activation system. Consists of nuclei that contain noradrenalin.

Long-term memory: Memories that last a long time—in some cases a lifetime.

Long-term potentiation (LTP): Long-term strengthening of synapses that leads to a change in both pre- and post-synaptic cells. Also known as "cellular memory".

Malleable: Can be shaped.

Medulla: Marrow.

MEG-scan (magnetoencephalography): Uses sensitive superconductors to measure tiny changes in the brain's magnetic field. The method provides good temporal and spatial resolution.

Melatonin: Neurochemical that is synthesized from the amino acid tryptophan. Produced in the pineal gland and released when it is dark, and the organism prepares for going to sleep.

Mid-brain (diencephalon): The mid-brain consists of a large number of nuclei, for example, the thalamus and hypothalamus, which are involved in coordinating information from the brain-stem. Among other functions, it collates sensory information and distributes it to other brain regions, and it regulates homoeostatic functions and automatic movements.

Monoamines: Category of chemicals that includes serotonin, dopamine, and noradrenalin. Monoamines act as neurotransmitters and are only produced in a few areas of the brain, mostly in the brainstem.

MRI-scan (magnetic resonance imaging): Imaging technique that produces cross section images on every level. This technique makes it possible to distinguish between tissues that contain different amounts of specific atoms. The method is based on a measurement of magnetic resonance through the recording of the electromagnetic energy briefly radiating from the tissue after stimulation with a rotating electromagnetic field. The signals are computer-processed, and the result comes out as a two-dimensional image. The technique is based on mathematical calculations of huge quantities of data.

Myelin sheaths: White, fatty sheaths made of myelin from certain types of glial cells.

Narrative memory: Memory system that stores experiences in a story-like, narrative form.

Neocortex: A part of the cortex that consists of six separate layers, and which forms most of the surface of the brain cortex.

Neomammalian brain: In evolutionary terms the "new" mammalian brain, which is often associated with the neocortex, thinking, and the processing of emotions, planning, etc.

Neurons: Cells that are specialized in receiving and transmitting information. Consist of dendrites, which receive information, and axons, which pass information on.

Neuropeptides: Neuropeptides consist of neurochemicals that act as transmitters or as hormones. Neuropeptides can be inhibitory as well as excitatory, and the brain contains at least 100 different kinds. Neuropeptides may function as neurotransmitters in one region and as hormones in another.

Neurotransmitter: Substance that transmit nervous impulses in the synapses between two neurons or between a neuron and a muscle cell.

Noradrenalin: Also known as (nor)epinephrine. Neurotransmitter that is distributed throughout most of the central nervous system, and which is almost always inhibitory. Noradrenalin induces fight-or-flight behaviour, and maintains high signal levels, a high arousal level, alertness, attention, and efficient information processing.

Nucleus: Particularly dense clusters of neurons with the same task in the brain.

Nucleus accumbens: Structure in the basal ganglia that receives input from the limbic system and releases dopamine. The area probably relates emotions to movement and is essential for goal-oriented behaviour.

Occipital lobe: Contains the visual cortex, which receives information from the retina in the eye.

Oestrogens: Oestrogens are mainly produced in the female sexual organs and in the adrenal glands in both sexes. This hormone stimulates the synthesis of oxytocin.

Opioids: The body's own morphine system is referred to as the endogenous opioids. Among other functions, they help regulate pain, joy, and reward, reduce stress, and provide a sense of overwhelming calm.

Orbitofrontal cortex: A paralimbic structure situated in the prefrontal cortex. This area receives multimodal information from all sensory areas and collects representations of familiar faces and emotional expressions. The area is involved in the development of object permanence and the delayed response function.

Oscillator cells: Oscillating cells. Neurons that fire in a certain rhythm, and which enable synchronization with other nervous systems.

Oxytocin: Hormone that is synthesized in the hypothalamus, and which promotes typically feminine traits such as calm and caring behaviour. Oxytocin facilitates the establishment of attachment bonds between mother and child.

PAG (periaqueductal grey): A not particularly well-defined nucleus cluster located in the brainstem, which modulates pain perception and probably releases the body's endogenous opioids.

Palaeomammalian brain: The "old" mammalian brain, in evolutionary terms; often associated with the limbic system.

Para-: Next to, alongside.

Parasympathetic nervous system: Part of the autonomic nervous system; promotes the digestive process, slows the heart rate, and acts as a calming system.

Parcellation: Specialization.

Parietal lobe: Contains the somatosensory cortex, which helps provide a person with a sense of his/her placement in the world and an internal subjective space. It receives sensory impressions from skin, muscles, and joints.

Peptides: See neuropeptides.

Peripheral nervous system: Consists of sensory and motor nerve fibres that connect the "periphery", i.e. skin, muscles, and internal organs, with the spinal cord.

PET-scan (positron emission tomography): A brain-imaging technique where positrons are used to measure the positively charged anti-particles that are created with the annihilation of radioactive isotopes that are injected into a person's bloodstream when or soon after the person initiates a task.

Phenotype: The result of the genotype's reaction with the environment. Applies both to individual properties and the sum of an individual's properties.

Pineal gland: Also known as the epiphysis or the pineal body. It is situated near the centre of the brain and has no double. It produces melatonin and is crucial for the control of circadian rhythms and sleep rhythm.

Pituitary gland: Located under the hypothalamus, which it is connected to through the pituitary stem. The pituitary gland is a "master" endocrine gland, releasing hormones that regulate other endogenous glands.

Polymodal areas: Structures where separate sensory phenomena meet and form a coherent impression, e.g. vision, hearing, and touch.

Posterior: Towards the back.

Posterior cingulate gyrus: The back part of the cingulate gyrus, which regulates social behaviour, attachment and caring behaviour, and the ability to play.

Prefrontal cortex: A part of the frontal lobes that includes the orbitofrontal cortex and the dorsolateral prefrontal cortex, among others. The area is particularly highly developed in primates, and especially so in humans. It is a super-convergence zone that is connected with other parts of the brain. The prefrontal cortex is particularly important for emotional stability and control of behaviour. It inhibits impulses by overriding the reflexive and instinctive systems, and makes it possible to act on the basis of long-term plans and reason.

Premotor cortex: A part of the frontal lobes that is located in front of the motor cortex, and which coordinates impulses into motor patterns and enables volitional movement.

Primary process thinking: A form of imaginary thinking where "primitive" needs are expressed, and where the child does not distinguish between external reality and internal needs. The child is indifferent to whether the fantasies have any logical coherence.

Procedural memory: A memory system that is also known as non-declarative memory. It is a part of the implicit memory system that refers to automated functions.

Projection: Nerve paths that emit information to a particular cluster of neurons.

Proprioceptive sense (from Latin: proprius = own, capio = capture, receive): A general term for the sensory perception of joints, muscle, and balance. The awareness of sensations that come from the sensory organs on the basis of body impulses. The proprioceptive sense provides the basis for our ability to sense ourselves from within.

Putamen: Structure in the basal ganglia that controls automatic movements.

Raphe nuclei: Situated in the medial section of the reticular activation systems; uses the neurotransmitter serotonin.

Reptilian brain: The oldest evolutionary part of the brain; associated with structures in the brainstem.

Resilient: Limber, elastic.

Resonance (synchronous attunement, from Latin: re-sonate or return-sound): The vibrating strings of a musical instrument may cause other strings to swing along, i.e. to resonate.

Reticular formation: See reticular activation system.

Reticular activation system (RAS): Affects the state of consciousness and the activation of the neocortex. Springs from the base of the brainstem and projects all the way up through the brainstem. RAS consists of a diffuse neural network and controls breathing and heart rate, among other things.

Rhythm: Repetition of behaviour at regular intervals of time.

RIG (representations of interactions that have been generalized): Micro-interactive sequences that take place in momentary sequences of social behaviour and regulate affect, arousal, motivation, attention, intimacy, and attachment.

SAM (sympathetic adrenomedullary system): One of the two stress response systems of the organism that are related to sympathetic activation. The SAM system is regulated by CRF and activated by the startle response, among others.

Secondary process thinking: The form of thinking that is able to curb "primitive" needs, and which forms the basis for rational, reality-based ideas and executive functions.

Somatic markers: Body markers that connect emotions with body sensations.

Semantic memory: A part of the explicit/declarative memory system that includes general knowledge, for example the name of the capital of Denmark.

Serotonin: A neurotransmitter that is produced from the amino acid tryptophan. It contributes to all aspects of behaviour and cognition and stabilizes perceptual and cognitive information.

Short-term memory: The short-term memory lasts only a few seconds or minutes and holds small amounts of information for short periods of time, for example a meaningless list of numbers.

SPECT-scan (single photon emission tomography): Imaging technique that provides a three-dimensional image of the distribution of a radioactive substance. A low-cost and widely available method, but less accurate than MRI, MEG and PET scans.

Spindle cells: Spindle-like neurons, which are about four times larger than ordinary neurons. Found in particular in the front section of the cingulate gyrus in humans and great apes.

Splenium: The posterior area of the corpus callosum, which is larger in women than in men.

Striatum: Part of the basal ganglia and important in relation to affect regulation. It consists of putamen and caudate nucleus.

Support cells: Also known as glial cells. This cell type is specialized in nourishing and supporting the neurons. The number of glial cells far exceeds the number of neurons. Some glial cells play a role in regulating synaptic neurotransmitters, while others form myelin sheaths around the axons.

Substantia nigra: Dopamine-producing neuron group situated in the brainstem region that sends impulses to the basal ganglia, among other functions.

Sulcus (plural = sulci): Groove between two gyri.

Sulcus temporalis superior (STS): An area on the surface of the temporal lobe, which is activated, for example, when the person observes the functional behaviour of other living beings.

Superior: Towards the top or on top.

Suprachiasmatic nuclei: Neurons in the front section of the hypo-thalamus, which receive input from the retina in the eye. The area is involved in regulating the circadian rhythm in relation to light input.

Sympathetic nervous system: A part of the autonomous nervous system that is activated in stressful situations, for example, when one feels threatened, and in situations characterized by high levels of positive energy, for example, playfulness.

Synapse: The gap between a neuronal terminal and a dendrite that neurons communicate through by transmitting neurochemical substances. The synaptic gap is a space of 0.0002 mm.

Synaptogenesis: Strengthening of neural circuits through the formation of synapses.

Synchronicity: Two events that take place simultaneously.

Synaptic pruning: The elimination of weaker synaptic contacts in favour of stronger connections.

TDF (testis-determining factor): When the Y-chromosome is activated the production of testosterone is induced by TDF.

Tectum, dorsal tectum: An area that is located towards the back and at the top of the brainstem, and which receives input from all sensorimotor modalities. The area is a convergence zone and provides a rudimentary representation of the entire body, i.e., a combination of internal and external body sensations.

Temporal lobe: The temporal lobe includes the auditory cortex and large parts of the limbic system.

Testosterone: The male sex hormone, which is mainly produced in the male sexual organs. Testosterone stimulates the synthesis of vasopressin.

Thalamus: An eggs-shaped structure in the mid-brain, often referred to as a relay station. It receives sensory impulses from the entire body and passes the information on to the appropriate part of the brain for further processing.

Trigeminal nerve (fifth cranial nerve, trigeminal or triplet nerve): Contributes with information about the facial muscles, partly through proprioceptive impulses.

Tryptophan: An amino acid and an essential substance in relation to the production of serotonin and melatonin.

Vagus nerve (tenth cranial nerve, "wandering nerve"): The longest of the twelve cranial nerves. It consists of fibres that convey impulses from the organs to the parasympathetic centres in the brainstem. It connects the brainstem with the heart, lungs, intestines, and stomach, among other things.

Vasopressin: A hormone that raises the blood pressure, partly by stimulating sympathetic functions that increase the release of CRF. It is mainly released via the male androgens and is essential in connection with reproductive behaviour in mammals. Vasopressin is also known as antidiuretic hormone.

Ventral: Facing the stomach or belly. In humans: towards the chin.

Ventral tegmental nucleus: Dopamine-producing neuron group in the brainstem situated in front of the substantia nigra. Stimulated by the care-giver's positive facial expression, among other things.

Vermis: The mid-section of the cerebellum. Co-ordinates emotional and motor functions.

Visuospatial: Concerning spatial relations within the field of vision.

Vitality affects: Fleeing affective qualities associated with dynamic, kinaesthetic expressions such as surging, fading away, fleeting, explosive, etc.

White matter: Nerve tissue that appears white due to the myelin sheaths, which consist of a fat-like whitish substance.

Working memory: A memory system that explicitly processes information stemming from the senses or from long-term memory. One of the most important aspects of the so-called central executive functions.

Wernicke's area: An area that is usually situated in the left hemisphere, where speech sounds are associated with meaning. The area produces the symbolic representation of information from several different sensory modalities.

REFERENCES

Allen, J. G. (2002). *Traumatic Relationships and Serious Mental Disorders*. New York: John Wiley.

Anders, T. F. (1989). Clinical syndromes, relationship disturbances, and their assessment. In: J. Sameroff & R. N. Emde (Eds.), *Relationship Disturbances in Early Childhood: A Developmental Approach* (pp. 125–144). New York: Basic Books.

Anders, T. F., & Zeanah, C. H. (1984). Early infant development from a biological point of view. In: J. D. Call, E. Galenson, & R. L. Tyson (Eds.), *Frontiers of Infant Psychiatry* (pp. 55–69). New York: Basic Books.

Andresen, J. (2002a). Lecture on neuropsychology (29 April). The Danish University of Education.

Andresen, J. (2002b). Noter til undervisning. Tiden, den fjerde dimension og dens betydning for kognition og indlæringsvanskeligheder. The Danish University of Education.

Andresen, Å., & Tuxen, A. (1977–1980). *Lademanns lægeleksikon*. Copenhagen: Lademann.

Austin, J. H. (1998). *Zen and the Brain*. Cambridge, MA: MIT.

Baddeley, A. D. (1986). *Working Memory*. Oxford: Clarendon Press.

Baron-Cohen, S. (2003). *The Essential Difference: Men, Women and the Extreme Male Brain*. London: Penguin.

Bartels, A., & Zeki, S. (2004). The neural correlates of maternal and romantic love. *NeuroImage*, *21*: 1155–1166.

Bartlett, F. C. (1932). *Remembering: A Study in Experimental and Social Psychology.* Cambridge: Cambridge University Press.

Beauchaine, T. (2001). Vagal tone, development, and Gray's motivational theory: toward an integrated model of autonomic nervous system functioning in psychopathology. *Development and Psychopathology*, *13*: 183–214.

Bechara, A., Damasio, H., & Damasio, A. R. (2003). Role of the amygdala in decision-making. *Annals of the New York Academy of Science*, *985*: 356–369.

Beebe, B., & Lachmann, F. M. (1988). Mother–infant mutual influence and precursors of psychic structure. In: A. Goldberg (Ed.), *Frontiers in Self Psychology, Volume 3* (pp. 3–27). Hillsdale, NJ: Analytic Press.

Beebe, B., & Lachmann, F. M. (2002). *Infant Research and Adult Treatment. Co-constructing Interactions.* Hillsdale, NJ: Analytic Press.

Belsky, J., & Isabella, R. A. (1988). Maternal infant and social–contextual determinants of attachment security. In: J. Belsky & T. Neworski (Eds.), *Clinical Implications of Attachment* (pp. 253–299). Hillsdale, NJ: Erlbaum.

Benes, F. M. (1994). Development of the corticolimbic system. In: G. Dawson & K. W. Fischer (Eds.), *Human Behaviour and the Developing Brain* (pp. 176–199. New York: Guilford.

Benjamin, L. S. (1996). An interpersonal theory of personality disorders. In: J. F. Clarkin & M. F. Lenzenweger (Eds.), *Major Theories of Personality Disorder* (pp. 141–220). New York: Guilford.

Bentzen, M. (2006). Shapes of experience-neuroscience, development psychology and somatic character formation. In: G. Marlock & H. Weiss (Eds.), *Handbuch der Körperpsychotherapie* (*The Handbook of Body-psychotherapy*). Stuttgart: Schattauer.

Bentzen, M., & Hart, S. (2005). Neuroaffektiv udvikling og det terapeutiske rum. *Psykolog Nyt*, *2*: 16–22.

Bergström, M. (1998). *Neuropædagogik. En skole for hele hjernen.* Copenhagen: Hans Reitzels.

Bertelsen, P. (1994). Kernen i det menneskelige tilværelsesprojekt er rettethed mod rettetheden. In: A. Neumann (Ed.), *Det særligt menneskelige. Udviklingspsykologiske billeder* (pp. 158–218). Copenhagen: Hans Reitzels.

Blair, J. (1999). Psychophysiological responsiveness to the distress of others in children with autism. *Personality and Individual Differences*, *26*: 477–485.

Blair, J., Morris, J. S., Frith, C. D., Perrett, D. I., & Dolan, R. J. (1999). Dissociable neural responses to facial expressions of sadness and anger. *Brain, 122*: 883–893.

Blair, J., Colledge, E., Murray, L., & Mitchell, D. G. V. (2001). A selective impairment in the processing of sad and fearful expressions in children with psychopathic tendencies. *Journal of Abnormal Child Psychology, 29*(6): 491–498.

Bliss, T. V. P., & Lomo, T. (1973). Longlasting potentiation of synaptic transmission in the dentate area of anaesthetized rabbit following stimulation of the perforanth path. *Journal of Physiology, 232*: 331–356.

Bowlby, J. (1969). *Attachment and Loss. Volume 1: Attachment.* London: Pimlico, 1997.

Bowlby, J. (1981). *Attachment and Loss. Volume 3: Loss, Sadness and Depression.* New York: Basic Books.

Bradley, S. (2000). *Affect Regulation and the development of psychopathology.* New York: Guilford.

Brazelton, T. B. (1992). *Touchpoints: Your Child's Emotional and Behavioural Development.* Reading, MA: Addison-Wesley.

Brazelton, T. B., & Cramer, B. G. (1990). *The Earliest Relationship.* Reading, MA: Addison-Wesley.

Brodén, M. B. (1991). *Mor og barn i ingenmandsland.* Copenhagen: Hans Reitzels.

Brodal, P. (2000). Sentralnervesystemet. Bygning og funksjon. Oslo: Universitetsforlaget.

Bruer, J. T. (1999). *The Myth of the First Three Years. A New Understanding Of Early Brain Development and Lifelong Learning.* New York: Free Press.

Bruner, J. S. (1986). *Actual Minds, Possible Worlds.* Cambridge, MA: Harvard University Press.

Bruner, J. S. (1990). *Acts of Meaning.* Cambridge, MA: Harvard University Press.

Cameron, J. (2001). Effects of sex hormones on brain development. In: C.A. Nelson & M. Luciana (Eds.), *Handbook of Developmental Cognitive Neuroscience* (pp. 59–78. Cambridge, MA: MIT.

Carter, R. (1998). *Tænkeboksen. Kortlægning af den menneskelige hjerne.* Copenhagen: Gyldendal.

Chalmers, D. J. (1999). The puzzle of conscious experience. *The Scientific American Book of the Brain* (pp. 287–296). New York: Lyons Press.

Chess, S., & Thomas, A. (1987). *Origins and Evolution of Behavior Disorders.* Cambridge, MA: Harvard University Press.

Chisholm, K. (1998). A three year follow-up of attachment and indiscriminate friendliness in children adopted from Romanian orphanages: *Child Development, 69*(4): 1092–1106.

Chugani, H. T. (1994). Development of regional brain glucose metabolism in relation to behavior and plasticity. In: G. Dawson & K. W. Fischer (Eds.), *Human Behavior and the Developing Brain*. New York: Guilford.

Chugani, H. T. (1996). Neuroimaging of development nonlinearity and developmental pathologies. In: R. Thatcher, G. Lyon, J. Rumsey, & N. Krasnegor (Eds.), *Developmental Neuroimaging. Mapping the Development of the Brain and Behavior* (pp. 187–195). San Diego, CA: Academic Press.

Chugani, H. T. (1999). Metabolic imaging: a window on brain development and plasticity. *The Neuroscientist, 5*(1): 29–40.

Chugani, H. T., & Phelps, M. E. (1986). Maturational changes in cerebral function in infants determined by FDG position emission tomography. *Science, 231*: 840–843.

Chugani, H. T., Phelps, M. E., & Mazziotta, J. C. (1987). Position emission tomography. Study of human brain functional development. *Annals of Neurology, 22*: 487–497.

Cicchetti, D., & Tucker, D. (1994). Development and self-regulation structures of the mind. *Development and Psychopathology, 6*: 533–549.

Clarke, A. S., Hedeker, D. R., Ebert, M. H., Schmidt, D. E., McKinney, W. T., & Kraemer, G. W. (1996a). Rearing experiences and biogenic amine activity in infant rhesus monkeys. *Biological Psychiatry, 40*: 338–352.

Clarke, A. S., Soto, A., Bergholz, T., & Schneider, M. L. (1996b). Maternal gestational stress alters adoptive and social behaviour in adolescent rhesus monkey offspring. *Infant Behavior and Development, 19*: 451–461.

Cozolino, L. (2006). *The Neuroscience of Human Relationships: Attachment and the Developing Social Brain*. London: W. W. Norton.

Cozolino, L. J. (2000). *The Neuroscience of Psychotherapy. Building and Rebuilding the Human Brain*. New York: W. W. Norton.

Damasio, A. R. (1994). *Descartes' Error. Emotion, Reason, and the Human Brain*. New York: Grosset/Putnam.

Damasio, A. R. (1998). Emotion in the perspective of an integrated nervous system. *Brain Research Reviews, 26*: 83–86.

Damasio, A. R. (1999). *The Feeling of What Happens: Body, Emotion and the Making of Consciousness*. London: Heinemann.

Damasio, A. R. (2003). *Looking for Spinoza: Joy, Sorrow, and The Feeling Brain*. London: Harcourt.

d'Aquili, E., & Newberg, A. B. (1999). *The Mystical Mind: Probing the Biology of Religious Experience*. Minneapolis, MN: Fortress Press.

Darwin, C. B. (1872). *The expression of emotion in man and animals*. London: Fontana Press, 1999.

Davidson, R. J. (1995). Cerebral asymmetry, emotion, and affective style. In: R. J. Davidson & K. Hugdahl (Eds.), *Brain Asymmetry* (pp. 361–385. Cambridge, MA: MIT.

Davidson, R. J. (2002). Synaptic substrates of the implicit and explicit self. *Science, 296*: 268.

Davidson, R. J., & Fox, N. A. (1982). Asymmetrical brain activity discriminates between positive versus negative affective stimuli in human infants. *Science, 218*: 1235–1237.

Davidson, R. J., & Fox, N. A. (1989). Frontal brain asymmetry predicts infants' response to maternal separation. *Journal of Abnormal Psychology, 98*(2): 127–131.

Davidson, R. J., & Hugdahl, K. (1995). *Brain Asymmetry*. Cambridge, MA: The MIT Press.

Davidson, R. J., & Irwin, W. (1999). The functional neuroanatomy of emotion and affective style. *Trends in Cognitive Neuroscience, 3*: 11–21.

Davidson, R. J., & Slagter, H. A. (2000). Probing emotion in the developing brain: Functional neuroimaging in the assessment of the neural substrates of emotion in normal and disordered children and adolescents. *Mental Retardation and Developmental Disabilities Research Reviews,6*: 166–170. New York: Wiley-Liss.

Davidson, R. J., Ekman, P., Saron, C. D., Senulis, J. A., & Friesen, W. V. (1990). Approach-withdrawal and cerebral asymmetry: emotional expression and brain physiology I. *Journal of Personality and Social Psychology, 58*(2): 330–341.

Davidson, R. J., Marshall, J. R., Tomarken, A. J., & Henriques, J. B. (2000). While a phobic waits: regional brain electrical and autonomic activity in social phobias during anticipation of public speaking. *Biological Psychiatry, 47*: 85–95.

Davidson, R. J., Putnam, K. M., & Larson, C. L. (2000). Dysfunction in the neural circuitry of emotion regulation. A possible prelude to violence. *Science, 289*: 591–594.

Dawson, G. (1994). Development of emotional expression and emotion regulation in infancy: contributions of the frontal lobe. In: G. Dawson & K. W. Fischer (Eds.), *Human Behavior and the Developing Brain* (pp. 346–380). New York: Guilford.

DeCasper, A., & Carstens, A. (1980). Contingencies of stimulation: effects on learning and emotions in neonates. *Infant Behavior and Development*, 4: 19–36.

DeCasper, A., & Fifer, W. (1980). Of human bonding: newborns prefer their mother's voices. *Science*, 208: 1174–1176.

DeCasper, A., & Spencer, M. (1986). Prenatal speech influences newborn's perception of speech sounds. *Infant Behavior and Development*, 9: 133–150.

Diamond, A. (2000). Close interrelation of motor development and cognitive development and of the cerebellum and prefrontal cortex. *Child Development*, 71(1): 44–56.

Edelman, G. (1987). *Neural Darwinism: A Theory of Neuronal Group Selection*. New York: Basic Books.

Edelman, G. M., & Tononi, G. (2000). *A Universe of Consciousness: How Matter Becomes Imagination*. New York: Basic Books.

Ekman, P. (2003). *Emotions Revealed*. London: Weidenfeld & Nicolson.

Eriksson, H. (2001). *Neuropsykologi. Normalfunktion, demenser och avgränsade hjärnskador*. Falköping: Elanders Gummessons.

Evrard, P. Marret, S., & Gressens, P. (1997). Environmental and genetic determinant of neural migration and postmigratory survival. *Acta Pædiatrica*, 422(Suppl.): 120–126.

Fanselow, M. S., & Lester, L. S. (1988). A functional behavioristic approach to aversively motivated behaviour: Predatory imminence as a determinant of the topography of defensive behaviour. In: R. C. Bolles & M. D. Beecher (Eds.), *Evolution and Learning* (pp. 185–212). Hillsdale, NJ: Erlbaum.

Field, T., & Fogel, A. (1982). *Emotion and Early Interaction*. Hillsdale, NJ: Erlbaum.

Field, T. M., Woodson, R., Greenberg, R., & Cohen, D. (1982). Discrimination and imitation of facial expression by neonates. *Science*, 218: 179–181.

Field, T., Schanberg, S., Scharfidi, F., Bauer, C., Vega-Lahr, N., Garcia, R., Nystrom, J., & Kuhn, C. (1986). Tactile/kinesthetic stimulation effects on preterm neonates. *Pediatrics*, 77: 654–658.

Fisher, H. (2004). *Why We Love: The Nature and Chemistry of Romantic Love*. New York: Henry Holt.

Fogassi, L., Ferrari, P. F., Gesierich, B., Rozzi, S., Chersi, F., & Rizzolatti, G. (2005). Parietal lobe: from action organization to intention understanding. *Science*, 308, 662–667.

Fonagy, P. (2003). The development of psychopathology from infancy to adulthood: the mysterious unfolding of disturbance in time. *Infant Mental Health Journal*, 24(3): 212–239.

Fonagy, P., Gergely, G., Jurist, E.L., & Target, M. (2002). *Affect Regulation, Mentalization and the Development of the Self.* New York: Other Press.

Fonagy, P., Steele, M., Steele, H., Leigh, T., Kennedy, R., Mattoon, G., & Target, M. (1995). Attachment, the reflective self, and borderline states: the predictive specificity of the Adult Attachment Interview and pathological emotional development. In: S. Goldberg, R. Muir, & J. Kerr (Eds.), *Attachment Theory: Social, Developmental, and Clinical Perspectives* (pp. 233–278). Hillsdale, NJ: Analytic Press.

Fox, N. A. (1994). Dynamic cerebral process underlying emotion regulation: biological and behavioural considerations. *Monographs of the Society for Research in Child Development*, *59*(2–3: 152–166.

Freud, S. (1954). *The Origins of Psychoanalysis. Letters to Wilhelm Fliess, Draft and Notes: 1887–1902.* New York: Basic Books, 1977.

Gabbard, G. O. (1992). Psychodynamic psychiatry in the "decade of the brain". *American Journal of Psychiatry, 149*: 991–998.

Gade, A. (1997). *Hjerneprocesser.* Copenhagen: Forlaget Frydenlund.

Gallese, V. (2001). The "shared manifold" hypothesis. From mirror neurons to empathy. *Journal of Consciousness Studies, 8*(5–7): 33–50.

Gallese, V., & Goldman, A. (1998). Mirror neurons and the simulation theory of mind-reading. *Trends in Cognitive Sciences, 2*: 493–501.

Gallese, V., Fadiga, L., Fogassi, L., & Rizzolatti, G. (1996). Action recognition in the premotor cortex. *Brain, 119*: 593–609.

Gardiner, J. M. (2000). On the objectivity of subjective experiences of autonoetic and noetic consciousness. In: E. Tulving (Ed.), *Memory, Consciousness, and the Brain: The Tallinn Conference* (pp. 159–172). Philadelphia, PA: Psychology Press.

Gardner, H. (1996). *De sju intelligenserna.* Falun: Brain Books.

Gazzaniga, M. S. (1999). The split brain revisited. *The Scientific American Book of the Brain* (pp. 129–139). New York: Lyons Press.

Gazzaniga, M. S., LeDoux, J., & Wilson, D. H. (1977). Language, praxis and the right hemisphere: clues to some mechanisms of sensuousness. *Neurology, 27*: 1144–1147.

Gerhardt, S. (2004). *Why Love Matters. How Affection Shapes a Baby's Brain.* New York: Brunner-Routledge.

Gershon, M. D., Kirchgessner, A. L., & Wade, P. R. (1994). Functional anatomy of the enteric nervous system. In: L. R. Johnson (Ed.), *Physiology of the Gastrointestinal Tract* (3rd edn) (pp. 381–422). New York: Raven Press.

Geschwind, N., & Galaburda, A. M. (1987). *Cerebral Lateralization. Biological Mechanisms, Associations, and Pathology.* Cambridge, MA: MIT.

Giedd, J. (2002). Inside the teenage brain. Interview. Frontline.

Giedd, J. N., Blumenthal, J., Jeffries, N. O., Castallanos, F. X., Liv, H., Zijdenbos, A., Paus, T., Evans, A. C., & Rapoport, J. L. (1999). Brain development during childhood and adolescence: a longitudinal MRI study. *Nature Neuroscience, 2*(10): 861–863.

Gjærum, B. & Ellertsen, B. (2002). *Hjerne og atferd. Utviklingsforstyrrelser hos barn og ungdom i et nevrobiologisk perspektiv.* Oslo: Gyldendal Norsk.

Glaser, D. (2004). Early experience, attachment and the brain. In: J. Corrigall & H. Wilkinson (Eds.), *Revolutionary Connections. Psychotherapy and Neuroscience* (pp. 117–133). London: Karnac.

Gleitman, H. (1995). *Psychology* (4th edn). New York: W. W. Norton.

Goldberg, E. (2001). *The Executive Brain. Frontal Lobes and the Civilized Mind.* Oxford: Oxford University Press.

Goldman-Rakic, P. S. (1987a). Development of cortical circuitry and cognitive function. *Child Development, 58*: 601–622.

Goldman-Rakic, P. S. (1987b). Circuitry of the primate prefontal cortex and regulation of behavior by representational memory. In: F. Plum & V. Mountcastle (Eds.), *Handbook of Physiology* (pp. 373–418). Bethesda, MD: American Physiological Society.

Goldman-Rakic, P. S. (1999). Working memory and the mind. In: A. Damasio (Ed.), *The Scientific American Book of the Brain,* (pp. 89–105). New York: Lyons Press.

Goldman-Rakic, P. S., Isseroff, A., Schwartz, M. L., & Bugbee, N. M. (1983). The neurobiology of cognitive development. In: P. H. Mussen (Ed.), *Handbook of Child Psychology* (4th edn) (pp. 281–344). New York: Wiley.

Goleman, D. (2003). *Destructive Emotions: How Can We Overcome Them? A Scientific Dialogue with the Dalai Lama.* New York: Bantam Bell.

Gopnik, A., Meltzoff, A. & Kuhl, P. (1999). *The Scientist in the Crib. What Early Learning Tells Us about the Mind.* New York: Perennial.

Goy, R. W., Bercovitch, F. B., & McBriar, M. C. (1988). Behavioural masculinization is independent of genital masculinization in prenatally androgenized female rhesus macaques. *Hormones and Behaviour, 22*: 552–571.

Greenough, W. T., & Black, J. E. (1992). Introduction of brain structure by experience: substrates for cognitive development. In: M. R. Gunnar & C. A. Nelson (Eds.), *Minnesota Symposium on Child Psychology. Volume 24: Developmental Behavioural Neuroscience* (pp. 155–200). Hillsdale, NJ: Lawrence Erlbaum.

Greenough, W. T., Black, J. E., & Wallace, C. S. (1987). Experience and brain development. *Child Development, 58*(3): 539–559.

Gunnar, M. R. (2001). Effects of early deprivation: findings from orphanage-reared infants and children. In: C. Nelson & M. Luciana (Eds.), *Handbook of Developmental Cognitive Neuroscience* (pp. 617–629). Cambridge, MA: MIT.

Gunnar, M. R., & Barr, R. G. (1998). Stress, early brain development and behaviour. *Infants and Young Children, 11*: 1–14.

Gunnar, M. R., & Cheatham, C. L. (2003). Brain and behaviour interface: stress and the developing brain. *Infant Mental Health Journal, 24*(3): 195–211.

Gunnar, M. R., Mangelsdorf, S., Kestenbaum, R., Lang, S., Larson, M., & Andreas, D. (1989). Stress and coping in early development. In: D. Chiccetti (Ed.), *Rochester Symposium on Development Psychopathology. Volume 1: The Emergence of a Discipline* (pp. 119–138). Hillsdale, NJ: Lawrence Erlbaum.

Hadley, J. (1992). Instincts revisited. *Psychoanalytic Inquiry, 12*: 396–418.

Hamburger, V. (1977). The developmental history of the motor neuron. *Neuroscience Research Progress Bulletin, 15*: 1–37.

Hamer, D., & Copeland, P. (1998). *Living with Our Genes.* New York: Doubleday.

Hansen, S. (2002). *Fra neuron til neurose.* Copenhagen: Gads.

Harlow, H. F. (1958). The nature of love. *American Psychiatry, 13*: 673–685.

Harlow, H. F. (1959). Love in infant monkeys. *Scientific American, 200*(6): 68–74.

Hebb, D. O. (1949). *The Organization of Behaviour: A Neuropsychobiological Theory.* New York: Wiley.

Hines, M. (1982). Prenatal gonadal hormones and sex differences in human behavior. *Psychological Bulletin, 92*: 56–80.

Hofer, M. A. (1970). Cardiac and respiratory function during sudden prolonged immobility in wild rodents. *Psychosomatic Medicine, 32*: 633–647.

Hofer, M. A. (1983). On the relationship between attachment and separation processes in infancy. In: R. Plutchik & H. Kellerman (Eds.), *Emotion: Theory, Research and Experience* (pp. 199–219). New York: Academic Press.

Hofer, M. A. (1984). Relationships as regulators: a psychobiologic perspective on bereavement. *Psychosomatic Medicine, 46*: 183–197.

Hofer, M. A. (1990). Early symbiotic processes: hard evidence from a soft place. In: R. A. Glick & S. Bone (Eds.), *Pleasure Beyond the Pleasure Principle* (pp. 55–78). New Haven, CT: Yale University Press.

Hofer, M. A., & Sullivan, R. (2001). Toward a neurobiology of attachment. In: C. Nelson & M. Luciana (Eds.), *Handbook of Developmental Cognitive Neuroscience* (pp. 599–616). Cambridge, MA: MIT.

Hubel, D. H., & Wiesel, T. N. (1970). The period of susceptibility to the physiological effects of unilateral eye closure in kittens. *Journal of Physiology*, 206: 419–436.

Huttenlocher, P. R. (1994). Synaptogenesis in human cerebral cortex. In: G. Dawson & K. W. Fischer (Eds.), *Human Behavior and the Developing Brain*. New York: Guilford.

Insel, T. R., & Young, L. J. (2001). Neurobiology of social attachment. *Nature Neuroscience Review*, 2: 129–136.

James, W. (1878–1899). *Psychology: Briefer Course*. The Library of America. Harvard College, 1992.

Johnson, S. (2004). *Mind Wide Open: Your Brain and the Neuroscience of Everyday Life*. New York: Scribner.

Joseph, R. (1993). *The Naked Neuron. Evolution and the Languages of the Body and Brain*. New York: Plenum Press.

Joseph, R. (1996). *Neuropsychiatry, Neuropsychology and Clinical Neuroscience. Emotion, Evolution, Cognition, Language, Memory, Brain Damage, and Abnormal Behaviour*. Baltimore, MD: Williams & Wilkins.

Kagan, J. (1990). *Emergence of Morality in Young Children*. New York: Basic Books.

Kagan, J. (1994). *Galen's Prophecy*. New York: Basic Books.

Kagan, J., Snidman, N. & Arcus, D.M. (1992). Initial reactions to unfamiliarity. *Current Directions in Psychological Science*, 1(6): 171–174.

Kalin, N. H. (1999). The neurobiology of fear. *The Scientific American Book of the Brain* (pp. 195–207). New York: Lyons Press.

Kandel, E. R. (2005). A new intellectual framework for psychiatry. In: E. R. Kandel. *Psychiatry, Psychoanalysis, and the New Biology of Mind* (pp. 27–59). Washington, DC: American Psychiatric Publishing.

Kandel, E. R., & Hawkins, R. D. (1999). The biological basis of learning and individuality. *The Scientific American Book of the Brain* (pp. 139–155). New York: Lyons Press.

Kaplan–Solms, K., & Solms, M. (2002). *Clinical Studies in Neuro–Psychoanalysis: Introduction to a Depth Neuropsychology*. New York & London: Karnac.

Karen, R. (1998). *Becoming Attached*. New York & Oxford: Oxford University Press.

Karr-Morse, R., & Wiley, M. (1997). *Ghosts from the Nursery. Tracing the Roots of Violence*. New York: Atlantic Monthly Press.

Kimura, D. (1987). Are men's and women's brains really different? University of Western Ontario. *Canadian Psychology, 28*(1): 133–147.

Kimura, D. (1999a). Sex differences in the brain. *The Scientific American Book of the Brain* (pp. 157–171). New York: Lyons Press.

Kimura, D. (1999b). *Sex and Cognition.* Cambridge, MA: MIT.

Kringelbach, M. L. (2004). *Hjernerum. Den følelsesfulde hjerne.* Copenhagen: People's Press.

Krystal, H. (1988). *Integration and Selfhealing: Affect–Trauma . . . Alexithymia.* Hillsdale, NJ: Analytic Press.

Lautrop, J. (2002). *Kirstens dagbog.* Aalborg: Socialministeriet.

Lecours, A. R. (1982). Correlates of developmental behaviour in brain maturation. In: T. G. Bever (Ed.), *Regressions in Mental Development: Basic Phenomena and Theories* (pp. 267–298). Hillsdale, NJ: Lawrence Erlbaum.

LeDoux, J. E. (1989). Indelibility of subcortical emotional memories. *Journal of Cognitive Neuroscience, 1*: 238–243.

LeDoux, J. E. (1993). Emotional networks in the brain. In: M. Lewis & J. M. Haviland (Eds.), *Handbook of Emotions* (pp. 109–118). New York: Guilford.

LeDoux, J. E. (1994). Emotion, memory and the brain. *Scientific American, 270*: 32–39.

LeDoux, J. E. (1998). *The Emotional Brain: The Mysterious Underpinnings of Emotional Life.* London: Weidenfeld & Nicolson.

LeDoux, J. E. (2001). *Synaptic Self: How Our Brains Become Who We Are.* New York: Viking.

LeVay, S. (1993). *The Sexual Brain.* Cambridge, MA: MIT.

Lewis, T., Amini, F., & Lannon, R. (2001). *A General Theory of Love.* New York: Vintage Books.

Luria, A. R. (1973). *The Working Brain.* New York: Basic Books.

Lutchmaya, S., & Baron-Cohen, S. (2002). Short communication. Human sex differences in social and non-social looking preferences, at 12 months of age. *Infant Behavior and Development, 25*: 319–325.

Lutchmaya, S., Baron-Cohen, S., & Raggatt, P. (2002). Foetal testosterone and vocabulary size in 18- and 24-month-old infants. *Infant Behavior and Development, 24*: 418–424.

Lyons-Ruth, K. (1998). Implicit relational knowing: its role in development and psychoanalytic treatment. *Infant Mental Health Journal, 19*(3): 282–289.

Mace, C. (2004). Psychotherapy and neuroscience: How close can they get? In: J. Corrigall & H. Wilkinson (Eds.), *Revolutionary Connections. Psychotherapy and Neuroscience* (pp. 163–174). London: Karnac.

MacLean, P. (1967). The brain in relation to empathy and medical education. *Journal of Nervous and Mental Disease, 144*: 374–382.

MacLean, P. D. (1970). The triune brain, emotion, and scientific bias. In: F. O. Schmitt (Ed.), *The Neurosciences. Second Study Program* (pp. 336–349). New York: Rockefeller University Press.

MacLean, P. D. (1973). A triune concept of the brain and behaviour. Lecture I. Man's reptilian and limbic inheritance. Lecture II. Man's limbic brain and the psychoses. Lecture III. New trends in man's evolution. In: T. Boag & D. Campbell (Eds.), *The Hincks Memorial Lectures* (pp. 6–66). Toronto: University of Toronto Press.

MacLean, P. D. (1985). Brain evolution relating to family, play, and the separation call. *Archives of General Psychiatry, 42*: 405–417.

MacLean, P. D. (1990). *The Triune Brain in Evolution: Role in Paleocerebral Functions*. New York: Plenum.

Maguire, E. A., Spiers, H. J., Good, C. D., Hartley, T., Frackowiak, R. S. J., & Burgess, N. (2000). Navigation-related structural change in the hippocampus of taxidrivers. *Proceedings of the National Academy of Science of the United States of America, 97*(9): 4414–4416.

Main, M. (1999). Epilogue. Attachment theory. Eighteen points with suggestions for future studies. In: J. Cassidy & P. R. Shaver (Eds.), *Handbook of Attachment: Theory Research and Clinical Applications* (pp. 845–887). New York: Guilford.

Marcovitch, S., Goldberg, S., Gold, A., Washington, J., Wasson, C., Krekewich, K., & Handley-Derry, M. (1997). Determinants of behavioral problems in Romanian children adopted in Ontario. *International Journal Development, 20*(1): 17–31.

Mathiesen, B. B. (2004). Psyken I hjernen, *Kroppen I psyken* (pp. 49–84). Copenhagen: Hans Reitzels.

Meltzoff, A. N. (1985). The roots of social and cognitive development: models of man's original nature. In: T. Field & N. Fox (Eds.), *Social Perception in Infants* (pp. 1–30). Norwood, NJ: Ablex.

Meltzoff, A. N. (1995). Understanding the intentions of others: re-enactment of intended acts by eighteen-month-old children. *Developmental Psychology, 3*: 838–850.

Meltzoff, A. N., & Moore, M. K. (1977). Imitation of facial and manual gestures by human neonates. *Science, 198*: 75–78.

Meltzoff, A. N., & Moore, M. K. (1999). Persons and representations: why infant imitation is important for theories of human development. In: J. Nadel & G. Butterworth (Eds.), *Imitation in Infancy* (pp. 9–35). Cambridge: Cambridge University Press.

Mesulam, M. M. (1985). *Principles of Behavioural Neurology.* Philadelphia, PA: Davis.

Michael, R. P., & Zumpe, D. (1998). Developmental changes in behavior and in steroid uptake by the male and female macaque brain. *Developmental Neuropsychology, 14*(2–3): 233–260.

Miller, P. J., & Sperry, L. (1988). Early talk about the past: the origins of conversational stories of personal experience. *Journal of Child Language, 15*: 293–315.

Mortensen, K. (2001). *Fra neuroser til relationsforstyrrelser: Psykoanalytiske udviklingsteorier og klassifikationer af psykopatologi.* Copenhagen: Gyldendal.

Nadel, L. & Zola-Morgan, S. (1984). Infantile amnesia: a neurobiological perspective. In: M. Moscovitch (Ed.), *Infant Memory. Its Relation to Normal and Pathological Memory in Humans and Other Animals* (pp. 145–166). New York: Plenum Press.

Nauta, W. J. H. (1971). The problem of the frontal lobe: a reinterpretation. *Journal of Psychiatric Research, 8*: 167–187.

Neisser, U. (1993). The self perceived. In: U. Neisser (Ed.), *The Perceived Self: Ecological and Interpersonal Sources of Self Knowledge* (pp. 3–21). New York: Cambridge University Press.

Nelson, K. (1984). The transition from infant to child memory. In: M. Moscovitch (Ed.), *Infant Memory. Its Relation to Normal and Pathological Memory in Humans and Other Animals* (pp. 103–128). New York: Plenum Press.

Nelson, K. (1993). The psychological and social origins of autobiographical memory. *Psychological Science, 4*(1): 7–14.

Nelson, K. (1996). *Language in Cognitive Development.* Cambridge: Cambridge University Press.

Nelson, K., & Gruendel, J. M. (1981). Generalized event representations: basic building blocks of cognitive development. In: M. E. Lamb & A. L. Brown (Eds.), *Advances in Developmental Psychology, 1* (pp. 131–158). Hillsdale, NJ: Lawrence Erlbaum.

Newberg, A., d'Aquili, E., & Rause, V. (2002). *Why God Won't Go Away. Brain Science and the Biology of Belief.* New York: Ballantine.

O'Keefe, J., & Nadel, L. (1978). *The Hippocampus as a Cognitive Map.* Oxford: Clarendon Press.

Olson, G. M., & Strauss, M. S. (1984). The development of infant memory. In: M. Moscovitch (Ed.), *Infant Memory. Its Relation to Normal and Pathological Memory in Humans and Other Animals* (pp. 29–48). New York: Plenum Press.

Panksepp, J. (1998). *Affective Neuroscience. The Foundations of Human and Animal Emotions.* New York: Oxford University Press.

Panksepp, J. (2005).Defining concepts for affective neuroscience: how the brain creates meaning by integrating emotions and cognitions. In: M. Jaffa (Ed.), *Neuroscientific and Psychoanalytical Perspectives on Emotion.* (pp. 85–124). International Neuro–Psychoanalysis Congress Proceedings, Vol. 1, London, 2000.

Perry, B. D. (1990). Adrenergic receptor regulation in posttraumatic stress disorder. In: E. L. Giller (Ed.), *Advances in Psychiatry: Biological Assessment and Treatment of Posttraumatic Stress Disorder* (pp. 87–115). Washington, DC: American Psychiatric Press.

Perry, B. D. (1994). Neurobiological sequelae of childhood trauma: posttraumatic stress disorders in children. In: M. Murburg (Ed.), *Catecholamine Function in Posttraumatic Stress Disorder: Emerging Concepts* (pp. 253–276). Washington, DC: American Psychiatric Press.

Perry, B. D. (1997). Incubated in terror: neurodevelopmental factors in the "cycle of violence". Cybrary version. In: J. Osofsky (Ed.), *Children, Youth and Violence: The Search for Solutions* (pp. 124–148). New York: Guilford.

Perry, B .D. (1999a). Memories of fear. How the brain stores and retrieves physiologic states, feelings, behaviors and thoughts from traumatic events. Cybrary version. In: J. Goodwin & R. Attias (Eds.), *Splintered Reflections: Images of the Body in Trauma.* New York: Basic Books.

Perry, B. D. (1999b). Posttraumatic stress disorders in children and adolescents. Academy version of article to appear in *Current Opinions in Pediatrics, 11*(4) Psychiatry: 121–132.

Perry, B. D. (2001). Violence and childhood: how persisting fear can alter the developing child's brain. Cybrary version from the neurodevelopmental impact of violence in childhood. In: D. Schetky & E. Benedek (Eds.), *Textbook of Child Adolescent Forensic Psychiatry* (pp. 221–238). Washington, DC: American Psychiatric Press.

Perry, B. D. (2002). Childhood experience and the expression of genetical potential: what childhood neglect tells us about nature and nurture. *Brain and Mind, 3*: 79–100.

Perry, B. D., Pollard, R. A., Blakely, T. L., Baker, W. L. M., & Vigilante, D. (1995). Childhood trauma, the neurobiology of adoption, and "use-dependent" development of the brain. How "states" become "traits". *Infant Mental Health Journal, 16*: 271–291.

Petrovitch, S. B., & Gewirtz, J. L. (1985). The attachment learning process and its relation to cultural and biological evolution: proximate and ultimate considerations: In: M. Reite & T. Field (Eds.), *The Psycho-*

biology of Attachment and Separation (pp. 259–291. Orlando, FL: Academic Press.

Piaget, J. (1973). The affective unconscious and the cognitive unconscious. *Journal of the American Psychoanalytic Association*, 21(2): 249–261.

Plomin, R. (1983). Developmental behavioural genetics. *Child Development*, 54: 252–259.

Plomin, R. (1999). Genetics of childhood disorders: III. Genetics and intelligence. *Journal of the American Academy Child Adolescent Psychiatry*, 38: 786–788.

Porges, S. W. (1995). Orienting in a defensive world: mammalian modifications of our evolutionary heritage. A polyvagal theory. *Psychophysiology*, 32: 301–318.

Porges, S. W. (1996). Physiological regulation in high-risk infants: a model for assessment and potential intervention. *Development and Psychopathology*, 8: 43–58.

Porges, S. W. (1997). Emotion: an evolutionary by-product of the neural regulation of the autonomic nervous system. In: C. S. Carter, B. Kirkpatrick, & I. I. Lederhendler (Eds.), *The Integrative Neurobiology of Affiliation* (pp. 62–77). New York: Annals of the New York Academy of Sciences.

Porges, S. W. (1998). Love: an emergent property of the mammalian autonomic nervous system. *Psychoneuroendocrinology*, 23(8): 837–861.

Porges, S. W. (2001). The polyvagal theory: phylogenetic substrates of a social nervous system. *International Journal of Psychophysiology*, 42: 123–146.

Post, R. M., Weiss, S. R., Smith, M., Li, H., & McCann, U. (1997). Kindling versus quenching. *Annals of New York Academy of Sciences*, 849–854.

Purves, D., Augustine, G. J., Fitzpatrick, D., Katz, L. C., LaMantia, A., McNamara, J. O., & Williams, S. M. (2001). *Neuroscience*. Sunderland, MA: Sinauer.

Ramachandran, V. (2003). *The Emerging Mind*. London: Profile Books.

Rizzolatti, G., & Arbib, M. (1998). Language within our grasp. *Trends in Neurosciences*, 21: 188–194.

Rizzolatti, G., Fadiga, L., Fogassi, L., & Gallese, V. (1999). Resonance behaviours and mirror neurons. *Archives of Italian Biology*, 137: 85–100.

Rodriguez, E., George, N., Lachaux, J. P., Martinevic, J., Renault, B., & Vareloa, F. J. (1999). Perception's shadow: long distance synchronization of human brain activity. *Nature*, 397: 430–433.

Rothbart, M. K., & Bates, J. E. (1998). Temperament. In: W. Damon & N. Eisenberg (Eds.), *Handbook of Child Psychology. Volume 3: Social, Emotional and Personality Development* (5th edn) (pp. 105–176). New York: Wiley.

Rovee-Collier, C. K., & Fagen, J. W. (1981). The retrieval of memory in early infancy. In: L. P. Lipsitt (Ed.), *Advances in Infancy Research (Volume 1)* (pp. 225–254). Norwood, NJ: Ablex.

Rutter, M., & Plomin, R. (1997). Opportunities for psychiatry from genetic findings. *The British Journal of Psychiatry, 171*: 209–219.

Rutter, M., & Rutter, M. (1997). *Den livslange udvikling.* Copenhagen: Hans Reitzels.

Rymer, R. (1993). *Genie: Escape from a Silent Childhood.* London: Michael Joseph.

Sander, L. (1977). The regulation of exchange in the infant-caretaker system and some aspects of the context-content relationship. In: M. Lewis & L. Rosenblum (Eds.), *Interaction, Conversation, and The Development of Language* (pp.133–156). New York: Wiley.

Sander, L. W. (1983). Polarity, paradox, and the organizing process in development. In: J. D. Call, E. Galenson, & R. L. Tyson (Eds.), *Frontiers of Infant Psychiatry (Volume 1)* (pp. 333–347). New York: Basic Books.

Sander, L. W. (1985). Toward a logic of organization in psycho-biological development. In: K. Klar & L. Siever (Eds.), *Biologic Response Styles: Clinical Implications* (pp. 20–36). Washington, DC: Monograph Series American Psychiatric Press.

Sander, L. W. (1988). The event structure of regulation in the neonate-care-giver system as a biological background for early organization of psychic structure. In: A. Goldberg (Ed.), *Frontiers in Self Psychology (Volume 3)* (pp. 3–27). Hillsdale, NJ. Lawrence Erlbaum.

Sapolsky, R. (1998). *Why Zebras Don't Get Ulcers. An Updated Guide To Stress, Stress-related Diseases, and Coping.* New York: W.H. Freeman.

Scaer, R. C. (2001). *Trauma, Dissociation, and Disease: The Body Bears the Burden.* New York: Haworth.

Schacter, D. L. (1996). *Searching for Memory. The Brain, The Mind, and The Past.* New York: Basic Books.

Schacter, D. L., & Moscovitch, M. (1984). Infants, amnesics, and dissociable memory systems. In: M. Moscovitch (Ed.), *Infant Memory. Its Relation to Normal and Pathological Memory in Humans and Other Animals* (pp. 173–209). New York: Plenum Press.

Schore, A. (1994). *Affect Regulation and The Origin of Self.* Hillsdale, NJ: Lawrence Erlbaum.

Schore, A. (2000a). Healthy childhood and the development of the human brain. *International Conference.* Healthy Children for the 21st Century. Healthy Children Foundation.

Schore, A. (2000b). Conference at the Dansk Psykoterapeutisk Selskab for Psykologer [Danish Psychotherapeutic Association for Psychologists] (6 October). Copenhagen.

Schore, A. (2001a). The effects of a secure attachment relationship on right brain development, affect regulation, and infant mental health. *Infant Mental Health Journal, 22:* 7–66.

Schore, A. (2001b). The effects of early relational trauma on right brain development affect regulation, and infant mental health. *Infant Mental Health Journal, 22:* 201–269.

Schore, A. (2002). Dysregulation of the right brain: a fundamental mechanism of traumatic attachment and the psychopathogenesis of posttraumatic stress disorder. *Australian and New Zealand Journal of Psychiatry, 36:* 9–30.

Schore, A. (2003a). *Affect Dysregulation and Disorders of The Self.* New York: W. W. Norton.

Schore, A. (2003b). *Affect Regulation & The Repair of The Self.* New York: W. W. Norton.

Shatz, C. J. (1999). The developing brain. *The Scientific American Book of the Brain* (pp. 3–17). New York: Lyons Press.

Siegel, D. J. (1999). *The Developing Mind. Toward a Neurobiology of Interpersonal Experience.* New York: Guilford.

Siegel, D. J. (2004). Seminar at the Danish EMDR Association (16 June). Copenhagen.

Smith, L. (2001). *Småbarnsalderens nevropsykologi.* Oslo: Gyldendal Akademisk.

Solms, M., & Turnbull, O. (2002). *The Brain and the Inner World.* New York: Other Press.

Sørensen, J. H. (2006). Introduktion. Affektregulering i udviklingspsykologi og psykoterapi. In: J. H. Sørensen (Ed.), *Affektregulering i udvikling og psykoterapi* (pp. 9–130. Copenhagen: Hans Reitzels.

Sørensen, L. J. (1996). *Særpræg, særhed, sygdom.* Copenhagen: Hans Reitzels.

Sowell, E. R., & Jernigan, T. L. (1998). Further MRI evidence of late brain maturation: limbic volume increases and changing asymmetries during childhood and adolescence. *Developmental Neuropsychology, 14*(4): 599–617.

Spear, L. P. (2000). The adolescent brain and age-related behavioural manifestations. *Neuroscience and Biobehavioural Reviews, 24:* 417–463.

Sroufe, L. A. (1979). Socioemotional development. In: J. Osofsky (Ed.), *Handbook of Infant Development* (pp. 462–516). New York: Wiley.

Sroufe, L. A. (1989a). Relationships, self, and individual adaptation. In: J. Sameroff & R. N. Emde (Eds.), *Relationship Disturbances in Early Childhood: A Developmental Approach* (pp. 70–94). New York: Basic Books.

Sroufe, L. A. (1989b). Relationships and relationship disturbances. In: J. Sameroff & R. N. Emde (Eds.), *Relationship Disturbances in Early Childhood: A Developmental Approach* (pp. 97–124). New York: Basic Books.

Sroufe, L. A. (1996). *Emotional Development. The Organization of Emotional Life in the Early Years.* New York: Cambridge University Press.

Sroufe, L. A., Cooper, R. G., & Deltart, G. B. (1992). *Child Development: Its Nature and Course* (2nd edn). New York: McGraw-Hill.

Stein, J. (1987). *Internal Medicine.* Boston, MA: Little Brown.

Stern, D. N. (1977). *The First Relationship: Infant and Mother.* Cambridge, MA: Harvard University Press.

Stern, D. N. (1984). Affect attunement. In: J. D. Call, E. Galensch, & R. L. Tyson (Eds.), *Frontiers of Infant Psychiatry (Volume 2)* (pp. 3–13). New York: Basic Books.

Stern, D. N. (1985). *The Interpersonal World of the Infant. A View from Psychoanalysis and Developmental Psychology.* London: Karnac.

Stern, D. N. (1989). The representation of relational patterns: developmental considerations. In: J. Sameroff & R. N. Emde (Eds.). *Relationship Disturbances in Early Childhood: A Developmental Approach* (pp. 52–69). New York: Basic Books [reprinted London: Karnac, 2005].

Stern, D. N. (1995). *The Motherhood Constellation. A Unified View of Parent–Infant Psychotherapy.* New York: Basic Books.

Stern, D. N. (1998). Seminar and workshop. DISPUK (18–19 June). Snekkersten.

Stern, D. N. (2001). Lecture. SIKON Conference (9 November). Copenhagen.

Stern, D. N. (2004). *The Present Moment in Psychotherapy and Everyday Life.* London: Karnac.

Strogatz, S. (2003). *Sync. The Emerging Science of Spontaneous Order.* New York: Theia.

Suomi, S. J. (1985). Response styles in monkeys: experiential effects. In: H. Klar & L. J. Siever (Eds.), *Biological Response Styles. Clinical Insight* (pp. 2–17). Washington, DC: American Psychiatric Press.

Suomi, S. J. (1991). Uptight and laidback monkeys: individual differences in the response to social challenges. In: S. Brauth, W. Hall, & R. Dooling (Eds.), *Plasticity of Development* (pp. 27–56). Cambridge, MA: MIT.

Suomi, S. J. (1997). Early determinants of behaviour: evidence from primate studies. *British Medical Bulletin, 53*: 170–184.

Suomi, S. J. (2000). A biobehavioral perspective on developmental psychopathology: excessive aggression and serotonergic dysfunction in monkeys. In: A. J. Sameroff, M. Lewis, & S. Miller (Eds.), *Handbook of Developmental Psychopathology* (pp. 237–256). New York: Plenum.

Suomi, S. J., & Levin, S. (1998). Psychobiology of intergenerational effects of trauma. In: Y. Danieli (Ed.), *International Handbook of Multigenerational Legacies of Trauma* (pp. 623–637). New York: Plenum.

Taylor, S. E. (2002). *The Tending Instinct. How Nurturing is Essential to Who We Are and How We Live.* New York: Times Books.

Teicher, M. H. (2002). Scars that won't heal: the neurobiology of child abuse. *Scientific American, March*: 54–61.

Teicher, M. H., Ito, Y., Glod, C. A., Andersen, S. L., Dumont, N., & Ackerman, E. (1997). Preliminary evidence for abnormal cortical development in physically and sexually abused children using EEG coherence and MRI. *Annals of the New York Academy of Sciences, 821*: 160–175.

Tetzchner, S. (2002). *Utviklingspsykologi. Barne- og ungdomsalderen.* Oslo: Gyldendal Akademisk.

Thatcher, R. W. (1997). Neuroimaging of cyclic cortical reorganization during human development. In: R. Thatcher, G. Lyon, J. Rumsey, & N. Krasnegor (Eds.), *Developmental Neuroimaging. Mapping the Development of the Brain and Behavior* (pp. 91–106). San Diego, CA: Academic Press.

Thatcher, R.W., Walker, R. A., & Giudice, S. (1987). Human cerebral hemispheres develop at different rates and ages. *Science, 236*: 1110–1113.

Thompson, R. A. (1990). Emotion and self-regulation. *Nebraska Symposium on Motivation* (pp. 367–467). Lincoln, NB: University of Nebraska Press.

Tienari, P. (1991). Interaction between genetic vulnerability and family environment: the Finnish adoptive family study of schizophrenia. *Acta Psychiatrica Scandinavica, 84*: 460–465.

Torras, C. (1985). *Temporal-pattern Learning in Neural Models.* Amsterdam: Springer.

Trevarthen, C. (1989). Development of early social interactions and the affective regulation of brain growth. In: C. Euler, H. Fossberg, & H. Lagercrantz (Eds.), *Neurobiology of Early Infant Behaviour* (pp. 191–215). Wenner-Gren International Symposium. New York: Stockton Press.

Trevarthen, C. (1990). Growth and education of the hemispheres. In: C. Trevarthen (Ed.), *Brain Circuits and Functions of the Mind* (pp. 334–363). Cambridge: Cambridge University Press.

Trevarthen, C. (2004). Neuroscience and intrinsic psychodynamics: current knowledge and potential for therapy. In: J. Corrigall & H. Wilkinson (Eds.), *Revolutionary Connections. Psychotherapy and Neuroscience* (pp. 53–78). London: Karnac.

Tucker, D. M. (1992). Developing emotions and cortical networks. In: M. R. Gunnar & C. A. Nelson (Eds.), *Minnesota Symposium on Child Psychology, 24. Developmental Behavioural Neuroscience* (pp. 75–128). Hillsdale, NJ: Lawrence Erlbaum.

Tucker, D. M., & Derryberry, D. (1992). Motivated attention: anxiety and the frontal executive functions. *Neuropsychiatry, Neuropsychology, and Behavioural Neurology, 5*(4): 233–252.

Tucker, D. M., & Williamson, P. A. (1984). Asymmetric neural control systems in human self regulation. *Psychological Review, 91*: 185–215.

Tulving, E. (1972). Episodic and semantic memory. In: E. Tulving & W. Donaldsen (Eds.), *Organization of Memory* (pp. 381–403). New York: Academic Press.

Uvnäs-Moberg, K. (1997a), Oxytecin linked antistress effects—the relaxation and growth response. *Acta Psychologica Scandinavia, Supplement, 640*: 38–42.

Uvnäs-Moberg, K. (1997b). Psychological and endocrine effects of social contact. In: C. S. Carter, I. I. Lederhendler, & B. Kirkpatrick (Eds.), *The Integrative Neurobiology of Affiliation* (pp. 146–163). New York: The New York Academy of Sciences Annals, volume 807.

Uvnäs-Moberg, K. (1998). Oxytocin may still mediate the benefits of positive social interaction and emotions. *Psychoneuroendocrinology, 23*: 819–835.

van der Kolk, B. A. (1987). *Psychological Trauma*. Washington, DC: American Psychiatric Press.

van der Kolk, B. A. (1994). The body keeps the score: memory and the evolving psychobiology of posttraumatic stress. *Harvard Review of Psychiatry, 1*: 253–265.

van der Kolk, B. A (1996). The body keeps the score: approaches to the psychobiology of posttraumatic stress disorder. In: B.A. van der

Kolk, A. C. McFarlane & L. Weisaeth (Eds.), *Traumatic stress: The Effects of Overwhelming Experience on Mind, Body and Society* (pp. 214–241). New York: Guilford.

van der Kolk, B. A. (2000). Seminar at the County Hall (3 July), Sorø.

van der Kolk, B. A., & McFarlane, A. C. (1996). The black hole of trauma. In: B. A. van der Kolk, A. C. McFarlane, & L. Weisaeth (Eds.), *Traumatic Stress: The Effects of Overwhelming Experience on Mind, Body and Society* (pp. 3–23). New York: Guilford.

van Ijzendoorn, M. H. (1995). On the way we are: on temperament, attachment and the transmission gap a rejoinder to Fox. *Psychological Bulletin, 117,* (3): 411–415.

van Ijzendoorn, M. H., Goldberg, S., Kroonenberg, P. M., & Frenkel, O. (1992). The relative effects of maternal and child problems on the quality of attachment: a meta-analysis of attachment in clinical samples. *Child Development, 63*: 840–858.

Varela, F., & Maturana, H. (1987). *The Tree of Knowledge. The Biological Roots of Human Understanding.* Boston & London: Shambhala Publications.

Weiger, W. A., & Bear, D. M. (1988). An approach to the neurology of aggression. *Journal of Psychiatric Research, 22*: 85–98.

Wilson, E. O. (1980). *Sociobiology.* Cambridge, MA: Harvard University Press.

Wilson, F. A. W., O'Scalaidhe, S. P., & Goldman-Rakic, P. S. (1993). Dissociation of object and spatial processing domains in primate prefrontal cortex. *Science, 260*: 1955–1958.

Wood, J. D. (1994). Physiology of the enteric nervous system. In: L. R. Johnson (Ed.), *Physiology of the Gastrointestinal Tract, Volume 1* (3rd edn) (pp. 423–482). New York: Raven Press.

Yehuda, R. (1997). Sensitization of the hypothalamic-pituitary-adrenal axis in post traumatic stress disorder. In: R. Yehuda & A. C. McFarlane (Eds.), *Psychobiology of Post Traumatic Stress Disorder* (821 pp. 57–75). New York: New York Academy of Sciences.

Zola-Morgan, S., Squire, L. R., Rempel, N. L., Clower, R. P., & Amaral, D. G. (1992). Enduring memory impairment in monkeys after ischemic damage to the hippocampus. *Journal of Neuroscience, 12*: 2582–2596.

INDEX